Reflections on the Greek Sovereign Debt Crisis: The EU Institutional Framework, Economic Adjustment in an Extensive Shadow Economy

Reflections on the Greek Sovereign Debt Crisis: The EU Institutional Framework, Economic Adjustment in an Extensive Shadow Economy

Edited by

Aristidis Bitzenis, Ioannis Papadopoulos and Vasileios A. Vlachos

CAMBRIDGE SCHOLARS

PUBLISHING

Reflections on the Greek Sovereign Debt Crisis:
The EU Institutional Framework, Economic Adjustment in an Extensive Shadow Economy,
Edited by Aristidis Bitzenis, Ioannis Papadopoulos and Vasileios A. Vlachos

This book first published 2013

Cambridge Scholars Publishing

12 Back Chapman Street, Newcastle upon Tyne, NE6 2XX, UK

British Library Cataloguing in Publication Data
A catalogue record for this book is available from the British Library

ISBN (10): 1-4438-4512-4, ISBN (13): 978-1-4438-4512-0

EDITORIAL NOTE

By the time this volume met the press, Cyprus agreed with the Eurogroup on the basic terms to receive financial assistance (see Eurogroup statement on Cyprus issued on 25/03/2013 at http://www.consilium.europa.eu/uedocs/cms_Data/docs/pressdata/en/ecofin/136487.pdf). The progression of the negotiations and the agreement reached for managing the Cypriot crisis are indicative of the differentiated management of the crisis across the euro-area. The bailout deal will have severe consequences for the Cypriot economy and alters further the perception of risk-free investment (i.e. risk in the euro-area, which has been rising at previously unmet levels for low-risk government bonds, has been also associated with bank deposits, which were considered risk-free). Thus, two pillars of fundraising for economic growth in advanced capitalism (i.e. sovereign bonds and bank deposits) have been dealt a severe blow by the management of the euro area systemic crisis. Although it is not possible to address and analyze here the arguments for and against the management of the Cypriot crisis, the efficiency of debt crisis mechanisms and their aftermath are two of the main topics of this volume.

TABLE OF CONTENTS

ACKNOWLEDGEMENTS

The editors are grateful to Mary Beth Hasty for proofreading the manuscripts.

The research titled *The Shadow economy (black economy) in Greece: Size, Reasons and Impact* is implemented through the Operational Program "Education and Lifelong Learning" and is co-financed by the European Union (European Social Fund) and Greek national funds.

All chapters in this book, except chapter 7, are part of this research.

Ευρωπαϊκή Ένωση
Ευρωπαϊκό Κοινωνικό Ταμείο

ΕΠΙΧΕΙΡΗΣΙΑΚΟ ΠΡΟΓΡΑΜΜΑ
ΕΚΠΑΙΔΕΥΣΗ ΚΑΙ ΔΙΑ ΒΙΟΥ ΜΑΘΗΣΗ
επένδυση στην κοινωνία της γνώσης
ΥΠΟΥΡΓΕΙΟ ΠΑΙΔΕΙΑΣ & ΘΡΗΣΚΕΥΜΑΤΩΝ, ΠΟΛΙΤΙΣΜΟΥ & ΑΘΛΗΤΙΣΜΟΥ
ΕΙΔΙΚΗ ΥΠΗΡΕΣΙΑ ΔΙΑΧΕΙΡΙΣΗΣ

ΕΣΠΑ
2007-2013
ΕΥΡΩΠΑΪΚΟ ΚΟΙΝΩΝΙΚΟ ΤΑΜΕΙΟ

Με τη συγχρηματοδότηση της Ελλάδας και της Ευρωπαϊκής Ένωσης

CHAPTER ONE

THE EURO-AREA SOVEREIGN DEBT CRISIS AND THE NEGLECTED FACTOR OF THE SHADOW ECONOMY

ARISTIDIS BITZENIS, IOANNIS PAPADOPOULOS AND VASILEIOS A. VLACHOS

1. How Did We Get Here?

How did the sovereign debt crisis that started in Greece develop into a crisis of the euro-area? The Greek governments mismanaged the Greek economy and deceived all stakeholders about the size and nature of their budgetary problems. However, this mismanagement regards only the outburst and development of the Greek sovereign debt crisis. Financial market institutions and euro-area authorities carry the full responsibility of letting the Greek crisis advance into a systemic crisis of the entire European Economic and Monetary Union (EMU).

The aftermath of the overconfidence in the self-adjusting ability of the financial system to manage crises has led from booming credit and assets prices to an underestimation of the consequences of accumulating debt and leverage (see inter alia Bianchi and Mendoza, 2011; Galati and Moessner, 2011). The dramatically destabilizing role of financial markets – that always seem to be shaped *a posteriori* and solely by overreacting expectations for trend progression – is accompanied by the failure of rating agencies to be proactive instead of "overreactive".[1] The rating

[1] The rating agencies were not only caught off-guard by the credit crisis that erupted in the United States (US), but also by the sovereign debt crisis that hit the emirate of Dubai. Since then, they started the downgrading of peripheral euro-area member states, even if the repayment of bonds has never been postponed like in the case of Dubai. The shortcomings in the current rating process are discussed in a paper – published recently by the European Central Bank (ECB) – that examines

agencies failed to forecast the financial crisis that hit the global economy in the summer of 2007 and has since developed into a global economic crisis unprecedented in post-war economic history. This economic crisis has now become a sovereign debt crisis that spreads across euro-area member states.

The sovereign debt crisis emerged so drastically due to the hesitation of the governments of euro-area member states to deliver an unambiguous and concise plan announcing their intentions and promptness to support Greece.[2] This hesitation did not manifest a solution. The default of a member of the EMU entails the risk of contagion that would automatically lead to an increase of the government bond yields of other members because of a generalized lack of confidence in the EMU stabilization mechanisms.[3] This contagion would affect the continuity of access to financial markets and that would, in turn, require governments of euro-area member states to adopt contractionary measures leading to, or sustaining, recession. Moreover, this contagion has also triggered a banking crisis that is spreading in the euro-area periphery, as the declining bond prices have led to large losses on banks' balance sheets.

The members of the EMU face a dilemma. On the one hand, it is tempting to resist a bailout[4] to signal that irresponsible governments will

---

the quality of credit ratings assigned to banks in Europe and the US by the three largest rating agencies over the past two decades and indicates that rating agencies assign more positive ratings to large banks and to those institutions more likely to provide the rating agency with additional securities rating business (Hau et al., 2012). In view of these facts, the European Parliament has put forward stricter rules on 16 January 2013 that will allow rating agencies to issue unsolicited sovereign debt ratings only on set dates, and enable private investors to sue them for negligence (see announcements of the European Commission at http://ec.europa.eu/internal_market/securities/agencies/index_en.htm.

[2] The contribution of the ECB to the expansion of the sovereign debt crisis concerns – within the existing institutional framework – only the eligibility of government debt that can be used as collateral in liquidity provision. Nevertheless, the failure of euro-area institutions to contain the expansion and halt the aggravation of the sovereign debt crisis generates the argument that the contribution of the ECB to this expansion concerns also its statutory incapacity of serving as fiscal backstop ("lender of last resort") to over-indebted euro-area member states.

[3] There already has been contagion, though its degree is not uniform. Strong contagion has been observed in Portugal, Spain and Ireland, and to a lesser extent Italy (Arghyrou and Kontonikas 2011).

[4] The no-bail-out clause of the Treaty leads legal skeptics to argue that financial assistance between member states is forbidden. However, as it is stated in Article 122 – ex article 100 of the Treaty of European Community – in Chapter 1

not be rescued.[5] On the other hand, a bailout may seem the lesser of two evils because of the contagious effects discussed above. However, this dilemma regards only an immediate response, as bailing out is nothing more than a resolution for the short-term. The long-term issues lie in the structural problems of the EMU, which the sovereign debt crisis has unveiled: an imbalance between the full centralization of monetary policy and the sovereignty of each member on matters of fiscal policy. This sovereignty cannot be restrained by the SGP – the appropriateness of which is largely criticized – and leads to budgetary divergences that affect both competitiveness and the size of sovereign debt.

The bailouts[6] delivered to date are in the form of a joint euro-area/International Monetary Fund (IMF) financing package by the joint European Community/IMF/ECB rescue mission. These packages are accompanied with severe austerity measures and structural reform programs aiming to generate surpluses on future government budgets. By lowering the current and future levels of debt, it is the hope that the budgets will be considered sustainable. The receivers of these packages are – in chronological order – Greece, Ireland and Portugal.[7] But are these

---

(Economic Policy) of Title VIII (Economic and Monetary Policy), part three (Union Policies and Internal Actions) of the Consolidated versions of the Treaty on European Union (EU) and the Treaty on the Functioning of the European Union (Official Journal of the EU, 2010: 98): "Where a Member State is in difficulties or is seriously threatened with severe difficulties caused by natural disasters or exceptional occurrences beyond its control, the Council, on a proposal from the Commission, may grant, under certain conditions, Union financial assistance to the Member State concerned."

[5] The morality of bailing out primarily concerns the "rewarding" of breaking out the Stability and Growth Pact (SGP) rules – which has been a common practice since the introduction of the euro – and transferring this cost to taxpayers of EU member states. Moreover, the second concern is about the belief that it is morally better to bailout a systemic part (state economy, financial intermediary, etc.) of an economic/financial system in order to avoid a financial meltdown that would eventually lead to economic depression. Nevertheless, the fiscal austerity programmes (and tax increases) that accompany these bailouts seem only to delay the inevitable – i.e. severe recessions which contract government revenue and fuel fiscal imbalances. As a result, both of these concerns reveal that this course of action is neither moral nor economically sound.

[6] The commonly used term of "bailout" is an alternate expression to "debt restructuring". This process postpones and/or extends the schedule of debt repayments without reducing the total level of the debt by providing the borrower with the funds needed to repay amounts falling due.

[7] Other member states – namely Spain, Italy and Belgium – have been indirectly financed through purchases of their bonds by the ECB on secondary debt markets.

the countries mostly affected by the euro-area debt crisis? Are the causes of their deteriorating public finances similar?

Judging by the level of interest-rate spreads between long-term government bonds issued by euro-area member states and the respective issued by the German government, the peripheral member states of the euro-area mostly affected by the sovereign debt crisis to date are (in alphabetical order) Cyprus, Greece, Ireland, Italy, Portugal, Slovenia and Spain.[8] Although these countries have accumulated on the whole – see ***Table 1*** for specific figures that differentiate them – considerable amounts of debt, run large excess account deficits, and it is believed in general that their level of nominal wages has been outpacing productivity gains,[9] the causes leading to the outbreaks of the sovereign debts crises are not similar. The cases of Greece, Italy and Portugal are different from Cyprus, Ireland and Spain (for an early discussion see Stein, 2011). In Cyprus, Ireland and Spain the private banking sector was the origin of the sovereign debt crisis, whereas in Greece, Italy and Portugal continuous problems of competitiveness and fiscal deficits were the origins. In brief:

a) Cyprus is the fifth euro-area member to ask for financial assistance from the rescue mission, as a loan from Russia is not enough for the recapitalization of the country's banking system that is heavily

---

Spain also received financial assistance for the recapitalisation and restructuring of its banking sector.

[8] Central government bond yields on the secondary market, gross of tax, with a residual maturity of around 10 years (see Eurostat country profiles at http://epp.eurostat.ec.europa.eu/portal/page/portal/user_interfaces/introduction/country_profiles) were over the German respective yield at the end of December 2012 by 5.7% for Cyprus, 12.03% for Greece, 3.37% for Ireland, 3.24% for Italy, 5.95% for Portugal, 4.03% for Slovenia, and 4.04% for Spain.

[9] Austerity measures accompany bailouts not only for the reduction of budgetary deficits and the level of government debt, but also for the improvement of competitiveness – via the renowned internal devaluation process – required for attracting FDI (or making exports less costly). The generation of a surplus may be difficult for a country grappling with excessive debt repayment obligations and limited or extremely expensive access to finance, but it gets even more difficult when that country is unable to use the exchange rate as a policy tool of external devaluation and, as a result, has to undergo a painful process of internal devaluation to restore competitiveness. Nevertheless, Cyprus, Greece, Portugal and Spain are among the seven euro-area member states that have improved their real unit labor cost position since 2005 (see Eurostat statistics database at http://epp.eurostat.ec.europa.eu/portal/page/portal/statistics/search_database, as accessed on 10 July 2012), and yet they still are facing major difficulties to exit from the crisis and attract considerable amounts of FDI.

exposed to the Greek treasury bonds. Cyprus' request follows a downgrade of the country's bonds by Fitch in late June 2012, which disqualified them from being accepted as collateral by the ECB.

b) The Greek sovereign debt crisis is the outcome of public finance mismanagement and diachronic generation of budget deficits. The main problem of the Greek banking sector is its exposure to Greek sovereign debt.[10]

c) Although before the financial crisis Ireland indicated budget surpluses, this picture changed dramatically after 2007. The collapse of the construction sector and the fall in real estate prices led to the insolvency of Irish banks. The Irish government was forced to bailout banking institutions after the eruption of the financial crisis and the continuous decrease of public debt was terminated in 2006. Even though Ireland has been praised for progress in its overall fiscal and competitiveness trends, growth perspectives remain low because of low levels of domestic consumer spending and falling external demand for its products. The country is still suffering from a high unemployment rate and the government remains burdened with the debt it took on to recapitalize its banks.

d) Like Spain, Italy has most of its debt controlled internally. Debt and deficits have sharply increased following the crisis that started in 2007 and the sustainability of the Italian fiscal policy has turned into a critical issue. With a rather conservative financial sector, a high savings rate and much smaller foreign imbalances, it is believed that somehow Italy will weather the storm. However, given the high level of public debt, avoiding deterioration of its saving position is crucial.

[10] The unrealistic expectations for the reduction of Greek sovereign debt – designated in the "Memorandums of Economic and Financial Policies" between the Greek government and the rescue mission – are exposed by a study indicating that an annual primary surplus of 8.4% of GDP is required on an average basis in order to reduce the debt ratio within the SGP limits of 60 percent of GDP eventually, at the year of 2034 (Darvas et al., 2011).

Table 1 – Government debt and deficit/surplus (percentage of GDP), GDP (billions PPS) and unemployment of member states hit by the sovereign debt crisis.

State/Indicator/Time		2002	2007	2008	2009	2010	2011	2012 Q2
Eurozone	Gross debt	-	-	-	80.0	85.4	87.2	91.6
	Net lending/borrowing	-	-	-	-6.4	-6.2	-4.1	-2.9
	Primary balance	-	-	-	-3.5	-3.4	-1.1	-
	GDP (annual change)	3.2	6.6	0.8	-4.9	3.8	3.3	0.4
	Unemployment	8.3	7.6	7.6	9.6	10.1	10.1	11.1
	Long-term unemployment	3.6	3.3	2.9	3.4	4.3	4.6	5.2
Cyprus	Gross debt	65.1	58.8	48.9	58.5	61.5	71.6	84.3
	Net lending/borrowing	-4.4	3.5	0.9	-6.1	-5.3	-6.3	-9.1
	Primary balance	-1.2	6.5	3.8	-3.6	-3.1	-3.8	-
	GDP (annual change)	2.9	9.2	8.3	-4.1	3.6	1.9	-1.1
	Unemployment	3.6	4.1	3.8	5.5	6.4	7.9	11.4
	Long-term unemployment	0.8	0.8	0.5	0.6	1.3	1.6	3.2
Greece	Gross debt	101.7	107.4	113.0	129.4	145.0	165.3	144.3
	Net lending/ borrowing	-4.8	-6.5	-9.8	-15.6	-10.3	-9.1	-8.1
	Primary balance	0.7	-2.0	-4.8	-10.4	-4.7	-2.2	-
	GDP (annual change)	8.2	3.5	3.2	-3.8	-0.9	-5.6	-7.2
	Unemployment	10.3	8.3	7.7	9.5	12.6	17.7	23.6
	Long-term unemployment	5.3	4.1	3.6	3.9	5.7	8.8	13.2
Ireland	Gross debt	31.9	24.8	44.2	65.1	92.5	108.2	111.5
	Net lending/borrowing	-0.4	0.1	-7.3	-14.0	-31.2	-13.1	-7.4
	Primary balance	1.0	1.1	-6.0	-12.0	-28.0	-9.7	-
	GDP (annual change)	9.5	9.1	-8.1	-9.5	4.1	2.6	2.2
	Unemployment	4.5	4.6	6.3	11.9	13.7	14.4	15.0
	Long-term unemployment	1.3	1.3	1.7	3.5	6.7	8.6	9.4

Italy	Gross debt	105.1	103.1	105.7	116.0	118.6	120.1	126.1
	Net lending/borrowing	-3.1	-1.6	-2.7	-5.4	-4.6	-3.9	-2.8
	Primary balance	2.5	3.4	2.5	-0.8	0.0	1.0	-
	GDP (annual change)	-1.4	5.9	1.1	-6.3	1.5	3.4	-1.6
	Unemployment	8.5	6.1	6.7	7.8	8.4	8.4	10.5
	Long-term unemployment	5.0	2.9	3.1	3.5	4.1	4.4	5.6
Portugal	Gross debt	56.6	68.3	71.6	83.1	93.3	107.8	117.5
	Net lending/borrowing	-3.4	-3.1	-3.6	-10.2	-9.8	-4.2	-5.9
	Primary balance	-0.6	-0.2	-0.6	-7.3	-7.0	-0.4	-
	GDP (annual change)	3.7	5.3	-0.6	-3.5	4.1	-0.4	-4.5
	Unemployment	5.7	8.9	8.5	10.6	12.0	12.9	15.2
	Long-term unemployment	2.0	4.2	4.0	4.7	6.3	6.2	7.3
Slovenia	Gross debt	27.8	23.1	21.9	35.3	38.8	47.6	48.1
	Net lending/borrowing	-2.4	0.0	-1.9	-6.1	-6.0	-6.4	-4.7
	Primary balance	-0.3	1.2	-0.7	-4.7	-4.4	-4.5	-
	GDP (annual change)	3.8	7.0	3.4	-7.8	1.2	0.6	-3.1
	Unemployment	6.3	4.9	4.4	5.9	7.3	8.2	8.2
	Long-term unemployment	3.5	2.2	1.9	1.8	3.2	3.6	3.9
Spain	Gross debt	52.6	36.3	40.2	53.9	61.2	68.5	76.0
	Net lending/borrowing	-0.2	1.9	-4.5	-11.2	-9.3	-8.5	-11.0
	Primary balance	2.5	3.5	-2.9	-9.4	-7.4	-6.1	-
	GDP (annual change)	7.6	7.6	0.6	-5.8	1.3	2.0	-1.4
	Unemployment	11.4	8.3	11.3	18.0	20.1	21.7	24.7
	Long-term unemployment	3.8	1.7	2.0	4.3	7.3	9.0	10.9

Source: Eurostat
(http://epp.eurostat.ec.europa.eu/portal/page/portal/statistics/search_database,
as accessed 14 January 2013).

Notes
1. Dash implies that data is not available.
2. Gross debt refers to "government consolidated gross debt" ("Maastricht debt"), which is the sum of government liabilities as defined in ESA95 in: a) currency and deposits, b) securities other than shares, excluding financial derivatives and c) loans outstanding at the end of the year, measured at nominal value and consolidated.

3. Net lending/ borrowing refers to "government surplus/deficit under Excessive Deficit Procedure", which is net lending (+)/net borrowing (-) of "general government" (as defined in ESA95), plus net streams of interest payments resulting from swaps arrangements and forward rate agreements.
4. Primary balance is government net borrowing or net lending, excluding interest payments on consolidated government liabilities.
5. GDP for 2012Q2 is expressed at market prices.

e) Similarly to the case of Greece, Portugal sustained fiscal/government budgetary policies with a diachronic contribution to the generation of budget deficits and an over-bureaucratized civil service. The civil service encouraged over-expenditure and undermined competitiveness, which led to large debt burdens. Despite austerity measures taken by the government, the country is currently facing difficulties in its fiscal adjustment path and a continually rising unemployment rate.
f) Slovenia is threatened by a debt crisis due to the fiscal burden of covering the liabilities of the undercapitalized Slovenian financial industry. Continuous downgrades of the country's government bonds, the requirement by the country's largest financial institutions for capital injections and the negative economic outlook indicate that the government will eventually require a bailout.
g) The Spanish banks were unable to repay their loans to international lenders after the collapse of housing prices caused by the financial crisis. Although Spain generated a budget surplus until the eruption of the financial crisis in 2007, fiscal expansion and bailouts to banks altered this picture. The country has been in recession in two out of the last three years because of the steep contraction brought by four consecutive austerity programmes. Many autonomous regions are in a dire fiscal situation, local banks and savings institutions are severely undercapitalized and have been deleveraging at a speedy pace, and the – especially youth – unemployment rate is the highest among Western countries, and still escalating.

In relation to the preceding discussion, ***Table 1*** depicts the level of general government consolidated gross debt, the government surplus/deficit under excessive deficit procedure, and the primary balance. As for some countries some of these indicators are not worse than the euro-area average, it is noted that debt ratios are considered in conjunction with key economic and financial variables, such as growth, interest rates and the maturity profile of the debt in order to determine their trend in medium-term scenarios. In addition, further information on the composition of external debt – such as external income, external assets, financial derivatives, and the economy's creditors – contribute to the analysis of debt sustainability (IMF, 2003: 171-183). Furthermore, ***Table 1*** also indicates the negative impact of austerity measures adopted by the member states hit by the sovereign debt crisis, on their economic prosperity – i.e. on economic growth or unemployment or both.[11]

In summary, the eruption of the financial crisis and the subsequent recession led to sharp rises in government debt not only due to the rising expenditures for the re-ignition of economic growth and the support packages to financial institutions, but also to the abrupt fall in tax revenues. Government debt surges fueled the subsequent "flight to quality",[12] which in turn caused the eruption of the sovereign debt crisis in Greece and its transmission to other peripheral member states. However, the treatment for both the prevention of its transmission and the cure has been responsible for the domino effect of the debt crisis within the euro-area. Even though this treatment was aiming at the restoration of market confidence, it nevertheless sustains three interlocked – banking, sovereign debt, and growth – crises that fuel a deflationary spiral of economic recession and sovereign debt expansion. More specifically, undercapitalized banks facing liquidity problems are financed through government debt expansion, which in turn is contained through fiscal austerity that contracts output, disposable income and domestic demand. Ultimately, the latter reduces tax receipts and leads to government deficits that require for further debt expansion or austerity measures and hence, the vicious downward spiral continues.[13]

---

[11] As structural unemployment increases significantly in economic downturns (Michaillat, 2012), fiscal austerity (Bagaria et al., 2012) and disinflation (Ball, 2009) during recession become the worst policy options with regard to employment levels.

[12] During times of turbulence and perceived risk increases, investors are attracted by assets where they are least likely to experience a loss of principal.

[13] The deflationary spiral that emerged as a consequence of the current inappropriate treatment for the sovereign debt crisis should have been predicted/anticipated, as it is closely related to the theory of debt-deflation (Fisher, 1933), and the models (see Keen, 1995) that relate it with the financial instability hypothesis (Minsky, 1994). Although at a glance the sovereign debt crisis does not seem to be supported by debt-deflation theory since it has not entailed significant deflation yet, the deflationary pressures from decreasing domestic demand are countered by inflationary pressures from tax increases and increases in energy products fostered by the oil crisis that followed the subprime mortgage crisis. For example, Greece's inflation rate is still positive amid depression due to the increase of taxation – despite the fact that Greek enterprises absorbed part of this

2. The Way Out

The sovereign debt crisis that erupted in Greece in late 2009 and spread across the euro-area periphery ever since has not been efficiently confronted to date. Fiscal consolidation – associated with austerity measures – has led euro-area economies to a deflationary spiral and to appeal for financial assistance. The failure of euro-area institutions to contain the expansion and halt the aggravation of the sovereign debt crisis has put in question the ability of current policies and raised concerns over the future of the euro. The threats of a recession, and even worse, of an emergence of a deflationary spiral, along with the growing consensus that Greece was a pretext for the outbreak of the crisis and not its real cause, have highlighted the appeal for measures, which are currently rejected due to concerns about moral hazard or because they are not ratified by any EU treaty to date. These measures entail a monetary expansion by the ECB via the purchase of bonds issued by states requiring financial assistance or via a future issuance and purchase of Eurobonds. Such measures have not materialized to date, as the ECB main refinancing operations fixed rate remains well above the respective rates of central banks from other advanced economies (e.g. the US), and as "Outright Monetary Transactions"[14] do not entail quantitative easing due to sterilization and moreover, presuppose an approved programme of fiscal austerity.

The policy mix adopted to date does not only ignore economic theory, but also lacks a sense of realism. Firstly, it ignores the deterioration of national savings and their consequent impact on capital stock by fostering a deflationary spiral – via fiscal austerity – that sustains the budget deficits and reduces disposable income and thus private savings. Moreover, the substitution of domestic investment with FDI is ruled out, as international

---

increase – and the upward price movements of energy products (oil, electricity) and imported goods (see report published in Greek; Τράπεζα της Ελλάδος, 2011: 98-101).

[14] Hereinafter, the reader should be aware that the authors acknowledge the potential of these transactions, and for that reason do not consider them as a tool of monetary expansion. These transactions, which are ECB's latest intervention tool (see ECB press release, "Technical features of Outright Monetary Transactions", 6 September 2012, at http://www.ecb.int/press/pr/date/2012/html/pr120906_1.en.html), replace the Securities Markets Programme and focus on sovereign bonds with a maturity of between one and three years. The start, continuation and suspension of these transactions are at ECB's discretion and require for the adoption of an adjustment programme that has to be approved and monitored by the IMF. Moreover, the liquidity created through these transactions will be fully sterilised.

investors shy away from heavily indebted states because deleveraging of sovereign debts generally results in an output rate lower than an economy's structural capacities for economic growth, financial repression, and weak foreign exchange values (see Crescenzi, 2011: 229-231). Secondly, the effect of a low policy rate diminishes due to the deterrents to lending activity, i.e. balance sheet capacity of financial intermediaries is lowered due both to continuous deleveraging and to increased levels of perceived risk attributable to rising default rates and gloomy prospects.

To sum up, bailouts and austerity measures are evidently not working. The financial fragility of the economy grew rapidly and favoured the emergence of debt-deflation when mortgage lending moved to asset-based lending, instead of income-based lending (Tymoigne, 2012). The deleveraging shock that followed is reflected in the "Minsky moment" and the "balance sheet recession", which indicate that a temporary rise in government spending is required in order to increase the spending of liquidity-constrained debtors (Eggertsson and Krugman, 2012).[15] Hence, decreasing demand levels, recession, and gloomy prospects for economic growth due to the unstoppable transmission of the sovereign debt crisis indicate the ineffectiveness of strictly relying on monetary policy – that will possibly lead to a liquidity trap – and the requirement for quantitative easing. The main question is about the form(s) that this quantitative easing will take.

The trend toward debt-deflation could be subsided, or even inversed, if the EU financed, or at least co-financed to an important degree, infrastructure investments to obtain Trans-European economies of scale in the development of "network economy" sectors (such as information and communication technologies, transportation, and energy) and in large training, research and development, and innovation projects. Such a development would give a decisive push to capital spending in a conjuncture of slumping demand, private capitals' flight to quality, and industrial disinvestment. Consequently, an initial public investment at European level would be able to stimulate the economy of the euro-area periphery by leveraging private capitals in public-private partnerships and by restoring confidence via publicly-guaranteed securities.[16]

[15] The Minsky moment occurs when an asset bubble bursts, and overpriced assets are sold in a mass, causing sharp declines in financial markets. The balance sheet recession that follows forces asset owners to fly to quality and the economy loses demand equal to the savings and debt repayments.

[16] An account of public investments as engines of growth and a proposal for European Project Bonds is made in Haug et al. (2011: 58-64).

Infrastructure projects have a definite multiplier effect by attracting additional private financing, boosting employment, creating new demand, and strengthening social and economic cohesion through the territorial diffusion of productive capital that generates long-term revenue. Yet, risk-aversion for these projects is high for private investors because, even if they are financially viable in the medium to long term, they face short-term risks, particularly in the construction phase and during the early years of operation.[17]

Risk aversion, especially in times of disinvestment crisis, is the main reason for a fiscal union to intervene in bridging the initial infrastructure financing gap via its financial arm, which is able to raise large amounts of capital through access to the debt capital market. The "Europe 2020 Project Bond" Joint Initiative by the European Commission and the EIB – the financial arm of the Union that will manage the initiative – is meant to be such a risk-sharing mechanism.[18] Project Bonds will be funded, on the EU side, by the EU's own resources committed in its Multiannual Financial Framework (MAFF).[19] Such long-term involvement of the EIB, with its widely acknowledged expertise in the management of innovative financial instruments and its AAA credit rating,[20] could be of vital

[17] See European Commission MEMO/11/121, "The Europe 2020 Project Bond Initiative: the consultation by the Commission", Brussels, 28 February 2011: 1.

[18] Project bonds were first announced by President Barroso at his State of the Union Address in September 2010, and highlighted one year later in his State of the Union Address 2011; see José Manuel Durão Barroso SPEECH/11/607, "European renewal – State of the Union Address 2011", Strasbourg, 28 September 2011. The legal basis for this new financial instrument is to be found in article 309 of TFEU that states in relevant part: "The task of the European Investment Bank shall be to contribute, by having recourse to the capital market and utilising its own resources, to the balanced and steady development of the internal market in the interest of the Union. For this purpose the Bank shall, operating on a non-profit-making basis, grant loans and give guarantees which facilitate the financing of the following projects in all sectors of the economy", implemented by article 16 par. 4 of the Protocol No 5 on the statute of the European Investment Bank: "The Bank may guarantee loans contracted by public or private undertakings or other bodies for the purpose of carrying out projects provided for in Article 309 of the Treaty on the Functioning of the European Union."

[19] As these lines were written, the EU was entering a phase of intense deliberations over its next MAFF (the so-called "Financial Perspectives 2014-2020"), after a first extraordinary European Council on 22-23 November 2012 that failed to reach an agreement and soon before a second one on 7-8 February 2013 dedicated to this highly controversial issue.

[20] Even though the EIB has the capacity to deliver subordinated (i.e. not necessarily its rating) loans and is not targeting an AAA rating for the projects it

importance for institutional investors such as pension funds and insurance companies, i.e. investors with a long-term liability structure and regulated rating requirements for their investments.[21]

Before the sovereign debt crisis, specialized institutions called "monoliners" used to provide insurance for the financing of large infrastructure projects via the capital markets, thus guaranteeing the full credit risk of senior lenders and raising their rating. However, due to losses on subprime-related guarantees and to pressure on banks' balance sheets because of the Basel III regulatory requirements, the monoliners have largely exited the financial insurance market generally. The Project Bonds intend to replace them by providing partial credit enhancement of infrastructure projects to project companies raising senior debt under the form of bonds sold to institutional investors.[22] The statutory rules of the EIB, i.e. its strict prudential requirements designed to preserve the optimal credit rating for the EIB[23] and the conditionality of every EIB loan "either on a guarantee from the Member State in whose territory the investment will be carried out or on other adequate guarantees, or on the financial strength of the debtor",[24] do not allow for a high leverage ratio. The Project Bond mechanism is designed to overcome this obstacle to sufficient capital concentration by providing the subordinated tranche of project companies' debt for infrastructures, increasing thus the credit quality of the senior tranche to a level where most institutional investors are comfortable holding the bond for a long period.[25]

The only problem is that, even though plans to introduce European project bonds to fund infrastructures have been tabled by the European Commission and supported by the European Parliament since 2010, the

---

will fund through Project Bonds, its strong and long-lasting track record as a financially secure institution will certainly attract hesitant private investors.

[21] European Commission memo, "The Europe 2020 Project Bond Initiative": 3.

[22] See the EIB webpage "The Europe 2020 Project Bond Initiative – Innovative infrastructure financing" at http://www.eib.org/about/news/the-europe-2020-project-bond-initiative.htm, as accessed on 23 October 2012.

[23] See article 16 par. 5 of the Protocol No 5 on the statute of the European Investment Bank.

[24] Article 16 par. 3 of the Protocol No 5 on the statute of the European Investment Bank.

[25] The mechanism is explained in the EIB webpage "The Europe 2020 Project Bond Initiative – Innovative infrastructure financing" at http://www.eib.org/about/news/the-europe-2020-project-bond-initiative.htm, and more analytically in the European Commission Communication "A pilot for the Europe 2020 Project Bond Initiative", COM(2011) 660 final, Brussels, 19.10.2011: 5-6, and its Staff Working Paper, SEC(2011) 1239 final, Brussels, 19.10.2011: 4-5.

mechanism is still not fully operational, despite the urgent need for counter-cyclical measures in the midst of a protracted balance-sheet recession and the beginnings of a liquidity trap in Greece. The pilot phase of the "Europe 2020 Project Bond Initiative," whose impact assessment has been completed since October 2011, will be launched for the period 2012-2013, still within the current Multiannual Financial Framework 2007-2013. It is clear by now that only a limited number of projects (approximately 5-10) could probably be funded during the pilot phase, as the budgetary resources available are limited and the remaining time horizon for implementation would be very short.[26] Once again, the rigidity of EU rules – budgetary rules in this case – blocks substantive and, above all, rapid progress in the containment of the unprecedented crisis that is sweeping the European Continent.

3. The Neglected Factor of the Shadow Economy

The chapter of professor Schneider included in this volume and several previous studies (see inter alia Schneider et al., 2010) indicate that the size of the shadow economy in southern euro-area periphery countries hit by the crisis is approximately 20% of GDP or over, at the same time as it is less than 15% in Germany (an assumed accepted level by rule of thumb). In 2011, the shadow economy in terms of GDP was 26% in Cyprus, 24.3% in Greece, 21.2% in Italy, 19.4% in Portugal, 19.2% in Spain, and 13.7% in Germany.[27] For the same year, ***Table 1*** indicates that the government deficit under the Excessive Deficit Procedure was 3.4% in Cyprus, 9.9% in Greece, 8% in Italy, 7.9% in Portugal, and 5.6% in Spain.

A straightforward conclusion arising from the simple comparison between the sizes of these figures is the pragmatic expectation for a relief from the sovereign debt crisis that climaxes across the southern euro-area periphery. A successful transfer of a part of the shadow economy to the formal economy – ideally minimizing its levels to the respective of Germany – could have a multiple positive impact, i.e. an increase of GDP, government revenue, and tax morale, an opportunity to circumvent fiscal austerity and/or raise taxes, and ultimately, a decrease of government deficit.

---

[26] See European Commission MEMO/11/370, "The pilot phase of Europe 2020 Project Bond Initiative (reissue)", Brussels, 23 May 2012: 2.

[27] Work in progress by Aristidis Bitzenis, Friedrich Schneider and Vasileios A. Vlachos.

The neglected factor of the shadow economy arises from the fact that no proper measures have been adopted to date, in the sense that there has not been any progress to transfer part of the shadow economy to the formal economy. Deterrence and control have to be at the core of the policy mix in order to be able to achieve such a transfer.[28] For example, the formulation of an electronic platform that would be monitored by the state and would record all business transactions in real time, target bonuses for companies that are willing to operate their VAT, social security and tax payments transactions through the official financial channels, along with the formation of a highly specialized tax evasion police force, would suppress, or at least strongly discourage, financial transactions in cash. Nevertheless, the measures have to be distinctive, as for example, the shadow economy in Greece is also systemic (bureaucratic) and has been nurtured by clientelism and rent-seeking behaviours.

Furthermore, the critical importance of the neglected factor of the shadow economy is identified through the failure of the economic policy mix adopted to date to manage and contain the sovereign debt crisis that climaxes across the southern euro-area periphery. ***Table 1*** depicts a significant slowdown/recession/depression – depending on the member state – and a tremendous rise in unemployment levels. For example – with regard to Greece – a recent report by the European Economic and Social Committee (see Lanara-Tzotze, 2012) implies that it is the failure to address tax evasion that requires for measures whose impact has been unevenly and severely felt by workers, pensioners and honest tax-paying citizens. An effective policy mix is required for an interlocked three-battling front: a reduction in the levels of corruption implies a reduction in the levels of tax evasion and the successful transfer of the shadow to the formal economy. This policy mix will contribute significantly to the relentless efforts of successive Greek governments to achieve a primary balance amid the sovereign debt crisis and during the country's worst and longest recession ever.

---

[28] An EU study indicates that a boost on tax morale and the benefits (i.e. audits and direct control) from electronic means of payments are more effective than punishment and monetary incentives for tackling the shadow economy (Jensen and Wohlbier, 2012). Low tax morale – mainly due to the systemic (political) part of the crisis – will probably be the major obstacle that Greek authorities will face in the formulation of an accommodating policy for transferring part of the shadow economy to the formal economy.

4. The Structure of this Book

This brief chapter is in lieu of introduction to the notions organized in three main themes/parts throughout this volume. The first part discusses the actions taken by the euro-area in the effort to quell the negativities and transmission of the sovereign debt crisis that spreads across its member states. The second part discusses the causes, effects and measures taken so far to quell the effects of the Greek sovereign debt crisis and moreover, puts forwards some pragmatic policy directions for the Greek economy to grow out of the crisis. The third section looks upon critical subjects of the euro-area sovereign debt crisis from a historical perspective. More specifically, it discusses the development and the arguments on the appropriateness of SGP, Greek budgetary discipline, and the reliability of Greek statistics. A brief summary of the chapters comprising each part follows.

The opening chapter of the first part is by Ioannis Papadopoulos, who analyzes the structural deficiencies of the Common Economic and Monetary Policies of the EU, starting from the Treaty itself and then proceeding to secondary European law (notably the preventive and corrective arms of the SGP), as well as EU macroeconomic practices. Papadopoulos thinks that the EU has fallen prey to a quintuple systemic crisis (sovereign and private debt, bank undercapitalisation, disinvestment, political/institutional, and social crisis) and has been mired in a self-inflicted deflationary tendency ever since the Greek crisis broke out. Through a comparison with the US federalist political and economic philosophy and institutional mechanisms, the author shows that the European political system has been largely improvising *ad hoc*, after-the-fact and costly ways of toughening up budgetary discipline, whereas coordinated solutions, not only to deficit and debt, but most importantly to competitiveness and growth problems, would have been a more rational way out of the crisis. Papadopoulos argues that the principles and macroeconomic presuppositions of the EMU's Economic and Monetary Policy have been woefully inadequate to counteract the competitiveness imbalances between its member states. The SGP's "one-size-fits-all" aim is overbroad, overly rigid and procyclical instead of countercyclical; at the same time, the monetarist objections to an enlargement of the European Central Bank's mandate to the protection of a possible implosion of the euro-area itself and to the effective promotion of maximum employment, as is the case with the US Federal Reserve, are self-defeating because they do not allow for a decisive solution to the European crisis.

Papadopoulos takes a hard look at the overall architecture and philosophy of economic governance in the EMU and insists on the problem of the lack of secondary rules to ascertain the possible spill-over effects of a national budgetary derailment and the nature of the crisis at hand (borrowing, liquidity, or solvency crisis). He analytically presents and assesses the new EU legislative framework (commonly called "six pack") that seeks not only to strengthen the preventive and corrective arms of the SGP, but also to widen its scope of enquiry and action also to the fundamental problem of macroeconomic imbalances inside the EMU. The author presents a typology of fiscal unions, following which he assesses whether the new EU Fiscal Compact[29] can be considered as a viable path towards a European Fiscal Union. Finally, he pursues the theoretical task of evaluating whether both the so-called "Lisbon Strategy,"[30] i.e. structural measures to stimulate growth and employment, and the EU budget, are inchoate. Papadopoulos pulls the threads together in his conclusion by linking the concept of "legitimation crisis" with the rationalisation process of the EMU's economic governance, federalisation, and the future of European integration.

Dimitrios V. Skiadas argues in the next chapter that the EU budgetary reaction to the global financial crisis indicated that there is scope, room and potential for improvement. The unprecedented economic and financial crisis experienced throughout the globe has created the need for integrated actions to meet the short-term and long-term challenges for the national financial, economic, social and political structures and systems. Within the EU framework, the most promising option, given the nature and characteristics of the EU legal order, has been the restructuring of the budgetary architecture of the Union, thus allowing for the modification of the overall cohesion policy developed and financed by the Union's member states. The author discusses the various parameters of this reaction and its importance for the EU budgetary architecture.

In the opening chapter of the second part, Vasileios A. Vlachos assembles a coherent presentation of the literature on the development of the financial predicament and its climax into a sovereign debt crisis, and the effect of the latter on the business environment of the Greek economy.

---

[29] Formally, part of the new "Treaty on Stability, Coordination and Governance in the Economic and Monetary Union",that was signed by all EU member states except the Czech Republic and the United Kingdom on March 2, 2012.

[30] The Lisbon Strategy has been renamed "Europe 2020 Strategy" and extended for ten more years, until 2020. See notably Communication from the Commission, "EUROPE 2020. A strategy for smart, sustainable and inclusive growth," COM(2010) 2020 final, Brussels, 3 March 2010.

The author explores the fundamentals of the Greek business environment by concentrating on issues such as competitiveness, openness and direct investment (domestic and foreign). The analysis finally turns to the appropriateness of the economic policies adopted so far in order to indicate how these have contributed to the generation of a deflationary spiral that deepens depression and to identify the nature of policy orientations that are able to put forward pragmatic plans for Greece's prolonged recovery.

In the fifth chapter of the second part, Aristidis Bitzenis and Vasileios A. Vlachos focus on the myths and present some facts about the Greek sovereign debt crisis. At first, the authors indicate that the causes of the liquidity crisis, the credit crunch, and the current disinvestment crisis are the country's gloomy growth prospects. A significant amount of wealth has been generated in Greece during the euro era; hence the unwillingness to invest this wealth is due to psychological reasons – i.e. increased perception of risk – and the lack of growth prospects imposed by the sovereign debt crisis, not to the false notion that generally, funds do not exist. Secondly, the authors discuss the perils involved in the eventuality that Greece opts for an exit from the euro and the adoption of a national currency. Finally, the dead end policy of internal devaluation and other hazardous measures that unarguably fuel the deflationary spiral and sustain the Greek economy in depression are discussed. The authors conclude that instead of blindly reducing the public sector, cutting public capital spending – i.e. public investments – and fueling the deflationary spiral, there should be attempts in increasing the efficient use of resources, reducing the levels of corruption and ultimately, transferring the biggest possible part of the shadow economy to the formal economy through a well-calibrated set of bonuses, smart sanctions, and reinforcing the regulatory and coercive mechanisms of the state.

In the sixth chapter, Friedrich Schneider discusses the determinants and size of the Greek shadow economy and provides comparative estimates of the development of the Greek shadow economy and the impact of corruption on the Greek formal economy. The focus on the interrelation between the size of the shadow economy and levels of corruption in Greece is of primary importance. A reduction in the levels of corruption implies a reduction in the levels of tax evasion and the size of the shadow economy. This will contribute significantly to the relentless efforts of successive Greek governments to achieve a primary balance amid the sovereign debt crisis and during the country's worst and longest recession ever.

In the seventh chapter, Kostas C. Chryssogonos and Georgios D. Pavlidis discuss the Greek sovereign debt restructuring as a case study from a legal and political point of view. Sovereign debt that cannot be serviced has to be restructured in a timely, equitable and orderly manner. That implies a suitable bankruptcy framework for a balanced protection of both the state's and the creditors' interests, which was lacking in the EU at the time the Greek crisis erupted during the winter of 2009-10. A full-fledged legal analysis of the Greek debt restructuring and of the so-called "Memoranda" (the institutional mechanism of support devised to fill this void[31]) is pursued by the authors. Chryssogonos and Pavlidis show that this mechanism is an asymmetric bankruptcy framework for the repayment of Greek government creditors, which embodies a *de facto* – but not *de jure* – transfer of economic sovereignty to the "troika" outside the scope of the Greek Constitution and International Law. An assessment of the compatibility of salary and pension cuts with constitutional and international law is made. Finally, the legal and practical implications of a possible withdrawal of Greece – unilateral, negotiated, or imposed – from the EMU are discussed.

The eighth chapter opening the final part of this book is by Aristidis Bitzenis and Ioannis Makedos, who make a vast historical overview and a critical assessment of the Maastricht Treaty and the SGP from its original form throughout today. The authors describe the Maastricht convergence and budgetary discipline criteria as well as the sanctions procedure (the so-called Excessive Deficit Procedure). They assess the significance and real impact of the entire SGP framework on the coordination and surveillance of national budgetary policies. According to the authors, the original SGP's unbalanced emphasis on the sole budget deficit criterion, that takes into account neither the debt/GDP criterion nor the cross-country differences with respect to the potential rate of growth, was very short-sighted. Bitzenis and Makedos conclude that the original SGP did not reach its objectives, since more flexibility was required in its constitutive features. They conclude by explaining the two revisions of SGP in 2004 and 2011 and their importance for the current situation, and also briefly

[31] The joint EU/IMF rescue mechanism for Greece, an instrument eventually generalized for Ireland and Portugal, contains a Draft Plan consisting of two Memoranda: the Memorandum of Economic and Financial Policies and the Memorandum of Understanding on Specific Economic Policy Conditionality. These texts contain quantitative fiscal objectives for the future, the economic reforms that need to be made in order to obtain those targets, and monitoring mechanisms. Together they determine the long-term economic, fiscal, and social policy of Greece.

present the European Financial Stabilisation Mechanism and the European Financial Stability Facility, as well as the European Stability Mechanism that took their place.

In the ninth chapter, Pyrros Papadimitriou and Yiannis Hadziyiannakis indicate that although the international economic crisis has played its part in precipitating the Greek crisis, the underlying roots were firmly implanted in successive years of poor fiscal management and unruly public finances. The authors focus on two specific dimensions of the Greek crisis. Firstly, they unravel some core elements of poor budget management by looking at budgetary data and discussing the ineffectiveness of basic processes in public financial management. Secondly, they discuss how the architecture of the euro-area may have contributed to fiscal unruliness by unwittingly creating a framework of perverse incentives. Finally, they focus on the proposals made by the European Commission in September 2010 to reform the SGP and conclude that Greece would have to consider revisiting certain basic principles in its budgetary management.

In the final chapter, Aristidis Bitzenis and Ioannis Makedos return to the hotly debated issue of the manipulation of Greek statistics, which is widely considered as one of the basic – if not *the* basic – reasons for Greece's loss of credibility in the financial markets and its subsequent economic downfall. The authors parse through all the ramifications of this complex problem by using abundant data and by retracing the interpretative conflict between Eurostat and successive Greek governments. Bitzenis and Makedos conclude that the highly politicised system in Greece certainly did not allow for an independent production and dissemination of economic data, but they also point out the responsibility of many other institutional players in the outbreak and deepening of the latest European financial crisis. At the end of the day, it is always the good-faith investors that are misled by the inadequacies of the established system of collection, assessment and dissemination of information relevant to the true default risk of entities, be they corporate or sovereign.

References

English

Arghyrou, M.G. and Kontonikas, A. (2011). The EMU sovereign-debt crisis: Fundamentals, expectations and contagion. *European Economy Economic Papers No. 436*. Brussels: European Commission (Directorate-General for Economic and Financial Affairs).

Bagaria, N., Holland, D. and Van Reenen, J. (2012). Fiscal consolidation during a depression. *National Institute Economic Review*, 221 (1): F42-F54.

Ball, L.M. (2009). Hysteresis in unemployment: Old and new evidence. *NBER Working Papers No. 14818*. Cambridge (Massachusetts): National Bureau of Economic Research.

Bianchi, J. and Mendoza, E. (2011). Overborrowing, financial crises and 'macroprudential' policy. *IMF Working Paper No. 11/24*. Washington DC: International Monetary Fund.

Crescenzi, T. (2011). *Beyond the Keynesian Endpoint: Crushed by Credit and Deceived by Debt – How to Revive the Global Economy*. New Jersey: FT Press.

Darvas, Z., Pisani-Ferry, J. and Sapir A. (2011). A comprehensive approach to the euro-area debt crisis. *Bruegel Policy Brief No. 491*. Brussels: Bruegel.

Eggertsson, G.B. and Krugman, P. (2012). Debt, deleveraging, and the liquidity trap: A Fisher-Minsky-Koo approach. *Quarterly Journal of Economics*, 127 (3): 1469-1513.

Fisher, I. (1933). The debt-deflation theory of great depressions. *Econometrica*, 1 (4): 337-357.

Galati, G. and Moessner, R. (2011). Macroprudential policy: A literature review. *BIS Working Paper No. 337*. Basel: Bank for International Settlements.

Hau, H., Langfield, S. and Marques-Ibanez, D. (2012). Bank ratings: What determines their quality? *ECB Working Papers Series No. 1484*. Frankfurt: European Central Bank.

Haug, J., Lamassoure, A. and Verhofstadt, G., in collaboration with Gros, D. and De Grauwe P. (2011). *Europe for Growth: For a Radical Change in Financing the EU*. Brussels: Notre Europe.

IMF (2003). *External Debt Statistics: Guide for Compilers and Users*. Washington, DC: International Monetary Fund.

Jensen, J. and Wohlbier, F. (2012). Improving tax governance in EU Member States: Criteria for successful policies. *European Economy*

Occasional Papers No. 114. Brussels: European Commission (Directorate-General for Economic and Financial Affairs).

Keen, S. (1995). Finance and economic breakdown: Modelling Minsky's Financial Instability Hypothesis. *Journal of Post-Keynesian Economics*, 17 (4): 607-635.

Lanara-Tzotze, Z. (2012). *The Impact of Anti-Crisis Measures, and the Social and Employment Situation in Greece*. Brussels: European Economic and Social Committee.

Michaillat, P. (2012). Do matching frictions explain unemployment? Not in bad times. *American Economic Review*, 102 (4): 1721-1750.

Minsky, H. (1994). Financial instability hypothesis. In Arestis, P. and Sawyer, M. (eds.), *The Edward Elgar Companion to Radical Political Economy*. Aldershot: Edward Edgar.

Official Journal of the EU, C 83 of 30 March 2010. *Consolidated versions of the Treaty on European Union and the Treaty on the Functioning of the European Union*.

Schneider, F., Buehn, A. and Montenegro, C. (2010). Shadow economies all over the world: New estimates for 162 countries from 1999 to 2007. *Policy Research Working Papers Series No. 5356*. Washington DC: The World Bank.

Stein, J.L. (2011). The diversity of debt crises in Europe. *Cato Journal*, 31 (2): 199-215.

Tymoigne, E. (2012). Measuring macroprudential risk through financial fragility: A Minskyan approach. *Levy Economics Institute Working Paper No. 716*. New York: Levy Economics Institute of Bard College.

Greek

Τράπεζα της Ελλάδος (2011). *Έκθεση του Διοικητή για το Έτος 2010*. Αθήνα: Τράπεζα της Ελλάδος.

PART 1:

THE EURO-AREA'S SOVEREIGN DEBT CRISIS MANAGEMENT

CHAPTER TWO

THE EFFICIENCY OF DEBT CRISIS MANAGEMENT BY EU MECHANISMS: LESSONS FROM THE GREEK CASE*

IOANNIS PAPADOPOULOS

1. Introduction – A Quintuple Systemic Crisis

Since the winter of 2009-2010, the attention of the media and of public opinions at large has undoubtedly been drawn to the so-called "Greek tragedy,", namely the unexpectedly precipitous and deep debt crisis of that member state of the European Union (EU), coupled with gradual revelations as to the extent of falsification of its statistical data on public deficit and debt. For several months, the focus was on the short-term operational dimension of a particular country's financial difficulties due to its budgetary derailment. Consequently, the issue discussed by EU institutions during that period was that of the inaptitude of a specific country's institutions to manage its sovereign debt. That, of course, is understandable because it is only human that what is actually happening always takes priority over longer-term problems or, even worse, over structural deficits of the common political tools we Europeans have devised. But by now, it is universally acknowledged that, even though in the history of Europe the "Greek tragedy" will be considered as an event of primary importance with dramatic overtones, there are underlying issues of economic governance of the euro area and of the EU itself

* One first short version of this Chapter was presented as a paper on May 22, 2010, on the panel "Recession and EU Budgetary Crisis" of the International Conference on International Business 2010 (ICIB 2010), Thessaloniki, Greece. A short version of Section 6 of this Chapter was presented as a paper on May 18, 2012, on the panel "European Union" of the International Conference on International Business 2012 (ICIB 2012), Thessaloniki, Greece. I thank PhD candidate Ilias Konstantinidis for his valuable secretarial assistance.

overall. Thus, the Greek case will have served as an instrument to help us prevent similar problems occurring in the future and provide stability for the common currency on a viable basis.

In order to assess the efficiency of the EU mechanisms to manage crises like the one we are living at present, we have to parse through the structural problems of the Common Economic and Monetary Policies of the EU, starting, of course, from the highest level: that of the Treaty itself, and then proceeding to secondary European law (notably the preventive and corrective arms of the Stability and Growth Pact – SGP), as well as EU macroeconomic practices. The imbalance between the monetary aspect of the Economic and Monetary Union (EMU), which is sufficiently consolidated and managed by an independent institution, and its economic dimension, which proved to be weak and problematic, has been amply pointed out, so I will not rephrase the same (totally justified) criticism.

In this Chapter, I will try to show, sometimes through a quick comparison with a federal model's analogous mechanisms (notably the American ones), that because of these structural deficits, European officials have been largely improvising after-the-fact and costly ways of toughening up budgetary discipline and proposing crisis-busting solutions, whereas coordinated solutions, not only to deficit and debt, but most importantly to competitiveness and growth problems, would be the only rational solution.

I will argue that Europe is going through a *quintuple systemic crisis*:

A Sovereign and Private Debt Crisis

This aspect of the crisis originates either in the banking sector (as is clearly the case in Ireland and Spain) or in the official sector (as is clearly the case in Greece). The two sources fold back the one into the other and are mutually reinforcing. We all know, by now, how excessive banking leverage and risky financial operations spread non-repayable private debt to a huge number of households in the USA and how this provoked the Lehman Brothers crash and the ensuing economic meltdown in Europe. Since 2008, the public debt/gross domestic product (GDP) ratio has been mounting in almost all European countries due to the economic downturn and a series of bail-outs designed to prevent EU member states from collapsing.

A Bank Undercapitalisation Crisis

This aspect of the crisis is due to the toxic assets European banks have accumulated over the years, mostly because of insufficient regulation. The European banking sector, especially, is in a dire position. Violent deleveraging after the 2008 financial meltdown and stricter prudential requirements brought about a severe banking undercapitalisation. This, in its turn, is a major cause of underinvestment in the real economy.

A Disinvestment Crisis

The credit crunch has provoked a huge wave of underinvestment, especially in capital spending for infrastructures, due to liquidity shortages in the banking sector. This, in its turn, has brought down growth and jobs, since there can be no economic development without a steady flow of investment in productive resources. Stagnant capitals are safely placed in "refuge values" (such as gold or the US dollar and Treasury bonds) and are not sufficiently invested in infrastructure projects, research and development (R&D), innovation, life-long learning, and training of human resources that can produce economies of scale and boost growth and jobs across Europe.

A Political and Institutional Crisis

This is a crisis both of the euro area and of the EU overall, expressed as a serious democratic deficit in the functioning of the EU's crisis management mechanisms and in the Economic and Monetary Union (EMU) economic governance. The euro zone crisis management has been disastrous from its very beginning in 2009-2010. Instead of tackling the problem head-on by re-profiling the distressed Greek debt into jointly guaranteed European debt and securitizing part of it under EU guarantee, ending thus in one fell swoop speculative movements and the debt crisis before even its outburst, the EU has been dragging its feet by refusing to consider the problem as a European instead of a national one out of fear for "moral hazard"[1]. This attitude has been seriously undermining the EU's political credibility vis-à-vis the capital markets and Europe's strategic partners as well as competitors. This, in its turn, has brought about a social crisis.

---

[1] For an analysis of this notion, see *infra* p. 53-54 and note 82.

A Social Crisis

Investors, depositors and, of course, workers, unemployed, retired and citizens at large have lost confidence in the capacity of the EU, an economic heavyweight but a political dwarf, to handle crises and bring a halt to the deflationary spiral, the debt and deficit traps, and the growing unemployment in many member states. The catastrophic mismanagement of the crisis has been eroding the output legitimacy of the Union. In other words, a secondary crisis induced by the EMU's structural deficiencies, macroeconomic presuppositions, and seriously flawed crisis-prevention and crisis-resolution mechanisms has brought social discredit to the EU's rules, institutions and mechanisms.

The above are intertwined strands of a *systemic crisis* that has been unfolding since the end of 2009, starting from Greece and expanding in the whole euro area. This crisis has had a serious impact on the real economy by tightening the lending standards of banks, thus squeezing credit for companies. That, in turn, has hindered economic development and has contributed to the recession of the euro area overall. The asset bubble, which was provoked by investment banks' extremely loose leveraging practices and burst with the default of Lehman Brothers in September 2008, resulted in the exact opposite trend: a deleveraging overreaction.

What we have been observing since the beginning of this crisis is that the intergovernmental factor in the EU governance has gained power to the detriment of the Community spirit. Instead of comprehensive plans prepared and piloted by the European Commission, under the democratic monitoring and control of the European Parliament and with the aid of the European Central Bank (ECB), it seems that EU leaders now let national bargaining lines and strategies take hold at the heart of the European integration process. This might seem as a purely formal remark, but is of the utmost importance. National rivalries not only produce lesser democratic legitimacy and alienate European citizens - especially those from the smaller and weaker member states - from the European project; they also bring about a lowered efficiency of decision-making. Intergovernmentalism by definition strives to reconcile a myriad of particular national needs and exigencies, instead of producing regulation that promotes the European collective interest over and above the particularistic, self-centered national interests (or what some political leaders erroneously conceive as such).

Even further, the European leaders have been exceedingly opening the door to co-regulation by external factors, such as banks and insurance companies (the private sector in general), credit rating agencies, third party countries (such as China), and international organisations (such as the International Monetary Fund – IMF). This is an institutional logic that forcibly brings about a worsening of the regulatory quality of decisions, since European decision-making will depend more and more upon variable – since they are external to the EU institutional design – factors that, of course, obey to other kinds of considerations and follow their own agenda instead of the European one.

The result of these developments is a growing insecurity of European citizens and international markets in front of the indeterminacy of the regulatory framework and the changeable, erratic practices followed. This has produced important and continuous strains in the stock exchanges and in the capital markets, since investors hate indeterminacy and insecurity and are generally risk-avert.

I will also argue that, due to the peculiarities of the "community method", we have more or less been striking *ad hoc* and hardly manageable compromises, and then generalising them in an inductive fashion, instead of laying down clear, strong, and efficient general rules of prevention and sanction in favour of macroeconomic stability and competitiveness. More specifically regarding the euro, despite the voices of many great European figures (such as that of Jacques Delors) who kept repeating for years that it is macro-economically irrational to have a single currency without coordinated state economic policies, we naively thought until recently that we could manage a monetary union only through some regulation and supervision, but with no true political union[2].

Nevertheless, the whole architecture of the Maastricht Treaty and the SGP, based on a strict system of purely national responsibility for the rates of public deficit and debt, a no-bail-out clause, and an ECB policy of no monetisation of public debts, is now drawing to an end, after having deceived even its most fervent supporters. I shall argue in favour of a *European Fiscal and Banking Union* with at least seven structural features as a *sine qua non* way out of the current systemic crisis conundrum. I believe that, since any kind of European fiscal union will necessarily limit the freedom of member states to determine in a sovereign manner their own policy mix through the discretionary use of their national budgets,

---

[2] The EMU is characterized and affected by "the asymmetry between monetary and fiscal policy in the Euro Area […], with the ECB setting a predictable policy based on price stability in the area as a whole and the member states setting fiscal policy individually subject to the joint arrangements of the Broad Macroeconomic Guidelines and the SGP process", David Mayes and Matti Virén, "The SGP and the ECB: an exercise in asymmetry," *Journal of Financial Transformation* 19 (2007): 172.

something that is at the core of their national sovereignty, the way towards a Fiscal Union has to gain *political legitimacy* through some kind of European federalization. Otherwise, the citizens will most probably reject this plan.

2. The Basic Structural Deficiencies of the Euro Area

As already pointed out briefly in the Introduction, most of the commentators now think that the euro area's basic shortfall has been the dividing line between a completely integrated monetary zone, on the one hand, and a political and economic union underpinning it that has a limited only capacity to resolve disagreements among member states and to take decisive steps to resolve difficulties, on the other[3]. A big currency area, such as the EMU, proved itself incapable of relying for its existence and sound working on the prudent management of bank credit and of economic policies by its member states. Guy Verhofstadt, president of the Alliance of Liberals and Democrats (ALDE) in the European Parliament, put it bluntly in a speech: "There never was a currency, and there is no currency in the actual world without a state's authority to guarantee the economic, financial and political conditions to do so."[4] Stated differently, there never was a successful monetary union that was not supported by a

---

[3] One of the foremost critics of this structural deficiency of the euro is the French economist Christian de Saint-Etienne, who in his book *La fin de l'euro* (Paris: François Bourin, 2009), made an accurate portrait of the ill-conceived features of the European common currency.
In 1997, one of the fathers of the euro, former President of the European Commission Jacques Delors, proposed an Economic Policies Coordination Pact between the EU member states that would complement and equilibrate the monetary union, but his proposal was not favourably received; see Jacques Delors, "Jacques Delors dénonce le 'coup de poker' de Sarkozy et Merkel," interview held by Alain Faujas and Claire Gatinois for *Le Monde*, October 19, 2011, http://www.regards-citoyens.com/article-jacques-delors-denonce-le-coup-de-poker-de-sarkozy-et-merkel-le-monde-86801055.html.

[4] Guy Verhofstadt, "How to break the European deadlock?" (speech given at the European Chamber of Commerce in Hong Kong, November 3, 2011). In an acclaimed article published at the very beginning of the euro in 2000, Niall Ferguson and Laurence J. Kotlikoff foresaw that, due to the lack of a fiscal union in the EMU, the ECB would be called upon continually to print money in order to monetize the EMU member states' public debt, which would not be a viable model. See Niall Ferguson and Laurence J. Kotlikoff, "The Degeneration of EMU," *Foreign Affairs* 79(2) (March/April 2000).

fiscal and political union, without a sovereign standing behind the common currency.[5]

This criticism is well-known. Yet, it is too simple to affirm that the problem lies only in the impossibility of combining a single currency with 17 different governments, economic strategies, and bond markets.[6] Because in fact, the model the EU chose for its EMU meant that once a country met the Maastricht criteria to join the Monetary Union (budget deficit of no more than 3 %, and government debt of no more than 60 %, of GDP), then all government debt issued by that country – regardless of the size or state of its national economy – was presumed to be essentially equal to all the others' in determining whether it could be used as collateral by the banks for ECB borrowing. This brought about a false pricing of sovereign risk across the euro area, in the sense that all sovereign obligations were deemed "risk-free debt". Thus, banks were not only allowed by the Basel II rules[7], but also encouraged to hold a great deal of such zero-risk debt, which enabled them to use it in order to obtain very high leverage.

The result was that interest-rate spreads across different euro area government bonds was just a few basis points – as if we had to do with government bonds issued by several states of a federal union. That practically meant that the borrowing costs of all the member states of the euro area was brought down and remained low for almost ten years, as currency risk disappeared and all interest rates converged with the already low German rates. Cheaper credit, combined with excessive credit expansion by the banking sector, helped Southern European countries to borrow and grow. But these countries did little to pursue in time structural reforms that would increase productivity and adopt technological innovation so as to produce high value added products and services; they did little also to regulate efficiently the financial sector so as to prevent overleveraging, i.e. lending much more than banks could afford given their capital adequacy. Thus, Southern European EMU member states never actually restructured their productive models to allow them to cope with an environment where they could no longer regain competitiveness

---

[5] See *infra* Section 6.1 on the notion of a "Fiscal Union".

[6] Verhofstadt, "How to break the European deadlock?".

[7] "Basel II" is the code name for a set of recommendations, adopted by the so-called Basel Committee on Banking Supervision in 2004, that intended to create an international risk-management standard for banking regulators' use. This standard was designed to ensure that the capital requirements of banks would be able to guard against the risks they expose themselves to through their lending and investment practices.

through external (i.e. currency) devaluation. Lacking the tool of external devaluation, they are currently being forced to sustain a long deflationary spiral that depresses aggregate demand and produces recession and mass unemployment, but also makes the servicing and repayment of debt all the more difficult because of the GDP fall.

Yet, the biggest structural deficiency of the EMU in its inception was the *underlying comparative competitiveness problem* of some member states vis-à-vis others. The foremost of all EU's institutional shortfalls underlying the current acute crisis we are living in Europe probably is the problem of the EU's incapacity to account for, and to handle, member states' external competitiveness deficits. Neither the so-called "preventive" nor the so-called "corrective" arms of the SGP[8] made any serious reference to the problem of competitiveness disequilibria between member states, as this can be revealed through a comparison between the long-term trends in national balances of payments. The SGP solely imposes medium-term *fiscal* objectives to all participating member states through a mechanism of mutual surveillance of national stability programmes' implementation. It is as if the SGP officially recognised the existence of *only* economic and budgetary heterogeneity in the Union.

Nonetheless, following credit expansion and the vast capital flows into the countries of the "eurozone periphery", labour costs, wages, and prices rose at an unsustainable rate in most Southern European countries, condemning thus their manufacturing sector to a severe loss in competitiveness. As a result, countries that had a roughly balanced trade in the beginning of the EMU in 1999 began running large trade deficits instead. Until recently at least, there was no European mechanism for the smooth adjustment of trade imbalances between EMU member states. As Stephen King puts it[9], "if, however, the adjustment in the euro area is to take place via shifts in competitiveness, it follows not only that the real exchange rates of southern Europe should decline but, that the real exchange rates of northern Europe should rise. We are back to the need for different inflation rates in north and south". Yet, what happens instead is a "lopsided adjustment:" a continuous pressure obliging the southern European nations to reduce their current account deficits and practically no pressure towards the northern European nations to reduce their current account surpluses.

---

[8] That we will analyse extensively *infra*, Section 3.1.

[9] Stephen King, "What Ptolemy tells us about Germany and Greece," *Financial Times*, February 20, 2012, http://www.ft.com/intl/cms/s/0/70a81998-5bb5-11e1-a447-00144feabdc0.html#axzz22PV0mQ9f.

In order to understand this extremely serious pitfall of the EMU, we need to take a closer look at the overall architecture and philosophy of economic governance in the European Economic and Monetary Union (EMU) (Section 3). Having done that, I will briefly discuss the problem of the lack of secondary rules to ascertain the possible spill-over effects of a national budgetary derailment and the nature of the crisis at hand (borrowing, liquidity, or solvency crisis)[10] (Section 4). Then I will present and assess the new EU legislative framework (commonly called "six pack") that seeks, apart from strengthening the preventive and corrective arms of the SGP, to widen the scope of enquiry and action of the EU and the euro area governance to the fundamental problem of macroeconomic imbalances inside the EMU (Section 5). Consequently, I will briefly discuss the necessary components to any type of fiscal union, following which I will assess whether the new EU Fiscal Compact[11] can be considered as a viable path towards a European Fiscal Union (Section 6). Finally, I will try to show that the EU's tools, centred around the so-called "Lisbon Strategy,"[12] to pursue stimulus measures for growth and employment, but also around the EU budget, are inchoate (Section 7). In this Chapter's conclusion (Section 8), I will develop some more theoretical ideas on the relations between the concepts of "legitimation crisis", rationalisation process of the EMU's economic governance, federalisation, and the future of European integration.

---

[10] In their fascinating book Carmen M. Reinhart and Kenneth S. Rogoff, *This Time Is Different: Eight Centuries of Financial Folly*, (Princeton and Oxford: Princeton University Press, 2009), 49-138, 275-292 and *passim*, the authors retrace the history of sovereign external debt crises through an impressive array of macroeconomic time series data. Regarding early warning signals of a possible forthcoming debt crisis in the several forms it can take, they state that there is a "well-entrenched tendency of policy makers and market participants to treat the signals as irrelevant archaic residuals of an outdated framework"; Reinhart and Rogoff, *This Time,* 281; hence the need for an improvement of institutions, especially of international financial regulatory ones (such as the IMF).

[11] Formally, part of the new "Treaty on Stability, Coordination and Governance in the Economic and Monetary Union" (TSCG), which was signed by all EU member states except the Czech Republic and the United Kingdom on March 2, 2012.

[12] The Lisbon Strategy has been renamed "Europe 2020 Strategy" and extended for ten more years, until 2020. See notably Communication from the Commission, "EUROPE 2020. A strategy for smart, sustainable and inclusive growth," COM(2010) 2020 final, Brussels, 3 March 2010.

3. Presentation and Criticism of the Foundational Principles of the EMU

According to the Treaty on the Functioning of the European Union[13], the guiding principles of the Union's Economic and Monetary Policy are the following: "stable prices, sound public finances and monetary conditions and a sustainable balance of payments."[14] The EU Common Economic and Monetary Policy is divided into two strands: 1) Economic Policy[15] and 2) Monetary Policy, specifically for member states that have adopted the euro as common currency.[16]

I shall take up these two EU policies in turn in order to expound and assess both their foundational principles and their concrete functioning vis-à-vis analogous mechanisms in federal states, most prominently the United States of America.

3.1 Principles and Presuppositions of the EU Economic Policy

Under the implicit influence of the New Classical Economics, and particularly of the Ricardian Equivalence Proposition (also known as the "Barro-Ricardo Equivalence Theorem")[17], the SGP has as its basic aim the attaining of a balanced budget, or otherwise the annihilation of public deficit. As is well known, Keynesian economics hold that each time an economy operates below its potential output and growth rate path, the state

---

[13] This Treaty (TFEU) has replaced, since the adoption of the Lisbon Treaty as of December 1st, 2009, the former Treaty establishing the European Community.

[14] TFEU, article 119, paragraph 3.

[15] TFEU, articles 120-126.

[16] TFEU, articles 127-133.

[17] According to Robert J. Barro, "Are Government Bonds Net Wealth?" *Journal of Political Economy* 82 (1974): 1095-1117, and "On the Determination of the Public Debt," *Journal of Political Economy* 87 (1979): 940-71, who provided a theoretical groundwork for an intuition by David Ricardo in his groundbreaking *Principles of Political Economy and Taxation* (1817), a government's choice of either raising tax revenue or issuing public debt has an equivalent effect on the economy, since in both cases an increase in public expenditure is counterbalanced by a decrease in private spending (in Barro's words, "shifts between debt and tax finance for a given amount of public expenditure would have no first-order effect on the real interest rate, volume of private investment, etc.", Barro, "On the Determination", 940). Therefore, any increase in public spending and consequently of public deficit is necessarily inefficient, since any impact on economic growth it might have will be defeated by an equivalent decrease of private consumption and an increase of private savings.

has to intervene by decreasing interest rates and taxes and by increasing public spending in order to replace falling aggregate demand and boost economic activity, since otherwise an economy can remain trapped in a low employment equilibrium[18]. In clear opposition to Keynesian economics, New Classical Economics claim that public deficits should in any case be proscribed, since they bring about an increase in the public debt ratio and, even when they are employed in a countercyclical manner in order to mitigate the effects of an economic downturn, they have an inherent tendency to become perennially established, since governments do not usually have the political courage to slash them once their country enters once again the virtuous phase of its economic cycle. Thus, according to New Classical Economics, fiscal policy should only allow for automatic stabilisers (tax revenues and public expenditure) to exert a countercyclical action as long as an economy is in recession, and this action will be offset during the growth phase of the cycle; accordingly, during the whole economic cycle the budget will be in balance and public debt will not rise. Consequently, there will be no need to raise new taxes or increase existing ones.

As a consequence of this basic macroeconomic presupposition, the SGP obliges all EU member states to "commit themselves to respect the medium-term budgetary objective of positions close to balance or in surplus"[19], which will allow them to deal with normal cyclical fluctuations while keeping the government deficit within the reference value of 3 % of GDP[20]. In that framework, member states "will launch the corrective

---

[18] John Maynard Keynes, *The General Theory of Employment, Interest and Money*, 2nd edition, eds., Geoffrey C. Harcourt and Peter A. Riach, 2 vols., (London: Routledge, 1997). On J. M. Keynes' main thesis that it is aggregate demand that determines the overall level of economic activity, see Keynes' biography by Robert Skidelsky, *John Maynard Keynes 1883-1946: Economist, Philosopher, Statesman*, (London: Penguin Books, 2003).

[19] European Council Resolution on the Stability and Growth Pact, Amsterdam, 17 June 1997, ch. THE MEMBER STATES, pt. 1.

[20] The ratio of 3% "of the planned or actual government deficit to GDP at market prices" is considered as "excessive" for Stability and Growth Pact purposes, according to the value references given in the Protocol No. 12 on the Excessive Deficit Procedure (EDP), article 1. For two possible justifications of the choice of the 3% ratio of public deficit/GDP as the value reference in the Maastricht Treaty, see Marco Buti and André Sapir, eds., *Economic Policy in EMU: A Study by the European Commission Services* (Oxford: Clarendon Press & New York, Oxford University Press, 1998), and Jean-Pierre Vesperini, *Relancer la Croissance de l'Europe. Propositions pour une nouvelle gouvernance européenne* (Paris: Economica, 2005), 20.

budgetary adjustments they deem necessary without delay on receiving information indicating the risk of an excessive deficit"[21]. The 1992 Maastricht Treaty that instituted the EMU, and for the implementation of which the SGP was enacted five years later, already stated that "Member States shall avoid excessive government deficits"[22] and set up a mechanism of correction of excessive deficits that proved gravely deficient during the Greek sovereign debt crisis.

Normally, the monetarist underpinning of the euro area's architecture should have provided for a rather rigid mechanism of prevention of possible, and correction of actual, public deficits and debts at EU level. Indeed, by posing caps to member state public deficits and debts through common reference values, the European founders of the Maastricht Treaty and the SGP aimed at avoiding the possible negative externalities that an excessive public deficit or debt could induce on the monetary variables that the ECB uses in order to design and implement its common monetary policy for the euro area. Yet, the whole functioning of the multilateral budgetary surveillance mechanism set up by the EU (and that proved in hindsight excessively lax) is based on a philosophy of *self-assumption of responsibility by the euro area member states themselves*, as is clearly revealed in the Protocol No. 12 on the Excessive Deficit Procedure[23]. This lack of primary co-responsibility for member states' public deficits and debts is strikingly in tension with the abovementioned theoretical foundation of the euro area, namely that of the probable *interdependence between national budgetary policies and common euro area monetary policy*[24].

---

[21] European Council Resolution on the Stability and Growth Pact, Amsterdam, 17 June 1997, ch. THE MEMBER STATES, pt. 4.

[22] TFEU, article 126, paragraph 1. As Marco Buti, Daniele Franco and Hedwig Ongena, "Budgetary Policies during Recessions – Retrospective Applications of the "Stability and Growth Pact" to the Post-War Period," *European Economy Economic Papers* 121 (May 1997): 3, write: "In practice, the Treaty prescribes that the original cause of the rise of the deficit above the 3% ceiling must be exceptional, that the deficit must not, in any case, exceed this threshold by too much, and must return promptly below it once the initial driving force is over. These three conditions need to apply simultaneously."

[23] See Protocol on the Excessive Deficit Procedure (EDP), article 3: "In order to ensure the effectiveness of the excessive deficit procedure, *the governments of the Member States shall be responsible under this procedure for the deficits of general government* […]. The Member States shall ensure that national procedures in the budgetary area enable them to meet their obligations in this area deriving from these Treaties" (emphasis added).

[24] On this fundamental problem, see also *infra*, section 4.

Indeed, a public deficit is normally financed, and refinanced, by the issuance of state bonds. However, the (re)financing of state deficits certainly does have some monetary implications in certain circumstances. Thus, if the amount of bonds issued is considered at some point to be excessive by the international financial markets, either because of a lack of trustworthiness of the government's fiscal policy, or because of a shortage of international capital available for investment in sovereign bonds, the interest rates of these bonds will necessarily tend to increase exponentially[25]. Also, an afflux of state bonds might dry up the market from private investments, especially in times of economic uncertainty, where private risk-taking tends to decrease. *A fortiori*, if at a certain point a public deficit is monetised, i.e. is financed by banks through the purchase of government securities, that policy might have a propensity of creating excessive liquidities[26] and thus inflation, which in turn might provoke an increase in interest rates and a drop in the currency's exchange rates.

Of course, a public deficit will also be liable to bring about an increase in the public debt-to-GDP ratio in certain circumstances. And a public debt considered to be excessive by international financial markets will in turn undoubtedly incite fears of government insolvency in some cases, bringing about massive sells of Treasury bonds, a sharp raise in interest rates and a drop in the currency exchange rates[27]. If such is the case, the budgetary adjustment that will be needed to cope with the crisis will have to be particularly harsh in order to stabilise the public debt, sometimes putting in jeopardy the sustainability of the debt itself[28].

---

[25] The first scenario was what actually materialised in the "Greek crisis" during the months since December 2009.

[26] On the monetary tool known as "quantitative easing", see *infra* p. 43-44.

[27] This scenario materialised in the "Greek crisis" during the months since December 2009.

[28] On the notion of "public debt sustainability", see INSEE, *L'économie française - Comptes et dossiers*, ed. 2006-2007, 68 ff. A "solvency" crisis, as opposed to a "liquidity" crisis, means that in the first case, it is absolutely necessary for a country to reduce its liabilities to such extent that it achieves, once again, a sustainable medium-term path for the servicing of its external debt. This distinction is not easy to determine. See *inter alia* Nouriel Roubini, "Debt Sustainability: How to Assess Whether a Country is Insolvent" (paper presented at Stern School of Business, New York University, December 20, 2001), http://people.stern.nyu.edu/nroubini/papers/debtsustainability.pdf. Michel Aglietta, *La crise. Les voies de sortie*, (Paris: Michalon, 2nd edition, 2010), 77, rightly qualifies long-term debt sustainability as a "crucial inter-temporal condition" of any successful budgetary reflation and calls for medium-term budgetary

Hence, the fear that an initially purely domestic sovereign debt crisis could evolve into a government insolvency crisis, which would eventually produce dire consequences for the EMU in its entirety, produced some purely *prudential* "no bail-out" rules enshrined both in the Treaty[29] and in the so-called "preventive" and "corrective" arms of the SGP[30]. This set of rules is prudential because it is based on the expected deterrent effect a possible sovereign debt crisis scenario would have on member states' fiscal policy, and therefore on the *ex ante* self-assumption of responsibility by each member state. Consequently, we are not in presence of (as could rationally be expected) a set of *political* rules at the EU level establishing strong economic governance structures *ex ante* and crisis management institutions *ex post*. In order to strongly deter governments from enacting overly lax or irresponsible budgetary policies, the SGP sets, at least as a trend, an objective of "zero deficit", and does not allow for a posterior granting of credit facilities to[31], nor a privileged access to financial institutions in favour of[32], nor a direct assumption of public debts of[33], any public body or organism. Yet, this sacrosanct objective is both an overbroad and a "one-size-fits-all" policy unfit for all countries at the same time; it also inherently tends to have a procyclical, rather than a countercyclical, effect, which in periods of economic downturn is both economically irrational and politically problematic.

The SGP's aim of always tending towards a balanced or a surplus budget is overbroad because there will always be sound economic motives for a well-functioning sovereign debt market to be organised. On the supply side, there are certain infrastructure investments, necessitated by the development of so-called "network economy" sectors (such as information and communication technologies, transportation, and energy), that can only be financed, or at least co-financed, by public investments

---

programming establishing a credible link between public investment expenditures and the post-crisis growth regime; Aglietta, *La crise,* 77-8.

[29] TFEU, articles 123-25.

[30] Regulation (EU) No. 1175/2011 of the European Parliament and of the Council of 16 November 2011 amending Council Regulation (EC) No. 1466/97 on the strengthening of the surveillance of budgetary positions and the surveillance and coordination of economic policies, OJ L 306, 23.11.2011, 12, and Council Regulation (EU) No. 1177/2011 of 8 November 2011 amending Regulation (EC) No. 1467/97 on speeding up and clarifying the implementation of the excessive deficit procedure, OJ L 306, 23.11.2011, 33, respectively. On the new "preventive" and "corrective" arms of the SGP see *infra* Section 5.

[31] TFEU, article 123.

[32] TFEU, article 124.

[33] TFEU, article 125.

due to the need to obtain economies of scale; the same applies for large educational, R&D and innovation projects. Unless these public investments are 100 % self-financed, a state will need at some point to allow for the issuance of state-guaranteed securities. On the demand side, investors will always feel the need to include in their portfolios a certain amount of low-risk securities, which necessarily leads to the formation of a sovereign debt market. Thus, as can be seen, both from a supply and from a demand viewpoint, it is rational to consider that there always will be the need for a certain amount of (fluctuating according to conjunctional reasons) sovereign debt.

The SGP's "one-size-fits-all" aim is also overly rigid, as it imposes the same requirements to every member state in terms of the maximum allowed public deficit and debt ratios, despite the empirically attested fact that the economies of the euro area countries still evolve around differentiated cycles, due to the fact that their economies are structurally diverse and therefore dissimilarly exposed to the hazards of the international conjuncture[34]. The 3 % public deficit and the 60 % public debt ratios also are indiscriminate as value references, in the sense that they do not differentiate between different types of public expenditure, namely between current and investment expenditures, or otherwise between consumption and capital spending, even though the latter is, in principle at least, capable of hastening the pace of growth in the long run, and thus of bringing down more quickly the government debt level[35].

---

[34] There is much empirical evidence attesting to the fact of a high degree of divergence in the economic cycles of the EU member states, especially between "core" and "periphery" economies; see, *inter alia*, Guglielmo Maria Caporale, "Is Europe an Optimum Currency Area? Symmetric Versus Asymmetric Shocks in the EC," *National Institute Economic Review* 144 (1993): 95-103, and Paul De Grauwe and Wim Vanhaverbeke, "Is Europe an Optimum Currency Area?: Evidence from Regional Data," in *Policy Issues in the Operation of Currency Unions*, ed. Paul R. Masson and Mark P. Taylor (Cambridge: Cambridge University Press, 1993), 111-29.
Of course, the theoretical possibility of allowing for a fluctuating public deficit ratio depending on the euro area conjunction, the cycle of each member state depending on the structure of its productive capacities, its nominal and real growth ratios, its public debt ratio, and its balance of payments, even though rational *in abstracto*, would present irresolvable problems of manageability.

[35] On the theoretical and practical objections to the introduction of such a differentiated approach (the so-called "golden rule" which would allow governments to borrow in order to finance investment), see Communication from the Commission to the Council and the European Parliament, "Public finances in EMU – 2003," COM(2003) 283 final, Brussels, 21 May 2003, 7-9.

Finally, the SGP's philosophy clearly is procyclical rather than countercyclical, in other words tends to *magnify* economic or financial fluctuations instead of decreasing them[36]. Thus, the SGP mechanisms are not activated when we are in the upward phase of the economic cycle, so that the eventuality of corrective measures remains distant for fiscally irresponsible governments. On the contrary, the SGP applies in full rigor when the economic cycle enters into a recession phase, fiscal revenues and employment automatically drop and the public deficit increases, sometimes beyond the 3 % cap. In such case, the state paradoxically has to implement a restrictive budgetary policy in order to lower the deficit ratio, which of course tends to *enhance* rather than constrict the already existing economic downturn effects[37]. The only rational way out of this conundrum is to officially recognize a distinction between *cyclical* and *structural* deficits, and subsequently to focus budgetary efforts on the reduction of structural deficits all along the economic cycle[38].

In conclusion, even though the need for containment of probable risks due to interdependence between national budgetary policies and common euro area monetary policy is considered as one of the main pillars of the EU common economic policy for the euro area, the economic policy mix

---

[36] Economists qualify this phenomenon as an "asymmetry"; see Vesperini, *Relancer*, 36. In New Classical macroeconomics, and particularly in the "optimal currency area" (OCA) theory (initiated by Robert A. Mundell, "A Theory of Optimal Currency Areas," *American Economic Review* 51 (1961): 657-65), the cost of a country's joining a monetary union is the loss of a major macroeconomic policy tool, namely that of independently manipulating its currency exchange rates; "asymmetric shocks" occur each time the economic cycles of two or more states are not synchronised, and exchange rates are supposed to protect economies against such state of affairs.

[37] On this problem, see Marco Buti, Daniele Franco and Hedwig Ongena, "Budgetary Policies during Recessions – Retrospective Applications of the "Stability and Growth Pact" to the Post-War Period," *European Economy Economic Papers* 121 (May 1997): 1-33. Antonio Fatás and Ilian Mihov have found recently that "the euro area displays the most procyclical policy [...], in contrast with the United States, that shows acyclicality or mild counter-cyclicality"; Antonio Fatás and Ilian Mihov, "The Euro and Fiscal Policy," in *Europe and the Euro*, eds. Alberto Alesina and Francesco Giavazzi (Chicago: University of Chicago Press, 2010), 287-324, 299-302.

[38] Such a state of affairs, even though correct and feasible in theory, faces the same kinds of theoretical and empirical objections identified in the case of the so-called "golden rule" (see *supra* note 35), since it is not always easy to identify each economy's path of potential GDP growth in order to distinguish between cyclical and structural debts.

chosen by the European founders of the Maastricht Treaty and the SGP is not rational. Indeed, a policy mix composed of:

1. a grant of primary responsibility for budget balance and debt sustainability to individual member states of a common monetary zone,
2. prudential rules *ex ante* based on the deterrent effect some far-off and politically uncertain corrective measures might hopefully have against undisciplined member states, and
3. overly rigid, overbroad and asymmetric rules *ex post* that only fortuitously will have an optimal budgetary adjustment effect instead of a recessive effect,

amounts to a voluntarily self-delusional approach and certainly could not withstand a grave fiscal crisis inside the euro area, such as the one Greece has been sustaining over the past three years.

In slight contrast to the rigid European approach, coupled with the strict legal requirement of achieving annual balanced budgets in the EU[39], in the USA, no binding constraint was imposed on federal spending until the Gramm-Rudman-Hollings Balanced Budget and Emergency Deficit Control Act (popularly known as "Gramm-Rudman") was voted in Congress in 1985[40], and in reality, no balanced federal budget emerged until the late 1990's. Even then, the Supreme Court held unconstitutional the Act's process for determining the amount of the automatic spending

---

[39] TFEU, article 310, paragraph 1 unequivocally states: "The revenue and expenditure shown in the budget shall be in balance". On the importance of the balanced budget rule in the EU context, see Robert Ackrill, "The European Union Budget, the Balanced Budget Rule and the Development of Common European Policies," *Journal of Public Policy* 20 (2000): 1-19. A survey of the Member States on behalf of the European Commission recently showed a quasi-unanimous consensus on the need to maintain the balanced budget rule for the EU; see Iain Begg et al., "Financing of the European Union Budget," Final Report to the European Commission, DG Budget, 29 April 2008, 61
http://ec.europa.eu/budget/reform/library/issue_paper/study_financingEU_de_en_fr.pdf).

[40] Pub.L. N° 99-177, tit. II, 99 Stat. 1037, 1038, codified in 2 U.S.C. § 200 (1985). See annotations on this Act in William G. Dauster, *Budget Process Law Annotated* (Washington, D.C.: Government Printing Office, 1993), 403-692. For a scholarly discussion of Gramm-Rudman's effect on the budget process, see Kate Stith, "Rewriting the Fiscal Constitution: The Case of Gramm-Rudman-Hollings," *California Law Review* 76 (1988): 593-668.

cuts[41], and Congress had to redraft a version of the law in 1987[42], which largely failed to prevent large budget deficits. Finally, rigidly fixed caps in budget deficits were replaced by a federal law limiting so-called "discretionary" spending and enforcing those caps through a new accounting and budgeting system and through a mechanism requiring across-the-board cuts within any category of credits to make up for any overages[43].

Thus, the 1990 federal legislative revision changed its focus from automatic deficit reduction to spending control. Even though Gramm-Rudman and its aftermath are widely acclaimed as signs of an American political reorientation towards more fiscal rigour, the USA mechanism does not automatically lead to balanced budgets or surpluses. Under the Clinton administration, an economic growth boom led to two consecutive federal budget surpluses (1998-1999), the first such budgets since 1969; however, the George W. Bush administration initiated large tax cuts and the so-called "war on terrorism" with its ensuing huge increase in defence spending, so that the effects of the bursting of the "Internet bubble" in 2001 produced once more a mounting deficit beginning with the 2002 budget, well before the huge financial crisis that started in 2007 and broke out in 2008[44].

---

[41] *Bowsher v. Synar*, 478 U.S. 714 (1986).

[42] Budget and Emergency Deficit Control Reaffirmation Act of 1987, Pub.L. N° 100-119, tit. I, 101 Stat. 754, codified in 2 U.S.C. § 900 (1987).

[43] Budget Enforcement Act of 1990, Pub.L. N° 101-508, tit. XIII, 104 Stat. 1388-573 (1990), codified in scattered sections of 2 U.S.C., 15 U.S.C. § 1022, 31 U.S.C. § 1105, 1341, 1342 (Supp. IV 1992).

[44] Even though James D. Savage, *Balanced Budgets and American Politics*, (Ithaca N.Y.: Cornell University Press, 1988), 235-36, states that the balanced-budget rule "is so deeply rooted in the nation's political culture that neither full-employment economics nor the presence of the huge deficits created during the Reagan presidency has shaken American politics free from its constraining influence", one can ascertain, as a fact, a diachronic tendency of the American federal institutional framework to produce alarmingly great amounts of deficits and public debts, clearly overwhelming the national median GDP growth rate. See Dennis S. Ippolito, "The Budget Process and Budget Policy: Resolving the Mismatch," *Public Administration Review* 53 (1993): 9.

3.2 Principles and Presuppositions of the Euro Area Monetary Policy

The monetary policy of the euro area is guided by two fundamental principles: i) the maintenance of price stability, and ii) the independence of the European Central Bank (ECB).

i. The maintenance of price stability

Even though several economists have criticised the vagueness of the concept of "price stability"[45] and, of course, the monetarist hypothesis of a direct link between the monetary variables and the level of prices has never been actually proven, given the profusion of non-monetary variables influencing prices, the basic criticism that can be made of the first principle of Common Monetary Policy is *the nature of the Treaty's objective* itself. According to the Treaty, "The primary objective of the European System of Central Banks [...] shall be to maintain price stability"; apart from and "without prejudice to" this primary objective, "the European System of Central Banks shall support the general economic policies in the Union with a view to contributing to the achievement of the objectives of the Union as laid down in Article 3 of the Treaty on European Union"[46].

It is, of course, perfectly normal for a Central Bank to defend the stability of its currency and to fight against inflationary tendencies; still, what is less rational is the self-imposed strict hierarchy of values placing *a priori* price stability at the forefront of monetary policy, irrespectively of the macroeconomic tendencies of the moment, even though there should constantly be taken into account the need to ponder between maintenance of price stability, on the one hand, and growth of economic activity and of employment levels, on the other. By contrast, the legislation on the

---

[45] See, e.g., Patrick Artus et al. eds., *La Banque centrale européenne*, rapport du Conseil d'analyse économique n° 38, (Paris: La Documentation française, 2002) specifically pp. 49 ff. (report by Charles Wyplosz) and 93 ff. (report by Patrick Artus).

"Price stability" is generally accepted to mean an average inflation rate of no more than 2%; on the hotly debated concepts of "price stability" and "inflation targeting", see Iain Begg, "Monetary Policy Strategies", in *Central banks in the Age of the Euro: Europeanization, Convergence, and Power*, eds. Kenneth Dyson and Martin Marcussen (Oxford: Oxford University Press, 2009), 356-72.

[46] TFEU, article 127, paragraph 1. These values notably include: sustainable development, a highly competitive social market economy, and a high level of environmental quality, as well as economic, social, and territorial cohesion and solidarity among member states.

Federal Reserve Bank (Fed) of the United States of America states that "The Board of Governors of the Federal Reserve System and the Federal Open Market Committee shall maintain long run growth of the monetary and credit aggregates commensurate with the economy's long run potential to increase production, *so as to promote effectively the goals of maximum employment, stable prices, and moderate long-term interest rates*"[47]. Thus, in order to fight against alarming deflationary tendencies, the Fed has injected enormous amounts of liquidities in the market through the purchase of long-term securities by issuing new money, a nonconventional monetary policy generally known as "quantitative easing"[48], even though this policy might carry important systemic risks,

---

[47] Federal Reserve Act, Section 2a, codified in 12 U.S.C. 225a (emphasis added). Fed's chairman, Ben S. Bernanke, characteristically declared recently at a Congressional hearing that "the Fed would 'not actively seek' to raise inflation but if inflation and unemployment both rose above its targets, it could choose to reduce inflation more slowly in order to reduce unemployment more quickly." Binyamin Appelbaum, "Republicans Sharply Question Bernanke for Fed's Focus on Job Market," *New York Times*, February 2, 2012. For a discussion of the so-called "dual mandate" of the Fed, see Nicolas Jabko, "Transparency and Accountability" in *Central banks in the Age of the Euro: Europeanization, Convergence, and Power,* ed. Kenneth Dyson and Martin Marcussen (Oxford: Oxford University Press, 2009), 398-400.

[48] The Federal Open Market Committee (FOMC) announced on November 3, 2010, that it would purchase a further $600 billion of longer-term Treasury securities by the end of the second quarter of 2011, a pace of about $75 billion per month; see FOMC, "Press Release," November 3, 2010, accessed November 3, 2010, http://www.federalreserve.gov/newsevents/press/monetary/20101103a.htm, and Federal Reserve Bank of New York, "Statement Regarding Purchases of Treasury Securities," accessed November 3, 2010, http://www.newyorkfed.org/markets/opolicy/operating_policy_101103.html.
See the hospitable attitude of Ben S. Bernanke, "Central Bank Independence, Transparency, and Accountability" (speech presented at the Institute's for Monetary and Economic Studies International Conference, Bank of Japan, Tokyo, Japan, May 25, 2010), http://www.federalreserve.gov/newsevents/speech/bernanke20100525a.htm. There, the Fed's chairman, after describing this monetary policy tool as one via which a central bank "provides additional support for the economy and the financial system by expanding the monetary base, for example, through the purchase of long-term securities", and after drawing attention to the fact that quantitative easing "can have fiscal side effects", goes on to say: "Nevertheless, I think there is a good case for granting the central bank independence in making quantitative easing decisions, just as with other monetary policies. Because the effects of quantitative easing on growth and inflation are qualitatively similar to those of more conventional monetary policies, the same concerns about the potentially adverse

not only for the United States' economy, but for the stability of the international monetary system as well[49]. Despite the "moral hazard" brought by any kind of monetary easing, i.e. the risk that, by buying time through liquidity injections, political systems and economic actors lose their incentive to further necessary changes in fiscal policy and thus delay return to sustainable growth, a real-world effect of quantitative easing is to lower borrowing costs by reducing the supply of debt available to investors, pushing them to accept lower interest rates and to shift money into riskier assets[50].

In an important paper, Professor Paul De Grauwe convincingly shows that "The solution to the contagion problems of the banking system is exactly the same solution for a monetary union. Contagion between sovereign bond markets can only be stopped if there is a central bank willing to be the *lender of last resort*, i.e. willing to guarantee that the cash will always be available to pay out the bondholders."[51] Only a central bank can reassure depositors, investors, and bondholders by guaranteeing them financial stability. This amounts to an "insurance mechanism"[52]. Nevertheless, the central bank always runs the risk of incurring some losses

---

effects of short-term political influence on these decisions apply". Indeed, the Bank of Japan, acknowledging that conventional policies have reached their limits to reverse the tendency and boost Japan's stagnant economy, has already employed a form of quantitative easing. Of course, in the United States, the Federal Reserve Bank has already purchased both Treasury securities and securities guaranteed by government-sponsored enterprises.

Finally, on September 13, 2012, the FOMC pledged a third and open-ended round of quantitative easing by buying mortgage-backed securities at a pace of $40 billion each month and until the outlook for the labour market improves "substantially." According to the FOMC's estimation, "a highly accommodative stance of monetary policy will remain appropriate for a considerable time after the economic recovery strengthens." ; see FOMC, "Press Release," September 12, 2012, accessed October 23, 2012,
http://www.federalreserve.gov/newsevents/press/monetary/20120913a.htm

[49] Ricardo J. Caballero, "A Caricature (Model) of the World Economy" (paper first presented as a keynote speech for the Ninth Macroeconomic Policy Research Workshop 'Understanding Financial Frictions', Magyar Nemzeti Bank, Budapest, October 27, 2010).

[50] Binyamin Appelbaum, "Three Central Banks Act to Stimulate More Borrowing," *New York Times*, July 5, 2012,
http://www.nytimes.com/2012/07/06/business/global/markets-look-to-europes-central-bank-for-action.html?_r=1.

[51] Paul De Grauwe, "Only a more active ECB can solve the euro crisis," CEPS Policy Brief No. 250, August 2011, 2 (emphasis added).

[52] Paul De Grauwe, "Only a more active ECB", 2.

by buying government bonds in open market, if those are not repaid in full. In such case, De Grouwe boldly states that "In contrast to private firms, the central bank can live happily with negative equity, because the central bank can always fill the holes *by printing money*"[53].

The fundamental monetarist objection to such an enlargement of the European Central Bank's mission is, of course, that if the ECB is able and willing to buy unlimited amounts of government bonds in open market as a lender of last resort, that would necessarily breed inflation, since it would increase the circulating money stock. Nevertheless, Professor De Grauwe has proven that this monetarist axiom does not hold true in periods of credit crunch, when deflationary tendencies gain momentum[54]. In such periods, as is the case after the 2008 financial meltdown, there is a clear tendency for the money base[55] aggregate to disconnect itself from the money stock (M3) aggregate, which is actually what the ECB uses as an indicator of inflation[56]. Practically, that translates into a "liquidity trap", whereby banks put aside the cash they receive for their capital adequacy and continue to deleverage. They thus avoid flooding businesses and households with money, which would bring about inflationary tendencies.

---

[53] (emphasis added). Professor De Grauwe follows Willem Buiter, who has shown that "As long as central banks don't have significant foreign exchange-denominated liabilities or index-linked liabilities, it will always be possible for the central bank to ensure its solvency though monetary issuance (seigniorage)"; Willem Buiter, "Can Central Banks Go Broke?" CEPR Policy Insight, No. 24, London, May 2008, 11.

[54] Paul De Grauwe, "Only a more active ECB," 3-4. Milton Friedman himself understood, against the monetarist vulgate, that when a financial crisis erupts, if the central bank fails to perform its role as lender of last resort and does not supply cash, it turns the financial crisis into a recession and probably a depression; that happened in the United States after the 1929 stock market crash because the Fed at the time did not increase the US money base sufficiently. See Milton Friedman & Anna Jacobson Schwartz, *A Monetary History of the United States, 1867-1960* (Princeton, NJ: Princeton University Press, 1993, 1st ed. 1963), especially 407-19.

[55] The currency in circulation and the banks' deposits at the central bank.

[56] According to the ECB's definition of the euro area monetary aggregates, "Broad money (M3) comprises M2 and marketable instruments issued by the MFI sector. Certain money market instruments, in particular money market fund (MMF) shares/units and repurchase agreements are included in this aggregate. A high degree of liquidity and price certainty make these instruments close substitutes for deposits. As a result of their inclusion, M3 is less affected by substitution between various liquid asset categories than narrower definitions of money, and is therefore more stable", "The ECB's definition of the euro area monetary aggregates," European Central Bank,
http://www.ecb.int/stats/money/aggregates/aggr/html/hist.en.html/.

ii) The independence of the European Central Bank (ECB)

The principle of the independence of the ECB is enshrined in the Treaty, which states: "When exercising the powers and carrying out the tasks and duties conferred upon them by the Treaties and the Statute of the ESCB and of the ECB, neither the European Central Bank, nor a national central bank, nor any member of their decision-making bodies shall seek or take instructions from Union institutions, bodies, offices or agencies, from any government of a Member State or from any other body"[57].

Of course, it is well established by now that the biggest central banks in the world are independent[58]. In particular, one undue government influence on the central bank's independent decision-making that needs to be avoided concerns quantitative easing decisions; in Ben Bernanke's words, "such influence might be tantamount to giving the government the ability to demand the monetization of its debt, an outcome that should be avoided at all costs"[59]. Nevertheless, a central bank can only produce an optimal monetary policy if it has a political interlocutor, namely a government capable of defining aims of economic growth and employment and of arranging its means to obtain those aims. In other words, a common monetary policy by an independent bank can be efficient if it applies on a homogeneous economic zone regulated by federal authorities (which is the case in the USA), but not if the common monetary zone is fragmented into multiple countries, each having its own economic structures and cycle. Since this continues to be the case in the EU, the ECB is not so much "independent" as a sole player on the field. That state of affairs necessarily brings about an imbalance between integrated monetary policies and not-yet integrated economic policies.

The philosophical difference between a full-fledged federal system – such as that of the USA – and an independent, yet timorous quasi-federal system of monetary governance – such as that of the euro area – can

---

[57] TFEU, article 130.

[58] On the hotly debated issue of the independence of central banks, see *inter alia* Alberto Alesina and Lawrence H. Summers, "Central Bank Independence and Macroeconomic Performance: Some Comparative Evidence," *Journal of Money, Credit and Banking*, 25 (1993): 151-62; Alex Cukierman, *Central Bank Strategies, Credibility, and Independence: Theory and Evidence*, (Cambridge, Mass.: MIT Press, 1992); Alex Cukierman et al., "Central Bank Independence, Growth, Investment, and Real Rates," *Carnegie-Rochester Conference Series on Public Policy*, 39 (1993): 95-140; and Alex Cukierman, Steven B. Webb, and Bilin Neyapti, "Measuring the Independence of Central Banks and Its Effect on Policy Outcomes," *World Bank Economic Review* 6 (1992): 353-98.

[59] Ben S. Bernanke, "Central Bank Independence."

probably be understood best by the treatment of the abovementioned "moral hazard" problem in the two respective cases. In the USA, because of the existent fiscal union mechanisms[60], the Fed did not really hesitate to expand the monetary offer thrice, disregarding any probable side-effects on the federal, state and sub-state governments' propensity towards lax fiscal policy. Yet, during the European sovereign debt crisis, even though "it is particularly ridiculous to suppose that sovereigns can provide effective insurance against their own default"[61], and despite the fact that there still is no core inflation problem in sight in the euro area, the ECB has been particularly hesitant to openly expand the euro monetary basis.

The reluctance of the ECB is due, to a great extent, to the "moral hazard" problem. The argument runs like this: if the ECB stepped in, providing potentially unlimited liquidity[62] to states that needed refinancing of their long-term debt, that would give all the wrong signals to spendthrift political systems to continue their fiscal derailment by overspending. The knowledge that the ECB would feel compelled to intervene would ultimately transform a liquidity crisis into a full-blown solvency crisis because of the permanent lack of any counter-incentive against the production of fiscal deficits. Of course, in such a case, it would only be unjust to hold the tax-payers of virtuous member states of a currency zone liable for the heavy cost of another sovereign's default. Hence the tension that leads to the hesitancy of the ECB to adopt a more Fed-like aggressive stance[63], even though it is often difficult to distinguish a liquidity from a solvency crisis in concrete cases[64].

---

[60] See *infra* Section 6.

[61] As Martin Wolf puts it nicely in an article for the *Financial Times*; Martin Wolf, "Be bold, Mario, put out that fire," *Financial Times*, October 26, 2011.

[62] A tool known as "bazooka" in markets language.

[63] The ECB did, however, adopt two open market operations to soothe the markets. Firstly, the Governing Council of the ECB initiated a Securities Markets Programme (SMP) on May 9, 2010, whereby the Eurosystem started purchasing both public and private securities in open market in order to "address the malfunctioning of securities markets and [to] restore an appropriate monetary policy transmission mechanism" (ECB press release, "ECB decides on measures to address severe tensions in financial markets," May 10, 2010); see Decision of the European Central Bank of 14 May 2010 establishing a securities markets programme (ECB/2010/5). The SMP has been mainly targeted towards the repurchase in the secondary market of distressed sovereign bonds issued by countries such as Greece, Spain, or Italy in order to restore confidence and to temporarily at least reduce the yields between the German 10-year *Bund* (that serves as the reference basis) and public securities under pressure by the capital

In conclusion, we have to deduce from the concrete functioning of the euro area's monetary policy tools, compared to the analogous federal tools in the USA, that the EU's fundamental monetary principles are rigidly self-restraining and sub-optimal. As a result, once economic crises break out, the ECB, even though it is commonly considered as a "federal" institution in the euro area[65], does not normally conceive itself as having the same ability to use the monetary tools the Fed has at its disposal.

---

markets. The SMP has purchased an outstanding amount of more than 211 billion euros up to 27 July 2012; "Liquidity analysis," ECB, http://www.ecb.int/mopo/liq/html/index.en.html#portfolios.
This programme has been recently superseded by the "Outright Monetary Transactions" programme that focuses on an unlimited purchase of sovereign bonds with a maturity of between one and three years in secondary bond markets. The start, continuation and suspension of these transactions are at ECB's discretion and presuppose the adoption of an adjustment (i.e. fiscal austerity) programme that has to be approved and monitored by the IMF. Moreover, the Eurosystem accepts the same (*pari passu*) treatment as private or other creditors with respect to bonds purchased by euro area member states, and the liquidity created through these transactions will be fully sterilised. See ECB press release, "Technical features of Outright Monetary Transactions", 6 September 2012, at http://www.ecb.int/press/pr/date/2012/html/pr120906_1.en.html
Secondly, the ECB has also provided direct support to troubled banks by granting them the opportunity to refinance via three-year loans at an interest rate of 1%. There have been two Long-Term Refinancing Operations (LTROs) by the ECB up to now, one in December 2011 and one in February 2012. Before that, ECB loans generally had to be repaid within about a year at most. Now, through LTROs, banks can borrow virtually unlimited amounts for three years at a 1% interest rate, well below what they would pay to borrow elsewhere. The ECB money comes with no strings attached, so banks can invest or lend it as they please. See David Enrich & Charles Forelle, "ECB gives banks big dollops of cash," *The Wall Street Journal*, March 1, 2012, http://online.wsj.com/article/SB10001424052970203986604577252803223310964.html. Banks and financial institutions have borrowed cheaply more than 1 trillion euros via the two rounds of LTROs.
For a critical appraisal of those two types of open market operations, see Ansgar Belke, "Driven by the markets? ECB sovereign bond purchases and the securities markets programme," *Intereconomics* 45, Number 6 (2010): 357-63.

[64] Paul De Grauwe, "Only a more active ECB can solve the euro crisis," 3.

[65] See e.g. Marvin Goodfriend, "The Role of a Regional Bank in a System of Central Banks, July 1999," Federal Reserve Bank of Richmond Working Paper No 99-4. According to Goodfriend, the Eurosystem shares the basic structure of the Federal Reserve System, but still, "[p]ower in the Eurosystem is more decentralized than in the Federal Reserve System" (Goodfriend, "The Role," 16). Cf. Dieter Gerdesmeier, Francesco Paolo Mongelli and Barbara Roffia, "The

* * *

Some commentators[66] had predicted that if one day a member state defaulted on its sovereign debt, the EU regulatory framework would implode because of the deficient macroeconomic foundations of the Maastricht Treaty and the SGP; as a result, a *political* solution to that situation would have to be devised at EU level. Others[67], on the contrary, believe that there is *too much* political discretion in the Council's decision to enforce sanctions against recalcitrant euro area member states, and try to devise ways to render more automatic the imposition of gradual sanctions. The conclusion is that the euro area governance rules continue to be plagued with a *radical ambiguity between political and monetarist considerations*. This tension assuredly replicates the built-in tension in the basic EMU architecture since its inception.

4. What Makes a Budgetary Crisis "Global"?

The fundamental ambiguity plaguing the original EMU governance principles can also be traced in the fact that the *interdependence between Member States' economies*, particularly in the euro area, was not fully accounted for. As the European Commission rightly acknowledges in its May 12, 2010 communication[68], "The recent financial crisis and pressure on the financial stability in Europe have underlined more clearly than ever

---

Eurosystem, the US Federal Reserve and the Bank of Japan: Similarities and Differences, March 2007," European Central Bank Working Paper No. 742, 7-12, according to whom, even though the legal status and several of the tasks of these three monetary institutions differ somewhat because of different historical conditions and national characteristics, there are fewer differences in their institutional structures, monetary policy frameworks, as well as the use of policy instruments. For other authors, such as Guillaume Courty and Guillaume Devin, *La construction européenne*, (Paris: La Découverte, 3ème éd., 2010), 15, the ECB is simply "a federal institution".

66 Vesperini, *Relancer*, 24.

67 Not least the European Commission itself, which pushed forward a new "reverse voting mechanism" in order to reduce discretion in the enforcement of sanctions against fiscally undisciplined member states (see *infra* Section 5). Under the new voting rules, which will apply when imposing sanctions, a Commission proposal will from now on be considered adopted unless the Council overturns it by a qualified majority. *Contra* Vesperini, *Relancer*, 51.

68 Communication, "Reinforcing economic policy coordination," COM(2010) 250 final, Brussels, May 12, 2010, 3. This important strategic document, that launched the process of modification and enrichment of the surveillance instruments of the Treaty, was of course adopted *after* the outburst of the borrowing crisis in Greece.

the interdependence of the EU's economies, in particular inside the euro area. […] However, these recent experiences also showed gaps and weaknesses in the current system, underlining the need for stronger and earlier policy co-ordination, additional prevention and correction mechanisms and a crisis resolution facility for euro area Member States". Herein lies the basic ambiguity of the euro area's philosophy that has to do with the possible negative externalities of unsustainable state finances on the monetary variables of the euro area in its entirety. As the Commission puts it, "Special consideration to the aggregate stance should be given in the cases of serious economic stress in the euro area, when sizeable fiscal policy measures taken by individual Member States are likely to produce important spill-overs"[69]. So the question might be formulated as follows: is there a safe way to determine beforehand the instances in which one or more euro area member states' fiscal policies are likely to produce sizeable negative externalities on common monetary variables[70]?

The experience with the "Greek crisis" clearly indicates that the answer to that question is "no". It seems that the EMU principles were implicitly based on the *a priori* rational, but in the end of the day misguided, presupposition that member states with "small" (or "peripheral") economies cannot, by definition, influence the monetary variables in the euro area whatever happens, whereas member states with "big" (or "core") economies, as well as a group of member states "whose economies share common cyclical traits", might impact on the euro, so that their budgetary surveillance should be tighter[71]. At the very least, according to Jean-Pierre Vesperini, the second and third sub-groups should be required to submit to

---

[69] *Idem*, p. 8.

[70] The first paper to provide evidence on intra-euro area spill-overs based on simulations of four macroeconomic models was Daniel Gros and Alexandr Hobza, "Fiscal Policy Spillovers in the Euro Area: Where are they?" CEPS Working Document No. 176, November 2001. The researchers found that at that time, cross-country spill-over effects of fiscal policy were indeed of uncertain sign and magnitude; they also accurately found that the most important channel of international spill-over transmission is the financial market channel, and that there is not a linear relationship between the average spill-overs in the euro area and the economic weight of country/ies undertaking the fiscal expansion (*ibid.*, 19, 22).

[71] Vesperini, *Relancer*, 32, who builds his case in favour of changes in the SGP on the assumption that we should differentiate between "countries of small dimension" (whose fiscal policy has "by definition" no influence on the monetary variables of the euro area), "big countries" (whose fiscal policy is "by definition" capable of having an influence on the monetary variables of the euro area), and lastly, "a group of countries sharing similar conjunctures" (whose fiscal policies as a whole are liable to have an influence on the monetary variables of the euro area).

a "principle of consultation" (*principe de concertation*) as to the reorientation of their national fiscal policies at the highest political level, namely that of the Council or the Eurogroup, or even of the ECB, every time they produce negative externalities for the euro area in its entirety[72], contrary to smaller countries who should be let alone in fiscal matters, in accordance with the principle of subsidiarity[73]. Theoretically, one can even say *a fortiori* that unbridled fiscal discretion of member states as a matter of principle – as long as the latter does not impact negatively on the monetary variables of the euro-zone – is even more necessary in the case of member states who have handed over their monetary policy to a monetary zone (as is the case for members of the euro area) in order to be able to exert some leverage and stimulate their economic growth[74].

Yet, it is quite ironical that a small-to-medium country like Greece, which according to this macroeconomic rationale "should decide by itself the extent to which it accepts to bear the eventual negative consequences of its own fiscal policy" and should not even be obliged to respect the Maastricht criteria[75], was the catalyst that revealed the flawed structure of the euro area by hastening to ask for financial aid from its European partners once it became clear that it could no longer refinance its sovereign debt from financial markets on acceptable interest rates. And, of course, the Greek experience has definitely proven wrong one specialist's prediction that once "a lax fiscal policy [of a country of small dimension]

---

[72] Vesperini, *Relancer*, 50.

[73] The Treaty on European Union (TEU) defines the principle of subsidiarity as follows (article 5, paragraph 3): "[…] in areas which do not fall within its exclusive competence, the Union shall act only if and in so far as the objectives of the proposed action cannot be sufficiently achieved by the Member States, either at central level or at regional and local level, but can rather, by reason of the scale or effects of the proposed action, be better achieved at Union level". The principle of subsidiarity is one of the fundamental principles of the overall EU institutional framework, and is by now more carefully enforced through a new mechanism expounded in Protocols Nos 1 and 2 to the Treaty (Protocol on Role of National Parliaments in the European Union, and Protocol on the Application of the Principles of Subsidiarity and Proportionality, respectively).

[74] Vesperini, *Relancer*, 51.

[75] Vesperini, *Relancer*, 33, 48. Cf. the opinion by Patrick Artus, "Y a-t-il un lien entre les *spreads* souverains (vis-à-vis de l'Allemagne) dans la zone euro et l'ampleur du choc subi par les pays dans la crise?" *Natixis Special Report* N° 105, April 6, 2009, according to whom dispersion of sovereign spreads of different euro area countries is too strong to be solely explained by their risk of default on their fiscal sovereign debt, which in other words means that fiscal solvency does not necessarily command the level of long-term interest rates.

has negative effects, for example in the form of an increase in the interest rate spreads, […] we can imagine that that country's government will modify its policies as a consequence, particularly under the pressure of its opposition"[76].

Thus the first, and foremost, problem EU institutions have proven unable to manage – or even to predict its existence – is that of assessing when an acute financial problem showing up in one or more EU member states can be qualified as a short-term borrowing, a mid-term liquidity, or a long-term solvency crisis. In other words, we have not yet been able to lay down our secondary economic rules (i.e. the rules on the production, reform, interpretation, and abolishment of rules)[77], namely who is responsible, and in what circumstances, to say authoritatively that it is the *euro area* and not a *specific member state* that is facing an overall debt crisis, and also to decide that the problem is a *conjunctional/cyclical* or a *structural* one.

As we followed the unravelling of the "Greek crisis" from December 2009 onwards, we could not but observe that many euro area governments hid behind the sacrosanct rule "no default, no bail-out, no exit from the EMU" for member states in order to deny, for a long period of time, that there even *was* any solvency problem for a member state. Unfortunately, this state of denial invited speculator short-selling practices (which remain largely unregulated until very recently[78]) and eventually brought about a

---

[76] Vesperini, *Relancer*, 48.

[77] On the notion of "secondary rules", see the classic book by the legal philosopher H. L. A. Hart, *The Concept of Law*, 2nd ed., eds. Peter Cane, Tony Honoré and Jane Stapelton (Oxford: Oxford University Press, Clarendon Law Series, 1994, 1st ed. 1961), 79 ff. According to the terminology introduced by Hart, laws that impose duties or obligations on individuals are described as "primary rules of obligation", whereas "secondary rules" are necessary in order for a system of primary rules to function effectively by providing an authoritative statement of all the primary rules ("rules of recognition"), by allowing legislators to introduce changes in the primary rules if those rules are found to be defective or inadequate ("rules of change"), and by enabling courts to resolve disputes over the interpretation and application of the primary rules ("rules of adjudication").

[78] For the latest efforts of the EU to regulate the operation of hedge funds, see Directive 2011/61/EU of the European Parliament and of the Council of 8 June 2011 on Alternative Investment Fund Managers, OJ L 174, 1.7.2011, 1, and Communication from the Commission "European financial supervision," COM(2009) 252 final, Brussels, May 27, 2009. On December 16, 2010, a reform of the EU framework for financial supervision established a European Systemic Risk Board (ESRB), which is designed to provide macro-prudential oversight of the financial system in order to eliminate henceforth the deficiencies exposed

contagion of the Greek crisis, which revealed the existence of a *systemic* crisis of the whole euro area structure.

The only legal basis that could be found in the Treaty for a coordinated EU response to a financial crisis is article 122, par. 2 TFEU, that states: "Where a Member State is in difficulties or is seriously threatened with severe difficulties caused by natural disasters or *exceptional occurrences beyond its control*, the Council, on a proposal from the Commission, may grant, under certain conditions, Union financial assistance to the Member State concerned[79]". Yet, the continuous tergiversations and the prevalence of short-sighted electoralism reflexes among some European governments considerably delayed this interpretation of the Treaty.

By contrast, in federal systems such as that of the USA, where there necessarily is a Federal Treasury Department and a Central Bank, financial regulation in general and the assessment of financial risks in particular are not left to the political judgment of an intergovernmental organ such as the Eurogroup[80], but action is instead taken up by federal authorities to evaluate and contain possible systemic risks. Expediency and celerity of action are critical in such cases, and only centralised federal agencies can ensure that[81].

Moreover, elimination of "moral hazard" is very important in this context[82], because the internalised belief that governments, central banks

---

during the financial crisis, as well as three European authorities to supervise the banking, insurance, and securities sectors; see Regulation 1092/2010 of the European Parliament and of the Council of 24 November 2010 on European Union macro-prudential oversight of the financial system and establishing a European Systemic Risk Board, OJ L 331, 15.12.2010, 1.

[79] (Emphasis added).

[80] The Eurogroup is composed by the ministers of finance of the member states whose currency is the euro, and meets regularly to discuss questions related to the specific responsibilities these member states face; see TEU, article 137, and Protocol No. 14 on the Eurogroup.

[81] For an overview of the American banking and securities regulators and of their methods of risk assessment, see United States Government Accountability Office (GAO), *Review of Regulators' Oversight of Risk Management Systems at a Limited Number of Large, Complex Financial Institutions*, Testimony Before the U.S. Senate, March 18, 2009, 5-9, http://www.gao.gov/assets/130/121973.pdf.

[82] "Moral hazard" describes any situation in which one party freely makes decisions about how much risk to take, while being insulated from the consequences of these decisions, since another party will bear the cost for the risk-taker (will "bail him out") if things turn out badly. See Paul Krugman, *The Return of Depression Economics and the Crisis of 2008* (New York and London: W.W. Norton, 2nd ed., 2009), 62-3. On the understanding of "moral hazard" in the

or other public institutions will at some point provide for a financial bail-out of lending institutions can encourage risky lending in the future, since financial risk-takers might come to believe that they will not have to carry the full burden of losses for their own choices. The counterpart to irresponsible fiscal policies by governments clearly is excessive risk-taking by "too big to fail" financial institutions. These companies lend money to governments with the assuredness that the most risky loans have the potential for making the highest return, whereas if the investment turns out badly the lender will be bailed out by the taxpayers in order to avoid a severe liquidity shortage, and thus a possible systemic crisis, that will eventually cause it to default[83].

With the recent Dodd-Frank Wall Street Reform and Consumer Protection Act (Dodd-Frank Act) that was signed into law by President Obama on July 21, 2010, the most sweeping change was passed in financial regulation in the United States since the Great Depression in the 1930's[84]. This federal law revamped the entire American financial regulatory environment, created a host of new federal agencies, and gave new powers and tools to existing ones in order to allow them to respond to financial crises.

The Act's Title I on Financial Stability outlines two new agencies, the Financial Stability Oversight Council (FSOC) and the Office of Financial Research (OFR), tasked, among others, with monitoring systemic risk and

---

microeconomics of contract theory, which analyses the behaviour of decision-makers in settings of asymmetric information according to optimisation algorithms, see, among a vast literature, Prajit K. Dutta and Roy Radner, "Moral Hazard," *in Handbook of Game Theory with Economic Applications,* vol. 2, chap. 26, eds. Robert Aumann and Sergiu Hart (Amsterdam: Elsevier, coll. "Handbooks in Economics," 1994), 869-903 and Richard J. Arnott and Joseph E. Stiglitz, "Labor Turnover, Wage Structures and Moral Hazard: The Inefficiency of Competitive Markets," *Journal of Labor Economics* 3 (1986).

[83] On the exacerbation of moral hazard and of the "too big to fail" rationale by the financial crisis of 2008 and its aftermath, see the excellent analysis by Aglietta, *La crise*, 96-99.

[84] Pub.L. 111-203, H.R. 4173. For an informative presentation of the most important stakes of this new federal law, enacted as a political response to the severe 2007-2010 financial crisis, see "Dodd-Frank Act Becomes Law," The Harvard Law School Forum on Corporate Governance and Financial Regulation, http://blogs.law.harvard.edu/corpgov/2010/07/21/dodd-frank-act-becomes-law/. and the "Dodd–Frank Wall Street Reform and Consumer Protection Act," Wikipedia article, accessed on August 06, 2012, http://en.wikipedia.org/wiki/Dodd%E2%80%93Frank_Wall_Street_Reform_and_Consumer_Protection_Act#cite_note-6.

researching the state of the economy. These new agencies are attached to the Treasury Department, with the Treasury Secretary being Chair of the FSOC, and the Head of the OFR being a Presidential appointment with Senate confirmation. The FSOC is explicitly charged with identifying threats to the financial stability of the United States, promoting market discipline, and responding to emerging risks to the stability of the United States financial system. It is the FSOC's duty to eliminate moral hazard "by eliminating expectations on the part of shareholders, creditors, and counterparties of such companies that the Government will shield them from losses in the event of failure"[85].

Even before the July 2010 financial reform, one of the four duties explicitly assigned to the Federal Reserve System was that of maintaining the stability of the financial system and containing systemic risk that may arise in financial markets[86]. The enactment of the Dodd-Frank Act "strengthens the consolidated supervision of systemically important financial institutions, gives the government an important additional tool to safely wind down failing financial firms, creates an interagency council to detect and deter emerging threats to the financial system, and enhances the transparency of the Federal Reserve while preserving the political independence that is crucial to monetary policymaking"[87]. Indeed, the new federal law established a new position of "Vice Chairman for Supervision", who is responsible for developing policy recommendations to the Board of Governors regarding supervision and regulation of financial institutions supervised by the Board, which reports regularly to Congress to disclose the activities and efforts of such institutions[88].

Additionally, the Comptroller General of the United States[89] is now required to conduct several audits, not least "a one-time audit of all loans and other financial assistance provided during the period beginning on December 1, 2007" after having assessed, among others, "the operational integrity, accounting, financial reporting, and internal controls of the credit

---

[85] Sec. 112(a)(1)(B).

[86] Federal Reserve Board, *The Federal Reserve System: Purposes and Functions* (Washington, D.C., 9th ed. 2005: Board of Governors of the Federal Reserve System), 1.

[87] Board of Governors of the Federal Reserve System press release, "Statement by FED Chairman Ben S. Bernanke," last modified July 15, 2010, http://www.federalreserve.gov/newsevents/press/other/20100715a.htm.

[88] Sec. 1108(a) and 1108(b).

[89] Director of the Government Accountability Office (GAO), a legislative branch agency founded by Congress in 1921 to ensure the fiscal and managerial accountability of the federal government.

facility" and "the effectiveness of the security and collateral policies established for the facility in mitigating risk to the relevant Federal reserve bank and taxpayers"[90]. The Fed is also required to establish a host of new prudential standards for the institutions it supervises with the aims of integrating sound risk management practices in the financial sector and protecting taxpayers from losses[91]. Finally, and very importantly, the new law retains responsibility to set supervision and regulatory policy to the Fed Board of Governors; in other words, it *maintains at the most centralised level possible*, i.e. the Board of Governors, financial regulation and supervision by abolishing the possibility of delegating these tasks to a Federal Reserve Bank[92].

After having lived the painful experience of a rapid propagation of the financial crisis from the US to Europe in 2007-2008, which highlighted the weaknesses in monitoring and assessing potential threats and risks arising from the interaction between macro-economic developments and the worldwide financial system, the EU too moved to create a European Systemic Risk Board (ESRB), giving a prominent place to the European System of Central Banks (ESCB). In doing that, the EU was inspired by the USA's decision to create a systemic risk monitoring body within the Federal Reserve. The ESRB shall henceforth be able "to assess and prevent potential risks to financial stability in the EU properly and swiftly[93]".

In conclusion, we observe that in the American context, several federal agencies (both old and new) and the Fed are required by federal law to identify, measure, monitor, and mitigate risks to the financial stability of the United States at a centralised level and according to sound risk management standards. This practically means that financial regulation and crisis management are insulated from the political pressure of haphazard state, or even local, electoral cycles[94]. The EU has started recently to follow suit.

* * *

---

[90] Sec. 1109(a)(1), 1109(a)(2)(A) and 1109(a)(2)(B).

[91] See notably Sec. 1101(a).

[92] Sec. 1108(c).

[93] European Commission, "New financial supervision architecture: Q&A on the European Systemic Risk Board / the macro-supervision part of the package," Memo/09/405, Brussels, September 23, 2009, 1.

[94] "At the macroeconomic level, the central banks must assume financial stability as a permanent objective, of the same importance as price stability" (Michel Aglietta, *La crise*, 94).

Resuming the above analyses, the founding principles of the euro area, namely the lack of co-responsibility for member states' public debts and the separation between monetary and budgetary policies (popularly known as the "no-bail-out clause" of articles 123-125 of the Treaty), were devised, conspicuously after the insistence of German political authorities at the time the Maastricht Treaty was enacted in 1991[95], in order precisely to prevent a European mutualisation of national deficits and a monetisation of debts that would have resulted in inflationary tendencies, according to a monetarist presupposition. Yet, the Greek crisis has showed that in reality, the abovementioned fundamental principles are endangered by financial assistance to a defaulting member state *only* when direct transfers are made without any concern for the underlying competitiveness disequilibria between member states. In other words, our principles are more endangered by the lack of any indicator or reference value on competitiveness in our treaties than by the imaginary danger of having euro area members assume sovereign debts of their partners or of the ECB continually expanding the monetary mass by buying euro area public and private bonds in the secondary markets.

From the outset, it seems extremely difficult to treat the EU's underlying comparative competitiveness problem (much more so than the debt problem). That is so because Germany, as the main European exporting force, needs to freeze salary increases and thus to squeeze its internal demand in the name of its external competitiveness, whereas its euro area partners need to regain some of the external competeveness they have lost since the beginning of the EMU, and the ECB has as its principal statutory objective the maintenance of price stability. These three objectives cannot be fulfilled at the same time and there certainly is no Treasury Department-type institution in the EU yet to impose some political priorities here. The economic logic, as well as the long-term interest of the euro area ensemble, seems to me to demand from the German government a fiscal stimulus of its internal demand, and a slightly – yet permanently – higher inflation rate. The only problem is that in the EU institutional setting these requirements might take the form of recommendations by the ECB or the European Commissioner for Economic and Financial Affairs, but have no normative force whatsoever.

---

[95] The euro clearly embodies German "soft" power, since it is a construction based on the German central banking template; see Kenneth Dyson and Kevin Featherstone, *The Road to Maastricht: Negotiating Economic and Monetary Union* (Oxford: Oxford University Press, 1999).

5. New Mechanisms of Coordination of Debt Management and of Macroeconomic Surveillance

Greece is currently facing grave problems, notably the continuous shrinking of its industrial basis, high unemployment rates, especially among young people and women, an expanding brain drain; but above all, its main structural problem is that of a political system of extremely poor quality and of the subsequent lack of state administrative capacity due to extensive corruption and lawlessness. The country is facing the spectrum of a deflationary spiral and deep internal recession, only partly recompensed by imported growth through the increase of exports. The problem was aggravated by many mistakes in its handling by the Greek government and the delay of the solution by EU institutions. In such a context, the fiscal adjustment measures negotiated between the tripartite Stabilisation Mechanism (the so-called "Troika" comprised of the European Commission, the ECB, and the IMF) and the Greek government, that Greece is obliged to activate in order to drastically cut its public deficit and later on stabilize its public debt to sustainable levels, is rash and extremely hard, since it drastically compresses internal demand by slashing through public expenditure, raising the overall tax pressure and imposing a steep internal devaluation (i.e. wage deflation). Such a bail-out will certainly not achieve soon the pursued objective of allowing the country once more to refinance its sovereign debt in open markets, even though there was an unprecedented restructuring and reprofiling of the Greek sovereign debt through so-called PSI (Private Sector Involvement) in February 2012, combined with a second bail-out deal[96].

---

[96] According to Silvia Ardagna and Francesco Caselli, "The Political Economy of the Greek Debt Crisis: A Tale of Two Bailouts," CEP Special Report No. 25 (London: Centre for Economic Performance (London School of Economics and Political Sciences), 2012): 13, "PSI provided no meaningful benefits in terms of debt reduction, and caused considerable havoc through contagion", therefore "not having included PSI in the final deal [of July 21, 2011] might have been Pareto improving".
The IMF's synopsis of PSI is as following: "By involving private creditors and private enterprises in crisis-fighting, the international community aims to limit both moral hazard (the perception that international rescues encourage risky investments) and a 'rush for the exits' by private investors during a crisis. Involvement of the private sector in the resolution of financial crises is appropriate in order to have the burden of crisis resolution shared equitably with the official sector, strengthen market discipline, and, in the process, increase the efficiency of international capital markets and the ability of emerging market borrowers to protect themselves against volatility and contagion. An additional goal is avoiding

In the wake of the Greek crisis, and in the midst of an escalating contagion of the confidence crisis from the periphery to the core itself of the euro area, the EU decided to reinforce the SGP's preventive and corrective mechanisms providing for a multilateral surveillance of state fiscal discipline, and for the first time, to prevent and correct macroeconomic imbalances that can prove deleterious to the Union as a whole because of their possible systemic impact throughout the euro area.

After two communications[97] on the issue, the European Commission presented on September 29, 2010 a set of six legislative propositions ("six pack"), secondary EU law with two complementary aims: first, the strengthening of the Stability and Growth Pact[98], and second, the prevention and correction of macroeconomic imbalances[99]. I will present a summary of them in this order.

---

moral hazard—the encouraging of imprudent or unsustainable behavior by creditors or debtors that can increase the potential magnitude and frequency of future crises."; "The IMF and the Private Sector: A Factsheet," International Monetary Fund, Washington, DC: International Monetary Fund, accessed August 2001, http://www.imf.org/external/np/exr/facts/privsec.htm. On an analysis of PSI as a "positive-sum game" bringing welfare benefits both to debtors and creditors, see Andy Haldane, "Private sector involvement in financial crisis: analytics and public policy approaches," *Financial Stability Review* (November 1999): 184-202.

[97] Communication from the Commission to the European Parliament, the European Council, the Council, the European Central Bank, the Economic and Social Committee and the Committee of the Regions, "Reinforcing economic policy coordination," COM(2010) 250 final, Brussels, May 12, 2010, and Communication from the Commission to the European Parliament, the European Council, the Council, the European Central Bank, the Economic and Social Committee and the Committee of the Regions, "Enhancing economic policy coordination for stability, growth and jobs – Tools for stronger EU economic governance" COM(2010) 367/2 final, Brussels, June 30, 2010.

[98] Regulation (EU) No. 1173/2011 of the European Parliament and of the Council of 16 November 2011 on the effective enforcement of budgetary surveillance in the euro area, OJ L 306, 23.11.2011, 1; Regulation (EU) No. 1175/2011 of the European Parliament and of the Council of 16 November 2011 amending Council Regulation (EC) No. 1466/97 on the strengthening of the surveillance of budgetary positions and the surveillance and coordination of economic policies, OJ L 306, 23.11.2011, 12; Council Regulation (EU) No. 1177/2011 of 8 November 2011 amending Regulation (EC) No. 1467/97 on speeding up and clarifying the implementation of the excessive deficit procedure, OJ L 306, 23.11.2011, 33; and Council Directive 2011/85/EU of 8 November 2011 on requirements for budgetary frameworks of the Member States, OJ L 306, 23.11.2011, 41.

[99] Regulation (EU) No. 1174/2011 of the European Parliament and of the Council of 16 November 2011 on enforcement measures to correct excessive macroeconomic

5.1 Strengthening of Fiscal Discipline through Secondary EU Law

The Commission proposed to reinforce Member States' compliance with the Stability and Growth Pact (SGP) by deepening their fiscal policy coordination. Thus, the Commission decided to treat excessive deficits and excessive debt on an equal basis, reinforce the preventive arm of the SGP that had proven inefficient, introduce a wider range of sanctions and incentives, move the sanctions provided for in the SGP more upstream, and also propose minimum requirements for national fiscal frameworks so that they are in line with Treaty obligations[100].

i. The "preventive arm" of the SGP

The multilateral surveillance procedure is detailed in article 121 paragraphs 3 and 4 TFEU. Its "preventive arm" aims at ensuring that member states follow "prudent fiscal policies", so as not to put fiscal sustainability at strain and thus, to prevent any potential spill-over effect of a state fiscal derailment that might have severe negative consequences for the EMU as a whole. Each member state will continue to present a stability and convergence programme that will outline the measures it will take in order to meet its medium-term budgetary objectives (MTO), expressed as a percentage of GDP in structural terms (i.e. adjusting for the effect of the cycle and excluding one-off and temporary measures). A faster adjustment path towards the medium-term budgetary objectives will henceforth be required for member states faced with a debt level exceeding 60 % of GDP, or with pronounced risks in terms of overall debt sustainability.

The novelty here is the new principle of "prudent fiscal policy-making," that will provide the benchmark against which the member states' fiscal plans in the stability and convergence programme will be examined. The point is to ensure that when the cycle is upward, the rate of growth of public expenditure does not exceed, in principle, a prudent

---

imbalances in the euro area, OJ L 306, 23.11.2011, 8; and Regulation (EU) No. 1176/2011 of the European Parliament and of the Council of 16 November 2011 on the prevention and correction of macroeconomic imbalances, OJ L 306, 23.11.2011, 25.

100 President José Manuel Durão Barroso, "Opening remarks on economic governance," Joint press conference with Commissioner Olli Rehn, SPEECH/10/494, Brussels, September 29, 2010. An overview of the new legislation is provided in European Commission, "Economic governance package (1): Strengthening the Stability and Growth Pact," MEMO/10/455, Brussels, September 29, 2010.

medium-term rate of growth of GDP, unless the MTO has been significantly overachieved, or the excess of expenditure growth over the prudent medium-term rate is matched by discretionary revenue measures. A temporary departure from prudent fiscal policy-making is of course allowed in case of severe economic downturn in order to facilitate economic recovery, or of an unusual event outside the control of the member state that has a major impact on the structural balance of the general government of at least 0.5 % of GDP in one single year. For a temporary departure from the MTO, the implementation of major structural reforms (such as systemic pension reforms) can also be taken into account.

The basic aim of the strengthened preventive arm is to prevent, at an early stage, the occurrence of excessive general government deficits through a form of surveillance now more stringent than in the past, and also to prevent that revenue windfalls over time are spent rather than being allocated to debt reduction. From a macroeconomic point of view, these rules can be understood through a monetarist frame of thought that prioritizes the slashing of public debt during the growth phase of the cycle over the medium term, all the more so for countries overburdened with debt. This comprehension of economic realities may well contain the danger of a so-called "double dip", i.e. a recession followed by a short period of growth, only to be followed again by a remission because the amount of money channelled to the repayment of debt may limit expansionary spending, and growth may be too fragile to continue without fiscal stimulus.

As far as the enforcement mechanism is concerned, apart from an initial warning from the Commission and a recommendation by the Council to take corrective action in case of a persistent or particularly serious infraction, the scheme becomes tighter for the euro area member states, whose fiscal problems represent the greatest systemic risks for the entire European Union. The Council recommendation to a recalcitrant member state can be backed by an interest-bearing deposit amounting to 0.2 % of GDP. The deposit will be imposed by a "reverse voting" mechanism: on proposal by the Commission, the deposit will become due on the issuance of the recommendation by the Council, unless the Council within ten days decides the contrary by qualified majority. Needless to say that the new "reverse voting" mechanism was hailed by all the proponents of strict fiscal discipline as being more automatic and less contingent upon political considerations inside the Council.

ii. The "corrective arm" of the SGP

The "corrective arm" of the SGP has as its axis the Excessive Deficit Procedure (EDP) of article 126 TFEU. It is meant to correct deviations in budgetary policies that may put at risk the sustainability of public finances and potentially endanger the EMU itself, before gross fiscal errors arrive at a domino effect[101]. Here too, the fundamental macroeconomic presuppositions remain the same as before, but three major changes of perspective are brought:

First, the debt criterion of the EDP is taken into account on par with the deficit criterion and is made operational through the adoption of a "numerical benchmark" to gauge whether the debt ratio is diminishing sufficiently rapidly towards the required 60 % of GDP threshold. Still, even though the pace of fiscal consolidation is thus becoming faster, since a debt-to-GDP ratio above 60 % is to be considered sufficiently diminishing if its distance with respect to the reference value has reduced over the previous three years at a rate of one-twentieth per year, in fact a compromise was struck for less automaticity. In case of failure to reduce the debt ratio at the required pace, the decision to place a country in excessive deficit is by no means automatic and still takes into account relevant economic factors, such as whether very low nominal growth is hampering debt reduction, risk factors linked to the structure of the debt, private sector indebtedness and implicit liabilities related to demographic changes.

Another change induced by an effort to change the philosophy of the SGP is the effort to upstream sanctions. Those that come too late in the process do not really serve as deterrents of fiscal derailment at all, since the dire financial situation that an undisciplined member state will endure will be so deteriorated that any talk about imposing financial sanctions will simply not be credible[102]. Thus, sanctions kick in earlier in the excessive deficit procedure and use a graduated approach. A non-interest-bearing deposit amounting to 0.2 % of GDP may be imposed already when decision has been taken to subject a country to the excessive deficit procedure. If the Council's recommendation for correcting the deficit is not followed, a fine will then be imposed.

Lastly, always for the sake of making more credible the threat of initiation of an EDP procedure against a fiscally irresponsible government,

---

[101] On a philosophical analysis of that notion, see Ioannis Papadopoulos, "Two types of domino," in *Domino*, ed. Thessaloniki Center of Contemporary Art (Thessaloniki: Thessaloniki Center of Contemporary Art, 2011) 40-53, particularly 40-43, where the notion of "systemic domino" (as opposed to the "praxeological domino") is analysed.

[102] See the criticism against that flawed model of deterrence *supra* Section 3.1.

the European Parliament and the Council agreed to reduce discretion in the enforcement by establishing a "reverse voting" mechanism for the imposition of the new sanctions. Upon each step of the EDP, the Commission will make a proposal for the relevant sanction, and this will be considered adopted unless the Council decides within ten days against it by qualified majority.

One decisive step towards a fiscal union[103] undoubtedly is the enactment of a new directive on requirements for the budgetary framework of the member states, so that the objectives of the SGP are adequately reflected in the national budgetary frameworks, i.e. in the set of elements that form the basis of national fiscal governance. This directive sets out minimum requirements to be followed by all member states. Accounting and statistical issues, as well as forecasting practices, will thus be able to reflect minimum European standards to facilitate transparency and the monitoring of fiscal developments. Member states will be able to follow the EU's medium-term objectives more easily, since a multi-annual fiscal planning will be adopted in national budgetary frameworks, despite the traditional rule of annual budgets. Finally, every member state will put in place numerical fiscal rules that are able to lead to the respect of the deficit and debt thresholds.

5.2 Prevention and Correction of Macroeconomic Imbalances inside the EMU

It is the thesis of this Chapter that the basic structural deficiency of the euro area, and more specifically of the original Stability and Growth Pact, is that it only focused on the budgetary positions (the level of public deficit and debt ratios), that are in a certain sense only the symptoms of a malady, and not on the true cause, i.e. the *underlying comparative competitiveness problem* of some member states vis-à-vis others inside a common currency zone.

The Commission communication "EMU@10: successes and challenges after 10 years of Economic and Monetary Union", had already pointed out clearly the need to "broaden surveillance to address macroeconomic imbalances. Developments within Member States such as the growth of current account deficits, persistent inflation divergences or trends of unbalanced growth need to be monitored given that the occurrence of spill-over effects and the growing interdependence of euro-area economies

---

[103] See the analysis of this notion *infra* Section 6.

mean these developments represent a concern not just for the country in question but for the euro area as a whole"[104].

The Commission proposed a new framework for identifying and addressing macroeconomic imbalances at an early stage, including deteriorating competitiveness trends and large current account deficits of member states. This framework, comprising two regulations that outline a novel "excessive imbalance procedure", and introducing the possibility of fines being imposed on member states found to be in an "excessive imbalance position", closes a very significant gap in the EMU economic governance framework[105].

The axis of this innovative process that broadens surveillance of member states beyond their budgetary policies is a "scoreboard" comprising a limited set of macroeconomic and macrofinancial indicators relevant to the detection of both short-term and long-term (structural) macroeconomic imbalances, together with country-specific qualitative expert analysis that takes into account heterogeneous economic circumstances[106]. Those tools

---

[104] Communication from the Commission to the European Parliament, the Council, the European Economic and Social Committee, the Committee of the Regions and the European Central Bank, "EMU@10: successes and challenges after 10 years of Economic and Monetary Union," Brussels, COM(2008) 238 final, May 7, 2008: 9.

[105] An overview of the new legislation is provided in European Commission, "Economic governance package (2): Preventing and correcting macroeconomic imbalances," MEMO/10/454, Brussels, September 29, 2010.

[106] Regulation (EU) No. 1176/2011 reads, in relevant part:

> "The scoreboard shall, inter alia, encompass indicators which are useful in the early identification of,
>
> (a) internal imbalances, including those that can arise from public and private indebtedness; financial and asset market developments, including housing; the evolution of private sector credit flow; and the evolution of unemployment
>
> (b) external imbalances, including those that can arise from the evolution of current account and net investment positions of Member States; real effective exchange rates; export market shares; changes in price and cost developments; and non-price competitiveness, taking into account the different components of productivity.
>
> 4. In undertaking its economic reading of the scoreboard in the alert mechanism, the Commission shall pay close attention to developments in the real economy, including economic growth, employment and unemployment performance, nominal and real convergence inside and outside the euro area, productivity developments and its relevant drivers such as R&D and foreign and domestic investment, as well as sectoral developments, including energy, which affect GDP and current account performance".

will help identify timely imbalances emerging in different parts of the economy and will trigger an "alert mechanism" for the early detection of them. Concretely, each time an "alert threshold", i.e. an indicative value defined as a threshold for each one of the macroeconomic indicators of the scoreboard, is reached, and the imbalance is considered to be excessive, the member state concerned could be subject to an excessive imbalance procedure, and would be called upon to adopt a corrective action plan within a specific timeframe. It is accepted that the crossing of one or more indicative thresholds need not necessarily imply that macroeconomic imbalances are emerging, as economic policy-making should take into account interlinks between macroeconomic variables; therefore, the thresholds will not be interpreted in a rigid or mechanical way.

The Commission gained an enhanced role in the surveillance procedure (assessments, monitoring, on-site missions, recommendations and warnings). This is obviously a victory for the Community, as against the intergovernmental, spirit, since the Commission will take in charge and steer the procedure: it will release the results of the scoreboard on a regular basis and attach a Commission report putting it into perspective. On the basis of all available information, the Commission will draw a list of member states deemed at risk of imbalances.

The basic novelty here, and a prerequisite for any successful future fiscal union[107], is the so-called "in-depth review" following a detailed investigation of the underlying problems in the member states identified by the Commission. Such an in-depth review does not presume the existence of an imbalance, but encompasses a thorough analysis of potential sources of imbalances in the member state under review, taking due account of country-specific economic conditions and circumstances and of a wider set of analytical tools, indicators and qualitative information of a country-specific nature. When such an in-depth review is opened by the Commission, the member state has to cooperate to ensure that the information available to the Commission is as complete and correct as possible, and on the other side, the Commission has to give due consideration to any other information which is relevant in the opinion of the member state. This framework, which allows for continuous surveillance and prevention of severe macroeconomic imbalances and

---

Regulation (EU) No. 1176/2011 on the prevention and correction of macroeconomic imbalances, articles 4, paragraphs 3 and 4.

[107] Specifically regarding the proper functioning of a European Treasury that will manage jointly European public debt through the issuance of eurobonds, constantly review budgetary positions, and monitor the macroeconomic parameters of each EU member state; see *infra* Section 6.

possible spill-overs to other member states, is able to reduce the risk of negative externalities that can quite easily degenerate into a real EMU-wide systemic crisis[108].

Another extremely important novelty is the following: It is explicitly mentioned in the Regulation No 1176/2011 on the prevention and correction of macroeconomic imbalances that member states tending to accumulate large current-account surpluses represent also a potential threat to the financial stability in the EU, as a source of macroeconomic imbalances. The Regulation explicitly states in relevant part: "Policies should aim to identify and implement measures that help strengthen their domestic demand and growth potential"[109].

If the Commission considers that macroeconomic imbalances (or the risk thereof) do exist, it will come forward with preventive recommendations for the member state(s) concerned. But if the alert mechanism points to severe imbalances in a member state, the Council may open an "excessive imbalance procedure": on a recommendation from the Commission, it can adopt recommendations on a corrective action plan that the concerned member state will have to draft. That practically means that a member state falling under an excessive imbalance procedure will be driven by peer pressure to set up a roadmap of implementing policy measures within a specified deadline. The Commission will monitor the implementation of corrective action by the member states concerned, which will have to issue on a regular basis progress reports.

In case of persistent non-compliance of a euro area member state with the Council recommendations, then a phase of financial sanctions will be opened: the member state will have to pay a yearly fine, until the Council establishes that corrective action has been taken. If the member state fails repeatedly to draw up a corrective action plan to address the Council recommendations, it will be equally subject to a yearly fine adopted by a "reverse voting" mechanism in the Council, on proposal of the Commission. This yearly fine will equal 0.1 % of the GDP of the member state concerned in the preceding year.

* * *

[108] See *supra* Section 4.

[109] Regulation (EU) No. 1176/2011 of the European Parliament and of the Council of 16 November 2011 on the prevention and correction of macroeconomic imbalances, Explanatory statement 17; see also article 3, paragraph 2.

The second – and this time major – revision of the SGP rules comes as a response to the obvious failure of the previous institutional setting of the EU to prevent the grave financial crisis plaguing Europe since 2010.

As far as the new fiscal discipline measures are concerned (the "preventive" and "corrective" arms of the SGP), even though they clearly represent an advance compared to the lacunae of the previous framework, they still see the problem through a distorted lens: *Fiscal laxity and profligacy played only a minor role in the euro area's sovereign debt crisis.* It is only the Greek solvency crisis that can be traced back to a continuous fiscal derailment over the years after the country's accession to the EMU. Neither Ireland nor Spain ever breached the rules of the SGP: their combined real estate bubble and banking crises would never have been prevented or corrected by the rules of secondary EU law. Greed for cheap credits and overleveraging would never have been sanctioned by the SGP's rules. As for Portugal, its main problem was a lagging real economy due to productivity stagnation, in other words, private sector imbalances and lack of a real capacity to modernise the country's productive basis.

On the contrary, *the new rules on the prevention and correction of macroeconomic imbalances in the EMU are promising.* The effort to give the European Commission the means to detect and correct, at the earliest possible stage, macroeconomic imbalances, from the side either of the current-account deficit countries or of the current-account surplus countries, is surely positive. The new EU institutional scheme fits nicely with the Euro Plus Pact[110], that promotes the objectives of fostering competitiveness and employment, and therefore of contributing further to the sustainability of public finances and to the reinforcement of financial stability. By designing concrete policy commitments and by monitoring

---

[110] The Euro Plus Pact was agreed by the euro area Heads of State or government, joined by Bulgaria, Denmark, Latvia, Lithuania, Poland, Romania, in the European Council of March 24-25, 2011, in order to "strengthen the economic pillar of the monetary union, achieve a new quality of economic policy coordination, [and] improve competitiveness, thereby leading to a higher degree of convergence" (European Council conclusions of March 24-25, 2011, Annex I "The Euro Plus Pact – Stronger Economic Policy Coordination for Competitiveness and Convergence," 13). For an account of the facts that led to the announcement of a Franco-German "Pact for Competitiveness" to harmonize economic governance in the euro area on February 4, 2011 that was eventually opened to non euro area member states and was renamed "Euro Plus Pact", see Brigitte Young, "Economic Governance in the Eurozone: A New Dawn?" *Economic Sociology_The European Electronic Newsletter* 12(2) (2011): 11-6,
http://econsoc.mpifg.de/archive/econ_soc_12-2.pdf#page=11.

processes with the aid of macroeconomic and macrofinancial indicators that now enter officially into the EU institutional software, we are laying the foundations for sustainable growth and employment in the future and deepening the European integration.

6. Is the Fiscal Compact a Path Leading the European Union towards a Fiscal Union?

Lately, a lively discussion about a European Fiscal Union as a possible way out of the EMU crisis has been going on. In this Section, I will detail seven necessary components to any type of fiscal union. I will present the American historical experience and will argue that any kind of fiscal union needs *strong political legitimacy*, since the changes that it will induce to the existing EU architecture not only are important, but will put under pressure states' fiscal sovereignty.

I will also present briefly the European Fiscal Compact (the fiscal part of the TSCG), which was signed by all EU member states except the Czech Republic and the United Kingdom on March 2, 2012), and will articulate a political and macroeconomic criticism to it, since it is presented by some European stakeholders as a path towards a European Fiscal Union.

6.1 The Necessary Components of a Fiscal Union – the American Experience

History teaches us that the fate for currency unions has been eventual failure and dissolution, unless there is some form of *centralised political union* in place or, in technical terms, a *fiscal union*. One only has to bring in mind the fate of the Latin and Scandinavian Monetary Unions in the 19th century, and of course, the Gold Standard that developed internationally from the 1870's to the 1930's[111]. All of these currency areas or fixed

[111] The authoritative work on the mishaps and the demise of the Gold Standard in the interwar period is Barry Eichengreen, *Golden Fetters: The Gold Standard and the Great Depression, 1919-1939* (Oxford: Oxford University Press, 1996). Of course, the greatest foe of the Gold Standard was Lord Keynes; Keynes repeatedly attacked the Gold Standard in the 1920's until its abandonment by Great Britain in 1931 because, by ruling out the possibility of external (currency) devaluation, it trapped countries into deflationary policies, depressing thus industrial activity, at exactly the time when countercyclical expansionary measures were called for to stimulate aggregate demand and fight against rising unemployment after the 1929 Wall Street crash. See John Maynard Keynes, *A Tract on Monetary Reform*

exchange rates systems broke apart because there was no central institution to enforce common monetary policy, and because of the inability of member states to harmonise their divergent fiscal policies due to domestic concerns. In short, any monetary union that is not backed by a strong and politically integrated fiscal union is doomed to fail. This seems to have been understood in the EU. The American historical experience opens the way to an understanding of the *sine qua non* components of any Fiscal Union that I will shortly present in Section 6.1. Nevertheless, the basic path chosen towards the shaping of such a union, the so-called Fiscal Compact, does not seem to fulfil the high expectations in this regard, as I will argue in Section 6.2.

The notion of "fiscal federalism"[112], under the banner of which takes place a discussion over fiscal unions, is quite ambiguous: some authors have taken a "New Federalist" stance by claiming as its advantages its high decentralization of economic policymaking, whereas others have been arguing in its favour because of the need for more coordination and a stronger role for the federal government. In this ongoing theoretical debate, I will explicitly take the side of federalism-as-centralization, even though I will develop my own conceptualisation of fiscal unions.

(Amherst, NY: Prometheus Books, 1999, 1st edition 1923), and his pamphlet *The Economic Consequences of Mr. Churchill* (London: L. and V. Woolf, 1925).
On the Latin Monetary Union, that strived unsuccessfully to become the basis of the first European Monetary Unification from 1865 to 1873 but eventually ceased to bind its members since, in the meantime, it had converted into a pure gold standard, and was officially disbanded in 1927, see Luca Einaudi, *Money and Politics: European Monetary Unification and the International Gold Standard (1865-1873)* (Oxford: Oxford University Press, 2001).
The Latin Monetary Union influenced the Scandinavian Monetary Union, established between Denmark and Sweden in 1873 and joined by Norway two years later. The aim was to do for Scandinavia what the Latin Monetary Union was attempting more broadly for Europe as a whole; it, too, effectively ceased to function on the outbreak of World War I, and was formally brought to an end in 1924. See David Cannadine, "A Point of View: Making friends the shared currency way," *BBC News Magazine*, February 24, 2012, http://www.bbc.co.uk/news/magazine-17140379.

[112] There is a vast literature on the notion of "fiscal federalism" that was reinvigorated after the groundbreaking books by Wallace E. Oates, *Fiscal Federalism* (New York: Harcourt Brace Jovanovich, 1972), and by Geoffrey Brennan and James M. Buchanan, *The Power to Tax: Analytical Foundations of a Fiscal Constitution* (Cambridge: Cambridge University Press, 1980), were published. These authors were proponents of the so-called "New Federalism", i.e. of the need to decentralize regulation of both expenditure and revenues ("devolution").

According to Bruno Frey[113], the advantages of centralization in federal unions are the following:

- Spillovers can be taken into account by central coordination
- Economies of scale can be exploited
- Better coordination is assured
- Minimal provision of certain public goods can be guaranteed
- Redistribution policy becomes feasible
- Effective stabilization policy becomes feasible[114].

In a short but influential 1992 article, Robert P. Inman and Daniel L. Rubinfeld argued, for several reasons, in favour of a more centralized fiscal regime for the European Union based on the United States experience[115]. As they clear-sightedly argued, "[i]n open, integrated economies, deficit financed demand creation may be of only limited usefulness to small member states," since "the demand stimulus of deficit financing is dissipated through import demands from other union states" and, even if running deficit policies were economically feasible, "[i]n interdependent economic unions, the benefits from local demand creation through deficit financing may spill over to other member states via import expansion, while the interest costs of deficits remain with the borrowing state"[116]. The result could be that member states could not be able to provide expansionary fiscal policies when needed; that is why central government fiscal policies stand as the policy alternative[117].

In any case, central to any kind of fiscal union are the ideas of *direct transfers* and of a *central fiscal actor*. I will start the presentation of the necessary components of any fiscal union by discussing a test case: the bankruptcy of a member state of such a union (say, the United States of America). If the state government goes bankrupt:

---

[113] Bruno S. Frey, *Democratic Economic Policy* (Oxford: Blackwell, 1983).

[114] This concentrated presentation of the advantages, together with the disadvantages, of centralization can be found in Reiner Eichenberger, "The Benefits of Federalism and the Risk of Overcentralization," *Kyklos* 47(3) (1994): 403-19.

[115] Robert P. Inman and Daniel L. Rubinfeld, "Fiscal Federalism in Europe: Lessons from the United States experience," *European Economic Review* 36 (1992): 654-60.

[116] *Ibid.*, 655. This is *exactly* what has happened in Greece.

[117] Robert P. Inman and Daniel L. Rubinfeld, "Fiscal Federalism in Europe," 655, following Oliver Hart, "A model of imperfect competition with Keynesian features," *Quarterly Journal of Economics* 97 (1982): 109-38.

- First and foremost, the Federal Reserve stands ready to act as a lender of last resort to any state bank through the opening of an emergency credit line, and also to the state government itself by buying municipal bonds in open market.
- Borrower companies with healthy balance sheets will continue to have access to credit from the banks of the rest of the union. In fiscal unions, there is by definition no "state sovereign risk" the way there is, for example, Greek sovereign risk, since borrowers operate under a *federally guaranteed* legal regime (Banking Union).
- Citizens automatically get welfare checks and other transfer payments (e.g. unemployment benefits) from the federal government as automatic stabilizers
- Workers move easily and can easily seek jobs elsewhere in the union, since the labour market is very flexible and fluid and human resources very mobile.
- Discretionary measures, such as excess fiscal spending, extraordinary assistance and debt relief, can always be taken at the federal level through the political channels of the federal political system.

The direct support and benefits that residents of the bankrupt state get from the federal government transfers implies that there is no expectation that the federal government will ever need to bail out a state government[118]. This support limits the economic and political fallout of the state, contrary to what happens e.g. in Greece, where the bankruptcy of the Greek government condemns the entire Greek financial system and economy to a downfall.

Thus, in a fully integrated fiscal union such as the USA, a state has given up its full sovereignty by accepting the reach of federal laws and regulations, and has, in its turn, become part of a common governance structure based in the federal capital. This allows for automaticity (in

---

[118] In a recent working paper, C. Randall Henning and Martin Kessler note that within the US system the federal government does not mandate balanced budgets nor, since the 1840s, does it bail out states in fiscal trouble. Balanced budget rules have been viable in the US states because the federal government has a broad set of fiscal powers, including countercyclical fiscal action, and a Banking Union (a unified bank regulation and a common fiscal pool for restructuring the banking system) allows for bank rescues without undue strains on the sovereign debt level; C. Randall Henning and Martin Kessler, "Fiscal Federalism: US History for Architects of Europe's Fiscal Union," Petersen Institute for International Economics Working Paper 12-1, January 2012.

other words, no conditionality requirement) in credit and financial assistance and, of course, a consciousness of belonging together in a political community, instead of intergovernmental strife and nationalistic resentment, which make resolution of crises much harder. The notion itself of "moral hazard", i.e. of a moral deresponsabilization of economic actors by guaranteeing that there will always be a financial assistance as a last refuge to fiscal laxity, is completely ruled out in the context of a fiscal union.

The term "Fiscal Union" does not imply the existence of a unitary fiscal system. It refers to a federal type of structure, where a central authority that has its own resources and enjoys budgetary powers coexists with states that are fiscally sovereign, albeit with the safety net of revenue transfers for the execution of various federal programs. In a fiscal union, member states are not *obliged* to run balanced or surplus budgets, although most do; state authorities' bonds cannot generally be used as collateral for banks to borrow from the Federal Reserve; and there are no interstate bail-outs for failing state governments. This is basically the product of a political genius, the American Federalist Alexander Hamilton[119].

Before 1790, the United States of America was effectively bankrupt and had no banking system, no functioning securities market, no national currency, and no tax collection system. As the first secretary of the Treasury after the Independence and a prominent Federalist, Alexander Hamilton devised a brilliant plan to create a viable American financial system out of nothing. His First Report on Public Credit presented to the House of Representatives on January 14, 1790 included probably the single most groundbreaking idea in the history of public finance: the "debt assumption plan", i.e. the assumption of state debts incurred to prosecute the War of Independence by the federal government via the issuance of a federal debt instrument, precursor of today's Treasury Bond, and a voluntary swap of old debt for new bonds, backed by the tax base of the federal government. The operation, which met with enormous success, was actually accompanied by debt restructuring, both of prior federal debt and of the newly assumed state debt.

Hamilton's main ideas deserve a quotation in full because of their importance for the contemporary debt crisis in the EU[120]:

---

[119] For the account that follows, I have been drawing on C. Randall Henning and Martin Kessler, "Fiscal Federalism," 3-5.

[120] Alexander Hamilton, "First Report on Public Credit, January 9, 1790," http://www.gwu.edu/~ffcp/exhibit/p13/p13_3.html.

> "And as on the one hand, the necessity for borrowing in particular emergencies cannot be doubted, so on the other, it is equally evident, that to be able to borrow upon *good terms,* it is essential that the credit of a nation should be well established.
>
> For when the credit of a country is in any degree questionable, it never fails to give an extravagant premium, in one shape or another, upon all the loans it has occasion to make. Nor does the evil end here; the same disadvantage must be sustained upon whatever is to be bought on terms of future payment.
>
> From this constant necessity of *borrowing* and *buying dear,* it is easy to conceive how immensely the expences of a nation, in a course of time, will be augmented by an unsound state of the public credit."

Hamilton did not conceive of his plan as "simply a way to secure credit for the government, or even to establish a national financial system, but as a grand political project"[121]. He thought that the plan would, *inter alia*, secure for the federal government the allegiance of the holders of federal debt (since bondholders would have a direct financial interest to help the new United States government survive and thrive), shore them up to a deep and well-functioning financial system, give them incentive to stimulate the economy by using the new federal bonds as collateral for loans, and more generally bind the states to the Union:

> "In so strong a light nevertheless do they appear to the Secretary, that on their due observance at the present critical juncture, materially depends, in his judgment, the individual and aggregate prosperity of the citizens of the United States; their relief from the embarrassments they now experience; their character as a People; the cause of good government"[122].

Later on, Alexander Hamilton (the "Federalist") was fiercely opposed to Thomas Jefferson (the "Democratic-Republican") over his proposal for a Bank of the United States, the precursor of the Federal Reserve System. The bipolarization of American political life among two opposite theories of government, Hamilton's stance of centralisation in the hands of a strong national government, and Jefferson's decentralized, agrarian, small-government ideal of politics and economy, finds its source in this controversy.

The American historical experience has proven by now that a monetary union must be combined with some form of economic and fiscal union to be viable and strong. If we take the case of the euro area, a single

---

[121] C. Randall Henning and Martin Kessler, "Fiscal Federalism," 4.

[122] Alexander Hamilton, "First Report on Public Credit."

currency with seventeen different governments, seventeen different bond markets, and seventeen different economic strategies simply cannot work.

I would now like to detail the *seven necessary components*, in my view, *of any type of fiscal union*, and consequently of a European Fiscal Union:

1. A Treasury Department (or Finance Ministry)

Such a central authority is intended to impose common fiscal rules, like the well-known Maastricht criteria (public debts no higher than 60 % and budget deficits no higher than 3 % of GDP). It will also manage European public debt through the issuance of jointly guaranteed bonds (Eurobonds or "stability bonds" or "blue bonds") backed by important EU revenue so as to maintain an excellent credit rating. This mutualisation of debts can only happen logically if the Treasury constantly reviews budgetary positions of member states and monitors the macroeconomic patterns of each EU member state so as to prevent in time excessive macroeconomic imbalances, especially concerning the connection between productivity and wages, the viability of pension and social security systems, inflationary or deflationary tendencies, the growth rate of private debt for housing and consumption, and more generally the balance of payments of each member state[123].

2. A Treasury bond (Eurobond)

A single European market for jointly guaranteed bonds will certainly close the gap for the unbearable spreads between Europe's national bond markets, and will thus protect vulnerable member states of a Union from the markets in their effort to refinance their outstanding debt. It will also attract much liquidity from private savings, from inside the state and outside, and will help finance European recovery. A deep European bond market will refinance public debt at the lowest cost and recapitalise banks.

3. A Central Bank as lender of last resort to euro zone member states

As I have shown, the basic structural deficiency of the European Central Bank (ECB) is that, according to its statute, it is basically concerned with inflation, and does not pursue a double objective of price stability and full employment, as is the case for the Federal Reserve in the USA. The ECB has been using a more innovative approach since May 2010 by buying up sovereign bonds in the secondary market, or by giving long-term and cheap loans to commercial banks in order to fight against the lurching credit crunch. Yet, the strict rule-bound (*ordoliberalismus*) variation of monetarism underlying the Stability and Growth Pact does not

---

[123] See analytically *supra* Section 5.

allow the ECB to fully play its role in order to restore confidence in the real economy, by fear of medium-term inflationary tendencies[124]. Once markets comprehend that the ECB is not really willing to provide a safety net by monetary expansion, i.e. by printing more money, they will condemn the weakest national economies by driving up their borrowing costs[125].

4. A system of direct transfers

As already analyzed above, a system of direct transfers works like an automatic stabilizer for a fiscal union. It absorbs a big part of the asymmetric shocks that are due to divergent economic cycles or to purely conjunctional reasons such as energy shocks. The existence of direct transfers presupposes a serious rise in the EU's own resources in order to finance Europe-wide economies of scale, programs and operations. It also necessarily implies a mechanism of solidarity and redistribution, generally referred to under the code name "fiscal federalism," through some sort of European tax, such as a financial transactions tax or a carbon tax.

5. A strong Investment Bank

Every fiscal union has to have a financial arm able to raise large amounts of capital through the issuance of project bonds and the leveraging of private resources in order to finance industrial reinvigoration, Trans-European infrastructures, R&D, innovation, sustainable development, life-

---

[124] "The central and defining concern of ordoliberalism was to establish 'order' as a set of legal rules for a society of essentially self-reliant decision makers whose actions are controlled and co-ordinated by market competition"; Manfred E. Streit and Michael Wohlgemuth, "The Market Economy and the State Hayekian and Ordoliberal Conceptions," in *The Theory of Capitalism in the German Economic Tradition: Historism, Ordo-Liberalism, Critical Theory, Solidarism*, ed. Peter Koslowski (Berlin - Heidelberg: Springer Verlag, 2000), 230. The specialist of German politics Stephen Padgett gets it right in his quote: "A central tenet of ordoliberalism is a clearly defined division of labor in economic management, with specific responsibilities assigned to particular institutions. Monetary policy should be the responsibility of a central bank committed to monetary stability and low inflation, and insulated from political pressure by independent status. Fiscal policy—balancing tax revenue against government expenditure—is the domain of the government, whilst macroeconomic policy is the preserve of employers and trade unions" (Wikipedia article "Ordoliberalism," last modified 26 February 2013, http://en.wikipedia.org/wiki/Ordoliberalism).

[125] See analytically *supra* Section 3.2.

long learning, and capital spending in general, through public-private partnerships and economies of scale[126].

6. A Monetary Fund

A European Monetary Fund, i.e. a large, flexible and credible safety net against the possibility of a member state failure, is a prerequisite for the normal functioning of a sub-optimal currency zone. The sometimes necessary national debt restructurings cannot produce beneficial effects unless they are managed by experienced staff, and not by one-size-fits-all policies favored by the International Monetary Fund, that intervenes all over the world[127]. And finally,

7. A Banking Union, together with a Union-wide risk capital market and regulation of systemic risks, financial derivatives, and hedge funds

A Banking Union is a federal-type mechanism comprising at least three strands:

- a Union-wide deposit insurance scheme that will prevent abrupt and gregarious transfers of capitals from one member state's banks to another's in times of crisis ("bank runs")
- a unified bank monitoring and regulation scheme for at least the systemically important financial institutions, those that might produce negative externalities and spillovers of such dimensions and unforeseeable consequences as to be potential sources of systemic risk, and
- a common fiscal pool for the direct recapitalization of undercapitalized banks and a common scheme for the restructuring of the Union-wide banking system more generally.

For the financing of innovative SMEs, we need new forms of risk-sharing financing facilities, and above all, a demand stimulus for innovative products and services. Finally, no real fiscal union can be conceived that does not have Union-wide independent regulators for banks, hedge and pension funds, and insurance companies. The fragmentation of banking

---

[126] The role of the European Investment Bank (EIB) in leveraging capital for Europe-wide infrastructure projects through the issuance of "project bonds" will not be discussed in this Chapter. An account of it is made in the Introduction.

[127] In a renowned paper, Daniel Gros and Thomas Mayer, "How to deal with sovereign default in Europe: Towards a Euro(pean) Monetary Fund," CEPS Policy Brief No. 202, May 17, 2010, http://www.ceps.eu/book/towards-european-monetary-fund, called for the creation of a European Monetary Fund so as to avert the threat of a disorderly default in the euro area and of an ensuing systemic financial instability at European and global level.

and macro-prudential regulations across national lines is not efficient, since it tends to undermine common rules by simple trans-frontier movements of capital.

From this overview of its *sine qua non* components, it must be obvious that any kind of Fiscal Union will need *strong political legitimacy*. The only logical outcome is to organize the quickest possible truly European elections to vote, not only for a European Parliament with budgetary powers, but also for a European Commission that will evolve into a true government and that will reflect the equilibrium between European political parties.

6.2 A Criticism of the Fiscal Compact

I wish to articulate a brief political and macroeconomic criticism to the intergovernmental European Fiscal Compact[128], since this text is presented by some European stakeholders as a path towards a European Fiscal Union.

The basic questions here can be formulated as follows: What is the level of fiscal autonomy that member states continue to have after the signature (but not yet ratification) of this text, and are the presuppositions of the Fiscal Compact really amenable to a European Fiscal Union, such as I have described it?

The Fiscal Compact contains the following basic rules:

General government budgets shall be balanced or in surplus[129]. That shall be deemed to be respected if the annual structural deficit does not exceed 0.5 % of GDP[130]. Such a rule will also be introduced in member states' national legal systems "through provisions of binding force and permanent character, preferably constitutional, or otherwise guaranteed to be fully respected and adhered to throughout the national budgetary processes"[131]. The rule will contain an automatic correction mechanism that shall be triggered in the event of deviation and will be defined by each member state on the basis of principles proposed by the European Commission[132]. The Court of Justice shall have jurisdiction to verify the transposition of this rule at national level and its respect by the signing

[128] TSCG, Title III (articles 3-8), which was signed by all EU member states except the Czech Republic and the United Kingdom on 2 March 2012.

[129] TSCG, article 3, paragraph 1(a).

[130] TSCG, article 3, paragraph 1(b).

[131] TSCG, article 3, paragraph 2.

[132] TSCG, article 3, paragraphs 1(e) and 2.

parties, and it will impose the payment of an appropriate lump sum or a penalty not to exceed 0.1 % of GDP in case of non compliance[133].

Countries with government debt levels significantly below 60 % and where risks in terms of long-term sustainability of public finances are low can reach a structural deficit of at most 1 % of GDP[134]. Member States whose government debt exceeds the 60 % reference level shall reduce it at an average rate of one twentieth (5 %) per year as a benchmark[135]. Member States shall converge towards their specific reference level, according to a calendar proposed by the European Commission taking into consideration country-specific sustainability risks[136]. Member states in Excessive Deficit Procedure shall submit to the Commission and the Council for endorsement an economic partnership programme detailing the necessary structural reforms to ensure an effectively durable correction of their excessive deficits. The monitoring of the implementation of such programmes, and the yearly budgetary plans consistent with them, will take place under the existing procedures of the SGP[137]. Finally, a mechanism will be put in place for the *ex ante* reporting by member states of their national debt issuance plans to the Commission and the Council[138].

The main intention of the text is to commit the member states to a stricter budgetary discipline, backed by automatic sanctions. Unfortunately, it strives to obtain that through strict predetermined rules in a context of great uncertainty, which demands a more flexible and responsive approach to macroeconomic problems. The text transposes the so-called "Golden Rule," which limits the annual structural deficit (meaning the "annual cyclically-adjusted balance net of one-off and temporary measures"[139]) to 0.5 % of GDP. Yet, instead of constitutionalizing the Golden Rule through permanent and binding provisions, the Compact should have adjusted the fiscal targets of the Union into a *medium-term* economic cycle, after having taken into account the realistic growth perspectives inside this same cycle. Thus, due to the often divergent economic cycles between different member states, it should have clearly and unequivocally accepted the creation of countercyclical deficits in a country caught in a

---

[133] TSCG, article 8.

[134] TSCG, article 3, paragraph 1(d).

[135] TSCG, article 4, and Council Regulation (EU) No. 1177/2011 of 8 November 2011 amending Regulation (EC) No. 1467/97 on speeding up and clarifying the implementation of the excessive deficit procedure, article 2, paragraph 1a.

[136] TSCG, article 3, paragraph 1(b).

[137] TSCG, article 5.

[138] TSCG, article 6.

[139] TSCG, article 3, paragraph 3(a).

downward spiral, so as to halt this trend through investments, and impose big budgetary surpluses during the upward trend of the cycle, after the creation of wealth and employment by the private sector will have started to compensate for cuts in public spending.

The Fiscal Compact seems thus unfortunately skewed towards a philosophy of unilateral fiscal consolidation, and not towards a balanced approach between discipline and growth. Of course, the text refers to the "country-specific medium-term objective" and to the "adjustment path towards it" of each member state[140], as did the original SGP, and distinguishes between structural and cyclical deficits[141]. Yet, this reference is incomplete and unproductive because *no real distinction* is made between deficits that occur for capital spending and productive investments (such as broadband networks, energy efficiency of buildings, hard and soft infrastructures), on the one hand, and deficits stemming from the consumption demands of some spendthrift, unproductive, and parasitic, public sector, on the other.

In brief, productive public investments, *as long as they are monitored and authorized by a European Ministry of Finance*, should *not* be taken into account at all in the balanced or surplus budgetary positions that each country is obliged to seek. These vital expenditures should be *exonerated* altogether from the calculation of the maximum percentage of deficit allowed. The extremely strict "one-size-fits-all" Golden Rule is clearly a straightjacket: not only will it not lead to more fiscal discipline and harmonization, but on the contrary, it will push more and more member states towards its violation in order to activate some growth tools when their economies enter into a recession phase.

What is more, in a single currency area, where by definition there is no way to regain some lost competitiveness by external devaluation, if external competitiveness is only calculated on the basis of comparative

---

[140] TSCG, article 3, paragraphs 1(b) and 1(e).

[141] TSCG, article 3, paragraph 1(b): "the rule under point (a) shall be deemed to be respected if the annual structural balance of the general government is at its country-specific medium-term objective, as defined in the revised Stability and Growth Pact, with a lower limit of a structural deficit of 0,5 % of the gross domestic product at market prices. The Contracting Parties shall ensure rapid convergence towards their respective medium-term objective. The time-frame for such convergence will be proposed by the European Commission taking into consideration country-specific sustainability risks. Progress towards, and respect of, the medium-term objective shall be evaluated on the basis of an overall assessment with the structural balance as a reference, including an analysis of expenditure net of discretionary revenue measures, in line with the revised Stability and Growth Pact".

salary costs between several member states, that will produce a "race to the bottom", a continuous social dumping, and a war of all against all. Dumping, in its turn, will most certainly result in a disastrous deflation that will open a never-ending and self-fulfilling cycle of recession, destruction of values, disinvestment and unemployment. By focusing exclusively on fiscal consolidation through the requirement of the Golden Rule not to exceed a 0.5 % rate of structural public deficit, the Fiscal Compact, if not intertwined with an EU Growth Pact, will most certainly have the opposite result than the one expected. A violent and short-term public debt reduction through the priority use of any public revenues to repay bonds at maturity before the private sector has the time to develop its productive basis to produce growth, surplus value and employment, is simply catastrophic for the economy.

The absence of any direct transfer mechanism for financial resources, that remain idle in zero-risk German Bunds or bank accounts, in other words the lack of any mechanism for the recycling of excessive liquidities in some countries of the EMU, whereas other countries are suffering from a liquidity crisis, will certainly not be conducive to a true Fiscal Union[142].

---

[142] *Contra* Yves Bertoncini, "Tribune: 'Fiscal Compact', sovereignty and austerity," *Notre Europe*, July 26, 2012, http://www.notreeurope.eu/uploads/tx_publication/FiscalPact_Viewpoint_NE_July12.pdf, who believes that European discipline is not necessarily a synonym for austerity, since the target of the efforts to reduce public debt through gradual adjustments is "to *boost investor confidence* and thus to bring down the rates at which governments borrow, thereby increasing their margins for manoeuvre in this area too"; Yves Bertoncini, "'Fiscal Compact'", 2 (emphasis added). This conception is what Nobelist Paul Krugman calls "growsterity", i.e. a form of austerity that allows for some targeted structural measures to encourage growth by establishing confidence in an economy's long-term capacity to grow. Krugman has been chastising this conception as the "confidence fairy": "According to this doctrine, governments should respond to a severely depressed economy not the way the textbooks say they should — by spending more to offset falling private demand — but with fiscal austerity, slashing spending in an effort to balance their budgets" because "[c]onfidence-inspiring policies will foster and not hamper economic recovery" (Paul Krugman, "Death of a Fairy Tale," *New York Times*, April 26, 2012). Empirical evidence from the euro area periphery has shown, not only that fiscal austerity in depressed economies is self-defeating because the shrinking of the economy and the lowering of long-term tax revenues make the debt outlook worse rather than better, but also that it never managed to restore the bond markets' confidence.

7. The EU's Inchoate Tools to Pursue Stimulus Measures for Growth and Employment

It is quite obvious that one lesson learned from the crisis is that fiscal policy should never be looked at in isolation; efforts should be made, instead, to integrate indispensable fiscal consolidation measures into a broader EU macroeconomic surveillance framework, so as to avoid large macroeconomic imbalances as well as persistent divergences in competitiveness performances between member states.

Since both Europeans and Americans find themselves in the midst of an unprecedented since the Second World War – yet initially underestimated – crisis, it is rather doubtful that classical budgetary stimuli such as tax cuts or financial assistance to enterprises in difficulty will have long-term beneficial effects. What our real economies need in an era of prolonged budgetary restrictions is no less than a complete restructuring of our models of production and consumption, a smart rearrangement of our sources of fiscal revenues and top-priority public expenditures in order to liberate our potential for both sustainable growth and an ambitious level of employment.

Indeed, the Greek case has clearly shown the danger of entering into the vicious circle of a deflationary spiral once we focus excessively on fiscal consolidation, to the detriment of well-calibrated measures spurring economic growth. Such a scenario brings about a real parade of horrors:

- a decrease in the available income, and thus a sharp fall of consumption because of the generalised economic insecurity,
- an inability to borrow from international markets at a reasonable cost,
- an underinvestment of the private sector due to its massive efforts of debt pay down,
- a devaluation of work as a production factor because of the massive and often durable unemployment, and ultimately,
- a heavy tendency of degradation of our human capital because of prolonged periods of un- or underemployment of our productive forces, especially of young people, women, and seniors, that are caught in the pangs of a systemic crisis[143].

Because the Maastricht Treaty's and the original SGP's only quantified objectives addressed to member states are those concerning the two fiscal

[143] See the very acute remarks on the basic recessionary and deflationary features by Aglietta, *La crise*, 61-3, 116-18.

variables (deficit-to-GDP and debt-to-GDP ratios) I discussed above, it was only natural that governments would eventually focus almost exclusively on these indicators and leave aside extremely important long-term *growth* ones, such as demographic trends, levels of employment and unemployment, rise in per capita productivity, capital intensity, quality of human resources (through the wide diffusion of education and life-long learning), performances in research and technological innovation, investment in information and communication technologies and infrastructures, and so on[144]. Michel Aglietta puts it nicely when he writes that "the question must not be that of budgetary austerity, but that of a restructuring both of revenues and of expenditures to obtain a rise in potential growth, which will ensure the sustainability of the debt"[145]. In short, sound macroeconomic management is not – and should never be – conceptually and politically detached from long-term structural policies tending to inject dynamism into the economy, since without the return of growth into an economy in stagnation, even the most well designed fiscal adjustment is doomed to fail because public deficits will not be brought down in the long run. Or, to put it even more boldly, *budgetary discipline and fiscal adjustment can be conceived of as necessary preconditions of sound and sustainable growth, but certainly not to be cherished* per se.

Therefore, the real issues can be formulated as follows: Are the EU growth policies efficient? Do they successfully marshal and coordinate member states' growth efforts through sufficiently clear and coherent sectoral and horizontal policies? And, in the last resort, do they mobilise European citizens' human resources, talents and productive capacities to a satisfactory degree?

If there is but *one* lesson to be learned from the Greek case, that is that systemic crises – that break out regularly in capitalist economies – in regional economic and monetary zones such as the EMU cannot be efficiently managed without *integrated* common policies in favour of entrepreneurship, competitiveness, and innovation in every economic sector. Growth policies can be figuratively illustrated as gears, instruments that can be used to accelerate the movement of a vehicle (the economy) and thus produce more output (social wealth). The thesis defended in this Chapter is that the use of these gears must not be left to the complete discretion of multiple pilots – the national governments of the twenty-seven EU member states – in a common vehicle – the Union –, especially since the launch of the EMU.

---

[144] Vesperini, *Relancer*, 47-8.

[145] Aglietta, *La crise*, 119 (my translation).

Of course, not only is it reasonable that there always exist political divergences between several national and regional policies, but that is a highly desirable state of affairs, since federal experience has shown how productive it is for member states and infra-state levels of decision-making (i.e. local and regional governments) to experiment alternative ways of reaching commonly decided goals[146]. The solidity of a political union often passes through *emulation* between different political actors in pursuit of common aims, especially in the field of social and economic regulation; in that sense, guidelines, best practices, benchmarking, individualised recommendations, and other methods of mutual learning and evaluation[147] are crucial for the successful outcome of commonly designed policies in a union.

Nevertheless, if we install from the outset a very loose coordination framework and detach long-term structural and growth policies (assigned primarily to the individual member states) from fiscal discipline measures (assigned to member states, but within the framework of mutual surveillance containing also an array of sanctions in cases of serious deviation), the divergence between national and infra-national growth policies might eventually end up in disintegration. Public policies in a commonly designed framework (such as that of the Lisbon Strategy) ought to be able to mobilise productive forces, especially dormant or underused human and technological resources, in pursuit of a common destination; they ought to bring them together to achieve economies of scale and gain critical mass in the ongoing international competition. Especially in times of severe systemic crisis, the EU member states ought to *act in common*, through the impulse of the European Commission if not the European Council, in order to stimulate economic activity in the face of recessionary tendencies.

---

146 For the classical view depicting states as "laboratories of social and economical experimentation" in the USA, see the famous dissenting opinion by Supreme Court Justice Louis D. Brandeis in *New State Ice Co. v. Liebmann*, 285 U.S. 262, 311 (1932): "To stay experimentation in things social and economic is a grave responsibility. Denial of the right to experiment may be fraught with serious consequences to the nation. It is one of the happy incidents of the federal system that a single courageous state may, if its citizens choose, serve as a laboratory; and try novel social and economic experiments without risk to the rest of the country". Recently, though, an author denied that the Brandeis opinion has anything to do with federalism issues; see G. Alan Tarr, "Laboratories of Democracy? Brandeis, Federalism, and Scientific Management," *Publius* 31 (2001): 37.

147 On these forms of "soft law", see the analysis of the so-called Open Method of Coordination *infra* p. 89-94.

Indeed, as Pierre-Alain Muet has shown, the absence of coordination between EU member states in order to implement common stimulus measures necessarily brings about a profound *asymmetry* between diverse and disparate policies; thus, policies in favour of labour flexibility and gains in external competitiveness through the freezing of labour costs tend to be excessively used, whereas policies boosting demand or favouring offer through the take-up of technological innovations tend to be devalued and underused[148]. As this author nicely puts it, "This restrictive bias of European policies is partly *the cost of the political non-Europe*. The European economies are interdependent almost as much as those of the American states, but we lack federal and democratic institutions that would allow us to manage the economic zone we have created"[149]. Muet's conclusion is that to define a comprehensive policy mix geared towards both growth and price stability, we need to give incentives to EU member states to promote growth policies, the costs of which they would bear alone, while all their partners would share their benefits; and this cannot be done without some sort of *political* institution able to coordinate economic policies or, otherwise said, without establishing, alongside the Monetary Union, "a 'European government' sufficiently credible in order for central banks to accept to initiate economic recovery"[150].

I will outline, at least roughly, desirable growth policies that can normatively serve as standards for the evaluation of the EU's effective growth and employment policies (regrouped under the code name "Lisbon Strategy", recently renamed "Europe 2020 Strategy"[151]). The master word here is *innovation*. Indeed, only through a use of innovation as a regulative idea[152] of European growth policies can we go beyond a strictly

[148] Pierre-Alain Muet, "Déficit de croissance européen et défaut de coordination : une analyse rétrospective," in *Coordination européenne des politiques économiques*, rapports du Conseil d'Analyse Economique, (Paris: La Documentation française, 1998), 13-4, 26.
[149] *Ibid.* (emphasis added) (my translation).
[150] *Ibid.*, p. 30 (my translation).
[151] Communication from the Commission "Europe 2020: A strategy for smart, sustainable and inclusive growth," COM(2010) 2020 final, Brussels, March 3, 2010.
[152] In the first part of the "Appendix to the Transcendental Dialectic" of his *Critique of Pure Reason*, entitled "On the Regulative Use of the Ideas of Pure Reason," Immanuel Kant attempts to identify some proper "immanent" use for reason. In its most general terms, Kant is here concerned to establish a necessary role for reason's principle of systematic unity. The regulative use of human reason posits a unifying faculty which unites the manifold of knowledge gained by the understanding. See Paul Guyer and Allen W. Wood, "Introduction to the *Critique*

accounting treatment of our economic problems in order to restructure our policy mix of revenues and expenditures.

A basic stimulus of innovation on the revenue side would be that of reorienting our fiscal basis at European level so as not to tax work but instead, for example, the externalisation effects of pollution through some form of European "carbon tax"[153]. Such a strategic choice, if combined with correlative tax reliefs reducing labour cost and, on the expenditure side, public investments to aid R&D efforts, particularly by the private sector, will inevitably increase EU competitiveness and leverage private investment[154]. Other such investments on the expenditure side would include financing of large-scale infrastructures and of green growth, namely of a set of R&D and technological innovation production and take-up policies lying at the intersection between the sectors of energy, environment and information and communication technologies (ICT), such as energy efficiency, promotion of renewable energies, smart grids, low- or zero-energy consuming housing and transports, etc.

Indeed, one basic priority of every EU growth policy should be to augment the public investment in R&D, life-long learning, and innovation of every sort (technological and non-technological, manufacturing and services, linear and open[155]), since the qualifications, skills, and employability of human capital increasingly depend on the amount and quality of expenditure on higher education and on the performances according to some basic R&D and innovation indicators, such as the ratio of researchers to the general population, the amount of business

---

of Pure Reason," in Immanuel Kant, *Critique of Pure Reason*, The Cambridge Edition of the Works of Immanuel Kant, transl. and eds. Paul Guyer and Allen W. Wood, (Cambridge: Cambridge University Press, 1998, 1st ed. 1781), 13-5. On the differences between the regulative and the constitutive principles in Kant's philosophy, see *ibid.*, 14, 18, 45, 297-98, 520-24, 547, 552, 567-78, 591, 602-04, 606-23, 659-60.

[153] The Commission has officially launched the discussion on a European tax on carbon dioxide emissions as one of several options for a new European tax to augment the Union's own resources and boost eco-innovation. See Communication from the Commission to the European Parliament, the Council, the European Economic and Social Committee, the Committee of the Regions and the National Parliaments "The EU Budget Review," COM(2010) 700 final, Brussels, October 19, 2010, 20-1.

[154] Aglietta, *La crise*, 119-20.

[155] From a large body of literature on innovation, see Henry Chesbrough, Wim Vanhaverbeke and Joel West, eds., *Open Innovation: Researching a New Paradigm*, (Oxford and New York: Oxford University Press, 2006), a book which assembles a vast research project on the processes of innovation.

investment in R&D, the ratio of patents per capita, technology balance of payments flows, the percentage of innovative small and medium enterprises (SMEs), and the extent of the diffusion of ICT and of business broadband access[156]. In all the abovementioned sectoral and horizontal policies, it is crucial that public monies leverage private investment, and that structural reforms are made so as to ease introduction of innovation processes in the entire life-cycle of products, avoid overlapping of national expenditures, and achieve economies of scale and critical mass to compete with advanced and emerging economies. We need an ample and long-term development project, a "European dream"[157], not only to boost our growth potential, but also to proceed to technology transfers towards emerging countries, which are already at the forefront of economic progress worldwide. Even though it is conceivable – and of course desirable – that each one of the abovementioned measures and policies be adopted and implemented at the local/regional, national, or transnational level, what is truly needed is a *Europe-wide effort* of financial support and institutional empowerment[158].

To be sure, the enormous challenge of a smart, sustainable, and inclusive growth for Europe comprising five interrelated and quantified "EU headline targets" for 2020 cannot reasonably be pursued without a revamped and ambitious *EU budget*[159]. Indeed, the need for a budgetary overhaul at EU level is *even more* pressing in times of economic crisis, since the decline in economic activity has had a massive downward impact

---

[156] For a thorough and comprehensive survey of innovation indicators and performances in the EU, see the latest annual edition of European Commission, "European Innovation Scoreboard (EIS) 2009: Comparative Analysis of Innovation Performance," PRO INNO Europe paper No. 15, March 2010, 10-1 and *passim*.

[157] Cf. the high-order reflection by Jeremy Rifkin, *The European Dream. How Europe's Vision of the Future Is Quietly Eclipsing the American Dream* (New York: Penguin Books, 2004), where the author boldly claims that the economy of the EU is stronger, and, in many ways, healthier than that of the USA, because it is based on the quest for "connectivity", community relationships, and quality of life, instead of private property, individual autonomy, and accumulation of wealth, respectively.

[158] Vesperini, *Relancer*, 72.

[159] The five headline targets are comprised in the Europe 2020 Strategy, 5, 10-1. On the need for a reinforcement of the EU budget see, among many others, Simon Hix, *The Political System of the European Union* (Basingstoke and New York: Palgrave Macmillan, 2nd ed., 2005), 336-38; Muet, "Déficit de croissance," 29; Gauron, "Coordination des politiques économiques," 103 ff., particularly 105; Aglietta, *La crise*, 82, 89-90.

on European budget resources. In the current economic predicament, many member states are short-sightedly tempted to call for a *more restrictive* approach to the EU budget, despite having very recently expanded the Union's competencies with the Lisbon Treaty[160]. Now, the Interinstitutional Agreement between the European Parliament, the Council and the Commission on budgetary discipline and sound financial management of 2006 (IIA) unequivocally states: "Should a Treaty revision with budgetary implications occur during the multiannual financial framework 2007 to 2013 (...), the necessary adjustments will be made accordingly"[161]. Nevertheless, the issue of a possible readjustment of the EU budget has been lagging in the EU institutional organs ever since.

After the final agreement on the IIA was achieved in 2006, the annual average ceiling on the EU's Own Resources for payments made from the EU budget amounts to 1.00 % of EU-27 Gross National Income (GNI), with an available margin of only 0.24 %. Thus, it is clear that the reference framework for budgetary discipline, binding on all EU institutions and applying to all expenditure covered by the multiannual financial framework 2007-2013, cannot exceed a ridiculously low percentage of the aggregate wealth produced in the EU[162]. No wonder

---

[160] The Lisbon Treaty has expanded the EU's competence in many policy sectors, amongst which energy (TFEU, articles 4, paragraph 2i, 122 paragraph 1, 192 paragraph 2c, 194) and climate change (TFEU, article 191, paragraph 1, indent 4), space (TFEU, articles 4, paragraph 3, 189), and civil protection (TFEU, articles 6f , 196), and has instituted the European External Action Service (EEAS) (TEU, article 27, paragraph 3) that is intended to give the Union a greater role in foreign policy.

[161] Interinstitutional Agreement between the European Parliament, the Council and the Commission on budgetary discipline and sound financial management of May 17, 2006, pt. 4.

[162] According to the European Commission, the "own resources ceiling" of 1.24 % of the EU GNI corresponds to approximately 293 € per EU citizen on average. See Commission, *The European Union budget at a glance*, Publications Office of the European Union, 2010, 7. Of course, the EU budget forecasts both commitments (i.e. legal pledges to provide finance, provided that certain conditions are fulfilled) and payments (i.e. cash or bank transfers to the beneficiaries), and appropriations for commitments often are slightly higher than appropriations for payments because multiannual programmes and projects are usually committed in the year they are decided and are paid over the years, as the implementation of the programme or project progresses. Nonetheless, total commitment appropriations for the period 2007-2013 do not exceed a meager 1.13 % as a percentage of the EU GNI.

many major EU projects, such as Galileo[163], or large-scale infrastructures where the EU is actively involved as an international partner, such as ITER[164], have been underfinanced from their beginning. Not only has not the EU budget increased in time to meet more and more challenges in a globalised and increasingly complex world, but on the contrary, *it has been decreasing* as a percentage of national wealth, despite successive enlargements in 2004 and 2007[165]. The Commission itself has admitted that margins under all ceilings of the multiannual financial framework are becoming very tight and that overall, the remaining margin for manoeuvre within the Multiannual Financial Framework for years to come is severely

---

[163] The financing needs of the Galileo project necessitated an amendment of the multiannual financial framework and an increase in the ceilings for heading 1a of the multiannual financial framework for the years 2008 to 2013 by a total amount of EUR 1.6 billion in current prices, offset by an equivalent reduction of the ceiling for heading 2 for the year 2007; see European Commission, Report to the European Parliament and the Council on the functioning of the Interinstitutional Agreement on budgetary discipline and sound financial management, COM 2010(185) final, Brussels, April 27, 2010, 5, 10.

[164] For ITER, the international experimental thermonuclear reactor whose construction is planned to last for several decades and that will be built in Cadarache, France, total construction costs were estimated at around €5.9 billion in 2001, and construction was expected to be completed over a ten-year period. However, expected costs have now almost tripled to €16 billion, with critics claiming that the final bill could be even higher, and construction has not yet started. The exact additional financial needs still have to be determined, so that "[t]he estimated additional commitment appropriations for ITER to be provided by the EU budget under the present Multiannual Financial Framework might be well above one billion euro" (Report to the European Parliament and the Council on the functioning of the Interinstitutional Agreement on budgetary discipline and sound financial management, 6). Thus, to ensure European financing for the project in 2012-2013, the Commission recently adopted a proposal for the short-term funding needs of €1.4 billion to build the ITER initial demonstration reactor, by drawing on unused funding from the EU budget (€940 million) and by redeployment of €460 million from the EU's 7th Framework Programme for Research (FP7); see Proposal for a Decision of the European Parliament and the Council amending the Interinstitutional Agreement of 17 May 2006 on budgetary discipline and sound financial management as regards the multiannual financial framework, to address additional financing needs of the ITER project COM(2011) 226 final, Brussels, April 20, 2011.

[165] See the European Commission table of the relative size of the EU budget as a percentage of the EU GNI, http://en.goldenmap.com/Budget_of_the_European_Union#, where it is clearly shown that the average for the 2007-2013 period forecast has dropped to 1.05 % from 1.21% for the 1993-1999 period.

limited, since the remaining margins and possibilities for redeployment offer only limited scope at best to respond to future eventualities[166].

Any reasonable person would say that in order to be able to deal with challenges ahead, the EU needs to ensure that sufficient financial means are given to do so, and that securing a sustainable economic recovery in times of economic uncertainty calls for new Community responsibilities.

Hence the European Parliament has sent a message to the Council: the review of current financial perspectives cannot be put off any longer, as it is necessary for settling next budgets. Neither can the political debate be postponed with a view to identifying positive synergies between the Community budget and national budgets.

Yet, the Lisbon Strategy notoriously failed on both aspects[167]. It never succeeded in mustering the necessary resources at both EU and national level in order to close the gap on investment and it never managed to build a sufficiently strong institutional framework in order to achieve the EU Lisbon strategic goal of becoming "the most competitive and dynamic knowledge-based economy in the world capable of sustainable economic growth with more and better jobs and greater social cohesion"[168]. And one of the basic reasons for this failure is the *inchoate character of the political framework of cooperation* utilised to obtain growth and jobs through the Lisbon Strategy, regrouped under the code name *"Open Method of Coordination"* (OMC)[169]. Indeed, this innovative at the time

---

[166] In European Commission, "Report to the European Parliament and the Council on the functioning of the Interinstitutional Agreement on budgetary discipline and sound financial management," COM 2010(185) final, Brussels, April 27, 2010, 9 and *passim*. Concerns along these lines have already been expressed by the European Parliament resolution of 25 March 2009 on the Mid-Term Review of the 2007-2013 Financial Framework (2008/2055(INI)).

[167] The failure of the Lisbon Strategy is widely acknowledged in the doctrine, and is attested by the European Commission itself in the relaunch of the Strategy in 2005 as "EU Partnership for Growth and Jobs" after its Mid-Term Review; see Communication from President Barroso in agreement with Vice-President Verheugen to the Spring European Council, "Working together for growth and jobs: A new start for the Lisbon Strategy" COM(2005) 24 final, Brussels, February 2, 2005, 3-6.

[168] Lisbon European Council, 23-24 March 2000, Presidency conclusions, pt. 5.

[169] The OMC is mentioned for the first time in the Lisbon European Council conclusions of March 2000 that launched the famous Lisbon Strategy; see pt. 7: "Implementing this strategy will be achieved by improving the existing processes, introducing a *new open method of coordination* at all levels, coupled with a stronger guiding and coordinating role for the European Council to ensure more coherent strategic direction and effective monitoring of progress. A meeting of the

intergovernmental method is a form of "soft law" based on the determination of certain political orientations – sometimes quantified – at EU level, accompanied by a supple monitoring procedure, data dissemination through reporting concerning the performances of member states vis-à-vis the orientations fixed, benchmarking (i.e. the process of systematically identifying, analyzing, comparing, and adapting best practices to improve an organization's performance), and peer pressure (i.e. mutual evaluation of member states' performances), with the Commission's role being limited to surveillance[170].

The heads of states and governments of the EU that conceived the OMC considered it as *a totally decentralised method*, to be implemented at all levels of decision-making (local/regional, state, and EU) and leaving

---

European Council to be held every Spring will define the relevant mandates and ensure that they are followed up", and pt. 37: "Implementation of the strategic goal will be facilitated by applying *a new open method of coordination as the means of spreading best practice and achieving greater convergence towards the main EU goals*. This method, which is designed to help Member States to progressively develop their own policies, involves:

- fixing guidelines for the Union combined with specific timetables for achieving the goals which they set in the short, medium and long terms;
- establishing, where appropriate, quantitative and qualitative indicators and benchmarks against the best in the world and tailored to the needs of different Member States and sectors as a means of comparing best practice;
- translating these European guidelines into national and regional policies by setting specific targets and adopting measures, taking into account national and regional differences;
- periodic monitoring, evaluation and peer review organised as mutual learning processes.

(emphasis added)".

[170] For a synthetic presentation of the OMC in the whole policy-making process of the EU, see European Commission, "White Paper on European Governance," COM(2001) 428 final, Brussels, July 25, 2001, 21-2. There, the OMC is described as follows: "The open method of co-ordination is used on a case by case basis. It is a way of encouraging co-operation, the exchange of best practice and agreeing common targets and guidelines for Member States, sometimes backed up by national action plans [...]. It relies on regular monitoring of progress to meet those targets, allowing Member States to compare their efforts and learn from the experience of others". On the concept of benchmarking in business organization, see Robert J. Boxwell, Jr., *Benchmarking for Competitive Advantage* (New York, San Francisco and Washington, D.C.: McGraw-Hill, 1994), 17-34.

sufficient leeway for the participation of non-governmental actors[171]. From its inception, the OMC was heralded as a smart and flexible policy tool complementing the somewhat more rigid community method, which makes systematic recourse to European integration through legislation[172]. Thus, in some policy sectors, the OMC is centred on the convergence of member states around certain general objectives, eventually specified by guidelines that give rise to national action plans submitted to peers and evaluated on the basis of certain indicators[173]. Yet in others, the OMC

---

[171] Lisbon European Council, 23-24 March 2000, Presidency conclusions, pt. 38: "A fully decentralised approach will be applied in line with the principle of subsidiarity in which the Union, the Member States, the regional and local levels, as well as the social partners and civil society, will be actively involved, using variable forms of partnership. A method of benchmarking best practices on managing change will be devised by the European Commission networking with different providers and users, namely the social partners, companies and NGOs".

[172] See e.g. Joanne Scott and David M. Trubek, "Mind the Gap: Law and New Approaches to Governance in the European Union," *European Law Journal* 8 (2002): 1-18, and Vesperini, *Relancer*, who thinks that, despite criticism, the OMC can contribute to the development of a "logic of incentives" in favour of national measures pursuing specific growth objectives (*ibid.*, 95), and talks about the need for a "principle of coordination, aiming to establish, between all member states of the euro area, or only between some states that will decide so, a coordinated budgetary policy with the goal of promoting growth" (*ibid.*, 85) (my translation).
The OMC has given rise to an abundant literature; see, among others, the exhaustive analysis by Stéphane De La Rosa, *La méthode ouverte de coordination dans le système juridique communautaire* (Brussels: Bruylant, coll. "Travaux du CERIC", 2007), Renaud Dehousse, ed., *L'Europe sans Bruxelles? Une analyse de la méthode ouverte de coordination* (Paris: L'Harmattan, coll. « Logiques Politiques », Paris, 2004); Caroline De la Porte and Philippe Pochet, eds., *Building Social Europe through the Open Method of Coordination* (Brussels, Bern, Berlin, Frankfurt, New York, Oxford and Wien: P.I.E.-Peter Lang, 2nd ed., 2003); Maria Joao Rodrigues, ed., *The New Knowledge Economy in Europe: A Strategy for International Competitiveness and Social Cohesion* (Cheltenham and Northampton: Edward Elgar, 2002); and Jonathan Zeitlin and Philippe Pochet, eds., *The Open Method of Coordination in Action: The European Employment and Social Inclusion Strategies* (Brussels: P.I.E.-Peter Lang, 2005).

[173] For example, in the field of Social Protection and Social Inclusion, EU member states work together under an OMC containing common objectives and common indicators, which show how progress towards these goals can be measured; then national governments translate the common objectives into national strategic reports, which are assessed by the Commission and Council in joint reports that reflect what EU-level initiatives have achieved in individual countries. See Council (COREPER I), "Draft Joint Report on Social Protection and Social Inclusion 2010," Brussels, February 15, 2010, chap. "Governance," 13-14.

framework is much looser, since it is centred on monitoring and the determination of indicators, but with no political aim of convergence towards commonly determined objectives (even though member states can voluntarily establish national objectives), or even looser, on a simple exchange of best practices between member states[174].

In 2002, well before the mid-term review of the Lisbon Strategy by the Kok Reports, Professor Mario Telò considered that "the question of political leadership is open in the EU"[175], and wrote the following: "The new methods of governance [i.e. of the Lisbon Strategy] imply a new model of government [...] The institutional innovation underway in the government of the Union is a double one: firstly, the global character of the OMC *can only strengthen the centripetal demand for coherent coordination*, capable of counter-balancing the articulation and decentralisation of governance practices arising from the 'Lisbon Strategy' [...] Secondly, the European Council, as the super network of prime ministers, takes up again its strategic role of guidance by situating it in the framework of the essential goals of economic and social modernisation"[176]. And two years later, changing somewhat his tone in his preface to the French edition of the book, the same author wrote: "The shortfalls of the Lisbon Strategy can be summarized in a principal cause: the discontinuity at the leadership level, notably of the European Council, the fragmentation of the Council, the difficulty of the Commission to master and centralise its implementation within the Member States"[177].

---

[174] For example, in the field of Best and "pseudo-Best" Projects coordinated by European Commission DG ENTR, an external evaluation of the OMC found that, in order for those projects to be successful at EU level, they need notably to have clear objectives and should not be one-off projects but part of a long-term strategy, and there need to be follow-up events such as monitoring, feedback reporting and post-project workshops to maintain the member states' focus on the dissemination of results and the implementation of recommendations. See GHK / Technopolis Report, "Evaluation of the Open Method of Coordination activities coordinated by DG Enterprise and Industry," Brussels, September 20, 2006, 7. Here we obviously have the loosest possible form of OMC.

[175] Mario Telò, "Governance and government in the European Union: The open method of coordination", in *The New Knowledge Economy in Europe*, 242-271, 257.

[176] *Ibid.*, 256-257 (emphasis added).

[177] Mario Telò, "Préface", in *Vers une société européenne de la connaissance : La stratégie de Lisbonne (2000-2010)*, dir. Maria Joao Rodrigues (Bruxelles: Editions de l'ULB, 2004), VII ff., XII (my translation). However, the same author writes – incorrectly in my view – that "the Lisbon Strategy would be inconceivable without the open method of coordination, the only way to overcome the existing

Things could not have been said better. The Lisbon Strategy failed to reach its aims by 2010[178] because of a deficit in political will and ownership, to the extent that the whole process was not taken up by some cognizable and credible institution or authority. This was to be expected, since the different OMC structures, designed to coordinate common actions within a more or less loose framework in the name of the principle of subsidiarity and the freedom of member states' growth initiatives, generated many institutional tensions: a tension between the Council (that paid practically no attention to the process) and the Commission (that would have liked to pilot more actively the process by using its right of initiative, but lacked the competence and political clout to do it); and a tension between the Community (i.e. the centralised level of decision-making) as a whole and the several member states, local governments and non-governmental actors (i.e. the decentralised level of decision-making)[179].

The second Kok Report, drafted as an independent mid-term review of the Lisbon Strategy and presented in November 2004, left no doubt as to the inefficiency of the political framework of the OMC: "The open method of coordination has fallen far short of expectations. If Member States do not enter the spirit of mutual benchmarking, little or nothing happens. But neither has the Community method delivered what was expected. Member States are lagging behind the implementation of what has been agreed [...] If governments do not show commitment to implementation nationally, this remains a huge problem"[180]. The disappointing delivery of the Lisbon targets at that time was seen as due to an overloaded agenda, poor coordination and conflicting priorities, as well as the lack of determined

---

oppositions within the majority of the States against the expansion of community competences"; *ibid.*, XII (my translation). *Contra* Stéphane De La Rosa, who thinks, on the contrary, that it is necessary to "surpass that entanglement [between the Lisbon Strategy and the OMC]", (De La Rosa, *La méthode*, 120) (my translation).

[178] Michel Aglietta even goes all the way to write about a "total fiasco of the famous Lisbon Strategy launched in 2000" in his article "La longue crise de l'Europe," *Le Monde*, May 18, 2010 (my translation).

[179] De La Rosa, *La méthode*, 111. De la Rosa perspicaciously considers that "we are in presence of a recurrent failure linked to the contradiction between a centrality in the conception and formulation of objectives, on the one hand, and in principle, a strong decentralisation for the conversion of guidelines at national level" (my translation).

[180] High Level Group chaired by Wim Kok Report, "Facing the challenge - the Lisbon Strategy for growth and employment", Luxembourg: Office for Official Publications of the European Communities, November 2004, 42.

political action – all the above meaning that if the EU as a whole does not take action in a consistent, and not just piecemeal, fashion, it will never succeed in closing the growth and employment gap with North America and Asia. "The task is to develop national policies in each Member State, *supported by an appropriate European-wide framework*, that address a particular Member State's concerns and then *to act in a more concerted and determined way*. The European Commission must be prepared to report clearly and precisely on success and failure in each Member State. *National and European Union policies, including their budgets, must better reflect the Lisbon priorities*"[181].

The Kok Report, widely acclaimed at the time of its publication, and followed to a great extent by the Spring European Council of March 2005, thus points out to the democratic and structural deficiencies of the institutional framework set up in order to administer the Lisbon reforms agenda. If we read between the lines of the text, we can understand that the outlines of reform all move towards the direction of a *democratisation* and *centralisation* of the Lisbon process: "[T]he European Parliament needs to be involved much more in this process. It must hold the European Commission accountable for the progress it is making and the way it is discharging its responsibilities"[182]; "The EU budget should be reshaped so that EU spending reflects the priority accorded to growth and employment"[183]; and most importantly, "The High Level Group proposes a radical improvement of the process [through] [t]he establishment by the European Council of a more limited framework of 14 targets and indicators offer[ing] the opportunity to improve the working of the instrument of peer pressure"[184]. Characteristically, the Kok Report recommends the establishment of tables of member state rankings according to their performances on certain specified targets and indicators, coupled with a mechanism of "naming, shaming, and faming"[185] (i.e. praising those that have performed well and blaming those who have not).

---

[181] *Ibid.*, 7 (emphasis added); and analytically, *ibid.*, 39-44. Cf. Communication from President Barroso in agreement with Vice-President Verheugen to the Spring European Council, "Working together for growth," that points out to the need to "simplify the myriad of existing reports under the Open Method of Co-ordination (OMC), which the Commission will review" (29).

[182] *Ibid.*, 41.

[183] *Ibid.*, 42.

[184] *Ibid.*, 42-3.

[185] *Ibid.*, 43.

Now, this proposal stands witness to the "rationalisation of [institutional] impotence"[186] of the EU vis-à-vis a federal state like the USA that has at its disposal integrated macroeconomic policy tools, such as common employment and social security policies. So, the real question – once more – is "[h]ow to implement ambitious objectives in sectors where the European Union has no competence"[187]. In other words, in order for public policies to have a real leveraging effect, member states definitely need to delegate more competences to the Union, which will start to act as a true federation does.

8. Conclusion

In this Chapter, I tried to show that the European Monetary Union needs to be complemented with an appropriate institutional and political framework that will allow us to draft and implement a coherent, at least, economic policy at EU level. The community method, dear to Jean Monnet, and more recently the open method of coordination, have carried through the project of European integration after the early collapse of the federalist project of building a "top-down" European Defence Community in the 1950's[188]. But they seem to have lost their momentum, as the "Greek crisis" (that actually unveiled a systemic crisis of the euro area in its entirety) showed in 2010, because of their fundamental ambiguity: it is indubitable that the national economies are by now increasingly "Europeanised" because of the gradual progress in European integration; yet, on the other hand, European political institutions continue to be weak and democratically deficient; this growing hiatus creates a *tension*.

---

[186] Philippe Aghion, Elie Cohen et Jean Pisani-Ferry, *Politique économique et croissance en Europe*, rapport du Conseil d'analyse économique, Paris: La Documentation française, 2006, 80-4, 82.

[187] *Ibid.*, 82.

[188] The European Defence Community (EDC) Treaty was signed on May 27, 1952, with the intention of including West Germany, France, Italy, and the Benelux countries into a pan-European defence as a rival of the Soviet bloc and as an alternative to Germany's proposed accession to NATO. Yet, the plan collapsed when it failed to obtain ratification in the French Parliament on August 30, 1954 because of fears that the EDC threatened France's national sovereignty, constitutional concerns about the indivisibility of the French Republic, and fears about Germany's remilitarization. On this founding moment for post-war Europe, see Kevin Ruane, *The Rise and Fall of the European Defense Community: Anglo-American Relations and the Crisis of European Defense, 1950–55* (Houndmill, Basingstoke: Macmillan, 2000), and Tony Judt, *Postwar: A History of Europe Since 1945* (New York: Penguin Books, 2005), 241 ff.

Now, fiscal and macroeconomic regulation is situated inside this gray area of ambiguity and tension, since all available policy tools – fiscal and monetary – either have been withdrawn altogether from the hands of national governments (monetary unification of the euro area) or have little by little been submitted to procedures of coordination or consultation with the EU partners (mechanism of multilateral budgetary surveillance, open method of coordination of growth measures). Yet, we still have not developed truly *European* instruments of financial and macroeconomic management, monitoring and regulation to cope with the global and systemic nature of the financial crisis in an efficient manner.

Can we go on like this? In the United States, the Great Depression of the 1930's signalled the opportunity for a vast reinforcement of central government under the New Deal, for the consolidation of a truly federal budget, and a correlative rise in federal spending for long-term structural reforms. All in all, those were the times of a shift of macroeconomic paradigm. Now, in a situation of economic recession[189] once more, the EU definitely needs a rebalancing, in the sense of a better command of all the available tools of economic policy in a now-single market. Can we achieve this overhaul without a really radical change of course? Will we genuinely be able to manage efficiently crises like the Greek one in the future without some mechanism of fiscal transfers for solidarity at EU level, a pan-European mechanism of prudential control and risk management, and a permanent European Monetary Fund protecting the "weak links" in periods of massive speculative attacks? Can we continue to have nationally differentiated mechanisms for the issuance of treasury bonds to refinance public debts, at a moment when sovereign debt markets are global and negative externalities of national economies tend sometimes to produce severe domino effects for the rest of the partners and the common currency? And, all things considered, does it really make sense to have a monetary union without some centralised mechanism of fiscal coordination and macroeconomic surveillance, or can we do without it as long as we have a uniform rule of fiscal consolidation (the Stability and Growth Pact) or an unwieldy intergovernmental organ of economic coordination (the Eurogroup)?

If the answer to all the above questions is "no", then the real question is: taking into account the history of the American economic and monetary system, can we imagine of any other model that might work better in times of crisis than a *federal* one? The incremental and cautious step-by-step posture of the community method probably is one of the reasons for the

[189] And downright depression for Greece.

institutional failure of the Stability and Growth Pact and of the entire euro area's architecture, since the voices warning against the irrationality of an imbalance between a monetary union, on the one hand, and a preservation of national economic sovereignty, with "economic policies [only regarded as] a matter of common concern [to be] coordinate[d]"[190], on the other, were easily suppressed in the name of political prudence and in order to preserve the sacrosanct national sovereignty in fiscal matters.

Quite ironically, though, the community method's anti-ideological and purely pragmatic stance that has marked the European Communities from the beginning[191] might be of use at a time when the whole European integration experiment, based on the said method, is under severe distress[192]. Indeed, we are forced to the conclusion that the old and recurring ideological debate between European federalists and intergovernmentalists might not have any rational sense in the context of an ongoing *legitimation crisis* of a system supposedly establishing an economic union between national sovereign states, but painfully discovering it is not sufficiently protected against the systemic outputs of a possible default of one of them[193].

---

[190] TFEU, Article 121 paragraph 1.

[191] It is well-known that Jean Monnet's basic intuition was that union between individuals or communities is not natural; it can only be the result of an intellectual process having as a starting point the observation of the need for change and the consciousness of the existence of common interests between individuals or communities. Indeed, the entire community method was based on a strong belief in the cumulative sagacity of institutions; Monnet was fond of quoting Swiss philosopher Henri Frederic Amiel: '[e]ach man begins the world afresh. Only institutions grow wiser; they store up their collective experience; and, from this experience and wisdom, men subject to the same laws will gradually find, not that their natures change, but that their behavior does'; see François Duchene, *Jean Monnet: The First Statesman of Interdependence* (New York: W. W. Norton, 1994), 401.

[192] *Contra* Giandomenico Majone, who thinks that the community method has become obsolete since it is too rigid and is inspired by a failed federalist vision, whereas a European federal superstate would lack legitimacy and would thus be unable to act decisively even in areas where close cooperation is needed; Giandomenico Majone, *Dilemmas of European Integration. The Ambiguities and Pitfalls of Integration by Stealth* (Oxford: Oxford University Press, 2005).

[193] In the Parsonian systems theory, every social system needs to solve four fundamental problems in order to maintain and to reproduce itself: a) pattern maintenance, b) goal-attainment, c) adaptation, and d) integration; see Talcott Parsons and Neil J. Smelser, *Economy and Society*, (London, Routledge and Kegan Paul, 2001, 1st ed. 1956), 14-20. The economy is the functionally differentiated sub-system of the society with primary reference to the *adaptive* function of the society as a whole (*ibid.*, 20), which requires that the system be responsive to

A large rationalisation process[194] of the economic governance of the euro area, and even of the EU political system overall, is underway since May 2010, as a result of the severe financial crisis, for which Greece was finally but the catalyst[195]. This process in all probability expresses the quintessence of the community method, as opposed to the intergovernmental one: a sufficient amount of interdependence between member states and entanglement between national interests is liable to set in motion a process

---

changes in the external environment so that its successful maintenance and reproduction is immunized against the impact of strictly exogenous factors. With the progressive differentiation between the different social sub-systems (economy, polity, culture and motivation, and law and social control), each subsystem is no longer functionally self-sufficient, but instead relies on inputs from the others, and in turn, produces generalized resources employed throughout the society (interchange relations). Therefore, according to Parsons, "the goal of the economy is not simply the production of income for the utility of an aggregate of individuals. It is the maximization of production relative to the whole complex of institutionalized value-systems and functions of the society and its sub-systems" (*ibid.*, 22). "Legitimation", in that sense, means a generalized form of consent to the basic institutional processes and outcomes; it is a structural question about the quality of interchange relations between different social sub-systems.
In conclusion, every time social agents have not sufficiently internalized values through the process of socialization (pattern maintenance), or are not willing and motivated to labour (adaptation) and to show solidarity to one another through collective self-regulation (integration), there will be a "legitimation crisis", a lack of symbolic resources for the justification of political action. Now, this is clearly what is happening in the EU in the present context, since its adaptive and integrative outputs are excessively low.

[194] In the Weberian ideal type sense of the term, for which the development of a critical attitude toward authority and the problematization of received practices – normative phenomena consubstantial to modernity – must be understood as a process of societal rationalization that allows agents to reorganize social institutions so as to make them more calculable, efficient, systematic, and predictable. See Max Weber, *Economy and Society: An Outline of Interpretive Sociology,* 2 vols., 1st edited 1922 (Berkeley and Los Angeles: University of California Press, 1978).

[195] Cf. the rephrasing of the famous "legitimation crisis" thesis by Jürgen Habermas in his *Between Facts and Norms: Contributions to a Discourse Theory of Law and Democracy*, transl. William Rehg, Cambridge, Polity Press, 1996, 385-386: "The political system is vulnerable on both sides to disturbances that can detract from the effectiveness of its achievements and the legitimacy of its decisions, respectively. The regulatory competence of the political system fails if the implemented legal programs remain ineffective or if the regulatory and steering performances give rise to disintegrating effects in the action systems that require regulation".

of "an ever closer union among the peoples of Europe"[196], especially after a crisis such as the Greek one of 2010. Still, if we grasp the opportunity, leave aside the emotionally charged ideological underpinnings of federalism and make use of the pragmatic and a-dramatised attitude of the community method to inaugurate a truly European economic government, springboard for "a kind of United States of Europe"[197], we will have achieved a major institutional and philosophical breakthrough, a true paradigm shift.

Bibliography/ Resources

Ackrill, Robert. "The European Union Budget, the Balanced Budget Rule and the Development of Common European Policies," *Journal of Pubic Policy* 20 (2000): 1-19.

Aglietta, Michel. *La crise. Les voies de sortie*. Paris: Michalon, 2nd edition, 2010.

—. "La longue crise de l'Europe." *Le Monde*, May 18, 2010.

Aghion, Philippe, and Elie Cohen et Jean Pisani-Ferry, Politique économique et croissance en Europe, rapport du Conseil d'analyse économique, Paris: La Documentation française, 2006.

Alesina, Alberto, and Lawrence H. Summers. "Central Bank Independence and Macroeconomic Performance: Some Comparative Evidence", *Journal of Money, Credit and Banking* 25 (1993): 151-62.

Appelbaum, Binyamin. "Republicans Sharply Question Bernanke for Fed's Focus on Job Market." *New York Times*, February 2, 2012.

—. "Three Central Banks Act to Stimulate More Borrowing." *New York Times*, July 5, 2012.

Ardagna, Silvia, and Fransesco Caselli. "The political economy of the Greek debt crisis: A tale of two bailouts." *CEP Special Report No. 25*. London: Centre for Economic Performance (London School of Economics and Political Sciences), 2012.

Arnott, Richard J., and Joseph E. Stiglitz. "Labor Turnover, Wage Structures and Moral Hazard: The Inefficiency of Competitive Markets." *Journal of Labor Economics* 3 (1986): 434-62.

Artus, Patrick, Charles Wyplosz, Anton Brender and Jean-Victor Louis, éds. *La Banque centrale européenne*. Paris: La Documentation française, 2002.

[196] Preamble to the TFEU.

[197] Winston Churchill, "Speech to the Academic Youth of the World," University of Zurich, September 19, 1946.

Artus, Patrick. "Y a-t-il un lien entre les *spreads* souverains (vis-à-vis de l'Allemagne) dans la zone euro et l'ampleur du choc subi par les pays dans la crise?" *Natixis Special Report* N° 105, April 6, 2009.

Barro, Robert J. "Are Government Bonds Net Wealth?" *Journal of Political Economy* 82 (1974): 1095-117.

—. "On the Determination of the Public Debt." *Journal of Political Economy* 87 (1979): 940-71.

Barroso, José Manuel Durão. "Opening remarks on economic governance." Joint press conference with Commissioner Olli Rehn, SPEECH/10/494, Brussels, September 29, 2010.

Begg, Iain, Henrik Enderlein, Jacques Le Cacheux, and Mojmir Mrak. "Financing of the European Union Budget", Final Report to the European Commission, DG Budget, 29 April 2008. http://ec.europa.eu/budget/reform/library/issue_paper/study_financing EU_de_en_fr.pdf.

Begg, Iain. "Monetary Policy Strategies." In *Central banks in the Age of the Euro: Europeanization, Convergence, and Power,* edited by Kenneth Dyson and Martin Marcussen, 356-72. Oxford: Oxford University Press, 2009.

Belke, Ansgar. "Driven by the markets? ECB sovereign bond purchases and the securities markets programme", *Intereconomics* 45, Number 6 (2010): 357-63.

Bernanke, Ben S. "Central Bank Independence, Transparency, and Accountability." Speech presented at the Institute's for Monetary and Economic Studies International Conference, Bank of Japan, Tokyo, Japan, May 25, 2010. http://www.federalreserve.gov/newsevents/speech/bernanke20100525a .htm.

Bertoncini, Yves. "Tribune: 'Fiscal Compact', sovereignty and austerity." *Notre Europe*, July 26, 2012. http://www.notre-europe.eu/uploads/tx_publication/FiscalPact_ Viewpoint_NE_July12.pdf.

Board of Governors of the Federal Reserve System press release. "Statement by FED Chairman Ben S. Bernanke." Last modified July 15, 2010. http://www.federalreserve.gov/newsevents/press/other/20100715a.htm.

Bowsher v. Synar, 478 U.S. 714, July 7 1986. http://law2.umkc.edu/faculty/projects/ftrials/conlaw/bowsher.html.

Boxwell, Robert J. Jr. *Benchmarking for Competitive Advantage*. New York, San Francisco and Washington, D.C.: McGraw-Hill, 1994.

Brennan, Geoffrey, and James M. Buchanan, *The Power to Tax: Analytical Foundations of a Fiscal Constitution*. Cambridge: Cambridge University Press, 1980.

Buiter, Willem. "Can Central Banks Go Broke?" CEPR [Centre for Economic Policy Research] Policy Insight, No. 24. London, May 2008.

Buti Marco, and André Sapir, eds. *Economic Policy in EMU: A Study by the European Commission Services*. Oxford: Clarendon Press & New York, Oxford University Press, 1998.

Buti, Marco, Daniele Franco and Hedwig Ongena. "Budgetary Policies during Recessions – Retrospective Applications of the "Stability and Growth Pact" to the Post-War Period." *European Economy Economic Papers* 121 (May 1997): 1-33.

Caballero, Ricardo J. "A Caricature (Model) of the World Economy." Paper first presented as a keynote speech for the Ninth Macroeconomic Policy Research Workshop 'Understanding Financial Frictions', Magyar Nemzeti Bank, Budapest, October 27, 2010. http://econ-www.mit.edu/files/6011.

Cannadine, David. "A Point of View: Making friends the shared currency way." *BBC News Magazine*, February 24, 2012. http://www.bbc.co.uk/news/magazine-17140379.

Caporale, Guglielmo Maria. "Is Europe an Optimum Currency Area? Symmetric Versus Asymmetric Shocks in the EC." *National Institute Economic Review* 144 (1993): 95-103.

CEPS. Policy Brief No. 202, May 17, 2010. http://www.ceps.eu/book/towards-european-monetary-fund.

Chesbrough, Henry, Wim Vanhaverbeke and Joel West, eds., *Open Innovation: Researching a New Paradigm*. Oxford and New York: Oxford University Press, 2006.

Churchill, Winston. "Speech to the Academic Youth of the World." University of Zurich, September 19, 1946.

Communication from President Barroso in agreement with Vice-President Verheugen to the Spring European Council "Working together for growth and jobs: A new start for the Lisbon Strategy." COM (2005) 24 final, Brussels, February 2, 2005.

Communication from the Commission "European financial supervision." COM (2009) 252 final, May 27, 2009.

Communication from the Commission. "Europe 2020: A strategy for smart, sustainable and inclusive growth." COM (2010) 2020 final. Brussels, March 3, 2010.

Communication from the Commission to the Council and the European Parliament. “Public finances in EMU – 2003.” COM (2003) 283 final. May 21, 2003.

Communication from the Commission to the European Parliament, the Council, the European Economic and Social Committee, the Committee of the Regions and the National Parliaments. “The EU Budget Review.” COM (2010) 700 final. Brussels, October 19, 2010.

Communication from the Commission to the Council, the European Economic and Social Committee, the Committee of the Regions and the European Central Bank. “EMU@10: successes and challenges after 10 years of Economic and Monetary Union.” COM (2008) 238 final. Brussels, May 7, 2008.

Communication from the Commission to the Council, the European Council, the Council, the European Central Bank, the Economic and Social Committee and the Committee of the Regions. “Enhancing economic policy coordination for stability, growth and jobs – Tools for stronger EU economic governance.” COM (2010) 367/2 final, Brussels, June 30, 2010.

Communication from the Commission to the Council, the European Council, the Council, the European Central Bank, the Economic and Social Committee and the Committee of the Regions. “Reinforcing economic policy coordination.” COM (2010) 250 final, Brussels, May 12, 2010.

Council of the European Union (COREPER I). “*Draft Joint Report on Social Protection and Social Inclusion 2010.*” Brussels, February 15, 2010, chap. “Governance”.

Council Directive 2011/85/EU of 8 November 2011 on requirements for budgetary frameworks of the Member States, OJ L 306, 23.11.2011.

Council Regulation (EU) No 1177/2011 of 8 November 2011 amending Regulation (EC) No 1467/97 on speeding up and clarifying the implementation of the excessive deficit procedure, OJ L 306, 23.11.2011, 33.

Courty, Guillaume, and Guillaume Devin. *La construction européenne*. Paris: La Découverte, 3ème éd., 2010.

Cukierman, Alex. *Central Bank Strategies, Credibility, and Independence: Theory and Evidence*. Cambridge, Mass.: MIT Press, 1992.

Cukierman, Alex, Pantelis Kalaitzidakis, Lawrence H. Summers and Steven B. Webb. “Central Bank Independence, Growth, Investment, and Real Rates.” *Carnegie-Rochester Conference Series on Public Policy* 39 (1993): 95-140.

Cukierman, Alex, Steven B. Webb, and Bilin Neyapti. "Measuring the Independence of Central Banks and Its Effect on Policy Outcomes." *World Bank Economic Review* 6 (1992): 353-98.

Dauster, William G.. *Budget Process Law Annotated.* Washington, D.C.: Government Printing Office, 1993.

De Grauwe, Paul, and Wim Vanhaverbeke. "Is Europe an Optimum Currency Area?: Evidence from Regional Data." In *Policy Issues in the Operation of Currency Unions*, edited by Paul R. Masson and Mark P. Taylor, 111-29, Cambridge: Cambridge University Press, 1993.

De Grauwe, Paul. "Only a more active ECB can solve the euro crisis." CEPS [Centre for European Policy Studies] Policy Brief No 250, August 2011.

Dehousse, Renaud, ed., *L'Europe sans Bruxelles? Une analyse de la méthode ouverte de coordination*. Paris,

L'Harmattan, coll. « Logiques Politiques », 2004.

De la Porte, Caroline, and Philippe Pochet, eds., *Building Social Europe through the Open Method of Coordination.* Brussels, Bern, Berlin, Frankfurt, New York, Oxford and Wien: P.I.E.-Peter Lang, 2nd ed., 2003.

De La Rosa, Stéphane. *La méthode ouverte de coordination dans le système juridique communautaire*. Brussels, Bruylant: "Travaux du CERIC", 2007.

Delors, Jacques. "Jacques Delors dénonce le 'coup de poker' de Sarkozy et Merkel." Interview held by Alain Faujas and Claire Gatinois for *Le Monde*, October 19, 2011.

De Saint-Etienne, Christian. *La fin de l'euro*. Paris: François Bourin, 2009.

Duchene, François. *Jean Monnet: The First Statesman of Interdependence.* New York: W. W. Norton, 1994.

Dutta, Prajit K., and Roy Radner. "Moral Hazard." In *Handbook of Game Theory with Economic Applications,* vol. 2, chap. 26, edited by Robert Aumann and Sergiu Hart, 869-903. Amsterdam: Elsevier, coll. "Handbooks in Economics", 1994.

Dyson, Kenneth, and Kevin Featherstone. *The Road to Maastricht: Negotiating Economic and Monetary Union.* Oxford: Oxford University Press, 1999.

Eichengreen, Barry. *Golden Fetters: The Gold Standard and the Great Depression, 1919-1939*. Oxford: Oxford University Press, 1996.

Eichenberger, Reiner. "The Benefits of Federalism and the Risk of Overcentralization." *Kyklos* 47 (3) (1994): 403-20.

Einaudi, Luca. *Money and Politics: European Monetary Unification and the International Gold Standard (1865-1873).* Oxford: Oxford University Press, 2001.

Enrich, David, and Charles Forelle. "ECB gives banks big dollops of cash." *The Wall Street Journal*, March 1, 2012. http://online.wsj.com/article/SB10001424052970203986604577252803223310964.html.

European Central Bank. "Liquidity analysis." http://www.ecb.int/mopo/liq/html/index.en.html#portfolios.

—. Press release, "ECB decides on measures to address severe tensions in financial markets." 10 May 2010.

—. "The ECB's definition of the euro area monetary aggregates." http://www.ecb.int/stats/money/aggregates/aggr/html/hist.en.html.

—. Press release, "Technical features of Outright Monetary Transactions", 6 September 2012. http://www.ecb.int/press/pr/date/2012/html/pr120906_1.en.html.

European Commission. "*The European Union budget at a glance*." Publications Office of the European Union 2010.

—. "Economic governance package (1): Strengthening the Stability and Growth Pact." MEMO/10/455, Brussels, September 29, 2010.

—. "Economic governance package (2): Preventing and correcting macroeconomic imbalances." MEMO/10/454, Brussels, September 29, 2010.

—. "European Innovation Scoreboard (EIS) 2009: Comparative Analysis of Innovation Performance." PRO INNO Europe paper No 15, March 2010.

—. "New financial supervision architecture: Q&A on the European Systemic Risk Board / the macro-supervision part of the package." Memo/09/405, Brussels, September 23, 2009.

—. "Report to the European Parliament and the Council on the functioning of the Interinstitutional Agreement on budgetary discipline and sound financial management." COM 2010(185) final, Brussels, April 27, 2010.

—. Table of the relative size of the EU budget as a percentage of the EU GNI. http://en.goldenmap.com/Budget_of_the_European_Union#.

—. "White Paper on European Governance." COM (2001) 428 final. Brussels, July 25, 2001.

European Council conclusions of March 24-25, 2011, Annex I "The Euro Plus Pact – Stronger Economic Policy Coordination for Competitiveness and Convergence."

European Council Resolution on the Stability and Growth Pact.

Amsterdam, June 17,1997.

European Parliament and Council Regulation (EU) No 1175/2011, November 16, 2011.

Fatás, Antonio, and Ilian Mihov. "The Euro and Fiscal Policy." In *Europe and the Euro*, edited by Alberto Alesina and Francesco Giavazzi. Chicago: University of Chicago Press, 2010.

Federal Reserve Bank of New York. "Statement Regarding Purchases of Treasury Securities." November 3, 2010. http://www.newyorkfed.org/markets/opolicy/operating_policy_101103.html.

Federal Reserve Board. *The Federal Reserve System: Purposes and Functions* (Washington, D.C., 9th ed. 2005: Board of Governors of the Federal Reserve System.

Ferguson, Niall, and Laurence J. Kotlikoff. "The Degeneration of EMU." *Foreign Affairs* 79(2) (March/April 2000): 110-21.

FOMC press release, November 3, 2010. http://www.federalreserve.gov/newsevents/press/monetary/20101103a.htm.

FOMC press release, September 12, 2012. http://www.federalreserve.gov/newsevents/press/monetary/20120913a.htm.

Frey, Bruno S. *Democratic Economic Policy*. Oxford: Blackwell, 1983.

Friedman, Milton, and Anna Jacobson Schwartz. *A Monetary History of the United States, 1867-1960*. Princeton, NJ: Princeton University Press, 1993 (1st ed. 1963).

Gerdesmeier, Cf. Dieter, Francesco Paolo Mongelli, and Barbara Roffia. "The Eurosystem, the US Federal Reserve and the Bank of Japan: Similarities and Differences, March 2007." European Central Bank, Working Paper No 742, 7-12.

GHK / Technopolis Report. "Evaluation of the Open Method of Coordination activities coordinated by DG Enterprise and Industry." Brussels, September 20, 2006.

Goodfriend, Marvin. "The Role of a Regional Bank in a System of Central Banks." Federal Reserve Bank of Richmond Working Paper 99-4, July 1999.

Gros, Daniel, and Alexandr Hobza. "Fiscal Policy Spillovers in the Euro Area: Where are they?" CEPS [Centre for European Policy Studies] Working Document No. 176, November 2001.

Gros, Daniel, and Thomas Mayer. "How to deal with sovereign default in Europe: Towards a Euro(pean) Monetary Fund." CEPS Policy Brief No. 202, May 17, 2010. http://www.ceps.eu/book/towards-european-monetary-fund.

Guyer. Paul, and Allen W. Wood. "Introduction to the *Critique of Pure Reason.*" In Immanuel Kant, *Critique of Pure Reason*, The Cambridge Edition of the Works of Immanuel Kant. Translated and edited by Paul Guyer and Allen W. Wood. Cambridge: Cambridge University Press, 1998. 1st ed. 1781.

Habermas, Jürgen. *Between Facts and Norms: Contributions to a Discourse Theory of Law and Democracy.* Translated by William Rehg. Cambridge: Cambridge Polity Press, 1996.

Haldane, Andy. "Private sector involvement in financial crisis: analytics and public policy approaches." *Financial Stability Review* (November 1999): 184-202.

Hamilton, Alexander. "First Report on Public Credit, January 9, 1790." http://www.gwu.edu/~ffcp/exhibit/p13/p13_3.html.

Hart, H. L. A. *The Concept of Law*, 2nd ed., edited by Peter Cane, Tony Honoré and Jane Stapelton. Oxford: Oxford University Press, Clarendon Law Series, 1994. 1st edition 1961.

Hart, Oliver. "A model of imperfect competition with Keynesian features." *Quarterly Journal of Economics* 97 (1982): 109-38.

Henning, Randall, and Martin Kessler. "Fiscal Federalism: US History for Architects of Europe's Fiscal Union." Petersen Institute for International Economics Working Paper 12-1, January 2012.

High Level Group chaired by Wim Kok Report. "Facing the challenge - the Lisbon Strategy for growth and employment." Luxembourg, Office for Official Publications of the European Communities, November 2004.

Hix, Simon. *The Political System of the European Union*. Basingstoke and New York: Palgrave Macmillan, 2nd ed., 2005.

Inman, Robert P., and Daniel L. Rubinfeld. "Fiscal Federalism in Europe: Lessons from the United States experience." *European Economic Review* 36 (1992): 654-60.

INSEE. *L'économie française - Comptes et dossiers*. Edition 2006-2007.

International Monetary Fund. "The IMF and the Private Sector: A Factsheet." Washington, DC: International Monetary Fund, accessed August 2001. http://www.imf.org/external/np/exr/facts/privsec.htm.

Ippolito, Dennis S. "The Budget Process and Budget Policy: Resolving the Mismatch." *Public Administration Review* 53 (1993): 9-14.

Jabko, Nicolas. "Transparency and Accountability." In *Central banks in the Age of the Euro: Europeanization, Convergence, and Power,* edited by Kenneth Dyson and Martin Marcussen, 391-406. Oxford: Oxford University Press, 2009.

Judt, Tony. *Postwar: A History of Europe Since 1945*. New York: Penguin Books, 2005.

Keynes, John Maynard. *A Tract on Monetary Reform.* Amherst, NY: Prometheus Books, 1999, 1st edition 1923.

—. *The Economic Consequences of Mr. Churchill.* London: L. and V. Woolf, 1925.

—. *The General Theory of Employment, Interest and Money*. 2nd edition. Edited by Geoffrey C. Harcourt and Peter A. Riach. 2 vols.. London: Routledge, 1997.

King, Stephen. "What Ptolemy tells us about Germany and Greece." *Financial Times*, February 20, 2012.

Krugman, Paul. "Death of a Fairy Tale." *New York Times*, April 26, 2012.

—. *The Return of Depression Economics and the Crisis of 2008*. New York and London: W.W. Norton, 2nd ed., 2009.

Lisbon European Council, 23-24 March 2000, Presidency conclusions.

Majone, Giandomenico. *Dilemmas of European Integration. The Ambiguities and Pitfalls of Integration by Stealth.* Oxford: Oxford University Press, 2005.

Mayes, David, and Viren Matti. "The SGP and the ECB: an exercise in asymmetry." *Journal of Financial Transformation* 19 (2007): 159-75.

Muet, Pierre Alain. "Déficit de croissance européen et défaut de coordination : une analyse rétrospective." In *Coordination européenne des politiques économiques*, rapports du Conseil d'Analyse Economique. Paris: La Documentation française, 1998.

Mundell, Robert A. "A Theory of Optimal Currency Areas." *American Economic Review* 51 (1961): 657-65.

Oates, Wallace E. *Fiscal Federalism.* New York: Harcourt Brace Jovanovich, 1972.

Papadopoulos, Ioannis. "Two types of domino." In *Domino*, ed. Thessaloniki Center of Contemporary Art . Thessaloniki: Thessaloniki Center of Contemporary Art, 2011.

Parsons, Talcott, and Neil J. Smelser. *Economy and Society.* 1st ed. 1956. London: Routledge and Kegan Paul, 2001.

Reinhart, Carmen M., and Kenneth S. Rogoff. *This Time Is Different: Eight Centuries of Financial Folly*. Princeton and Oxford: Princeton University Press, 2009.

Rifkin, Jeremy. *The European Dream. How Europe's Vision of the Future Is Quietly Eclipsing the American Dream*. New York: Penguin Books, 2004.

Rodrigues, Maria Joao, ed., *The New Knowledge Economy in Europe: A Strategy for International Competitiveness and Social Cohesion.* Cheltenham and Northampton: Edward Elgar, 2002.

Roubini, Nouriel. "Debt Sustainability: How to Assess Whether a Country is Insolvent." Paper presented at Stern School of Business, New York University, December 20, 2001. http://people.stern.nyu.edu/nroubini/papers/debtsustainability.pdf.

Ruane, Kevin. *The Rise and Fall of the European Defense Community: Anglo-American Relations and the Crisis of European Defense, 1950–55.* Houndmill, Basingstoke: Macmillan, 2000.

Savage, James D. *Balanced Budgets and American Politics*, Ithaca N.Y.: Cornell University Press, 1988.

Scott, Joanne, and David M. Trubek. "Mind the Gap: Law and New Approaches to Governance in the European Union." *European Law Journal* 8 (2002): 1-18.

Skidelsky, Robert. *John Maynard Keynes 1883-1946: Economist, Philosopher, Statesman*. London: Penguin Books, 2003.

Stith, Kate. "Rewriting the Fiscal Constitution: The Case of Gramm-Rudman-Hollings." *California Law Review* 76 (1988): 593.

Streit, Manfred E., and Michael Wohlgemuth. "The Market Economy and the State Hayekian and Ordoliberal Conceptions." In *The Theory of Capitalism in the German Economic Tradition: Historism, Ordo-Liberalism, Critical Theory, Solidarism*, edited by Peter Koslowski, 224-69. Berlin - Heidelberg: Springer Verlag, 2000.

Tarr, G. Alan. "Laboratories of Democracy? Brandeis, Federalism, and Scientific Management." *Publius* 31 (2001): 37-46.

Telò, Mario. "Préface". In *Vers une société européenne de la connaissance : La stratégie de Lisbonne (2000-2010)*. Bruxelles: Editions de l'ULB, 2004.

The Harvard Law School Forum on Corporate Governance and Financial Regulation. "Dodd-Frank Act Becomes Law." http://blogs.law.harvard.edu/corpgov/2010/07/21/dodd-frank-act-becomes-law/.

United States Government Accountability Office (GAO), *Review of Regulators' Oversight of Risk Management Systems at a Limited Number of Large, Complex Financial Institutions*, Testimony Before the U.S. Senate, March 18, 2009, 5-9. http://www.gao.gov/assets/130/121973.pdf.

Verhofstadt, Guy. "How to break the European deadlock?" Speech given at the European Chamber of Commerce in Hong Kong, November 3, 2011.

Vesperini, Jean-Pierre. *Relancer la Croissance de l'Europe. Propositions pour une nouvelle gouvernance européenne.* Paris: Economica, 2005.
Weber, Max. *Economy and Society: An Outline of Interpretive Sociology.* 2 vols., 1st edited 1922. Berkeley and Los Angeles: University of California Press, 1978.
Wikipedia article "Ordoliberalism." Last modified July 26, 2012. http://en.wikipedia.org/wiki/Ordoliberalism.
Wikipedia. "Dodd–Frank Wall Street Reform and Consumer Protection Act." Last modified August 06, 2012. http://en.wikipedia.org/wiki/Dodd%E2%80%93Frank_Wall_Street_Reform_and_Consumer_Protection_Act#cite_note-6.
—. "Ordoliberalism." Last modified 26 February 2013. http://en.wikipedia.org/wiki/Ordoliberalism
Wolf, Martin. "Be bold, Mario, put out that fire." *Financial Times,* October 26, 2011.
Young, Brigitte. "Economic Governance in the Eurozone: A New Dawn?" *Economic Sociology The European Electronic Newsletter* 12(2) (2011): 11-6. http://econsoc.mpifg.de/archive/econ_soc_12-2.pdf#page=11.
Zeitlin, Jonathan, and Philippe Pochet, eds., *The Open Method of Coordination in Action: The European Employment and Social Inclusion Strategies*. Brussels: P.I.E.-Peter Lang, 2005.

CHAPTER THREE

THE NEW BUDGETARY ARCHITECTURE OF THE EU IN VIEW OF THE FINANCIAL AND ECONOMIC CRISIS

DIMITRIOS V. SKIADAS

Introduction – The Concept of the EU Budget

The unprecedented economic and financial crisis experienced throughout the globe challenged the capacity of all institutional schemes, in terms of meeting all the short-term and long–term complications caused at national and international financial, economic, social and political level. The European Union (EU) demonstrated a somehow different than usual behaviour, acting in a timely and organized manner, in order to re-structure its budgetary architecture with a view to use the EU cohesion policy as a budgetary instrument to tackle the extreme conditions caused by the crisis. The aim of this Chapter is to examine this behaviour and highlight its main elements.

The discussion on the public finances of the EU (and before that the European Communities) is as old as the European Integration experiment itself. One of the principal institutional developments in the historical course of this process was the establishment of the Community Budget as a mechanism to provide resources in order to meet the needs of the implementation of the various policies developed by the European institutions. The various relevant procedures during the 1960s and 1970s were very intense – the main issue at the time being the establishment of the Communities' Own Resources System – and led to direct confrontation between the European Commission and various Member States (France, United Kingdom, etc).[1] The main innovations introduced at the time were

[1] For a detailed account of these events see F. Wooldridge, M. Sassela, Some recent legal provisions increasing the budgetary powers of the European

the democratisation of the budgetary process, through the reinforcement of the European Parliament's authority over the budget, as well as the establishment of the European Court of Auditors as a mechanism for external financial control over the management of the budget by the European institutions and the national authorities.

In the 1980s the enactment of the Single European Act included another reform of the budgetary provisions, aiming to a) introduce additional resources into the financing of the budget, b) increase the weight of the structural financial assistance and limit agricultural expenditure and c) distribute at a fairer rate the burden of financing the budget on behalf of the Member States.[2] These aims were seen at three interrelated levels: political, financial and legal. Politically, the principle of solidarity among the Member States and the purpose of the common market required a reduction of the differences in the level of development between the various regions. Financially, there was not only a need for assistance to the underdeveloped regions involving a redistributive action through the transfer of resources to such regions,[3] but also a need to assure better financial management of the Community's resources which could be seen as a burden on European citizens, given the nature of the EU's own resources system, which rely, inter alia, on sums paid by the citizens of the member states either for agricultural levies or for VAT.[4] Legally, the provisions introduced by the Single European Act provided for an amendment of the Structural Funds' operational rules.[5]

Similar and sometimes even more intense have been the discussions on the financial provisions of the Treaties during the last twenty years, especially within the framework of the negotiations on the financial perspectives of the Union. The last example of the negotiations for the

---

Parliament, and establishing a European Court of Auditors, *LIEI* (1976/2), 13-52, D. Chalmers, A. Tomkins, *European Union Public Law*, (2007), 13-15.

[2] T. Szemler, *EU Budget Milestones: From Fundamental Systemic Reforms to Organised Chaos*, EU-CONSENT Conference, Budapest 24.3.2006, 2.

[3] European Commission, *The EIB, the other financial instruments, and strengthening economic and social cohesion*, COM (88) 244, 3.

[4] For an analysis of the EU's Own Resources System see D. Skiadas, *The financial provisions of the Lisbon Treaty (in Greek)*, Hellenic Review of European Law, 2010/3, 325-344 at 334-337.

[5] For this multilevel approach of the EU Cohesion Policy see European Commission, *Vade Mecum on the Reform of the European Community's Structural Funds*, (1989), 11-12, A. Evans, *The EU Structural Funds*, (1998), 21-23. For more details on the legal requirements see European Commission, *Reform of the Structural Funds: 1) Commission Communication, 2) Comprehensive Proposal pursuant to Art. 130d of the EEC Treaty*, COM (87) 376 final, OJ 1987, C 245/3.

2007-2013 financial perspectives is very indicative of this atmosphere (see below).

This should not come as a surprise. Having and exercising authority over the European Budget has always been a focal point in the course of European Integration. A budget is defined as a procedure, according to which an administration forms its economic and financial policy, including its monetary aspects, and this policy is then accepted and implemented effectively.[6] The instrument of implementing the fiscal-monetary policy mix is decided by the competent governmental departments, who take into account the effects of government partisanship, the impact of central bank independence, and the use of policy instruments (deficits and interest rates), or the resulting macroeconomic performance (inflation, unemployment, and GDP growth). It is not only a financial statement, nor just a method of financial assumptions and forecasts, or a system of controlling expenditure, or a decision making instrument, or a report aiming to the economic and financial development of a country, but all of the above.[7] Practically the budget is a series of goals with price tags attached, a plan, a contract to accomplish certain ends, a means of control, and even a precedent, because what has been enacted in a given year is likely to be re-enacted in the following one.[8]

In the European Community context, a definition exists in Article 4 paragraph 1 of the Financial Regulation,[9] according to which the budget is the instrument that, for each financial year, forecasts and authorises all revenue and expenditure considered necessary for the European Community and the European Atomic Energy Community. This latter definition, setting the limits of the concept of the budget, is very helpful in identifying the importance of the budget in the institutional system of the EU.

From the above definitions the main functions of the budget in public finances are highlighted: estimation, authorisation, allocation/redistribution, and stabilisation.

The estimating function entails the arithmetical description of revenue and expenditure for the next financial year, thus having a futuristic perspective, as it takes place before the time of the budget's implementation. Its importance derives from the fact that it is an ex ante forecast of the relevant figures, which are precise as possible and have to

---

[6] A.E. Buck, *Public Budgeting*, (1929), 3.

[7] R. D. Lee, R .W. Johnson, *Public Budgeting Systems*, (1973), 2.

[8] A. Wildavsky, *The Politics of the Budgetary Process*, (1964) 1-4.

[9] Council Regulation 1605/2002 on the Financial Regulation applicable to the general budget of the European Communities, OJ 2002 L248/1.

be balanced. The lack of this forecast would make the budget practically inexistent as there would not be any financial limits set by this estimation.[10]

The authorising function is the provision of permission by the legislature to the executive to take the necessary action in order to collect revenue and pay expenditure during the financial year. Given the legal nature of the budget, this permission is considered to be an obligation for the executive, an obligation that has to be adhered to and the lack of which would transform the budget's nature from obligatory to indicative.[11]

The allocating/redistributive function refers to the process through which the annual resources are raised, collected, then cut between the competing claims of departments or agencies or social groups.[12] For instance, in the context of the EU, allocating resources through the budget is focussed mainly on agricultural and structural aid, in order to preserve food security and facilitate structural change in a period of rapid industrial change. The redistribution function is mainly exercised through the operations of the Structural Funds, in order to support the regional policy and the economic and social cohesion of the Union.

Finally, stability in EU public finances is a core element for the Economic and Monetary Union, which is supported indirectly through the EU budget, as this budget supports through its functions the national economies of the Member States, in the light of the provisions of the Stability and Growth Pact.[13] The effects of the ongoing global financial crisis on the economies of the Member States of the EU have highlighted that interrelation.

The budgeting process entails also two additional functions, which are not included in the concept of budgeting *stricto sensu*: the audit and the evaluation of financial and political programmes. In an overall assessment,

---

[10] N. Barbas, *Elements of Public Finance Law (in Greek)*, (2002) 20, L.G. Theocharopoulos, *Law of the State Budget (in Greek)*, Vol. A', (1976) 22-23, D. Korsos, *Public Finance Law (in Greek)*, Vol. A', (1980) 65, M. Stasinopoulos, *Lessons of Public Finance Law (in Greek)*, (1966) 32.

[11] D. Korsos, *Public Finance Law (in Greek),* Vol. A', (1980), 65, M. Stasinopoulos, *Lessons of Public Finance Law (in Greek)*, (1966), 32-33, N. Barbas, *Elements of Public Finance Law (in Greek)*, (2002), 21, L.G. Theocharopoulos, *Law of the State Budget (in Greek)*, Vol. A', (1976), 22-23.

[12] A. Gray, B. Jenkins, B. Segsworth, Perspectives on Budgeting, Auditing and Evaluation: An Introduction, in A. Gray, B. Jenkins, B. Segsworth (Eds), *Budgeting, Auditing and Evaluation – Functions & Integration in Seven Governments*, (1993) 6.

[13] For some indicative views on the interaction between the EU public finances and the European Monetary Union see J. Ferreiro, G. Fontana and F. Serrano (eds), *Fiscal Policy in the European Union*, Palgrave-Macmillan, 2008.

the fundamental task in budgeting is twofold: it predicts the future and evaluates the past. This task is described in the budgetary mechanism for making choices among competing claims for resources under conditions of scarcity.[14]

The historical course of the European Integration teaches us that negotiations over the Union's budget are inevitably becoming more complicated and complex. This is due not only to the increased heterogeneity of the EU, because of the heterogeneity produced by the entry of new Member States in terms of economic conditions, per capita income, policy preferences and cultural values and orientations, but also due to the variety of negotiated solutions between Member States on budgetary issues increases in accordance to the number of negotiators, or Member States.

Setting the New Scenery

It was the 15th of September 2008 when one of the biggest banks worldwide, Lehman Brothers Holdings Inc., filed for Chapter 11 bankruptcy protection, thus signifying the start of a – until then dormant[15] – financial and economic turmoil, with enormous social and political implications. This has been the culmination of a dramatic situation developing since 2002, as the inflow of funds in the U.S. economy allowed for low interest rates, thus facilitating loans of various types with easy credit conditions, and "motivating" consumers to assume unprecedented debt loads. The U.S. housing market developed the scheme of mortgage-backed securities, deriving their value from mortgage payments and housing prices, which attracted investors from all over the world. But as housing prices declined, reaching values below those of the mortgage loans, those participating in such schemes suffered significant losses, causing a foreclosure wave, which hit both consumers and financial

---

[14] J. McCaffery, Features of the Budgetary Process in R. T. Meyers (ed.), *Handbook of Government Budgeting*, (1999), 27.

[15] There have been warning signs for the upcoming crisis, in the form of financial imbalances caused by factors such as rising global imbalances (capital flows), monetary policy that might have been too loose, or inadequate supervision and regulation. For a detailed analysis of these causes of the global financial crisis see O. Merrouche, E, Nier, *What Caused the Global Financial Crisis?—Evidence on the Drivers of Financial Imbalances 1999–2007*, IMF Working Paper, WP/10/265, December 2010.

institutions. It was not difficult for the crisis to expand to other sectors of the economy throughout the world, reaching "pandemic" proportions.[16]

The impact of the crisis reached Europe through three "channels": a) the connections between the European and the American financial systems, b) the wealth and confidence effects on demand and c) the global trade.[17] The real GDP was reduced in 2009 by around 4% on average in the EU, making this recession clearly deeper than any recession since World War II. The effects, however, were not similar in all Member States, as in some the recession was more than the EU average (i.e. Hungary, Germany, Ireland), while others were much less affected, at least at the time (i.e. Poland, Cyprus, Malta).[18] The crisis is expected to have a long-lasting impact on the potential growth rate in the immediate future, given that financial crises weaken investment opportunities as demand prospects are likely to be poor, real cost of borrowing is high and credit is in short supply. In addition, a significant part of the unemployment caused by the crisis might prove to be structural, as displaced workers may find it hard to return to the labour market due to the new outlook caused by the structural economic changes and the reduction of wages.[19]

EU Budgetary Architecture before the Crisis

This crisis found Europe in a rather strange budgetary status. The balance achieved through the financial perspectives as agreed on December 15, 2005, was to be, in any case, reassessed, as it was stated in the 2006 Interinstitutional Agreement between the European Parliament, the Council and the Commission.[20] According to the agreement reached

---

[16] For details about the 2008 financial crisis see P. Krugman, *The Return of Depression Economics and the Crisis of 2008,* (2008), B. S. Bernanke, *Four Questions about the financial crisis*, Speech on April 14, 2009, Morehouse College, Atlanta, Georgia, available on line on May 1st, 2010, at http://www.federalreserve.gov/newsevents/speech/bernanke20090414a.htm.

[17] European Commission, *Economic Crisis in Europe: Causes, Consequences and Responses*, European Economy 7/2009, p. 24.

[18] European Commission, *Economic Crisis in Europe: Causes, Consequences and Responses*, European Economy 7/2009, p. 26-27.

[19] European Commission, *Economic Crisis in Europe: Causes, Consequences and Responses*, European Economy 7/2009, p. 31.

[20] I. Begg, Fr. Heinemann, *New Budget, Old Dilemmas*, Centre for European Reform, Briefing Note, 22.2.2006, pp. 1-2, Interinstitutional Agreement between the European Parliament, the Council and the Commission on budgetary discipline and sound financial management, OJ C 139, 14.6.2006, p. 15 (Declaration No 3).

during the meeting of the European Council in Brussels, the total appropriations available to the EU budget, for the period 2007-2013, were set to 862 billion Euros, which represent 1.045% of EU GNI. Out of this sum, the Structural Funds were allocated 308 billion euros, while the Common Agricultural Policy, along with actions supporting the environment, were allocated 371 billion euros.[21]

This agreement was reached after long and hard negotiations and it satisfied, at the time, all parties involved: The UK because it managed to conclude its term of Presidency with a successful deal over the budget; France because it maintained the status quo regarding the Common Agricultural Policy, which is very favourable for French farmers; Germany because it was deemed as the major mediator for achieving the budget agreement, despite the fact that it still remained the biggest net contributor to the EU budget; the so called "cohesion countries" (Spain, Portugal, Greece) because they maintained the bulk of the benefits they receive from the Union's structural and cohesion funds within the framework of the Union's regional policies; and the ten new Member States because they obtained a larger regional aid allocation than the one originally proposed.[22]

However, this was only the surface. A "*quid pro quo*" mentality has always been present during the workings of the European Councils' meetings. The enlargement of the EU by ten new Member States has set new challenges, especially due to its economic and social implications, which, in turn, have caused mounting concerns within the fifteen "old" Member States, especially with regard to income distribution, social policy, and impact on living standards.[23]

In terms of content, the agreement maintained the two major components of EU spending. The first is the cost of the Common Agricultural Policy. Although there was much criticism for this choice, the fact that most of the new Member States of the Union demonstrated a very high percentage of employment in the agricultural sector did not allow for a reduction of CAP expenditure. This was reinforced by the international economic environment, as it had been demonstrated during the workings of the Doha Round, which indicated a tendency of increasing agricultural

---

[21] European Council, *Presidency Conclusions*, Brussels 15-16 December 2005, Doc 15914/1/2005 and Doc 15915/2005.

[22] I. Begg, Fr. Heinemann, *New Budget, Old Dilemmas*, Centre for European Reform, Briefing Note, 22.2.2006, 1-2.

[23] T. Boeri, H. Brücker, *The Impact of Eastern Enlargement on Employment and Labour Markets in the EU Member States*, European Integration Consortium (DIW, CEPR, FIEF, IAS, IGIER), 2000, 1.

subsidies in the interest of development in poor countries. Furthermore, the protection of food sufficiency and quality calls for investment, especially in an age where food related health hazards are quickly spread across the globe. Consequently, it was deemed that there was not much scope for changing the 2002 agreement on agriculture, as reached by the European Council in Brussels, before the end of the current programming period. Alternatively, there were considerations of either changing the policy itself, i.e. reorienting the payments in a direction of rural development, in which all payments would not be direct but proportionate to the size of the farms, and the income capacity of the farmers, or even abolishing the entire common agricultural policy, in order to make room for free agricultural markets, in which any state subsidies would be monitored and evaluated closely.[24]

The second largest part of EU expenditure refers to the support of cohesion and regional policies. Despite all efforts, there are still criticisms about the effectiveness of the support provided by the Structural Funds, a support which leads to an increase of income in some regions, but only through a redistribution of resources instead of the implementation of a more substantive structural policy, i.e. a policy with more tangible results in terms of GDP growth or employment increase in the areas receiving the structural assistance. For the 2007-2013 period, the introduction of the Lisbon Strategy as an element of preparing the various interventions may result in more positive outcomes.[25]

This novelty was introduced in the 2006 reform of the European Cohesion Policy, which signified the actions financed by the EU Structural Funds as one of the principal Community measures for the delivery of the Union's growth and jobs agenda. While maintaining the traditional principles of cohesion policy (complementarity, consistency, coordination, compliance, programming, partnership, territorial level of implementation, proportional intervention, shared management, additionality, equality between men and women and non-discrimination and sustainable development), the reform introduced a number of new elements in recognition of the need to focus further the limited resources available on promoting sustainable growth, competitiveness and employment. This framework encourages Member States and regions to focus on those areas of investment that help to deliver the National Reform Programmes adopted within the Lisbon Strategy framework, while taking into account

[24] I. Begg, *The 2008/9 EU Budget Review*, EU-CONSENT, EU-Budget Working Paper No 3, March 2007, 18-20.

[25] I. Begg, *The 2008/9 EU Budget Review*, EU-CONSENT, EU-Budget Working Paper No 3, March 2007, 20-21.

national and regional circumstances. It retains the same three priorities which are at the heart of the growth and jobs strategy, namely: a) making Europe and its regions more attractive places to invest and work, b) encouraging innovation, entrepreneurship and the growth of the knowledge economy, c) creating more and better jobs. It is foreseen in the Structural Funds Regulations that Member States have to "earmark" the major part of their financial allocations for investments with the potential to make a significant contribution to realising the Lisbon objectives. Moreover, the introduction of new reporting mechanisms, focusing on the annual achievement of the Lisbon objectives through the earmarked investments, supported by the operational programmes, and implemented by the Member States, has reinforced significantly the links between the European Cohesion Policy and the Lisbon Strategy.[26]

The result of the European Council's summit in December 2005, being a temporary solution due to the abovementioned reassessment clause of the 2006 Interinstitutional Agreement, created a tangled web of regulations and conditions, based mainly on agreements of previous programming periods. Even the European Parliament rejected it initially. It took six months of long negotiations before reaching the current Interinstitutional Agreement on budgetary discipline and sound financial management.[27]

The final compromise has not been so radical, as it still gave relatively more weight to the financing of agriculture (CAP) and the reduction of development disparities (cohesion policy), and less weight to the Lisbon strategy objectives (competitiveness policy), other internal policies (freedom, security, justice and citizenship) and external policies (enlargement and development aid to non-EU and non-candidate countries).[28]

---

[26] For a detailed analysis of the interaction between the Lisbon Strategy and the European Cohesion Policy, see European Commission, *Member States and Regions delivering the Lisbon strategy for growth and jobs through EU cohesion policy, 2007-2013*, COM(2007) 798 final.

[27] For the use and the importance of the Interistitutional Agreements see D. Skiadas, *Reforming the European Budget: An Ongoing Tale*, Karamanlis Working Paper No 5 in Hellenic and European Studies, May 2008, The Constantine Karamanlis Chair in Hellenic and Southeastern European Studies, The Fletcher School of Law and Diplomacy, Tufts University, 18-19.

[28] M. Mrak, V. Rant, *Financial Perspectives 2007-2013: Domination of national interests*, EU-CONSENT, EU-Budget Working Paper No 1, July 2007, 5-6.

Reviewing the Architecture

For some, the most important element of the new Financial Perspectives agreement has been the commitment undertaken by the Union's Institutions to reassess the financial framework of the 2007-2013 period, by reviewing all aspects of EU spending and resources, and to prepare a relevant report in 2008/2009. This "review clause" allowed for mutual concessions to be made during the negotiations and also demonstrated that the Member States have, at last, realised the need for further budget reform.[29]

Others have adopted a more pessimistic approach, noting that there have been in the past very well documented studies on reforming the European budget, without, however, resulting in an effective solution.[30]

The European budget has developed into a historical relic, since the areas of expenditure reflected outdated needs of the Union, therefore a radical restructuring was in order.[31] The discussion on the European Budget Review has already indicated that there is scope for improvement for the Union's financial mechanism. Such a discussion sometimes goes back to basics, a characteristic caused by two interrelated factors. The first is the vagueness of the mandate on the review of the budget, using an ambiguous wording which did not clarify either the scope or the usefulness of the review.[32] The second is the fact that addressing such a complicated issue requires taking a step backwards and examining the entire structure and operation of the EU, before putting forward proposals for the reform of this financial system. Topics such as the modes of governance used by the Union's institutions (i.e. the regulatory function within the framework of the "Community method" in areas of EU exclusive competence, the budgetary function with regard to financing policies, the coordinating function with regard to the implementation of EU policies such as the Lisbon Strategy or the Stability and Growth Pact,

---

[29] I. Begg, Fr. Heinemann, *New Budget, Old Dilemmas*, Centre for European Reform, Briefing Note, 22.2.2006, 4.

[30] T. Szemler, *EU Budget Milestones: From Fundamental Systemic Reforms to Organised Chaos*, EU-CONSENT Conference, Budapest 24.3.2006, 11.

[31] Report of Independent High Level Group, *An Agenda for a growing Europe – Making the EU Economic System Deliver*, July 2003.

[32] E. Rubio, *EU Budget Review: Addressing the Thorny Issues*, Policy Paper no 32, Notre Europe, 2008, 3-5.

etc.) are being studied in order to be used in formulating a proposal for a new financial system of the Union.[33]

Some of the characteristics of the review process were the following: It has been an open procedure and all those interested, at local, national and international level, submitted their contributions, thus participating in the broad consultation process. Priority was given to EU expenditure, despite the fact that the revenues have been examined as well. The review adopted a policy-driven approach as all EU spending was examined in the light of EU political priorities and challenges. And there has been a considerable effort to separate the 2008/2009 review from the preparation of the negotiations for the next programming period, after 2013. In an overall approach, it has been noted that in order for the review to be successful, it must be inspired by the early reforms in the 1980s: As those reforms were affiliated with significant political choices, such as the establishment of the Single Market, and they resulted in considerable changes in the EU Financial system, any attempt for a new reform must be related to a new political agenda, such as the Lisbon Strategy, and it needs to focus on the structural problems by tackling all dimensions of the EU budgetary system (revenue, expenditure, procedures).[34]

The financial crisis created a new scenery in which the EU had to operate in a method and spirit which would put its potential as a financial as well as a political mechanism to the test. Therefore a new EU policy framework for crisis management was established, including policy instruments in the pursuit of: a) crisis prevention, b) crisis control and mitigation, and c) crisis resolution.[35] The European "cure" for the pandemic financial problem was to introduce a mixture of measures and policies, based on both the monetarist approach inspired by Milton Friedman's ideas on reducing state action and consequently government expenditure,[36] and the interventionist approach inspired by John Maynard Keynes's views on using taxation and public expenses in order to improve the demand in the market, thus controlling the effects of the crisis.[37]

---

[33] I. Begg, *The 2008/9 EU Budget Review*, EU-CONSENT, EU-Budget Working Paper No 3, March 2007, 4-7.

[34] E. Rubio, *EU Budget Review: Addressing the Thorny Issues*, Policy Paper no 32, Notre Europe, 2008, 13-22.

[35] European Commission, *Economic Crisis in Europe: Causes, Consequences and Responses*, European Economy 7/2009, p. 58-59.

[36] M. Friedman, *Capitalism and Freedom*, Chicago University Press - 40th Anniversary Edition, 2002.

[37] J. M. Keynes, *The General Theory of Employment, Interest and Money,* Harourt, Brace & World, 1936.

In that respect, the European Commission presented its proposal for a new architecture, as a recovery plan for Europe. This proposal is based on three pillars: a new financial market architecture at EU level, tackling the crisis' impact on the real economy and providing a global response to the crisis.[38]

Out of these three pillars, the third falls beyond the scope of this analysis. It entails an interactional approach and the need for action on behalf of international financial organisations, such as the International Monetary Fund, the World Trade Organisation, the Transatlantic Economic Council, as well as the renewal of bilateral negotiations between key players at world economic stage (i.e. U.S., China, Brazil, India, Russia, etc).

The first pillar also falls beyond the scope of this analysis, as it refers to actions related to the banking and credit markets at EU level and the role of the European Central Bank on this issue. However, it is interesting to note that until May 2009, the governments of the member states had approved an overall amount of 3,7 trillion euros to support the banks in Europe, including 311,4 billion euros in capital aid, 2,92 trillion euros in guarantees, 33 billion euros for the acquisition of problematic assets and 505,6 billion euros for liquidity aid of the banks. Similarly, it falls beyond the scope of this analysis to refer to the initiative of establishing a mechanism to provide financial support to its member states, in cooperation with the International Monetary Fund, and reviewing, at the same time, the entire scheme of national economic governance in the EU.[39]

---

[38] European Commission, *From financial crisis to recovery: a European framework for action*, COM (2008), 706 final, 29.10.2008.

[39] For more details on this initiative and its implementation see Statement by the Heads of State and Government of the Euro Area, Brussels, 25 March 2010, Council of the European Union, Extraordinary Council Meeting, Economic and Financial Affairs, Brussels, 9/10 May 2010, Press Release, 9596/10 (Presse 108). The legal instrument for this mechanism is Regulation (EU) 407/2010, OJ 2010, L 118/1, European Commission, *Reinforcing economic policy coordination*, COM (2010) 250 final, European Central Bank, *Reinforcing Economic Governance in the Euro Area*, June 2010, Council of the European Union, Economic and Financial Affairs, Brussels, 7 September 2010, Press Release, 13161/10 (Presse 229), European Council, *Presidency Conclusions*, Brussels, 16 September 2010, EUCO 21/10, Report of the Task Force to the European Council, *Strengthening the Economic Governance in the EU*, 21 October 2010, European Council, *Presidency Conclusions*, Brussels, 25 March 2011, EUCO 10/11.

The second pillar, i.e. supporting the real economy, entails various EU budgetary measures for tackling the crisis. The assessment of this scheme is made at two levels: the procedural and the substantive.

In terms of process, there has been severe criticism of the entire existing process of selecting a policy for funding. This process has been structured in certain stages, which have become more of a formality, instead of substantive elaboration of political choices and opinions. The usual sequence, including initial debates on the objectives of the budgetary settlement, the Commission's proposals and the Council's reactions, the exchange of views which can never be reconciled, the intensive efforts of the various Presidencies of the Council in order to reach a complex political agreement in which nobody really understands what they have actually agreed upon, and the indifference of the peoples of Europe, in the name of which all these take place, effectively blocks any prospect of reform.[40]

In dealing with the crisis, the institutions of the Union demonstrated a somewhat different approach and behaviour, being more result-oriented instead of process-focused. The Commission reacted immediately to the abovementioned events of September 2008 by presenting several consecutive proposals in October and in November 2008. The European Council, during its meeting in December 2008, approved these proposals, thus setting a new framework for action. It is noteworthy that perhaps for the first time in the long history of the EU and its budgetary and cohesion policy, the various decisions were adopted without the long delays caused by the various layers of consultation and the workings of the various bodies involved in such procedures. It is interesting to note that while the process for reaching agreement by all interested parties for the financial perspectives of the period 2007-2013 lasted for twenty-seven months (February 2004 - May 2006), the new budgetary architecture was agreed upon within only three months (October 2009 - December 2009).

In terms of substance, the contents of the new architecture have been set by the European Council. The measures referring to EU action entail:

- an increase in intervention by the European Investment Bank of 30 billion Euros in 2009/2010, especially for small and medium-sized enterprises, renewable energy and clean transport,
- the simplification of procedures and faster implementation of programmes financed by the Cohesion Fund, the Structural Funds and the European Agricultural Fund for Rural Development,

[40] I. Begg, *The 2008/9 EU Budget Review*, EU-CONSENT, EU-Budget Working Paper No 3, March 2007, 24-25.

- the mobilisation of the possibilities, in the context of the Community budget, for strengthening investment in sectors and geographical areas identified by the Commission,
- the mobilisation of the European Globalisation Adjustment Fund, in order to promote employment in key sectors of the European economy,
- the possibility, for the Member States that so wish, of applying reduced VAT rates in certain sectors,
- a temporary exemption of two years beyond the *de minimis* threshold for State aid in respect of an amount of up to 500.000 Euros,
- the use for 2009 and 2010 of the accelerated procedures in the public procurement directives, which is justified by the exceptional nature of the current economic situation, in order to reduce from 87 to 30 days the length of the tendering process for the most commonly-used procedures for major public projects.

These elements form a coherent framework for actions, which set a new, accelerated – in terms of procedural time frameworks in public procurement proceedings – rhythm for the implementation of the Union's budgetary policy.[41]

The European Economic Recovery Plan has two aspects, one regarding measures financed by the national budgets of the Member States and one regarding measures co-financed by the Union's budget, through the cohesion financial instruments. While the former is to be conducted within the limits set by the Stability and Growth Pact, the latter is closely connected to the priority areas of the Lisbon Strategy (i.e. people, business, infrastructure, and energy, research and innovation). The combination of funds and policies is seen as a catalyst for actions meeting the challenges set by the crisis and improves the perspectives for future investments.[42]

The new budgetary architecture described in the European Economic Recovery Plan has a very strong element of investment in human capital, in the form of a European Employment support initiative. This initiative aims at activating flexicurity strategies by promoting employment and long term employability rather than particular jobs through adaptation to change and easing transition between jobs while at the same time

---

[41] European Council, *Presidency Conclusions*, Brussels 11-12 December 2008, Doc 17271/1/08.

[42] European Commission, *A European Economic Recovery Plan*, COM (2008), 800 final, 26.11.2008.

matching skills to labour market needs. These measures are supported financially by the European Social Fund (ESF) in the form of specialised training, personal job counselling, apprenticeship, subsidised employment, grants and credits for self-employment and business start ups. The funding criteria are being simplified and the advance payments have been accelerated.[43]

Furthermore, new schemes for supporting entrepreneurship have been developed. Improving access to finance has been identified as a major need, therefore there has been an increase of the leverage of EU investments for the 2007-2013 period, through launching new schemes such as JEREMIE ("Joint European Resources for Micro to Medium Enterprises"), which targets new business creation and SME expansion, and JASMINE ("Joint Action to Support Micro-Finance Institutions in Europe"), which channels various forms of technical and financial assistance to primarily help non-bank micro-credit providers to improve the quality of their operations, to expand and to become sustainable. Innovative cluster creation and maintenance has been selected also as a business support measure, especially by exploiting the potential of ICT applications, low-carbon technologies and eco-friendly products, production techniques and energy efficient processes.

Strengthening the institutional and administrative capacity of the EU member states has been identified as a major goal. The creation of a stable business environment will promote structural adjustments and foster growth and jobs, especially by reducing regulatory and administrative burdens on businesses (i.e. ensuring starting up a business anywhere in the EU within three days at zero costs and via a single access point) and thus contributing to increasing productivity and strengthening competitiveness. Special attention is paid to the areas of transport and energy as sources of sustainable development through new – environmentally friendly – infrastructure. In that respect two new instruments have been developed: JASPERS ("Joint Assistance in Supporting Projects in European Regions"), providing assistance to managing authorities in the new member states of the EU to prepare major projects in priority EU infrastructure investments, and JESSICA ("Joint European Support for Sustainable Investment in City Areas"), accelerating and enhancing sustainable investments in energy efficiency, urban transport, ICT infrastructures, regeneration, etc., in the urban context.[44]

---

[43] European Commission, *Cohesion Policy: Investing in the real economy*, COM (2008), 876/3.

[44] European Commission, *Cohesion Policy: Investing in the real economy*, COM (2008), 876/3.

These new elements of the EU budgetary architecture necessitated the adoption of a new legislative framework, which has been included in a series of Regulations:

- Council Regulation (EC) 2008/1341 of 18 December 2008, OJ 2008, L 348/19 and Council Regulation (EC) 2009/284 of 7 April 2009, OJ 2009, L 94/10 amending Council Regulation (EC) 2006/1083 of 11 July 2006, OJ 2006 L 210/25, on general provisions on the European Regional Development Fund, the European Social Fund and the Cohesion Fund,
- Council Regulation (EC) 2009/397 of 6 May 2009, OJ 2009, L 348/19 amending Council Regulation (EC) 2006/1080 of 5 July 2006, OJ 2006 L 210/1 on the European Regional Development Fund,
- Council Regulation (EC) 2009/396 of 6 May 2009, OJ 2009, L 126/1 amending Council Regulation (EC) 2006/1081, of 5 July 2006, OJ 2006, L 210/12 on the European Social Fund.

These provisions include: a) measures to improve cash flow of the public authorities charged with delivering the national and regional programmes by allowing for an additional tranche of prefinancing in 2009 and accelerating the reimbursement of expenditure incurred under major projects and within the framework of state aid schemes, b) measures facilitating the launch of financial engineering instruments with a view to accelerating the use of access to finance measures, c) measures simplifying the use of flat rates and lump-sums costs to allow public authorities to more quickly prepare projects and measures and d) measures expanding the possibilities for support to investments in energy efficiency improvement and renewable energy in housing in favour of low income households in the EU 27.

Putting the New Architecture to Work

If setting the new Architecture was considered to be a difficult task, the completion of which is still to be achieved, in some respects, putting this Architecture to work has indeed proved to be a real challenge.

The Member States, in compliance with the European Economic Recovery Plan, prepared national recovery plans, in which they included targeted measures at short and medium term perspectives. These measures focused on structural reforms, while at the same time included the provision of financial support to sectors of the national economies that needed to be reinforced, in order to underpin growth and employment. The provided European budgetary support is estimated at over 600 billion euros for 2009 and 2010. Furthermore, steps have been taken in order to simplify the business environment, especially for small and medium sized enterprises, by reducing social charges and administrative burdens.[45]

It has been noted, however, that the amounts made available by the EU budget in order to meet the crisis appear far more than they actually are. These amounts include relatively little "new money," as they entail mainly bringing forward payments which were already planned. As for the national financial measures, these, in many cases, were not new initiatives, but measures which already existed in the national programmes and were going to be implemented in any case.[46] Furthermore, the main burden of tackling the crisis, assigned to the Member States, was seen as a risk of undermining the single market, the economic and monetary union, and the EU's role as a global actor, because this development could relapse into nationalistic and protectionist behaviour on behalf of the Member States.[47]

It is interesting to note that out of the total budgetary support, a quarter was provided to help industry save and create jobs or keep workers in employment, by supporting short time working arrangements, investing in skills and retraining, etc. Half of the budgetary support has been used to support the unemployed, households and vulnerable social groups. The last quarter of the budgetary support was allocated towards investments of a more long-term nature, such as infrastructure, energy efficiency, innovation, etc.[48] The overall idea is to make the social protection systems of the Member States more responsive to the economic cycle and especially to crises, like the recent one.[49] This approach has been welcomed as a means of achieving greater flexicurity results, an aim that

---

[45] European Commission, *Progress on the Implementation of the European Economic Recovery Plan*, June 2009, 1-2.

[46] European Economic and Social Committee, *Opinion on the European Economic Recovery Plan, COM (2008) 800, final*, Doc ECO/244 – CESE 50/2009, January 2009, 7. European Parliament, *Resolution of 11 March 2009 on a European Economic Recovery Plan*, Doc P6_TA(2009)0123, para 78.

[47] European Parliament, *Resolution of 11 March 2009 on a European Economic Recovery Plan*, Doc P6_TA(2009)0123, para 11, Committee of the Regions, *Opinion on the European Economic Recovery Plan and the role of Local and Regional Authorities*, Doc CdR 12/2009 fin, April 2009, 3.

[48] European Commission, *Progress on the Implementation of the European Economic Recovery Plan*, June 2009, 3.

[49] European Commission, *Growth, Jobs and Social Progress in the EU - A Contribution to the Evaluation of the Social Dimension of the Lisbon Strategy*, September 2009.

has been acknowledged as the most suitable solution for guaranteeing adequate social protection for all.[50]

The main structural reforms put forward by the Member States, within the framework of the European Economic Recovery Plan, have focused on three main objectives: i) easing labour market conditions and supporting vulnerable groups, ii) strengthening competitiveness and the business environment, and iii) investing in a greener, more knowledge-based economy.[51]

In a preliminary effort to assess the impact of these measures, the European Commission noted that they had significant influence in limiting the rise in unemployment at EU level. Involving the social partners in these schemes allowed the Member States to support flexible working arrangements (especially with regard to short time working), equip people with skills and incentives to progress in their working lives, and facilitate transitions in employment. All these efforts prevented substantial falls in the incomes of those worst affected by the crisis.[52] The OECD estimates that the various financial support schemes provided at world level have saved between 3.2 and 5.5 million jobs, with the EU accounting for over half of those.[53] In the field of business support, the measures adopted by the Member States facilitated access to finance at EU level, without resulting in protectionist tendencies. However, restoring credit flows to the corporate sector is a *conditio sine qua non* for the recovery to take hold.[54] As for the infrastructure and the "greening" of the economy, there have been variations of performance, given that, despite isolated successful measures for energy efficiency, a lack of provision of strong incentives in various Member States was noted. This is not surprising as the impact of public investment in infrastructure will be felt only in the long term and does not have immediate results. The comforting aspect is that many existing projects have been accelerated and a rapid absorption of funds

---

[50] European Economic and Social Committee, *Opinion on the European Economic Recovery Plan, COM (2008) 800, final*, Doc ECO/244 – CESE 50/2009, January 2009, 6, European Parliament, *Resolution of 11 March 2009 on a European Economic Recovery Plan*, Doc P6_TA(2009)0123, para 42.

[51] For a detailed overview of these measures, see European Commission, *Progress on the Implementation of the European Economic Recovery Plan*, June 2009, 4-9.

[52] European Commission, *Progress report on the Implementation of the European Economic Recovery Plan*, December 2009, 6.

[53] OECD *Economic Outlook*, No 85, OECD Paris, 2009.

[54] European Commission, *Progress report on the Implementation of the European Economic Recovery Plan*, December 2009, 9.

was realised.[55] With regard to innovation and research, the overall effort focused on supporting private spending on innovation, while the main concern is to make R&D spending a catalyst for an accelerated post-crisis recovery, within the framework of continuing the implementation of the European Research Area.[56]

In order to achieve these results, the EU made significant advance payments from the Structural Funds, allowing more money to be spent rapidly on priority projects. Total advance payments of 11.25 billion euros have been approved for 2009, including 5 billion euros of advance payments already foreseen for 2009, plus a further 6.25 billion euros as a crisis response measure. Of this total, ESF advances for 2009 amount to approximately 2.4 billion euros.[57]

The European Parliament and the European Council agreed to fund major energy and broadband infrastructure projects amounting to a total of 5 billion euros (4 billion for energy and 1 billion to help rural areas get broadband internet access, create new jobs and help businesses to grow). In that respect, it was suggested that promoting EU investments in sustainable development had to be a pivotal element of the budgetary review, not only in terms of the budgetary proceedings but also in terms of budgetary aims.[58] Disappointingly, however, only around 35% of the available funding is currently devoted to high-speed internet investments.[59] This is attributed partly to the lack of agreement within the Council (despite the consensus achieved at the European Council) and partly to long negotiations between the Commission and the Member States, regarding the possibility of the EU budget to support such projects, and such delays must be countered with an increased margin of maneuver with regard to unspent money, in order to facilitate the possibility of reallocating resources that are not used timely and effectively.[60]

---

[55] European Commission, *Progress report on the Implementation of the European Economic Recovery Plan*, December 2009, 10.

[56] European Commission, *Progress report on the Implementation of the European Economic Recovery Plan*, December 2009, 11.

[57] European Commission, *Progress report on the Implementation of the European Economic Recovery Plan*, December 2009, 12.

[58] European Parliament, *Resolution of 11 March 2009 on a European Economic Recovery Plan*, Doc P6_TA(2009)0123, para 75.

[59] European Commission, *Progress report on the Implementation of the European Economic Recovery Plan*, December 2009, 13.

[60] Committee of the Regions, *Opinion on the European Economic Recovery Plan and the role of Local and Regional Authorities*, Doc CdR 12/2009 fin, April 2009, 4, European Parliament, *Resolution of 11 March 2009 on a European Economic Recovery Plan*, Doc P6_TA(2009)0123, para 83.

In total, the European Economic Recovery Plan, and especially its budgetary aspects, has been deemed as too vaguely formulated, thus necessitating the submission, on behalf of the Commission, of additional evidence to the Budgetary Authority, in order to decide on the financing of an activity through the EU budget, and causing dangerous delays in the Plan's implementation.[61] However, this crisis provided the opportunity to the EU institutions of seeking methods to optimise the procedural aspects of their budgetary functions and especially the proceedings of administering the Structural Funds, at national and European level. The proposal and adoption of additional flexibilities within the Funds' regulations, the accelerated procedures of approving and financing investments, the careful use of derogations in financial and budgetary rules that did not allow for the offsetting of the relevant mechanisms, the coordination of the required multi-layered action in order to involve all necessary actors, taking into account the principle of subsidiarity, all these created a very interesting and useful experience that can be part of the basis for reassessing the European Budget, in terms of size, structure and procedures.[62]

Conclusion

The global financial crisis has provided the impetus for a much needed re-appraisal of the budgetary architecture of the EU. The speedy amendment of the relevant legislative provisions, as well as the establishment of new financial schemes within the EU Cohesion Policy and Lisbon Strategy frameworks, demonstrated that there is potential for change in the EU. The implementation of the new schemes, despite its teething problems, looks promising.

Before the crisis, it seemed that the Union could not decide whether it wanted a budget that redistributes money from one set of Member States to another or a budget that supports financially the implementation of certain EU-wide policies. Now there is an increased demand for budgetary efficiency.

This efficiency entails, inter alia, the timely and flexible allocation of resources in order to ensure the appropriate provision of the main public

---

[61] European Parliament, *Resolution of 11 March 2009 on a European Economic Recovery Plan*, Doc P6_TA(2009)0123, paras 76-77.

[62] Committee of the Regions, *Opinion on the European Economic Recovery Plan and the role of Local and Regional Authorities*, Doc CdR 12/2009 fin, April 2009, 4-6, European Parliament, *Resolution of 11 March 2009 on a European Economic Recovery Plan*, Doc P6_TA(2009)0123, paras 79-89.

goods required. The response to the crisis is an indication of such efficiency, at least with regard to the procedural aspects of the relevant effort. In terms of substance, however, it remains to be seen if the lessons learned from this process will be useful in the future attempts of the Union to set new financial perspectives and mechanisms of economic governance.

References

English

Begg, Iain, and Friedrich Heinemann. "New Budget, Old Dilemmas." Centre for European Reform, Briefing Note, February 22, 2006.

Begg, Iain. "The 2008/9 EU Budget Review." EU-CONSENT, EU-Budget Working Paper No 3, March 2007.

Bernanke, Ben S. "Four Questions about the financial crisis." Speech given on Morehouse College, Atlanta, Georgia, April 14, 2009. Accessed May 1, 2010. http://www.federalreserve.gov/newsevents/speech/bernanke20090414a.htm.

Boeri, Tito, and Herbert Brücker. "The Impact of Eastern Enlargement on Employment and Labour Markets in the EU Member States." European Integration Consortium (DIW, CEPR, FIEF, IAS, IGIER), 2000.

Buck, A. E. *Public Budgeting: A Discussion of Budgetary Practice in the National, State, and Local Governments of the United States.* New York: Harper & Bros, 1929.

Chalmers, Damian, and Adam Tomkins. *European Union Public Law: Text and Materials*, Cambridge: Cambridge University Press, 2007.

Committee of the Regions. "Opinion on the European Economic Recovery Plan and the role of Local and Regional Authorities." Doc CdR 12/2009 fin, April 2009.

European Central Bank. "Reinforcing Economic Governance in the Euro Area." 10 June 2010.

European Commission. "A European Economic Recovery Plan." COM (2008) 800 final, Brussels, November 26, 2008.

—. "Cohesion Policy: Investing in the real economy." COM (2008) 876/3 final, Brussels, December 16, 2008.

—. EU Economy – 2009 Review, "Economic Crisis in Europe: Causes, Consequences and Responses." Brussels, 2009.

—. Report "Growth, Jobs and Social Progress in the EU - A Contribution to the Evaluation of the Social Dimension of the Lisbon Strategy." Brussels, September 2009.

—. "From financial crisis to recovery: a European framework for action." COM (2008), 706 final, October 29, 2008.

—. "Member States and Regions delivering the Lisbon strategy for growth and jobs through EU cohesion policy, 2007-2013." COM (2007) 798 final, Brussels, December 11, 2007.

—. "Progress on the Implementation of the European Economic Recovery Plan." Brussels, June 2009.

—. "Progress report on the Implementation of the European Economic Recovery Plan." Brussels, December 2009.

—. "Reform of the Structural Funds: 1) Commission Communication, 2) Comprehensive Proposal pursuant to Art. 130d of the EEC Treaty." COM (87) 376 final/2, Brussels, August 24, 1987.

—. "Reinforcing economic policy coordination." COM (2010) 250 final, Brussels, May 12, 2010.

—. "The EIB, the other financial instruments, and strengthening economic and social cohesion." COM (88) 244 final, Brussels, December 23, 1988.

—. "Vade Mecum on the Reform of the European Community's Structural Funds." Brussels, 1989.

European Council. "Economic and Financial Affairs." Press Release, 13161/10 (Presse 229), Brussels, September 7, 2010.

—. "Extraordinary Council Meeting. Economic and Financial Affairs, Brussels." Press Release, 9596/10 (Presse 108), May 9/10, 2010.

—. "Presidency Conclusions." Brussels, December 15-16, 2005.

—. "Presidency Conclusions." Brussels, December 11-12, 2008.

—. "Presidency Conclusions." Brussels, September 16, 2010. EUCO 21/10.

—. "Presidency Conclusions." Brussels, March 25, 2011. EUCO 10/11.

European Economic and Social Committee. "Opinion on the European Economic Recovery Plan. COM (2008) 800 final", Doc ECO/244 – CESE 50/2009, January 2009.

Evans, Andrew. *The EU Structural Funds*. Oxford: Oxford University Press, 1998.

Ferreiro, Jesus, Giuseppe Fontana and Felipe Serrano, eds. *Fiscal Policy in the European Union*. Basingstoke: Palgrave-Macmillan, 2008.

Friedman, Milton. *Capitalism and Freedom*. Chicago: Chicago University Press - 40th Anniversary Edition, 2002.

Gray, Andrew, Bill Jenkins and Bob Segsworth, eds. "Perspectives on Budgeting, Auditing and Evaluation: An Introduction." in *Budgeting, Auditing and Evaluation: Functions & Integration in Seven Governments*, edited by Andrew Gray, Bill Jenkins and Bob Segsworth, New Brunswick: Transaction Publishers, 1993.

Heads of State and Government of the Euro Area, "Statement 25 March 2010." Brussels.

Independent High Level Group. *An Agenda for a growing Europe – Making the EU Economic System Deliver: The Sapir Report*. Oxford: Oxford University Press, 2004.

Keynes, John Maynard. *The General Theory of Employment, Interest and Money*. New York: Harcourt, Brace & World, 1936.

Krugman, Paul. *The Return of Depression Economics and the Crisis of 2008*. New York: Norton, 2009.

Lee, Robert D. Jr., Johnson, Ronald D. and Joyce, Philip G., eds., *Public Budgeting Systems*, Burlington: Jones & Bartlett Learning, 1973.

McCaffery, Jerry L. "Features of the Budgetary Process." in *Handbook of Government Budgeting*, edited by Roy T. Meyers, pages 3-29. Hoboken: Jossey-Bass Publishers, 1999.

Merrouche, Ouarda and Erlend Nier. "What Caused the Global Financial Crisis?—Evidence on the Drivers of Financial Imbalances 1999–2007." IMF Working Paper, WP/10/265, December 2010.

Mrak, Mojmir, and Vasja Rant. "Financial Perspectives 2007-2013: Domination of national interests." EU-CONSENT, EU-Budget Working Paper No 1, July 2007.

OECD. "Economic Outlook No 85." Paris, 2009.

Rubio, Eulalia. "EU Budget Review: Addressing the Thorny Issues." Policy Paper no 32, Notre Europe, 2008.

Skiadas, Dimitrios V. *Reforming the European Budget: An Ongoing Tale*, Karamanlis Working Paper No 5 in Hellenic and European Studies, May 2008, The Constantine Karamanlis Chair in Hellenic and Southeastern European Studies, The Fletcher School of Law and Diplomacy, Tufts University, May 2008

Szemler, Tamás. "EU Budget Milestones: From Fundamental Systemic Reforms to Organised Chaos." Paper presented at the EU-CONSENT Conference, Budapest, March 24, 2006.

Task Force of the European Council. Report on "Strengthening the Economic Governance in the EU." October 21, 2010.

Wildavsky, Aaron B. *The Politics of the Budgetary Process*, New York: Little, Brown, 1964.

Wooldridge, F., and M. Sassela. "Some recent legal provisions increasing the budgetary powers of the European Parliament, and establishing a European Court of Auditors." *Legal Issues of European Integration* 2 (1976): 13-52.

Greek

Θεοχαρόπουλος, Λουκάς. *Δίκαιον κρατικού προϋπολογισμού, Τόμος Α*. Θεσσαλονίκη: αυτοέκδοση, 1976

Κόρσος, Δημήτριος Ι. *Δημοσιονομικόν δίκαιον, Τόμος Α: Εισαγωγικαί έννοιαι, Πηγαί του δημοσιονομικού δικαίου, Δημόσιον λογιστικόν*. Αθήνα: Αντ. Ν. Σάκκουλας, 1980

Μπάρμπας, Νικόλαος *Στοιχεία δημοσιονομικού δικαίου*. Αθήνα: Σάκκουλα, 2002.

Σκιαδάς, Δημήτριος. "Οι δημοσιονομικές διατάξεις της Συνθήκης της Λισσαβόνας", *Ελληνική Επιθεώρηση Ευρωπαϊκού Δικαίου*, τόμος 30, τεύχος 3/2010, Ιούλιος - Σεπτέμβριος 2010, 325-344.

Στασινόπουλος, Μιχαήλ. *Μαθήματα Δημοσιονομικού Δικαίου*. Αθήνα: Σάκκουλας, 1966

PART 2:

THE GREEK SOVEREIGN DEBT CRISIS

CHAPTER FOUR

NOT BUSINESS AS USUAL

VASILEIOS A. VLACHOS[1]

1. Introduction

Greece has been a member of the European Union (EU) since 1981 and member of the Economic and Monetary Union (EMU) of the EU since June 2000 (officially from 1.1.2001). Greece's fulfilment of the convergence criteria for entering the euro-area has been the result of the fiscal and monetary policies pursued since the mid-1990s. These policies were seen as the foundation of macroeconomic stability that fostered an improved environment for investment and faster output growth, which peaked a year before the outbreak of the global financial crisis.[2]

The Greek labour force totaled approximately 5 million in 2010 and Greece comes second after Austria in the euro-area ranking of full-time employment working hours.[3] The annual gross domestic product (GDP) of the Greek economy expanded at an average annual rate of almost 4% in the time period 2004-2008 – one of the highest rates in the euro-area, since its formation. However, due to global recession and the Greek sovereign debt crisis, GDP (in purchasing power standards – PPS) decreased – approximately – in 2009 by 4%, in 2010 by 1% and in 2011 by 6% (see *Table 2*).

After the introduction of the euro in 2002, the Greek economy grew successively and displayed the highest GDP growth (in PPS) in 2006 (7.5%). The peak of 2006 was explained at that time by "financial market

---

[1] I would like to thank Ioannis Papadopoulos for his useful comments.

[2] For an overview of the economic performance of Greece in the late 20th century and the consecutive steps that led to the adoption of the euro see Bryant et al. (2001).

[3] Henceforth, all indicators – if not referring to a Table – are from Eurostat statistics database (http://epp.eurostat.ec.europa.eu/portal/page/portal/statistics/search_database), unless otherwise stated.

liberalization coupled with membership in monetary union, which led to a substantial reduction in borrowing costs; buoyant activity in export markets in South-East Europe (SEE); and the fiscal stimulus and focal point given by the Olympic games in 2004" (OECD[4], 2007: 11).

Recent evidence indicates that the growth of the Greek economy until the eruption of the global financial crisis has been the outcome of internal demand that was fostered by institutions other than those resulting from economic reforms (which of course would enhance directly Greece's level of competitiveness).[5] Greece suffers from high levels of political and economic corruption and low global competitiveness compared to other EU, and especially EMU, member states. By the end of 2009 and in the beginning of 2010, as a result of the global crisis[6] and uncontrolled government spending, economic scandals, huge black economy rates, high corruption and large numbers of bureaucratic procedures, the Greek economy faced its most severe crisis since 1974 as the Greek government revised its deficit from an estimated 6% to 15.4% of GDP in 2009.[7] Eventually, a joint European Commission (EC)/International Monetary Fund (IMF)/European Central Bank (ECB) rescue mission replied in mid-2010 to Greece's request for international financial assistance and

---

[4] Organisation for Economic Co-operation and Development.

[5] Recent evaluations indicate that Greece's highly politicized system managed to mislead both Eurostat and the bond markets despite the fact that the issues regarding the validity of statistics were outlined as early as 2004 (Sturgess, 2010).

[6] Henceforth, "crisis" in its global context, refers to the financial crisis that was triggered in the summer of 2007 and gradually developed into a global economic crisis without precedent in post-war economic history. This economic crisis has now become a sovereign debt crisis.

[7] The Greek sovereign debt crisis has stimulated a worldwide discussion on the deficiencies responsible for the Greek economic performance. The need for sustained fiscal consolidation and the issues of productivity and competitiveness have been acknowledged – at least officially – since 2003 (see Featherstone, 2003; Albers et al., 2004; OECD, 2005). Since the eruption of the crisis, a bibliography has been developed that covers several subjects. Only to name a few:

(a) For the paradox of strong growth with weak institutions see Mitsopoulos and Pelagidis (2009a; 2009b; 2010).
(b) For the inefficiency of government spending due to interest groups that compete with each other for fiscal privileges at the expense of the general public interest, see Angelopoulos et al. (2010), Katsimi and Moutos (2010) and Lyrintzis (2011) – however, such inefficiencies are also observed in the euro-area (Angelopoulos et al., 2011).
(c) For the path that Greece followed from euro-area accession to the crisis see Lynn (2011) and Manolopoulos (2011).
(d) For a collective work on the Greek crisis see Botsiou and Klapsis (2011).

concluded on a joint euro-area/IMF financing package that had to be accompanied by accommodating economic policies – i.e. liberalization of product and labour markets, fiscal consolidation and internal devaluation (see DG ECFIN[8], 2010d).

However, the success of this endeavour was not guaranteed and several reviews of the economic adjustment programme followed with the ultimate aim of constituting the level of Greek sovereign debt sustainable. The review put forward by the joint mission in February 2011 announced that without additional measures the fiscal target for 2011 would be missed, and that a reinvigorated economic adjustment programme with scaled up financing assistance over an extended time period would be necessary (DG ECFIN, 2011b: 1-4). A medium-term fiscal strategy that was prepared to ensure the durability of fiscal consolidation was approved by the Greek parliament in the summer of 2011. However, the instability of the economic environment due to the:

(a) rapid escalation and contagion/transmission of the sovereign debt crisis, and
(b) unprojected fiscal gap and contraction of the Greek economy,

has led to the approvals of adjusted versions of the same strategy in October 2011 (see DG ECFIN, 2011c) – as well as in 2012. Moreover, private sector involvement in Greek debt restructuring was deemed necessary for the sustainability of Greek sovereign debt and the agreement was concluded in March 2012. With the achievement of the particular agreement, the precondition for the second bailout of the joint EC/IMF/ECB rescue mission was met. Moreover, the stable progress of the coalition government – that formed after the election took place in mid-2012 – toward the fulfilment of the targets set by the economic adjustment programme secured the imbursement of the first bailout installment by the end of that year. Nevertheless, the continuity and fulfilment – in terms of targets – of the second bailout are still in question. Although the politically unstable period calmed down after the summer of 2012, political stability is not secured due to successive political and economic scandals. Moreover, the coalition government – which promised to renegotiate for a bailout repayment extension and, if possible, the orientation set by the economic adjustment programme – has put forward several measures that will further deepen the depression and sustain the deflationary spiral.

---

[8] Directorate-General for Economic and Financial Affairs of the European Commission

This chapter aims to achieve a coherent presentation of the literature on the development of the financial predicament and its climax into a sovereign debt crisis, and the effect of the latter on the business environment of the Greek economy. Greece experiences a sustained, long-term downturn in economic activity – more severe than a recession – which is not a part of the country's business cycle. The Greek economy currently faces three interlocked – banking, sovereign debt, and growth – crises that fuel a deflationary spiral: undercapitalized banks facing liquidity problems are financed through government debt expansion, which in turn is contained through tax increases, and fiscal austerity that contract output, disposable income and domestic demand, which in turn reduce tax receipts and leads to government deficits that require for further debt expansion and fiscal austerity measures and hence, the vicious downward spiral continues.

This chapter is organized as follows. Each of the first four sections presents a general discussion of "the rise of the crisis and its effects" – with several references to the Greek case – and acts as a prerequisite of the fifth section "the path to recovery". The second section depicts how the financial crisis has developed to a sovereign debt crisis and what was/is the impact and the role/necessity of the Stability and Growth Pact (SGP). The third section discusses the imbalances in the euro-area and the development of the main figures of the Greek balance of payments. The requirement for readjusting these imbalances and the appropriateness of fiscal consolidation – in terms of fiscal austerity – are also discussed. The fourth section discusses the arguments within the EU about the path to recovery. The fifth section analyzes the Greek business environment and concentrates on issues such as competitiveness, openness and direct investment, both domestic and foreign. The sixth section discusses the levels of Greek unemployment and their effect on the business environment. The seventh section discusses the plans for Greece's prolonged recovery. The eighth and final section concludes on the issues discussed.

2. The Global Crisis

The recent global economic contraction originated in a financial crisis that had repercussions for the real economy,[9] and was rapidly transmitted

[9] For a discussion on the causes leading to the financial collapse and the repercussions to the real economy see Posner (2010). The effects of financial market developments to the real economy have been also pinpointed by the United

from the United States (US) to the rest of the world.[10] The recent global recession has reduced the volumes of world trade with reference to 2008 – it took until 2011 for international trade to overcome the values of 2008 (see *Table 1*). In addition, a longer-term negative shock has been fostered by trade uncertainty,[11] the loss of confidence,[12] and the rapid awareness of neglected but persisting global imbalances.[13]

Nations: "Blind faith in the efficiency of deregulated financial markets and the absence of a cooperative financial and monetary system created an illusion of risk-free profits and licensed profligacy through speculative finance in many areas" (United Nations Conference on Trade and Development – UNCTAD, 2009: iii). Although the liberalization of private capital flows had been expected to increase the rate of fixed investment, the latter stagnated in most parts of the world, despite a significantly higher level of international financial flows (United Nations, 2010: 103).

[10] The European sovereign debt crisis followed the US financial crisis with a delay of one and a half years (European Economic Advisory Group at CESifo, 2011: 71).

[11] The uncertainty about the smooth functioning of the channels of future international trade can have an independent, and additional, adverse effect on the real economy (see Van Bergeijk, 2009).

[12] This is the notion of the confidence multiplier (see Akerlof and Shiller, 2009), which is unusually buoyant in the boom years. On the contrary, in deep recessions, when the confidence is low, the expansionary impact of the usual fiscal and monetary stimuli is sluggish.

[13] The persistence of global imbalances has not only consequences for international competitiveness, but also for debt servicing flows. For a definition of global imbalances see, inter alia, the threefold definition of Bracke et al. (2010), who refer to:

a) external positions (current account and financial positions);
b) systemically important economies (both deficit and surplus side);
c) distortions, and
d) risks, for distinguishing between imbalanced and balanced positions.

A number of studies (e.g. Dunaway, 2009; Freund, 2009; Blanchard and Milesi-Ferretti, 2010) argue that trade policy should become a substitute for, or applied in conjunction with the traditional instruments of stabilisation – fiscal/monetary – policy (given the constraints placed on the latter instruments because of the liquidity trap and the burgeoning debt following the financial crisis). The importance of imbalances on future economic policy also appears in a study by DG ECFIN, which indicates that the build-up of external imbalances in the EU and the euro-area during the decade before the eruption of the financial crisis could have acted as a signal of contingent budgetary risks (Barrios et al., 2010a).

Table 1 – The impact of the crisis: GDP, FDI and international trade (US$ billions at current prices).

Region-Indicator/Year		2005	2008		2009		2010		2011	
World	GDP	45,744.8	61,232.8	9,6%	57,960.1	-5,3%	63,064.0	8,8%	-	-
	Outward FDI stock	12,416.0	15,987.9	-16,2%	19,197.2	20,1%	20,408.3	6,3%	-	-
	Inward FDI stock	11,539.5	15,294.7	-14,3%	17,950.5	17,4%	19,140.6	6,6%	-	-
	Merchandise exports	10,502.1	16,124.2	15,1%	12,526.3	-22,3%	15,255.9	21,8%	18,197.1	19,3%
	Merchantise imports	10,795.1	16,462.3	15,5%	12,667.3	-23,1%	15,381.4	21,4%	18,277.0	18,8%
	Services exports	2,555.2	3,904.6	12,3%	3,476.9	-10,9%	3,819.4	9,8%	4,224.4	10,6%
	Services imports	2448.9	3698.8	14,0%	3304.8	-10,6%	3620.2	9,5%	3974.1	9,8%
Developed Economies	GDP	33,800.8	41,313.9	6,0%	38,861.4	-5,9%	40,417.1	4,0%	-	-
	Outward FDI stock	10,982.9	13,414.1	-17,7%	16,171.4	20,6%	16,803.5	3,9%	-	-
	Inward FDI stock	8,563.0	10,616.2	-16,6%	12,263.7	15,5%	12,501.6	1,9%	-	-
	Merchandise exports	6,335.2	9,093.8	11,3%	7,056.4	-22,4%	8,221.1	16,5%	9,558.7	16,3%
	Merchantise imports	7,103.7	10,105.3	11,6%	7,594.1	-24,8%	8,878.3	16,9%	10,373.2	16,8%
	Services exports	1,868.8	2,755.5	10,6%	2,442.4	-11,4%	2,583.6	5,8%	2,835.9	9,8%
	Services imports	1,682.2	2,381.0	11,2%	2,110.5	-11,4%	2,204.5	4,5%	2,361.4	7,1%
Developing Economies	GDP	10,846.2	17,577.2	16,6%	17,311.6	-1,6%	20,530.3	18,6%	-	-
	Outward FDI stock	1,281.1	2,342.7	-1,7%	2,688.1	14,7%	3,131.8	16,5%	-	-
	Inward FDI stock	2,701.0	4,251.7	-4,3%	5,060.1	19,0%	5,951.2	17,6%	-	-
	Merchandise exports	3,803.8	6,290.8	19,1%	4,991.0	-20,7%	6,417.0	28,6%	7,814.8	21,8%
	Merchantise imports	3,419.5	5,746.0	21,5%	4,663.3	-18,8%	6,012.6	28,9%	7,265.9	20,8%
	Services exports	629.3	1,036.3	15,6%	940.5	-9,2%	1,133.5	20,5%	1,267.1	11,8%
	Services imports	698.6	1,186.9	18,9%	1,087.4	-8,4%	1,292.0	18,8%	1,464.4	13,3%
Euro-area	Outward FDI stock	4,237.3	5,812.8	-8,3%	6,779.2	16,6%	6,634.2	-2,1%	-	-
	Inward FDI stock	3,323.4	4,574.8	-13,7%	5,197.7	13,6%	4,759.1	-8,4%	-	-
	Merchandise exports	3,176.9	4,613.1	10,1%	3,589.8	-22,2%	4,002.4	11,5%	4,663.8	16,5%
	Merchantise imports	3,103.4	4,635.0	12,4%	3,515.6	-24,1%	3,958.2	12,6%	4,609.3	16,4%
	Services exports	848.5	1,266.3	12,2%	1,112.9	-12,1%	1,147.2	3,1%	1,253.9	9,3%
	Services imports	793.7	1,148.9	12,5%	1,020.2	-11,2%	1,041.4	2,1%	1,117.5	7,3%

Source: UNCTAD (http://unctadstat.unctad.org/ReportFolders/reportFolders.aspx, as accessed 10 July 2012).
* Annual change (percentage of previous year) in right-hand column.
\- Not available.

2.1 The Roots of the Crisis

Although the causes of the crisis vary across countries (Rose and Spiegel, 2011) there is a consensus that the main contributing factors to the global financial and subsequent economic (and in some cases sovereign debt) crisis are (Swinburne, 2010):

(a) global imbalances,
(b) regulatory governance, and

(c) monetary policy.

With regard to global imbalances a number of studies regard that they were not causally related to the initiation of the crisis and instead, hold responsible the adoption of:

(a) expansionary monetary – and fiscal – policy (Bibow, 2008; Taylor, 2009), and
(b) institutions such as financial regulations and supervision, and the situation of moral hazard (Whelan, 2010).

Nevertheless, there are studies arguing that global imbalances were the leading cause of the crisis (Portes, 2009). For example, global imbalances relaxed the US credit constraint and perpetuated low US real interest rates, which in turn, stoked borrowing and the housing bubble (Sibert, 2010). The main determinants of the crisis when studies regard that it is mainly influenced and sustained by global imbalances are:

(a) the low cost of financing (for the particular see Feldstein, 2008; Swinburne, 2010),
(b) Asia's export-led growth strategy[14]
(c) the reserve build-up, and
(d) the exchange rate policies (for "b, c, d" see Bilbow, 2008; Obstfeld and Rogoff, 2009; Swinburne, 2010).

However, a survey of the academic and policy debate on the roots of global imbalances, their role in the inception of the global crisis, and their prospects in its aftermath, builds up to the conclusion that global imbalances were not among the major causes of the crisis (Serven and Nguyen, 2010). In support of this argument is also the observation that trade and current account deficits are due to the fact that capital is flowing from countries with low levels of investment and growth to countries experiencing fast-growth (Backus et al., 2009).[15]

2.2 An Overview to the Effects of the Crisis

The most important consequence of the banking crisis was its transmission to all sectors of the economy domestically, and its transnational

[14] The renowned Asian "savings glut" (Adams and Park, 2009).

[15] This observation is against the notion that the causa causans of the crisis is identified in the lack of profitable investment opportunities in advanced capitalist systems (for this notion see Ietto-Gillies, 2010).

contagion effects.[16] Although the interactions of the financial crisis with the real economy led to a short-term recession – except for Greece where continuous recession developed into depression – the fears for an immense global slow-down, or even worst, a return to negative growth rates are not yet overcome. The reasons behind these fears are simple: What will replace the shrinkage of credit consumption and what is considered to be a "risk-free" investment?

The direct fiscal costs of the financial crisis – i.e. the budgetary rescue measures for supporting the financial system – contributed to:

(a) fiscal unsustainability that was caused by the reduction of government revenue – which in turn was caused by the eruption of the asset bubble that contracted economic activity – and
(b) the expansion of government expenditure that was adopted as a remedy for the worldwide recession that started in 2008 and lasted in most advanced economies until the end of 2009.

Table 1 presents four major indicators that capture the effects of the global crisis. Although the contraction on the levels of GDP and international trade at a global level occurred in 2009, foreign direct investment (FDI) stocks decreased in 2008 and returned on the growth path in 2009. Contraction in GDP occurred in 2009 at a global level, after the termination of a rising trend in 2008. International trade flows have started to grow again since the second quarter of 2010 (see UNCTAD statistics) with merchandise trade both increasing and decreasing at a greater extent than services.

Similar to the global trends are the fluctuations of GDP growth of both developed (approximately two thirds of world GDP) and developing (less than one third of world GDP) economies – which increase at a greater extent than the former. Moreover, the global trends are similar to those of the euro-area (more than one fourth of world GDP) – and the EU (less than one third of world GDP) – only as far as international trade flows are concerned. Due to specificities arising by the sovereign debt crisis, the euro-area indicates contraction both in inward and outward FDI in 2010. The picture for FDI flows at a global level is different from that of international trade flows, as contraction in both inward and outward FDI

[16] The combination of all three elements of a systemic crisis – increased levels of risk and government debt, and bank liabilities – raised real and nominal interest rates and consequently depressed investment and lowered the productive capacity of economies (Cecchetti et al., 2009).

Table 2 – EU, euro-area, Greece: National accounts and unemployment (€ billions at current prices).

Region	Indicator/Year	2001		2004		2008		2009		2010		2011	
EU	GDP (billions of PPS)	8,625.3	4.0%	10,388.0	14.9%	12,476.0	0.6%	11,751.5	-5.8%	12,263.8	4.4%	12,638.0	3.1%
	Domestic demand (percentage of GDP in billions of PPS)	99.0	-	98.7	-	99.8	-	99.0	-	99.1	-	98.9	-
	General government revenue (percentage of GDP)	45.0	-	44.0	-	44.7	-	44.2	-	44.1	-	44.6	-
	General government expenditure (percentage of GDP)	46.3	-	46.9	-	47.1	-	51.1	-	50.6	-	49.1	-
	General government expenditure: Compensation of employees (percentage of GDP)	10.6	-	10.8	-	10.6	-	11.3	-	11.1	-	10.8	-
	General government expenditure: Gross fixed capital formation (percentage of GDP)	2.3	-	2.4	-	2.7	-	2.9	-	2.7	-	2.5	-
	General government expenditure: Subsidies (percentage of GDP)	1.3	-	1.2	-	1.1	-	1.3	-	1.3	-	1.2	-
	Unemployment rate	7.3	-	9.3	-	7.1	-	9.0	-	9.7	-	9.7	-
Euroa-area	GDP (billions of PPS)	6,877.7	6.8%	7,466.1	4.1%	8,839.9	0.8%	8,411.0	-4.9%	8,733.6	3.8%	9,019.9	3.3%
	Domestic demand (percentage of GDP in billions of PPS)	98.6	-	97.9	-	99.0	-	98.7	-	98.7	-	98.6	-
	General government revenue (percentage of GDP)	45.3	-	44.6	-	45.4	-	44.8	-	44.7	-	45.3	-
	General government expenditure (percentage of GDP)	47.2	-	47.5	-	47.2	-	51.2	-	51.0	-	49.4	-
	General government expenditure: Compensation of employees (percentage of GDP)	10.4	-	10.5	-	10.3	-	11.0	-	10.8	-	10.6	-
	General government expenditure: Gross fixed capital formation (percentage of GDP)	2.5	-	2.5	-	2.6	-	2.8	-	2.5	-	2.3	-
	General government expenditure: Subsidies (percentage of GDP)	1.4	-	1.3	-	1.2	-	1.4	-	1.4	-	1.3	-
	Unemployment rate	7.9	-	9.2	-	7.6	-	9.6	-	10.1	-	10.2	-
Greece	GDP (billions of PPS)	187.3	7.2%	224.4	6.1%	259.8	3.2%	249.9	-3.8%	247.6	-0.9%	233.7	-5.6%
	Domestic demand (percentage of GDP in billions of PPS)	113.2	-	110.1	-	114.4	-	111.4	-	108.9	-	107.5	-
	General government revenue (percentage of GDP)	40.9	-	38.1	-	40.8	-	38.2	-	39.7	-	40.9	-
	General government expenditure (percentage of GDP)	45.3	-	45.5	-	50.6	-	53.8	-	50.2	-	50.1	-
	General government expenditure: Compensation of employees (percentage of GDP)	10.4	-	11.5	-	10.3	-	11.0	-	10.8	-	10.6	-
	General government expenditure: Gross fixed capital formation (percentage of GDP)	3.6	-	3.5	-	3.7	-	3.1	-	2.2	-	1.6	-
	General government expenditure: Subsidies (percentage of GDP)	0.1	-	0.1	-	0.0	-	0.1	-	0.1	-	0.1	-
	Unemployment rate	10.7	-	10.5	-	7.7	-	9.5	-	12.6	-	17.7	-
	Unemployment rate: Extra-EU nationals	11.1	-	-	-	6.6	-	10.3	-	15.4	-	22.3	-
	Unemployment rate: EU nationals except Greeks	-	-	-	-	7.4	-	11.6	-	12.9	-	13.3	-
	Unemployment rate: Greeks	10.6	-	10.4	-	7.9	-	9.5	-	12.5	-	17.6	-

Source: Eurostat

Notes to Table 2:
(http://epp.eurostat.ec.europa.eu/portal/page/portal/statistics/search_database, as accessed 10 July 2012).
* Annual change (percentage of previous year) in right-hand column.
** EU(15) for 2001, EU(25) for 2004, EU(27) for 2008-2011
- Not available.

stock takes place in 2008. In 2009 both forms of FDI stock recover and reach previously unmet levels in 2010.

With regard to the EU and the euro-area (see *Table 2*), GDP is also back on the growth track from 2010 – except for Greece (and Portugal in 2011) – however, expectations for 2012 are mixed as there are fears for a "double dip". Although the optimistic scenario of "full recovery" in the euro-area (see DG ECFIN, 2009b) was initially regarded as a not too distant goal – since GDP growth continued in 2011 despite the escalation of the sovereign debt crisis – the negative impact of fiscal austerity holds back expectations for recovery. Moreover, there is a growing consensus that recovery requires measures to strengthen solidarity and boost sustainable growth and employment.

2.3 The Build up to the Greek Sovereign Debt Crisis

It is argued ex post facto that the sequence of events of the global crisis – i.e. what started as a financial crisis, developed into an economic crisis (the recent recession), and transformed into a sovereign debt crisis – should have been anticipated.[17] Private debt surges are a recurring antecedent to banking crises, which often precede or accompany sovereign debt crises. In addition, public borrowing accelerates before the materialization of a sovereign debt crisis, as governments often have

[17] There are several instruments/indicators that can act as warning signals. For example, the financial crisis could/should have been predicted, as the measures of global liquidity are considered reliable enough to perform as early warning indicators of costly asset price booms (Alessi and Detken, 2009). Furthermore, a very interesting observation concerning the repercussions of the financial crisis is that the set of policies that favor liberalization in credit markets are negatively correlated with countries' resilience to the global recession of 2009 (Giannone et al., 2010). Finally, early warning signals for excess government debt are the trend of the debt burden (interest payments/GDP) and the marginal product of government deficits vis a vis the interest rate of sovereign debt payments (Stein, 2011).

"hidden debts" that exceed the documented levels of external debt (Reinhart and Rogoff, 2011).[18]

It is generally observed that the current problems of fiscal unsustainability in most advanced economies have four common roots (Buiter and Rabari, 2010):

(a) The pro-cyclical behavior of the fiscal authorities during boom and recession periods.
(b) The end of asset booms and bubbles and the normalization/"sheer drop" of profits and pay in the financial sector are likely to produce a lasting reduction in the generation of funds.
(c) The direct fiscal costs of the financial crisis – the bailouts and other budgetary rescue measures – directed at propping up the financial system.
(d) The worldwide recession that started in 2008 and lasted in most of the advanced industrial countries until the end of 2009.

In relation to the above, the discussion should turn to fiscal and monetary policy orientations within the euro-area in order to determine their influence on the build up to the Greek sovereign debt crisis. For example, there are studies suggesting that tax policies have been contributing substantially to the volatility of business cycles. Given that discretionary measures can significantly affect tax elasticities, they can also alter the relationship between tax revenues and the business cycle, which in turn plays a key role in the EU fiscal surveillance framework. Discretionary measures affecting tax revenues were often pro-cyclical in the EU from 2000 until the crisis.[19]

A part of the literature suggests that EMU contributed substantially to the economic divergences which have aggravated the impact of the financial crisis in Southern Europe (Matthes, 2009). Aggregate demand in euro-area countries is significantly affected by the euro-area real interest rate, but not by national real-interest-rate differentials (Von Hagen and Hofmann, 2004). For example, during the period 2001-2005, the Greek economy grew significantly faster than the euro-area average, in which case Greece needed higher nominal interest rates to control inflation more

---

[18] The issue of "hidden debts" was also raised by the validity of Greek statistics (Sturgess, 2010).

[19] Barrios and Fargnoli (2010) reveal that governments – Greece not included in the study – were likely to implement tax cuts during expansionary phases and resorted to tax increases during periods of slowdown (especially for direct taxes).

effectively. From this perspective, it is argued that the low interest rates set by the ECB (Arghyrou, 2009; Arghyrou and Tsoukalas, 2011):

(a) over-stimulated Greek domestic demand and fuelled inflationary pressures;
(b) overvalued the real exchange rate and, ultimately,
(c) were the cause of historically high current account deficit levels.[20]

But what if inflationary pressures are not solely the outcome of domestic demand but rather the effect of rigidities in product and labour markets? There is ex post facto evidence on the Greek case indicating that such rigidities did not only contribute to the escalation of the crisis but also magnified its effect by damaging competitiveness and leading to depression.

There is a part of the literature related to the above that suggests that inflation differentials in the euro-area are largely driven by rigidities in product – in means of imperfect competition – and labour markets and not by ECB policies (see *Box 1*). Studies have shown that in a monetary union, inflation rate differentials may be substantial over the business cycle.[21] The mechanism of price discrimination is the most important in explaining these differentials, but moderate differences in the degree of openness have sizeable effects on the dispersion of inflation rates if idiosyncratic shocks predominate (Andres et al., 2009).[22] In addition, differences on the strength and density of product and labour market regulations across member states explain the differences of price competitiveness and dynamics in response to shocks – and business cycles – and their inertia (Biroli et al., 2010). The renowned Balassa-Samuelson effect is not considered as an important contributing factor to inflation rates in the EU (Egert, 2011) and is also of little importance for the inflation target of the ECB (Lommatzsch and Tober, 2006).[23]

---

[20] The Greek government borrowed heavily on an annual basis in order to balance budget and current account deficits.

[21] Although inflation differentials are highly persistent in the euro-area, they do not consistently intensify real divergence, once accounting for structural breaks (Gregoriou et al., 2011).

[22] For example, the "Diamond, Mortensen and Pissarides" model of labour market structure indicates that shocks affecting directly the wage setting process have a strong impact on inflation. On the other hand, reforms affecting directly the labour market flows have a strong impact on the level of unemployment (Christoffel, 2011).

[23] It is important to note here that after the eruption of the crisis "stability of core inflation can be explained to a large extent by stable inflation expectations,

Box 1 – The cause of inflation differentials in the euro-area: Labour and product market rigidities.

Wage and price staggering are complementary in generating monetary persistence (Merkl and Snower, 2009). The monetary authority aims to keep the price level constant in order to minimize the costs introduced by inflation under nominal rigidities (Schmitt-Grohe and Uribe, 2004).

Labour market rigidities provide stronger amplification effects to all types of shocks than financial frictions do (Aspachs-Braconsa and Rabanal, 2011). Labour market rigidities exhibit strong asymmetries between expansionary and contractionary phases; wage rigidity being the most important shock transmitter (Christoffel et al., 2009). Nominal wages increase more easily in expansions and limit vacancy posting and employment creation. Alternatively, during contractions, nominal wages decrease slowly, and result in shifting the main burden of adjustment to employment and hours worked (Abbritti and Fahr, 2011). This has been the case in the euro-area during the recent contraction in economic activity (Lamo and Smets, 2010). The view, however, that employment protection and social-security institutions are responsible for higher unemployment is empirically unfounded (UNCTAD, 2010: 81).

In the absence of labour and product market rigidities – which is the ultimate goal of the EU – inflation differentials in the euro-area would diminish. It is assumed that area-wide inflation stability and low inflation differentials are complementary (Angeloni and Ehrmann, 2007). Since the monetary policy of the ECB is geared at delivering and maintaining low and stable inflation rates, inflation persistence should also decrease in the other countries, which would in turn mitigate the persistence of euro-area inflation differentials (Hofmann and Remsperger, 2005).

Persistently high inflation in Greece appears to be mainly the result of non-competitive behavior and rigidities in product and labour markets; the Balassa-Samuelson effect seems also to be less important.[24] The

---

sluggish price adjustment and an only moderate impact of the output gap on inflation" (Montoya and Dohring, 2011: 24).

[24] The Balassa-Samuelson effect has been declining through time in Greece (Gibson and Malley, 2008). The persistence of a higher inflation rate than the respective average of the euro-area has been the outcome of domestic seasonal effects and product market rigidities (Pelagidis and Taun, 2007), while nominal rigidities and frictions in the labour market do not seem to play an important role (Mitrakos and Zonzilos, 2006). Nevertheless, product and labour market rigidities have not been the cause of inflation differentials between Greece and the euro-area since the eruption of the crisis. The inflation rate has been growing faster in Greece

persistence of the inflation differential between Greece and the euro-area average was around 1% over the 2000s (DG ECFIN, 2010a: 69). The rigidities responsible for inflation differentials have held back Greek competitiveness, which in turn caused sizeable current account deficits that required for continuous financing through government and private expenditure.

The expansion of the public sector is also considered as a major contributor to the enhancement of both the Greek budget deficit and domestic demand prior to the crisis.[25] This notion of fiscal stimuli by the Greek government, which is the primary direct (public sector), and indirect (subsidies, etc.) employer in the country, is not unfounded:

(a) EMU has had a direct positive impact on growth only in the core euro-area countries (Barrel et al., 2008). A great part of the literature suggests that Greece's buoyant growth before the crisis was not due to the low interest rates set by the ECB[26] or the

---

than in the euro-area during 2006-2009, at an average rate of 1%. In 2010 this differential increased at 3.1% despite the fact that Greece was experiencing an economic downturn, while the euro-area was on the path to recovery. The main causes behind this rapid increase were the increase of indirect taxation – despite the fact that Greek enterprises absorbed part of this increase – and the upward price movements of energy products (oil, electricity) and imported goods (see report published in Greek; Τράπεζα της Ελλάδος, 2011: 98-101).

[25] There are numerous highlights for the importance of government expenditure in the theory of economic growth. For example, according to Wagner's law, government spending is a "prerequisite to" or "requirement for" economic development in advanced economies. The increase of government expenditures with respect to economic activity in Greece confirms Wagner's law (Dritsakis and Adamopoulos, 2004). Wagner's law is also confirmed by all members of the OECD (Lamartina and Zaghini, 2011). As a result, if the Greek public sector is equivalent to the respective size (e.g. as a GDP percentage) of other euro-area member states, but still generates budget deficits and augments the size of sovereign debt, then the issue is not the size per se. The discussion that follows reveals that the issue at hand concerns the efficient allocation of resources, prompt tax collection and tax evasion (extensive shadow economy).

[26] The debt of Greek households contributes considerably to the internal demand for consumption and housing (Athanassiou, 2007). Although private credit replaced government deficit spending after 1997 as the main way to finance the expansion of consumption in Greece, the difference between the average rates of change in net credit issued by the private banking sector in the 1990s and 2000s is approximately 2% (Mitsopoulos and Pelagidis, 2009a: 401). Since private credit expansion was not a new trend after the introduction of the euro, the "cheap"

stimulus of the euro on international trade and FDI.[27] It was rather due to major investments in infrastructure and the steady inflow of EU funds (see OECD, 2007).[28]

(b) As inflation differentials and relative output movements interact, national fiscal policies have the most important role in containing internal macroeconomic disparities (Landmann, 2011). Greece followed an expansionary fiscal policy – after the introduction of the euro and before the crisis – accompanied by the structural funds of the Community Support Framework.

(c) Inflation differentials across euro-area countries arise mostly by the non-tradable sector (Altissimo et al., 2011). The public sector

---

access to funds (low cost of capital) was not that important to Greece's buoyant growth. For example:

(a) The wealth effect has been more important than the credit price effect for the rising trend of real estate prices considered as investment vehicles (Kapopoulos and Siokis, 2005).

(b) Credit expansion in Greece was hand to hand with a fast growing volume of deposits (Pagoulatos and Triantopoulos, 2009).

(c) Although several studies have shown that the term structure of interest rates is a good indicator for future output growth of advanced economies, credit expansion and the cost of capital are not always predictors and thus, this should not be considered as a rule of thumb (Sauer and Scheide, 1995; Nobili, 2007).

All the above indicate that the approximate – as already stated – 2% rise in net credit issued by private banking should not be regarded as a noteworthy stimuli for economic growth for after the introduction of the euro.

[27] The literature on the effect of the euro on international trade and FDI signifies its strong stimulus on these types of international flows (for example, see Baldwin et al., 2008). Nevertheless, there are certain limits as the effects of the euro depend on the central location of Belgium, Germany and Luxembourg that act as a hub for FDI flows in the euro-area (Petroulas, 2007). Moreover, there is evidence that the euro has decreased investments for financially unconstrained enterprises from countries that previously had strong currencies (Bris et al. 2006). Ultimately, a meta-analysis indicates that there is no Rose effect at all for the euro-area, and that there is something not entirely right with the "Rosean" literature applied on the euro-area (Havranek, 2010). The "Rosean" literature stems from the work of Rose (2000) on the effects of currency unions upon trade and a positive Rose effect within EMU is rooted in the monetary integration process, which consists in a trade-costs reduction and higher competition within the European Single Market.

[28] The influence of these two factors took place in conjunction with:

(a) the growth of Greek enterprises that expanded to the Balkans and adjacent countries,

(b) the 2004 Olympics, and

(c) liberalization of product and service markets (e.g. telecommunications).

constitutes most of the non-tradable goods and services sectors. Wage increases that occurred in advance of any sign of productivity growth – particularly to the "non-tradable" public sector – contributed to the increasing domestic demand in the Greek economy prior to the crisis.

Table 2 depicts – among others – government revenue and expenditures in Greece, EU and the euro-area. While Greek government expenditure as a percentage of GDP has been more or less similar to that of the euro-area and EU, Greek government revenue has been approximately 5% less of the last decade's average annual euro-area and EU receipts. Greek government expenditure as a percentage of GDP has been less or similar to the respective levels of the EU and the euro-area in the 2000s, except for the period 2007-2009 – where it was greater by approximately 3%. A part of the unproductive Greek government expenditure (for productive/unproductive public expenditure see Braunstein, 2012) – i.e. compensation of employees (as a percentage of GDP) – has been analogous to the respective of the EU and the euro-area in 2000s. On the other hand, productive Greek government expenditure has been less than the respective of the EU and the euro-area in 2000s. Subsidies were approximately 1% less than the respective of the EU and the euro-area. Gross fixed capital formation was greater until 2008 and then drops significantly compared to respective of the EU and the euro-area.

The other two indicators of *Table 2* are differentiated greatly from the EU and euro-area. Greek domestic demand expressed as a percentage of GDP remains persistently well above the average EU and euro-area levels, irrespectively of the pace – and existence – of economic growth. This excess in demand justifies the negative trade balance of goods (see *Table 3*), which in turn highlights the Greek competitiveness issues. Furthermore, the rate of unemployment follows a justifiable trend, as it decreased during economic growth and increased during recession. With respect to the euro-area, Greece's rate of unemployment decreased to average euro-area levels in 2008 but increased at a higher pace as recession persisted. The unemployment rate of Greek citizens was higher before the recession compared to that of extra-EU immigrants, while the opposite occurred afterwards.[29]

---

[29] Two conflicting views exist in the literature regarding the impact of immigrants on the rate of unemployment of the native workers: the substitution hypothesis and the segregation hypothesis. The latter implies that immigrants are employed in jobs, which are of no interest to the natives, and is mostly supported by studies on the Greek labour market (Cholezas and Tsakloglou, 2009).

Table 3 – Greek balance of payments (US$ billions at current prices).

Indicator/Year	1995	2000	2005	2008	2009	2010	2011
Current account balance (percentage of GDP)	-2.2	-7.7	-7.6	-14.9	-11.1	-10.1	-9.8
Current account balance: Goods (percentage of GDP)	-10.9	-15.9	-14.3	-18.9	-13.3	-12.4	-12.7
Current account balance: Services (percentage of GDP)	4.0	6.3	8.0	7.4	5.5	5.8	6.8
Current account balance: Income (percentage of GDP)	-1.3	-0.7	-2.9	-4.6	-3.9	-3.6	-4.2
Current account balance: Current transfers (percentage of GDP)	6.1	2.6	1.6	1.2	0.6	0.1	0.3
Financial account balance (percentage of GDP)	2.4	6.5	6.5	12.8	10.5	9.4	8.3
Degree of openness	-	63.2	55.7	62.7	49.7	51.9	55.5
Degree of openness towards the EU	-	34.3	30.5	33.9	29.1	27.9	29.2
Degree of openness towards the euro-area	-	-	22.0	24.0	20.5	19.1	19.9
Trade balance (percentage of GDP)	-	-13.5	-9.3	-14.4	-11.4	-8.9	-7.5
Exports of goods and services (percentage of GDP)	-	24.9	23.2	24.1	19.2	21.5	24.0
Imports of goods and services (percentage of GDP)	-	38.4	32.5	38.6	30.5	30.4	31.5
Exports of goods (percentage of total trade)	-	16.5	19.1	17.1	17.4	19.3	21.5
Exports of services (percentage of total trade)	-	22.8	22.6	21.4	21.2	22.1	21.8
Imports of goods (percentage of total trade)	-	47.3	48.2	50.3	49.6	45.9	45.5
Imports of services (percentage of total trade)	-	13.4	10.1	11.2	11.8	12.6	11.2

Source: Eurostat (http://epp.eurostat.ec.europa.eu/portal/page/portal/statistics/search_database, as accessed 10 July 2012).

* Degree of openness is the sum of export and import volumes as a share of GDP.

** GDP is measured at current prices.

*** EU(15) for 2001, EU(25) for 2004, EU(27) for 2008-2011

- Not available.

The figures on *Table 2* indicate that Greek government expenditure as a percentage of GDP has been more or less similar to that of the euro-area, while at the same time Greek government revenue as a percentage of GDP was 5% less of the last decade's average annual euro-area receipts. This data is the foreground of several studies which insinuate that the shortfalls of public revenue are primarily responsible for the expansion of budget deficits and the consequent growth of public debt in Greece.[30] While personal income taxation has been considered as the main source of public revenue shortfalls (Mitsopoulos and Pelagidis, 2011), the ease of settling debts – arising from direct and indirect taxes payable – to both enterprises and consumers, is also responsible for the generation of long repayment periods that frequently end up as bad debts.[31] Furthermore, the element of corruption[32] (and subsequently, the shadow economy) highlights the inability of Greek governments to tax underground activities (Katsios, 2006) – which contribute directly to the shortfalls of public revenue – and raises questions about the efficient allocation of public funds (Mitsopoulos and Pelagidis, 2009b).

The determinants of low competitiveness and shortfalls in public revenue that require immediate attention are extremely complex and rooted to the existing economic system. The part of the literature that explores the institutional setting that has led to the Greek sovereign debt crisis argues that if the institutional determinants remain unchanged there will not be an exit from the crisis, regardless of the rescue plans. It is argued that clientelism and rent-seeking behavior have contributed to the climax of the Greek political and economic crisis (Katsimi and Moutos,

---

[30] Tax revenues have been steadily decreasing in Greece since 2000 due to inefficiencies in tax administration that hamper tax collection (Servera and Moschovis, 2008). The failures of tax system's institutions – which are rooted in and at the same time reinforce failures of informal institutions (i.e. perceived fairness of the tax system and allocation of resources) – have played a key role in the exacerbation of fiscal deficits (Kaplanoglou and Rapanos, 2013). The weak institutional framework of budgeting and tax administration is held responsible for the fiscal developments that led to the escalation of the Greek crisis (Kaplanoglou and Rapanos, 2011).

[31] The Greek government published a list of major debtors – with outstanding debts from both direct and indirect taxes that is more than €150 thousand in each case – on 8 September 2011. The total accruing sum is more than €30 billion. The list is available online – in Greek – at *http://www.gsis.gr/debtors/kerdoskopika-np.html*.

[32] The link between corruption and the shadow economy becomes evident from the former's definition: i.e. the behavior which deviates from formal duties due to private gains (Nye, 1967).

2010; Lyrintzis, 2011). It is even argued that the Greek paradox of rapid growth in the 2000s – until the eruption of the crisis – is the outcome of rent-seeking groups. The control and distortion of product and labour markets by rent-seeking groups has led Greece to match the prosperity of advanced countries at the same time as the quality of governance and social coherence is closer to that of a developing country (Mitsopoulos and Pelagidis, 2009a).

The chronic problems of clientelism and rent-seeking have resulted in high levels of perceived corruption and tax evasion, which undermine competition and the effective delivery of public services and functions, and generate a welfare system that is expensive, wasteful and socially exclusive (Featherstone, 2008). The planned and prolonged institutional reforms required for overcoming the spiral of recession and contraction of government spending – and which have been repeatedly put forward by the joint EC/IMF/ECB rescue mission since the eruption of the crisis – indicate that the institutional setting seems to be the causa causans of the Greek crisis.[33] The blockage of reforms has been the outcome of both the sizeable power of rent-seeking clientelism and the demands of the average Greek voter who regards the expansion of government expenditure – i.e. public sector – as a free good (Mitsopoulos and Pelagidis, 2009a).[34]

2.4 The Impact of the Crisis on the Euro-area and the Role of the SGP

The impact of the financial crisis has been territorially asymmetric.[35] Across Europe, the crisis aggravated structural weaknesses of the economy, adding to what had been generated or petrified by stagnating

---

[33] The requirement for an alternate institutional setting indicates that the Greek crisis is not only an economic but also – and primarily – a political crisis.

[34] These rents are obtained and sustained due to extreme bureaucracy and lack of transparency (Mitsopoulos and Pelagidis, 2007). A clear cut example of clientelism is put forward by an empirical study, which indicates that rent-seeking competition from state coffers – i.e. rent-seeking competition in the public sector for higher subsidies and transfers, lower taxes and other extra fiscal privileges – leads to fiscal privileges at the expense of the general public interest (Angelopoulos et al., 2010).

[35] This is because the causes of the crisis varied across countries. The only common ground about the causes and consequences of the crisis is that countries with current account surpluses seem to be better insulated from slowdowns (Rose and Spiegel, 2011).

economic growth of the last decade.[36] Both government deficits and debt in the EU have deteriorated to unprecedented levels since 2007. However, expectations for these levels – within the euro-area – to begin shrinking by 2011 due to accommodating policies (DG ECFIN, 2010b: 1) have been partially met. Thirteen euro-area members (except from Estonia, Finland, Germany, and Luxembourg) had deteriorating excessive debt levels in 2011, and two had deteriorating primary balances (Cyprus and Slovenia).

The euro-area has experienced a severe recession at the end of the global financial crisis, followed by a sovereign debt crisis that erupted and spread in peripheral member states.[37] The pace of recovery is held back by the requirement for fiscal consolidation (OECD, 2010a: 19). Theoretically, government debt is likely to affect economic growth via a crowding-out effect on private investment – since national savings are reduced and the cost of funds increases due to risk premium[38] – and via an increase in taxes needed to service the debt (DG ECFIN, 2010b: 2).[39]

While the Greek rescue plan has (temporarily) suspended the crisis, its long-run consequences are drastic and dangerous (Wyplosz, 2010b). The Greek sovereign debt crisis – initially – and the sovereign debt crisis of the EU South periphery have delayed the ECB's exit from its current highly expansionary monetary policy stance. It has also complicated it since the ECB now holds considerable quantities of Greek sovereign debt and consequently, it is exposed to considerable credit risk (Gerlach, 2010).[40] Moreover, the Greek sovereign debt crisis is also responsible for a part of the euro depreciation (Kasimati, 2011).[41]

---

[36] These structural weaknesses imply that simply relying on relatively favorable macroeconomic conditions to ensure growth, jobs and competitiveness is not enough (Hubner, 2010).

[37] "The generalized increase in spreads in the early part of 2010 appears to be the result of spillovers from the situation in Greece... the contagion effects through a wider re-evaluation of the prospects for other economies with large imbalances and weak fiscal positions were important" (OECD, 2010a: 90).

[38] The financial crisis has forced governments to assume additional risk (De Broeck and Guscina, 2011).

[39] Although EU is on average a high-tax area, tax policies have played an important role in countering the crisis. Policy responses varied markedly between member states depending on the evolution of macroeconomic and financial conditions. However, tax composition shifted uniformly towards indirect from direct taxes (DG ECFIN, 2010c: 6).

[40] Strictly technically speaking, there is no such thing as "credit risk" for a central bank, since it is always able to recapitalize itself by "printing money".

[41] Current account imbalances, such as those considered responsible for the recent global crisis, tend to create exchange rate tensions (De la Dehesa, 2010). The

In relation to all the above, the escalation and impact of the crisis has raised criticisms for the role of the SGP. The SGP is supposed to replace the need for central fiscal policy in an effort to fulfil the criteria for an optimal currency area. The motivation behind the decision of leaving the control over the domestic fiscal policy in the hands of each respective government is sovereignty.[42] The budgetary discipline imposed by the SGP is considered able to promote development in the long-term – i.e. when the budget is in order, fiscal expansion is manageable, extra taxes are not necessary and interest rates remain at low levels.[43]

A major part of the literature argues that the debt crisis confirms the failure of SGP. Its failure lies in the dysfunctionality of member state institutions (with Greece in the forefront) and the imbalance of its design (Featherstone, 2011). It is argued that the solution is not to make the SGP stricter and more intrusive but to require from every euro-area member to have in place proper budgetary institutions (Wyplosz, 2010a). The crisis should not be seen solely as a problem but also as an opportunity to reform the SGP in a nonconventional way, through jurisprudence.[44] Moreover, it seems that the EU "needed" this crisis to enforce structural reforms – i.e. by limiting the fiscal policy of member states, moves towards further political integration (Eijffinger, 2010).

---

peculiarity of the Greek case comes in terms of possible contagion within the euro-area and the formation of expectations – a procedure where the media play a major role. The effects of the Greek crisis have been adopted differently by the press at an international level. For example, in 2010, while newspapers in Europe and America had presented the Greek crisis as a European matter, newspapers from Asia had regarded the Greek crisis as a predicament of international proportions due to expectations for pressures on the exchange rates in the presence of global imbalances (research published in Greek – Κέντρο Διεθνούς Πολιτικής Οικονομίας, 2010: 8).

[42] However, there are arguments about the appropriateness of the SGP as a substitute for fiscal integration. For example, the role of SGP as the "sentry" of the sovereignty of member states is contradicted by the arguments about the necessity of fiscal integration in a single currency area put forward by Kenen (1969), who developed the notion – set forth by earlier researchers – of optimum-currency-areas. For the reason that fiscal transfers are able to smooth asymmetric shocks in a monetary union, fiscal integration should be a criterion to judge optimality for participation (Dellas and Tavlas, 2009).

[43] The Canadian economy is a model that combines budgetary discipline and economic development (see Sancak et al., 2011).

[44] Such arguments have led to the so-called six-pack that has fundamentally strengthened the SGP and tightened fiscal governance across EMU.

Several studies argue that strengthening the SGP would be dangerous if it deprived member states of policy tools proven to be helpful in the crisis (Mathieu and Sterdyniak, 2010). The current debt frontiers (60% of GDP) of the SGP are questioned by recent research. For example, the relationship between government debt and real GDP growth is weak for debt/GDP ratios below a threshold of 90% of GDP, and above 90%, median growth rates fall by 1%, and average growth falls considerably more (Reinhart and Rogoff, 2010). As a result, a reformed version of the SGP is required, with broader macroeconomic surveillance and tighter enforcement mechanisms during expansion phases, and a crisis resolution mechanism at the EU level (Larch et al., 2010).

3. Imbalances in the Euro-area During the Crisis

The present predicament occurred in the presence of global imbalances. Cyclical and policy-induced factors have fostered the enlargement of global imbalances, which have been brought back to attention by the recent financial and economic crisis (Bracke et al., 2010).[45] The launch of the euro in 1999 saw many member states benefiting from lower interest rates – including Greece, Italy, Portugal, Spain and Ireland – and ultimately, being those that were mostly exposed by the financial crisis because of harmful imbalances in their economies (Swinburne, 2010). The reference to harmful global imbalances is that these euro-area members would today be better off if they had somehow kept a better competitiveness position and lower external deficits (Gross, 2010).

The euro-area crisis is considered as a balance of payments crisis at least as much as it is a fiscal crisis (Merler and Pissani-Ferry, 2012). During the decade preceding the crisis, the euro-area experienced a steady divergence in the competitive position and the current accounts of its member states. The divergence in the competitive position was caused, in

[45] The widening of global imbalances began in the 1990s (UNCTAD, 2010: 23). Firstly, the encouragement of credit influenced growth in domestic demand by the US since the 1990s, resulted in the aggravation of internal imbalances and the property bubble burst in 2006. Secondly, in the aftermath of the Asian crisis, several developing economies avoided current-account deficits by favoring competitive exchange rates and accumulating foreign exchange reserves. Furthermore, the escalation of oil prices in the 2000s magnified the surplus positions of oil-producing countries. Another example can be found in free-trade areas (such as the EU single market), which foster imbalances despite their positive impacts on competition, economic growth, etc.

part, by various domestic economic imbalances (e.g. inappropriate responses of wages to a slowdown in productivity, excessive credit growth in the private sector and housing bubbles). Current account deficits were caused by large capital inflows that led to an unsustainable accumulation of household and corporate debt, which in some cases aggravated by inappropriate fiscal policy responses. Current account surpluses, on the other hand, reflected structural weaknesses in domestic demand.

Most indicators of price and cost competitiveness during the crisis point to a further divergence in competitiveness within the euro-area. However, modest signs of convergence have come from labour costs, although this seems to reflect mostly cyclical factors. On the other hand, the crisis has prompted a significant reduction in current account differences across member states – which could be of temporary nature (as it is influenced by the crisis). Part of the correction of current account differences is of structural nature, since the crisis has triggered a partial unwinding of domestic imbalances (e.g. asset and real estate booms). The reduction of current account deficits occurred from drops in private sector demand and changes in the composition of domestic demand with a substitution of imports with domestic products. Then again, the reduction of current account surpluses was influenced by the slump in world trade.[46]

3.1 The Greek Balance of Payments

The volume of trade flows in Greece remains relatively low. The degree of openness, which decreased from 63.2% in 2000 to 55.5% in 2011, is relatively low when compared to the respective EU and euro-area averages, which were approximately 86% in 2011 (see *Table 3* for the Greek balance of payments).[47] The EU share (Greece's most important trade partner) in

---

[46] The discussion in this and the previous paragraph are from DG ECFIN (2010a: 1-4).

[47] The relatively low degree of openness of the Greek economy is due to the export of goods, which has been approximately half than the respective volumes of the EU and the euro-area during the 2000s. Consequently, the relatively low degree of openness can be easily translated into a comparatively low level of competitiveness. Furthermore, the relatively low degree of openness can also be considered as an indicator of the degree of Greece's business cycle synchronization with the EU and the euro-area, as it is observed that the level of trade integration fosters business cycle synchronization directly, while financial integration affects it indirectly (Dees and Zorell, 2011). However, there is an opposing view suggesting that the euro-area has not affected the characteristics of member states' business cycles (Giannone and Lenza, 2009), and several respective studies support the notion that integration is either neutral or has

Greek trade flows has progressively diminished by Greece's export specialization towards neighbours in SEE with high economic growth and the rise on the volumes of imports from Asia – China, South Korea, Japan, and Russia (DG ECFIN, 2010a: 68). Greece's main export competitors are China and the G-7 countries and the destination of Greek exports is highly diversified – compared to other South euro-area member states – due to the expansion of its exports into SEE (Moreno-Badia, 2008).

High economic growth, persistent fiscal imbalances and deteriorating competitiveness in the last decade have worsened the external balance of the Greek economy, with the current account deficit peaking at 14.9% in 2008, as the balance of income and current transfers continued to deteriorate over time (see *Table 3*).[48] The balance of the current account is significantly affected by the trade imbalance, which is mostly due to the permanent deficit of the trade in goods. The figure of inward FDI flows was, and remains relatively small, and as a result, the growing external imbalance was financed mostly through portfolio investment and government bonds.[49] This reflects a dynamic feedback between the current account deficit and debt accumulation and the role of the public sector in the origin of the current account deficit.

Trade in goods and services have a diachronically opposing influence on the balance of trade. Trade in goods constitutes approximately two thirds of total trade volume, of which imports of goods totals about 50% (see *Table 3*). On the other hand, exports of services is more than two thirds of the total trade in services, reflecting the strong performance of the most dynamic sectors of the Greek economy, the tourism industry and the sea freight transport services. For the period between the mid-1990s to 2006, exports remained concentrated in low- and medium-technology

---

negative effects. With regard to the negative effects, the EU and the euro-area are characterised by decreasing synchronization among members and an increase in the number of clusters (Papageorgiou et al., 2010; Aguiar-Conraria and Soares, 2011). Such findings indicate that the costs of giving up the exchange rate instrument have not diminished (i.e. optimum-currency-area theory stresses that they decline with the degree of openness and integration).

48 Domestic imbalances – captured by the diachronic gap between domestic saving and investment – have been the cause of the significant deterioration of the current account balance since 1999 (Brissimis et al., 2010).

49 "According to the Bank of Greece, foreign investors' purchases of government bonds have been the main source of net inflows under portfolio investment" (DG ECFIN, 2010a: 72).

sectors, and as a result, product variety and quality have declined.[50] The characteristics of this performance signify the importance of non-price factors for the improvement of competitiveness in international markets (Athanasoglou et al., 2010).

The performance of exports of goods is disappointing at the same time as imports of goods are three times their value. The presence of high import elasticity with respect to domestic demand signifies that the Greek economy is facing structural difficulties in substituting imports with domestic production and in adjusting to external petition. The geographical location of the destination of the Greek exports – extra-EU countries of SEE and the Mediterranean basin – can partly explain their poor performance. Firstly, because the market size of the destination economies is relatively small compared to the EU and the euro-area, and secondly, the demand of these economies for Greek goods depends on their economic growth and the exchange rate, two factors that have worsened with the crisis (DG ECFIN, 2010a: 70).

Table 4 presents the share of total imports and exports of product categories imported and exported respectively. The high-tech category of "machinery and transport equipment" came first from 2000 to 2009 and this category along with "mineral fuels, etc." represent approximately half of total imports in 2011. On the other hand, the category of "food, drinks and tobacco" has been the single – i.e. not an all encompassing category such as "other goods" – category with the highest share of exports until 2010.[51] The category of "mineral fuels, etc." represents the highest share of total imports and exports of product categories in 2011.

The volume of exports of services is much greater than the volume of exports of goods, and at the same time, imports of services remain at considerably lower levels than the respective of goods (see *Table 3*). Travel and sea transport services represent the majority of both total exports and imports of services (see *Table 4*). The exports of travel services are directed mainly to the euro-area, although tourism from Eastern Europe and Russia has grown considerably in the most recent years.[52] In addition, the exports of

---

[50] During the 1990s, Greece drastically shifted its export structure from textile and clothing towards transport and tourism, resulting to a significant increase in the export of services (Escolano, 2008: 9).

[51] More than two thirds of the exported products from this category are food products (see statistical reports of the "Hellenic Foreign Trade Board" at www.hepo.gr).

[52] Although the export of tourism has admittedly a notable contribution to Greece's economic growth, research indicates that there is no real causal relationship – only a Granger causal relationship exists – between international tourism earnings and economic growth (Dritsakis, 2004).

Table 4 – Greece: Imports and exports of goods and services.

Indicator/Year	1995	2000	2005	2008	2009	2010	2011
Percentage of total goods exported (x) or imported (m)							
Mineral fuels, lubricants and related materials (x)	6.1	13.8	9.5	11.5	9.3	11.1	30.2
Other manufactured goods (x)	43.5	38.1	34.4	33.4	30.3	29.9	25.3
Food, drinks and tobacco (x)	23.3	19.5	18.7	19.2	23.5	22.2	16.7
Chemicals and related products (x)	4.8	8.1	14.6	13.0	14.4	14.5	10.3
Mineral fuels, lubricants and related materials (m)	7.1	12.1	18.0	21.4	16.8	24.1	27.4
Other manufactured goods (m)	33.1	27.0	25.3	25.6	23.7	22.1	21.5
Machinery and transport equipment (m)	27.4	35.8	28.6	26.5	29.8	24.0	18.4
Chemicals and related products (m)	13.1	11.6	14.5	13.4	15.5	15.2	15.7
Food, drinks and tobacco (m)	15.2	10.7	10.7	9.8	11.5	11.5	13.0
Percentage of total services exported (x) or imported (m)							
Sea transport (x)	12.2	39.1	47.0	-	45.4	49.2	-
Travel (x)	37.7	48.0	40.0	34.2	38.5	33.7	36.7
Professional and technical business services (x)	20.2	4.2	-	-	-	4.8	-
Communication (x)	0.7	1.3	-	1.0	1.1	1.1	1.3
Insurance (x)	0.2	0.9	-	0.9	1.2	1.1	1.4
Sea transport (m)	17.3	29.4	39.2	-	33.4	38.9	-
Travel (m)	32.4	40.4	20.6	15.8	16.9	14.2	16.2
Professional and technical business services (m)	12.8	5.7	-	7.8	-	8.1	-
Insurance (m)	4.5	1.8	-	5.9	6.7	7.2	7.7
Air transport (m)	7.1	2.6	3.1	-	3.7	2.7	-
Communication (m)	2.3	2.5	-	2.6	3.4	2.6	2.8
Financial services (m)	3.8	0.7	-	1.0	1.4	2.2	2.3

Source: Eurostat (http://epp.eurostat.ec.europa.eu/portal/page/portal/statistics/search_database, as accessed 10 July 2012).

* GDP is measured at current prices.

\- Not available.

sea travel services are mainly directed outside the euro-area in the form of sea freight transport (DG ECFIN, 2010a: 69).

3.2 Readjustment of Current Account Balances

The EC made the case for deeper and broader macroeconomic surveillance in the euro-area to address the importance of macroeconomic imbalances (see DG ECFIN, 2008).[55] Private restructuring and public reforms are found to be more important than public transfers for the readjustment of intra-euro-area imbalances and the perverseness of economic stability in the long-term (Zemanek et al., 2010). For example, product market reform, wage moderation and fiscal consolidation can support/accelerate the correction of imbalances by increasing price competitiveness and improving trade/current account balances (Vogel, 2011).[56] Furthermore, regarding the most drastic solution of abandoning the euro as a prelude to devaluation – i.e. the return of national currencies in the periphery – it is argued that this abandonment would not change the requirement to cut the twin deficits since short-term export competitiveness is not the key issue and opportunities to boost exports (including tourism) are quite limited, especially as the European economy remains weak (Rossi and Aguilera, 2010). In view of Greece's weakened competitiveness in the euro-area and persistent current account deficits, adjustment in the context of the euro-area would be facilitated by relative price and cost adjustments and a shift of resources from the non-tradable to the tradable sector (DG ECFIN, 2010: 72).[57]

However, the need for fiscal consolidation and readjustment of current account balances is not an issue concerning only the euro-area but appears to have global proportions. For example, the financial market problems in the US that led to a global crisis were related to global imbalances that have been building up since the 1990s. *Box 2* highlights the key policies leading to a rebalanced growth from a global perspective.

---

[55] For a discussion of the main shortcomings of the present political system regulating the euro-area see Mamadouh and Van Der Wusten (2011).

[56] Nonetheless, it also mentioned that euro-area-wide reforms within this framework may only affect balances with the rest of the world and not reduce disparities between euro-area member states.

[57] The reduction of Greek imbalances is expected to assist Greece to exit from depression sooner. It is observed that current account reversals associated with improvements in external positions increase growth acceleration beyond those generated by real exchange rate effects (de Mello et al., 2011).

Box 2 – The requirements for a rebalanced growth.

A coordinated countercyclical action is needed in order to overcome the systemic crisis (see UNCTAD, 2009). The route leading to a rebalanced sustainable growth from the recent deep recession, and which is capable of addressing the problem of global current account imbalances, requires that (Freedman et al., 2010):

(a) governments must ensure the financial sector's health, because it affects productivity growth both in the short and the long-run.
(b) governments must avoid protectionist measures, because the latter create distortions in product and labour markets.
(c) governments must increase investment expenditures in infrastructure, because the latter enhances GDP growth.
(d) governments (except for USA) must encourage a decrease in private saving in order to stimulate recovery in the short run and help to rebalance current accounts across regions in the desired direction.
(e) governments of emerging Asia must encourage nominal and real appreciation of their currencies, for rebalancing current accounts in the global economy.
(f) the USA government must reduce fiscal deficits, because otherwise the latter will reduce world savings and fiscal space in the long-run, and thereby increase world real interest rates, and create a higher tax burden, respectively.

3.3 Is Fiscal Consolidation Appropriate During the Crisis?

The global financial crisis has led to a sharp deterioration of EU members' public finances, and the sovereign debt crisis that erupted initially in Greece spread later on to six other peripheral member states, namely Cyprus, Ireland, Italy, Portugal and Spain. Significant consolidation – in terms of fiscal austerity – is urgently required in order to reduce public debt and restore market confidence. Fiscal consolidations appear to be less successful in absence of financial crises and there is not conclusive evidence that exchange rates depreciation/devaluation would enhance their success (Barrios et al., 2010b). The current debt dynamics in the EU, which are coupled with rising debt servicing costs and much deteriorated growth outlook, require differentiated fiscal consolidation strategies across EU countries.[58]

---

[58] The repair of the banking sector is a pre-condition for fiscal consolidation to succeed in reducing debt levels (Barrios et al., 2010b).

The literature is currently divided into two different perspectives regarding the requirement and success of fiscal consolidation. On the one hand, it is observed that stronger fiscal rules would reduce sovereign risk in the euro-area (Iara and Wolff, 2010), and that fiscal expansion would be ineffective for two reasons:

(a) The rising level of interest payments to creditors of government debt cancels the effect of the fiscal multiplier (Athanassiou, 2009).
(b) Although cuts in direct taxes generate a positive effect on consumer and business confidence, higher government wage bills and government investment, which would have to be financed by higher future taxes, reduce confidence (Konstantinou and Tagkalakis, 2010).

A further case for fiscal consolidation is that a permanent reduction in public employment (even wage cuts) increases consumption of domestic goods and services (compared to foreign) and appreciates the domestic exchange rate, if it is matched by a reduction in taxes.[59] In addition, it is observed that announced reductions in domestic government employment and consumption have also the same effects (Ganelli, 2010).[60] Finally, the existence of an Abrams curve in the EU (Christopoulos et al., 2005), which indicates a positive relationship between unemployment and the size of the public sector, provides further support for positive externalities arising by the latter's contraction.

The "European Economic Recovery Plan" – launched in December 2008 – is considered able enough to provide the necessary amount of fiscal stimulus and is complemented by proposals to speed up structural reforms under the Lisbon Growth and Jobs Strategy.[61] The DG ECFIN proposes that with the support of the European Economic Recovery Plan, the governments of member states will be able to undertake the necessary fiscal consolidation and shift their focus from short-term demand management to supply-side structural measures (see DG ECFIN, 2009a).

Nonetheless, the arguments against fiscal austerity emphasize that the latter has short-term negative effects on key macroeconomic aggregates

---

[59] Tax reductions could take place through tax reforms that lead to higher levels of output, consumption and private investment by reducing the labour and capital income tax rates and increasing the consumption tax rate (Papageorgiou, 2009).
[60] High public wages induce too many unemployed to queue for public sector jobs, raising unemployment (Gomes, 2011).
[61] An extra fiscal stimulus is available to Greece through the "National Strategic Reference Framework".

such as output and consumption, although GDP will be higher in the medium and long-term (Coenen et al., 2008; Roeger and in 't Veld, 2010).[62] As a result, even when under a balanced budget policy the output-gap inflation-volatility trade-off is improved (Linnemann and Schabert, 2010), given that private consumption is positively correlated to fiscal shocks (Ganelli and Tervala, 2009), fiscal consolidation is not proper in the presence of the crisis.[63] Finally, in cases where growth-promoting spending is cut so much that the present value of future government revenues falls more than the immediate improvement in the cash deficit, fiscal adjustment occurs at the cost of future consumption and economic growth (Easterly et al., 2008).[64]

So, is fiscal consolidation appropriate during the crisis? A relatively recent paper (Price, 2010) exploring the political economy of fiscal consolidation indicates a number of factors that would aggravate the difficulty of consolidating during the crisis. Although expenditure cuts are the most accessible means of medium-term consolidation – allied with measures to improve public sector efficiency – their implementation involves severe problems of political economy. However, the use of discretionary fiscal policy as a stabilising device – in cases it can be an option – should be with caution, since the possibilities for opportunistic fiscal behaviour rise during the crisis and the difficulties of maintaining transparency increase as well.

4. Measures for Recovery Put Forward by the EU

The current instruments in the EU to deal with debt and liquidity crises include, inter alia, the European Financial Stability Facility – set up by the euro-area – and the European Financial Stabilisation Mechanism (for a

[62] Turrini (2012: 9) indicates "that fiscal consolidation has an impact on cyclical unemployment in the order of 0.1% of additional unemployment for each point of GDP of budgetary measures, stronger for expenditure measures, and which gradually fades away."

[63] Households facing an unemployment shock may be unable to continue servicing debt obligations and thus put at risk the efforts of the economy to recover (Daras and Tyrowicz, 2011).

[64] The need of Greece to generate positive primary surpluses for several years in order to facilitate a sustained de-escalation of the debt burden that would eventually restore state access to international credit markets requires aggressive and sustained fiscal consolidation (Monokroussos, 2010). As depression endures, this route will reduce the present value of future government revenues more than the immediate improvement in the cash deficit.

discussion see Belke, 2010). Moreover, in June 2012 it was agreed that the successor of these instruments – the European Stability Mechanism – will loan funds directly to stressed banks rather in order to avoid adding to sovereign debt. Furthermore, asset-based reserve requirements are put forward as a solution to restrain the excesses of the next credit bubble for small open economies, and as an alternative to "tax-breaks" to secure levels of investment during a downturn (O'Sullivan, 2010).[65] The provision of this form of "financial support" along with the implementation of policies, which are able to reduce deficits and improve competitiveness, are considered sufficient enough to restore the ability of a member state facing excessive deficits to access the international capital markets.[66]

However, the adoption of fiscal austerity measures that precede the appeal for a rescue plan, or the resort to the crisis mechanism (i.e. financial support accompanied by fiscal consolidation and structural reforms) have not been sufficient enough to restrain the rise of sovereign spreads.[67] Such problems, for example, have been evident with the Greek bailout as both the market's perception of implicit official seniority and the credibility of the fiscal package have not resulted to any reduction on the level of spreads (Chamley and Pinto, 2011). The insufficient crisis management could be due to the fact that some of the criteria that affect the probability of debt restructuring – and on which the discrimination of market-implied sovereign default probabilities between countries is based – are not met. These criteria (see Blundell-Wignall and Slovik, 2011) concern the level of primary deficit, the size of debt (as a share of GDP), the chances for

---

[65] There are, however, sizable differences in crisis responses within the EU, which depend on the degree that banking systems are exposed to bad assets, and on budgetary restrictions (Stolz and Wedow, 2010).

[66] However, this form of "financial support" increases considerably the size of debt, and high government debts could expose financial strains and suppress growth for several years. Since debt recovery rates and sovereign bond prices decrease with the level of debt, and bargaining power is correlated to both debt recovery rates and sovereign bond spreads, there is doubt on the final outcome of the EU "financial support" (for the issues of sovereign default and debt renegotiation see Yue, 2010). The EC, however, regards that the level of debt is set to be increasing despite the EU "financial support" due to the cost of ageing (DG ECFIN, 2010b: 2).

[67] Possibly because the measures adopted have failed to account for the probability of insolvency and the systemic interdependence between banking and sovereign crises and the interdependence across member states (Darvas et al., 2011). Another possible explanation could also be put forward by the role of institutions and policies of member states, as poor domestic institutional quality affects debt sustainability by generating credibility gaps (Panizza et al., 2010).

bailout, the need for the government to return to the capital markets, and the amount of sovereign debt held by domestic banks.[68]

With reference to the Greek case, the mode of fiscal consolidation proposed by the joint EC/IMF/ECB rescue mission faced fierce criticism domestically. There are arguments against the measures proposed (and partially adopted to present) that a less generous unemployment benefit system – rather than temporary caps on spending (e.g., wage freezes) – would contribute to the success of fiscal consolidation. Moreover, it has been pointed out that the advancement of product market deregulation and more flexible employment protection legislation do not contribute positively to fiscal consolidation (Tagkalakis, 2009).

4.1 Alternate Proposals for Recovery

Recent research – that emerged across continents since the eruption of the crisis – indicates that fiscal austerity (Bagaria et al., 2012) and disinflation (Ball, 2009) during recession are responsible for rising unemployment levels. Fiscal policy is the key tool for reinvigorating economic activity and compensating for the apathy of private investment. As a result, a great part of the literature suggests that the EU has to combine measures to increase income with appropriate control of spending. From the perspective of the member states it is argued that the emphasis must be placed on combating tax fraud (Alvarez, 2010). In addition, redistribution of income is considered necessary, as a more unequal distribution of income can weigh on a country's fiscal performance (Larch, 2010). It is also argued that while short-term remedies should include a shift in income distribution to increase consumption, in the medium to long-term governments should undertake large investment

[68] Blundell-Wignall and Slovik (2011) – the discussants of these criteria – argue that since the monetary expansion that would assist the four peripheral members states is against the ECB rules, only a synchronized reduction of the primary deficit of all member states accompanied by a reduction of the interest rate on the debt (through the issuance of EU bonds), and the restructuring of principals and interest rates (through EU bonds or within an ECB context) would lead to the fulfilment of these criteria. However, since EU bonds would create contingent liabilities for stronger member states (e.g. Germany), and the involvement of the ECB would generate the risk of quantitative easing, these options are ruled out. Nevertheless, the "need for pan-European coordination" and the "overhaul of euro-area institutions" is embraced by more than a few scholars (e.g. De Grauwe, 2011a; 2011b; Schalck, 2011; Valiante, 2011; Pisani-Ferry, 2012).

projects to improve conditions for profitable private sector investment (Ietto-Gillies, 2010).[69]

The argument that fiscal expansion is necessary in economic downturns is not new. Fiscal policy is effective in supporting economic activity, especially in the short-term, because the effect of the short-term fiscal multiplier is stronger for government investment (Furceri and Mourougane, 2010). It is also observed that private consumption responds positively to fiscal expansions due to the complementarity between public and private consumption (Ganelli and Tervala, 2009). Moreover, fiscal expansions that occur from increases in expenditure can be relatively effective in stimulating the economy when the nominal interest rate is kept unchanged for a prolonged period of time and prices are sticky (Coenen et al., 2010) – a situation similar to that of Greece.

An alternate measure for recovery beyond the utilisation of fiscal policy is the rapid advancement of EU cohesion policy and perfect competition – the latter highlights the role of small and medium enterprises (SMEs). EU cohesion policy, which has been a major source of public investment at regional level "is not only a way to immediately damp down the negative economic and social effects of the crisis but is also a long-term policy for combating the structural problems revealed and created..." by the crisis, "particularly as regards competitiveness and employment" (Kratsa-Tsagaropoulou, 2010: 7). This was evident at the end of 2008 – in the context of the financial and economic crisis – when EU cohesion policy was facing three major challenges (Hubner, 2010):

(a) Overcoming the liquidity constraints in a number of EU member states and regions, which had hampered the pre-financing of projects in the regional (multi-regional, national) development programmes under cohesion policy.
(b) Facilitating and accelerating investments in member states and regions.
(c) Improving productive capacity and competitiveness.

The "special committee on the financial, economic and social crisis" of the European Parliament criticizes the European and global development

[69] The failure of the "European Economic Recovery Plan" is visible via its inability to enhance the recovery of employment, while fiscal austerity could risk further deceleration of the recovery of employment. The share of the structurally or long-term unemployed has increased significantly in most developed countries since 2007 due to the crisis (United Nations, 2011: v).

model[70] and recommends that the innovative SMEs can be a driving force for EU recovery and future growth and welfare.[71]

5. The Greek Business Environment

The issue at hand is that Greece currently faces a crisis on two fronts: there has been a long-run build-up of public sector debt due to persistently high budget deficits, and a very rapid build up of excessive external debt[72] due to several years of massive current account deficits (Rossi and Aguilera, 2010). The joint EC/IMF/ECB mission regards that unsustainable fiscal policies – sustained by rising external debt – rigid labour and product markets, and the loss of competitiveness were the origins of the Greek sovereign debt crisis (DG ECFIN, 2010e: 9).

Over the past decade, Greece borrowed heavily in international capital markets to fund government budget and current account deficits. GDP growth along with euro-bias[73] had granted Greece access to international capital markets for funding government budget and current account deficits despite the fact that the size of these deficits has been in the centre of attention at least since the mid 2000s.[74] The profligacy of the

---

[70] This special committee argues that the negative growth and employment trends of European economies during the period preceding the crisis worsened after the credit crunch, which has assumed the overall characteristics of a structural crisis affecting the neo-liberal development model. The committee highlights the necessity to abolish the SGP and terminate measures aiming to increase competitiveness in terms of labour costs (Chountis, 2010). The inappropriateness of measures aiming to decrease labour costs is also indicated by the observation that the euro-area is in a wage-led demand regime (Stockhammer et al., 2009).

[71] For example, this special committee recommends – inter alia – the formation of a new Small Business Act that would embrace a strong social dimension; the development of one-shop-stop for every administrative issue for SMEs; tax incentives and subsidies for SMEs, etc. (Bastos, 2010).

[72] The progressive deterioration of the net external borrowing position of the Greek economy reflects both rising investment and falling savings. The public and private sectors have alternated during the last decade as the driving force of this deterioration (Moschovis and Servera, 2009).

[73] Greater market integration (and lower transaction costs) within the EMU led to portfolio euro bias: a situation where euro investors tend to hold large proportion of assets issued within the euro-area. Euro bias is not unrelated to the remarkable convergence in government bond yields in the euro-area during 2001-2007 (Balli et al., 2010).

[74] Although before the crisis – in terms of real GDP growth – the Greek economy had performed very well and had weathered the international slowdown in activity

government, weak revenue collection, and structural rigidities are typically cited as major factors behind Greece's accumulation of debt, while access to capital at low interest rates after adopting the euro and weak enforcement of EU rules concerning debt and deficit ceilings may also have played a role (see Nelson et al., 2010).

The escalation of the Greek sovereign debt crisis since November 2009 has been confirmed as the result of an unfavourable shift in country-specific market expectations.[75] The actual spreads, both before and during the crisis, deviate significantly from those estimated by long-term fundamental determinants, such as the deficits, competitiveness, economic activity and dependence on imported energy (Gibson et al., 2011).[76] Any attempt to estimate the time of recovery highlights the importance of restoring confidence, making thus, the other predicting factors less important (Azis, 2010). The profound necessity of structural, competitiveness-inducing reforms is highlighted as the primary tool that is able to generate favourable country-specific market expectations (Arghyrou and Kontonikas, 2011).

5.1 Competitiveness

Greece's high GDP growth rates until 2008, co-existed with low competitiveness and continued institutional weakness (see DG ECFIN, 2010d: 3-7). On the one hand, enormous inflows –from tourism and sea transport (see *Table 4*), structural funds from the European Community Support Framework,[77] and public borrowing – fuelled GDP growth, but left

---

better than most OECD countries, an OECD survey dating back to 2005 reveals that this has been achieved at the cost of a sharply widening fiscal deficit to very high levels and high and rising public indebtedness. The same report raised concerns over Greece's productivity and competitiveness and required immediate actions such as: competition policy reforms; fostering a knowledge-based economy; the liberalisation of product markets, in particular the energy, telecommunication and transport sectors; policies to foster entrepreneurship; the implementation of a better corporate governance regime (see OECD, 2005).

[75] The literature suggests that the determinants of government bond yield spreads in the euro-area are the credit and liquidity risk premium, and the actual and expected level of government debt and deficits (Attinasi et al., 2010).

[76] The gradual integration between credit default swaps and spreads of Greek sovereign bonds (Apergis et al., 2011) indicates the "importance of restoring confidence" and the "quality of domestic institutions", since the long-term fundamental determinants remained more or less unchanged before, during and after the crisis.

[77] Since the effectiveness of the structural funds on the economic performance of receiving member states is conditional on the quality of their institutions, the size

the real economy and economic institutions with obsolete and rigid structures. On the other hand, extensive market regulation, high administrative costs, an unfavourable business environment to entrepreneurship, weak convergence in real terms, and widespread corruption – vis-à-vis the size (and norm) of the shadow economy[78] – were and still are drivers and causes of Greece's low competitiveness.[79]

The diachronically opposing influence that trade in goods and services have on the balance of trade (see *Table 3* and *Table 4*) points to the competitiveness issues of the manufacturing and the agricultural sectors. Competitiveness in Greece has declined by 10% since 2000 – both in terms of relative prices and unit labour costs – and concerns mostly the agricultural and industrial sectors (Malliaropulos, 2010).

Part of the literature suggests that the level of productivity is neither reflected on the level of nominal wages, nor co-existed with the rate of GDP growth. On the one hand, nominal wage growth has been outpacing productivity gains, pushing up unit labour costs and eroding the competitiveness of the Greek economy (Moschovis and Servera, 2009). Another issue is that of collective bargaining that is positively related with downward wage rigidity, which in turn it is positively associated with the extent of permanent contracts. This effect is stronger in countries with stricter employment protection regulations, such as Greece (Babecky et al., 2010).[80]

---

of the effect of the structural funds on Greece's economic growth is ambiguous. The same occurs regarding the impact of the structural funds on inward FDI flows (Katsaitis and Doulos, 2009).

[78] The main causes for the development of the size of shadow economies are the tax burden and tax morale, labour and product market regulations, and poor quality of official public institutions and administration (Enste, 2010).

[79] Despite the reforms in the credit and telecommunications markets, and the accruing benefits from EMU accession, these drivers still persist (Pelagidis, 2010).

[80] Inter-industry wage differentials in Greece are consistent with rent-sharing occurring from collective agreements (Du Caju et al., 2010). This observation poses further limitations to the argument that productivity growth accompanies wage growth. Nevertheless, there is also contrasting evidence. For example, a study of a data sample preceding the introduction of the euro reveals that the role of skills has been decisive in the formation of wage differentials in Greece (Christopoulou and Kosma, 2011). Moreover, a study of a more recent data sample reveals that the correlation between the size of the enterprise (employer) and the size of nominal wages in Greece is explained by the correlation between the size of the enterprise and the size of labour productivity (paper published in Greek – Γιαννακόπουλος κ.α., 2010).

Uneven development across Greece highlights the role of national and local elites in shaping growth or decline, and the significance of political parties and clientelism (Liddle, 2009), and the insignificance of productivity and innovation. Greece's economic strategy up to now has had little if anything to do with entrepreneurship and innovation. The important determinants of innovation – intensity of R&D, strength in marketing, proportion of university graduates and engineers in the staff, proportion of staff with managerial responsibility, proportion of professional staff with previous experience in another company and incentives offered to the employees to contribute to innovation – were scarce in the Greek business environment; the highly innovative enterprises were the ones to overcome country-specific innovation barriers, such as negligible industrial R&D, general weakness in marketing, outdated educational system, limited labour mobility and cultural problems with involving shop-floor employees in the innovation process (Souitaris, 2002). Where public administration economic strategies and public universities have failed, privately owned universities and entrepreneurial parks could finally guide the economy towards the right path regarding entrepreneurship, innovation, and business clusters (Piperopoulos and Piperopoulos, 2010).

There has been, however, some progress regarding technology and competitiveness. During the period 1995-2005, Greece experienced simultaneously, a decline in competition – increase of market concentration – and an increase in relative export unit values[81], while it increased the quality of exports. The rapid increase of the technology content and diversification of exports was related to the catch-up process following EU and subsequently EMU memberships (Escolano, 2008: 12). Furthermore, the export of services enhanced competitiveness with substantial gains in export revenue, market share, and the terms of trade (Escolano, 2008: 13). However, despite concentration in medium high-tech industries increased in Greece during 1995-2005, low-tech specialization of production is still predominant (Ivaschenko, 2008).[82]

[81] Measured in each market as the export unit value relative to competitors, and aggregated according to the value of exports to that market.

[82] The importance of medium high-tech and especially, high-tech industries is revealed as both contribute significantly to the euro-area export market shares (see Task Force of the Monetary Policy Committee of the European System of Central Banks, 2005).

5.2 Degree of Openness and FDI Attractiveness

The structural competitiveness of an economy – human capital, infrastructure, product and labour market regulations, legal and institutional framework, and taxes – determines both export performance and attractiveness to foreign investors. Greece has been registering consecutively the worst scores in the euro-area – especially regarding the legal and institutional framework and the tax system – in the annual survey about world competitiveness of the "Institute for Management Development". Moreover, although Greece has progressed positively on the 5-year measure of cumulative change of "Doing Business" index – thus doing business has become easier – the country is ranked 100 out of 183 economies in the "Ease of Doing Business" index (see World Bank and International Finance Corporation, 2012).

FDI attractiveness in Greece follows a downward trend due to inefficient public governance, high taxation, inefficient infrastructure, and general macroeconomic conditions (Pantelidis and Nikolopoulos, 2008). The Greek accession both in the EU and the EMU has not increased the attractiveness of the country as a production base for multinational enterprises – MNEs (see Georgopoulos and Preusse, 2006). During the 1990s, the interaction of firm and industry characteristics with location affected the decision of MNEs to enter the Greek market (Barbosa and Louri, 2002). Until the introduction of the euro – and during the early years after EMU accession – the motives for inward FDI flows were those associated to market-seeking (Bitzenis et al., 2007). The respective barriers to inward FDI flows were bureaucracy, taxation, corruption, and the structure of the labour market (Bitzenis et al., 2009). After the introduction of the euro and prior to the crisis the size of inward FDI flows is explained by market size, trade openness, and labour costs; market size has been the determining factor during the crisis (Leitao, 2010).[83]

An improvement of the degree of openness of the Greek economy is able to lead quicker to an exit from the crisis. Import penetration, off-shore outsourcing and FDI are able to improve productivity and export performance of the Greek economy (Bennett et al., 2008):

(a) The composition of imports in Greece has shifted away from low-technology products and the demand for innovative, high-quality

[83] It is important to mention that the significance of "skills" disappears when "market potential" is important (Blonigen et al., 2007). The continuous importance of "market size" as a determinant of inward FDI flows denotes the expectations for market growth.

products has increased. A positive gain could arise from the positive correlation between import penetration and labour productivity (Schule, 2008).

(b) It is assumed that off-shore outsourcing reduces production costs for domestic enterprises and makes them more efficient, as a positive relationship between off-shore outsourcing and productivity has been observed (however, a causal relationship between off-shoring and competitiveness has not been established yet).[84]

(c) It is generally considered that FDI has a favourable impact on productivity and exports. It is assumed that the limited externalities of FDI on productivity and exports of the Greek economy to date are due to low inward FDI flows (Xiao, 2008).

Greek exports were influenced positively by the recovery of the global economy in 2010, increasing by 8.8% after the significant contraction of 15.9% in 2009 (see report published in Greek; IOBE, 2011β: 71). The most promising export sectors are pharmaceuticals, petroleum products, transport services, and tourism (DG ECFIN, 2011a: 10-11):

(a) The presence of MNEs in the pharmaceutical sector offers the opportunity for knowledge spillovers and access to R&D resources that have been scarce due to the large share of SMEs.

(b) The rise in demand for Chinese exports strengthen Greece's role as a regional transportation hub and gateway to SEE, which in turn can be significantly improved by investment in the infrastructure of other means of transport that would upgrade Greece's connectivity.

(c) Tourism is over-concentrated in four geographical regions and follows an intense seasonality. The development of unexploited potentials requires the generation of a strategy that would assist in overcoming these "symptoms".

5.3 Inward and Outward FDI

There have been doubts regarding the confirmation of the FDI-led growth hypothesis in Greece (Alexiou and Tsaliki, 2007), even though there is evidence of a long run relationship between inward FDI and economic growth (Georgantopoulos and Tsamis, 2011). These doubts, however, can be due, as already stated above, to low inward FDI flows

[84] Off-shore outsourcing enterprises are more productive (Gorg et al., 2008; Wagner, 2011). However, the sunk costs of engaging to off-shore outsourcing imply that only the most productive enterprises would engage.

(Xiao, 2008). Nevertheless, Greece's inward FDI does not only increase market concentration, but also its positive externalities are limited. On the other hand, outward FDI flows are connected with the preservation of export markets (Lipsey, 2004), and verify the dominance of Greek MNEs in various business sectors of SEE. The importance of outward FDI is also highlighted by the fact that Greek enterprises with internationalized activities are more competitive and have a competitive advantage over Greek enterprises that do not engage in international business.[85]

The diachronic size of outward FDI relative to inward FDI – until the eruption of the crisis – characterizes the country as one that is more a host than a home to FDI (see *Table 5*). The decline of inward FDI from 2010[86] onwards – mainly due to the contraction in domestic demand and the gloomy prospects for recovery – and the continuous increase of outward FDI (for the same reasons) have altered the trend and characterize the country as a host to FDI. Nevertheless, despite the steady growth of Greek outward FDI, it might take some time until the country catches up with other developed countries as a net outward investor, due to surges of inward FDI from prolonged privatizations – and the increase of domestic demand once the economy recovers. Although Greece's net outward FDI position places the country at the fourth stage of the investment development path, the author argues that the country – due to the negative effects of the crisis on inward FDI – belongs to the third stage where the ownership advantages of domestic enterprises develop at a stage that allows them not only to compete locally with foreign enterprises but also to expand their activity abroad.[87]

---

[85] This is a major finding from reports for several industries about the motives and barriers to internationalize, undertaken by the Federation of Industries of Northern Greece in 2008 (titles in Greek are available online at http://www.sbbe.gr/m2/m2_3.asp). This notion has earlier foundations and was mainly concentrated on labour cost. For example, an earlier study (Labrianidis et al., 2004) indicates that Greece's outward FDI to SEE and inflow of labour (migrants from the Balkans) represent the gains of Greek firms by adopting labour intensive strategies.

[86] Outward FDI increased by 3.5% in 2010, while inward FDI decreased by 14% (Bank of Greece: International investment position data). There is a difference for 2010 between these figures from the Bank of Greece and the Eurostat figures shown on Table 5. The discussion focuses on the figures from the Bank of Greece, as Eurostat continuously updates and evaluates recent bulk of data.

[87] However, it can be argued that Greece is, and will be on the fourth stage of the investment development path even if inward FDI catches up after the prolonged privatisations, etc. It is possible for fourth stage countries to generate a negative net investment position, as a result of their fewer endowment and generation of knowledge, or technologically-intensive intangible assets (Duran and Ubeda, 2001).

Table 5 – Greece: Direct investment in the euro era.

Indicator/Year	2001	2005	2008	2009	2010	2011
Outward FDI position (stocks as a percentage of GDP)	5.1	5.9	11.6	12.8	14.0	15.4
Inward FDI position (stocks as a percentage of GDP)	10.5	12.8	11.7	12.1	11.5	10.1
Gross fixed capital formation (percentage of GDP)	21.6	20.7	22.1	19.1	16.6	14.0
Gross fixed capital formation by private sector (percentage of GDP)	18.1	17.3	15.8	14.2	12.7	10.9
Gross fixed capital formation in (percentage of total):						
Real estate activities	33.1	46.8	35.3	31.8	31.1	-
Public administration and defence; compulsory social security	13.3	8.0	10.3	13.1	14.1	-
Water transport	5.2	4.2	11.8	9.9	12.3	-
Crop and animal production, hunting and related service activities	3.3	3.8	3.9	4.0	3.7	-
Wholesale trade, except of motor vehicles and motorcycles	1.5	2.9	3.1	3.3	3.0	-
Electricity, gas, steam and air conditioning supply	2.9	1.7	1.9	2.5	2.7	-
Accommodation and food service activities	1.7	1.6	2.3	2.5	2.6	-
Construction	2.7	1.9	2.6	2.7	2.3	-
Retail trade, except of motor vehicles and motorcycles	0.8	2.6	2.1	2.3	2.1	-
Rental and leasing activities	0.4	2.5	2.8	2.6	2.1	-
Land transport and transport via pipelines	2.8	2.4	1.7	1.9	1.9	-
Manufacture of food products; beverages and tobacco products	1.6	1.0	2.1	2.1	1.8	-
Telecommunications	7.4	3.5	1.6	1.6	1.7	-
Education	2.7	2.2	1.8	1.9	1.7	-

Source: Eurostat

Notes to Table 5:
(http://epp.eurostat.ec.europa.eu/portal/page/portal/statistics/search_database, as accessed 10 July 2012).
* GDP is measured at current prices.
** FDI data for 2011 is from Bank of Greece
(http://www.bankofgreece.gr/BoGDocuments/Πίνακας_διεθνής_επενδυτικής_θέσης.xls, as accessed 10 July 2012).
- Not available.

Regarding inward FDI, MNEs are eager to acquire the most efficient enterprises in Greece and actively engage in assisting them to up-grade their procedures (Georgopoulos and Preusse, 2009). MNEs select to enter sectors/regions of high productivity and their impact on domestic productivity is negative, particularly to enterprises engaging in non-manufacturing activities and high-tech sectors (Monastiriotis and Jordaan, 2010). Inward FDI is concentrated in the most developed regions and its externalities exhibit an equilibrating character, as productivity spillovers are mainly negative in the regions hosting the main urban areas, while they are mostly positive in peripheral regions (Monastiriotis and Jordaan, 2011). The majority of foreign MNEs is more productive than domestic MNEs, and in general, positive spillover effects are identifiable mainly to SMEs with intermediate productivity levels (Petroulas, 2008). For example, in the tourism industry, MNEs are generally larger in terms of size, out-perform their domestic competitors and make substantial use of local partners, who contribute with their knowledge of the local market (Anastassopoulos et al., 2009).

On the subject of outward FDI, the importance of SMEs and the Balkans for the size and direction of Greece's outward FDI remains significant from the early 1990s to date (Kalogeresis and Labrianidis, 2010).[88] The transition and Europeanization of SEE marked a gradual reconfiguration of Greece, and as a result, more than half of Greece's outward FDI stock is accumulated in the Balkans, Cyprus and Turkey.[89]

[88] The majority of enterprises with Greek interests in the 1990s were small and not directly related to a parent enterprise in Greece (Karagianni and Labrianidis, 2001).

[89] Based on OECD data, Greece accounted for a considerable share of the inward FDI stock of several countries: 51% in Cyprus, 24% in Albania, 14% in the FYR of Macedonia, 13.3% in Serbia, 6.7% in Turkey, 6.6% in Romania, and 4.2% in Bulgaria (Bitzenis and Vlachos, 2011). Greece is among the major investors in SEE and outperforms markets of similar or larger size in Chile, Saudi Arabia and Indonesia (Invest in Greece Agency, 2010).

Despite this notable achievement, Greece is underachieving in relation to most EMU member states in terms of the ratio of outward FDI stock to GDP. Moreover, in view of the ongoing crisis, since diversification and in particular, the establishment of a leading role have been both the outcome and the basis for potential expansion in the emerging Balkan region, a potential strategy of major cut-backs in the activities of foreign affiliates as a mean of cost reduction would have negative effects on the future of MNEs from Greece (Bitzenis and Vlachos, 2011).

The successful outward FDI projects of Greek – or Greek-based – MNEs tend to be located in developed countries, performed in a high-technology sector and linked to horizontal integration (Demos et al., 2004). Greek enterprises expand to open economies with small market size, similar to Greece. Rule of law and high bureaucratic quality remain essential for the decision of Greek enterprises to choose a foreign location, while the existence of high corruption acts as a disincentive (Stoian and Filippaios, 2008).

The basic motives for the expansion of Greek MNEs are the "search for new markets", the "acquisition of strategic resources," "low labour cost," "geographical proximity" and "absence of decisive western investment interest." Greek MNEs offer mature products/services ready for consumption – at the final stage of the production chain – which are adjusted to the needs of the host market. Other factors such as market size, openness, capital productivity and labour costs on the sectoral level are also influencing the decision of Greek enterprises to internationalise their activities (see report published in Greek; Παπαναστασίου, 2009; in addition, see Bitzenis, 2006; Bitzenis and Vlachos, 2011).

5.4 Domestic Direct Investment

Gross capital formation increased by 11% during Greece's induction in the euro-area and the aftermath of the Olympics (2000-2005), and decreased by 37% since the eruption of the crisis (2007-2010). *Table 5* indicates that gross fixed capital formation by private sector constitutes more than 70% of total gross fixed capital formation, while inward FDI stock increased steadily to approximately 70% of total gross fixed capital formation. The investment expenditure that is less affected by the crisis concerns assets in "real estate activity" and "water transport," while the largest decrease concerns assets in "telecommunications."

In the EU and the euro-area, investment activity decreased in 2009 by 21.9% and 24.8% respectively. The domestic collapse of Greek investment activity in 2009 – a fall of 44.8% – was due to the economic crisis and concerned all sectors of the economy. Although the technological advancements on the one hand and the motives to invest on the other were the main factors that influenced positively investment activity, the unfavourable effect of the Greek economic policy prevailed. The rate of taxation of profits and both the availability and the cost of capital[90] also influenced negatively investments in Greece. The direction of investments that took place in 2009 was equally shared to the replacement of existing capital equipment, the increase of existing productive capacity, the improvement of existing production techniques, and the enlargement of productive capacity for new products (see report published in Greek; IOBE, 2010α).

While recovery took place amidst fiscal problems and weakened expectations at a global level in 2010, recession in Greece expanded to all productive sectors (see report published in Greek; IOBE, 2010β). Investment activity in the EU and the euro-area decreased in 2010 by 2.7% and 7.8% respectively (see report published in Greek; IOBE, 2010γ). The postponement of investment plans in 2009 due to financial difficulties generated forecasts of a rise of investment activity in 2010 regarding the manufacturing sector by 5.6% (see report published in Greek; IOBE, 2010α). However, the budgetary debt crisis and the escalated depression had retained the margins of investments and cancelled most of investment planning in 2010 – a fall of 9.2%. A similar reduction to investment activity was also forecasted for 2011.[91]

From the factors that influenced investment activity in 2010, only developments in technological advancement had a positive effect, while those with a negative effect matched those of 2009. The investment expenditure of manufacturing enterprises was directed in 2010 for the most part towards the enlargement of productive capacity for new products and the replacement of existing capital equipment. A lesser share was allocated to the increase of productive capacity for existing products, and the improvement of existing production methods (see report published in Greek; IOBE, 2010γ).

In the first quarter of 2011, the fall of investment expenses escalated at 21.8% due to depression. Although there was a minor improvement of the

---

[90] The drops in the availability of capital and the increases on the cost of capital is due to the decreased credit extension of Greek banks, and more generally, the stricter criteria of issuing loanable funds that Greek banks have adopted due to the crisis.

[91] Nevertheless, an optimistic expectation is that all forecasts to-date do not account for the likely positive effects from prolonged institutional adjustments (fast-track licensing, reduction of corporate tax, etc).

climate in the manufacturing sector, and consumers' confidence began to improve – remaining however to historically low levels – stagnation in the services and the retail trade sector, and an extended fall in the construction sector endured. Led primarily by continuous export increases, the manufacturing sector is the only sector that presents a stable yet weak improvement (see report published in Greek; IOBE, 2011γ).

From the factors that influenced investment activity in 2011, only developments in technological advancement had a positive effect. Half of the investment expenditure of manufacturing enterprises was directed in 2011 for the most part towards the enlargement of productive capacity for new products and the replacement of existing capital equipment. The other half was allocated to the increase of productive capacity for existing products and the improvement of existing production methods (see report published in Greek; IOBE, 2011δ).

5.5 Entrepreneurial Activity

Greece is placed on the 149th position of the "starting a business" 2011 ranking where issues like how to start a business or protecting investment are very poorly handled (see www.doingbusiness.org). Although these rankings indicate an unfriendly business environment, the size of entrepreneurial activity in Greece has always been relatively higher to the respective EU average due to the large preference for self-employment. This preference can be partly explained by the rising rate of "necessity-driven" individual owner-managers of new enterprises that Greece has been exhibiting during 2002-2010 (Kelley et al., 2011: 52).[92] Moreover, the choice for self-employment becomes more and more preferable for the youths because youth unemployment (less than 25 years old) in Greece has rocketed to more than 40% due to the depression caused by the crisis (for a study on the determinants of youth entrepreneurship see Ierapetritis et al., 2010).

Entrepreneurial activity is an important foundation of the Greek economy due to the relatively high preference of Greeks for self-

---

[92] The relatively high rate of self-employment in Greece is also attributed to activities of the shadow economy. Although administrative barriers to entry to self-employment make it unattractive, the advantages of the potential benefit of tax evasion and the savings from the social security payments – which effectively increase for higher incomes – become a forceful motive to prefer it from salaried full-time or part-time employment (Mitsopoulos and Pelagidis, 2011). Although not for Greek case, empirical findings suggest that an extensive shadow economy may favour entrepreneurial entry (Estrin and Mickiewicz, 2010).

employment and the vital contribution of SMEs to the levels of GDP and employment. Successful self-employment is driven by achievement, motivation and responsibility, which are the most significant discriminating factors between entrepreneurial and professional chief executive officers (Apospori et al., 2005).

The importance of entrepreneurial activity is crucial for many sectors of the Greek economy. For example, in the tourism industry,[93] performance is not only subject to industry and governance structures (for these issues see Buhalis, 2001) but depends also on the quality/ability of Greek entrepreneurship – in terms of education/training – to conform with a demanding and rapidly evolving business environment (Papageorgiou, 2008).

The impact of entrepreneurial networking on the likelihood of entrepreneurship participation depends on culture. Approximately half of total entrepreneurs in Greece are networking, i.e. have a personal relationship with someone who started a business in the last 2 years. Networking in Greece has a weak effect on entrepreneurship participation in all three stages of the entrepreneurship (discovery, start-up, young business), though it is most important in the startup stage (Klyver et al., 2008).

Inelastic household obligations differentiate the factors influencing the entrepreneurial activity of men and women. Men have greater odds of being self-employed than women. Self-employment is negatively correlated to centralization as individuals residing in the capital have lesser odds of being self-employed than individuals working outside the capital (Livanos, 2009a). In Greek urban areas, women prefer starting up a newly established business, and push factors such as low family income and unemployment and pull factors mainly in terms of incentives are very important in influencing their engagement to entrepreneurship (Sarri and Trihopoulou, 2005; Apergis and Pekka-Economou, 2010). Women entrepreneurship in Greek rural areas differs considerably from that of urban, as it is not always driven by personal goals and entrepreneurial ideals and the family plays a decisive role (Iakovidou et al., 2009).

Furthermore – and with regard to the differentiating factor of nationality – immigrants' entrepreneurship is embedded within the dynamics of immigrants' integration and the emergence of distinct ethnic business communities by migrants (Labrianidis and Hatziprokopiou,

[93] The dependence on mainly foreign tourist agents and the monopsonistic power of MNEs force Greek SMEs – that constitute the majority of the Greek accommodation sector – to operate on very thin profit margins (Papageorgiou, 2008).

2010). Self-employment for immigrants is an income-generating option towards inclusion and a strategy for escaping discrimination and exclusion (Lazaridis and Koumandraki, 2003; Hatziprokopiou, 2008). It comprises formal and informal activities – as it is part of Greece's large shadow economy – but it is not necessarily part of organized crime (Antonopoulos et al., 2011).

With regard to the types of entrepreneurial activity, in 2008, when the crisis was more an international than a Greek phenomenon, an explosive rise in "total early-stage entrepreneurial activity"[94] took place (see report published in Greek; Ιωαννίδης κ.α., 2009). In 2009 – by the end of which the Greek sovereign debt crisis emerged – the main cause of suspending possible entrepreneurial activity was the lack of sufficient profitability and the most important motives for undertaking enterprising action were "opportunity-driven" and "necessity-driven" entrepreneurial activities.[95] "Total early-stage entrepreneurial activity" decreased lightly, mainly because of the decrease of nascent entrepreneurs. On the other hand, the activity of established business owner-managers marked its higher rise since 2005 (see report published in Greek; Ιωαννίδης κ.α., 2010).

Greece showed a substantial decrease in "total early-stage entrepreneurial activity" during 2010 (Kelley et al., 2011: 25). Moreover, the "fear of failure" among all economies participating to GEM entrepreneurship survey was highest in Greece, indicating a strong aversion to risk, which is confirmed by the relatively high employment protection rate (Kelley et al., 2011: 20). Financial difficulties were the primary reason for discontinuing business activities. The majority of entrepreneurs states that it is harder to start a business in 2010 compared to 2009, and that turbulent economic conditions can diminish prospects for new start-ups (Kelley et al., 2011: 55).

---

[94] Percentage of the 18-64 age-group who are either a nascent entrepreneur or owner-manager of a new business. Nascent entrepreneurs are actively involved in setting up a business they will own or co-own; this business has not paid salaries, wages or any other payments to the owners for more than three months. Owner-managers of a new business own and manage a running business that has paid salaries, wages or any other payments to the owners for more than three months, but not more than 42 months (Kelley et al., 2011: 63).

[95] "Opportunity-driven" entrepreneurs are driven by the opportunity of increasing their income, or just maintaining it. "Necessity-driven" entrepreneurs are involved in entrepreneurship because they have no other option for work (Kelley et al., 2011: 64).

6. Unemployment in Greece during the Crisis

How is unemployment related to the business environment in Greece during the crisis? The depression has a direct negative impact on domestic demand, which in turn forces Greek enterprises to cut costs and increase their market share in the domestic market and, ultimately, to seek new markets abroad. The strategy adopted by the enterprises during the crisis leads, inevitably, to a downward adjustment of the rate of employment (see report published in Greek; Τράπεζα της Ελλάδος, 2011: 90). The adopted strategy broadly consists of two phases:

(a) The initial reaction is that enterprises seek to make their product more competitive by reducing operating costs, prices and profit margins, and increasing productivity. These actions aim to increase their share of the shrinking market and to avoid a reduction of their production.
(b) In the case that the enterprises fail to increase their market share despite the measures taken, they are forced to reduce their production levels.

Most enterprises have failed to increase their market share and the rising pressures on the Greek labour market are the outcome of their ultimate measures for survival. These ultimate measures include: expansion of working hours with no compensation for overtime, permanent leave, implementation of individual (non-collective) working agreements, job rotation, non-renewal of fixed-term employment contracts, and, ultimately, lay-offs.

The Greek government has adopted several measures in order to control the decline of both the employment rate and domestic demand during the crisis. Traditional measures designed to support the unemployed, such as unemployment benefits, have been accompanied by programmes aiming to facilitate the reintegration of the unemployed into the labour market, e.g. by subsidizing the salaries of new recruits (or the insurance contributions paid by employers), subsidizing self-employment, and training programmes. *Table 2* indicates that these measures have not managed to restrain the rise of unemployment, which reached 17.7% in 2011 (22.6% in the first quarter of 2012).[96] However, increasing

[96] Nevertheless, any kind of measures in the presence of fiscal consolidation seem to be effortless, since in countries with high employment protection legislation systems – such as Greece, at least until 2012 – fiscal consolidation is associated

unemployment has not proportionally affected the size of domestic demand, as the latter remains well over the size of GDP. The comparatively unaffected size of domestic demand indicates the importance of public sector employment – and government expenditure in general – to its composition.

Table 2 indicates that the rate of unemployment has been declining until 2008 and that employment follows a downward trend from 2009 onwards. All forms of employment declined further in 2010 – wage employment, self-employed with staff (employers) and without staff, as well as assistants in family businesses – and the only industry in which there was a rise in the number of employees was that of the health services (see report published in Greek; Τράπεζα της Ελλάδος, 2011: 85). Employment will continue to decline at least until the end of 2012 – and as long as the depression continues – and the rate of all categories of unemployed (sex, age, etc.) will continue to rise. Moreover, long-term unemployment has increased from 3.9% in 2009, to 5.7% in 2010, to 8.8% in 2011, to 12.3% in the first quarter of 2012 and the unemployment compensation system has resulted in increasing numbers of ineligible jobseekers as unemployment benefits in Greece expire after 12 months.[97] This tremendous increase of structural unemployment implies the lack of proper policy measures and the demand contraction that shocked the Greek economy.

Studies indicate that apart from gender and marital status, urbanisation and regionality have an important impact on employment – i.e. residents of regions outside Athens have a higher probability of being unemployed (Livanos, 2009b; Rodokanakis and Vlachos, forthcoming). Furthermore, the subject that an individual has studied affects the probability of being unemployed more than the qualification achieved (Livanos, 2009b) and the age-group of 15-24 years old has the lowest odds to being employed – with respect to other age-groups (Rodokanakis and Vlachos, forthcoming).

Young employees – less than 30 years of age – are among the most vulnerable population groups hit by the current economic crisis, mainly because they are usually employed for a fixed term and have less experience than older workers. Youth unemployment – less than 25 years of age – in Greece rose continuously from 22.1% in 2008, to 25.8% in 2009, to 32.9% in 2010, to 44.4% in 2011, and to 52.2% in the first quarter of 2012. The particular rise in the unemployment rate among youths

---

with a stronger reduction in job creation and a higher incidence of long-term unemployment (Turrini, 2012).

[97] The older someone gets the greater the odds of being long-term unemployed are (Livanos, 2007).

appears to be due to the increased number of young people who have lost their employment and the lengthening of the time of transition from education to employment (see report published in Greek; Τράπεζα της Ελλάδος, 2010: 91-92).[98]

The roots of this problematic situation are discussed in a relatively recent study, which indicates that the participation rates of young employees in the Greek labour market are among the lowest in OECD (see OECD, 2010b). In contrast to the practice of members of both the EU and the OECD, youth unemployment in Greece is influenced by the fact that to date:

(a) there is no minimum wage set for apprenticeship;
(b) the social security contributions made by employers are not differentiated by the age of the employees;
(c) a continuous "protection" of the employment of older individuals against that of young employees has been developed. This trend has been the outcome of prevailing social perceptions and is encouraged by the legal framework.
(d) the trial period of two months – on average – is not sufficient for induction; neither as a training period nor as an assessment for offering long-term vacancies;
(e) the number of jobs created by the private sector in contrast to the public sector is relatively lower – even in boom periods. This difference in job creation is largely due to the extensive regulatory interventions of public authorities, which hinder entrepreneurial activity.
(f) there is a mismatch between skills developed through education and skills required by the labour market.

High unemployment rates on the one hand, and unprecedented minimum wage levels for new entrants to the labour market on the other, force young people to seek employment abroad. Immigration of young prospective employees – particularly those of higher education – formulates a business environment that is based more on comparatively lower (than the euro-area) labour costs and less on innovation.

[98] For a detailed study about the transition from higher education to employment in the Greek labour market see Karamessini (2010).

Greece's relatively higher unemployment rate from both the EU and the euro-area – see *Table 2* – increases the preference for shadow economic activities (Danopoulos and Znidaric, 2007).[99] Except for the negative impact on employment, the strategy of Greek enterprises amid the crisis – as mentioned above – would also have a direct impact on the shadow economy. Since the Greek labour market entails a vast number of shadow economic activities,[100] it is rational to expect that the practices of Greek enterprises will inflate further the already enormous size of the Greek shadow economy.[101]

The enduring depression requires for continuous cost reduction measures as an ultimate effort for the survival of the shrinking private sector. The failure of domestic enterprises to expand their market share domestically – or abroad – leads to higher levels of unemployment. The demand for flexicurity, along with the enduring depression, suppress wage levels and elasticize the obligations of employers. These elements contribute to the formulation of a business environment where competitiveness will be based on labour cost and lesser skills. Furthermore, the shadow economy – which is also encouraged by the rising levels of taxation – will be the foreground of unfair competition between entrepreneurs utilizing the informal economy, compared to those remaining on the official economy.

[99] Danopoulos and Znidaric (2007) assert that Greece's relatively high unemployment rate and the non-stop – geographically influenced – provision of undocumented immigrant workers encourage shadow economic activities. They conclude that the relatively high Greek shadow economy is influenced by the relatively high poverty levels in Greece.

[100] Although not detected by the household budget survey and empirical literature, 10% of all firms inspected by the Social Insurance Foundation in 2008 failed to pay social contributions, while 27% of all employees remained unregistered (Matsaganis and Flevotomou, 2010).

[101] For the size of the Greek shadow economy see Schneider et al. (2010). Greece exhibits the largest shadow economy (as a percentage of GDP) among high income developed countries.

7. The Greek Exit from the Crisis and the Prolonged Recovery

The combination of private and official sector involvement in Greek debt restructuring[102] and the financial assistance under the second economic adjustment programme for Greece aim at putting Greece's public debt ratio on a downward path reaching approximately 120% of GDP by 2020 and bringing Greece's government deficit below the EU's reference value of 3% of GDP. The programme entails a number of structural reforms (see DG ECFIN, 2011a to c; DG ECFIN, 2012) – a part of which has already been accomplished – and is accompanied by strengthened monitoring of their implementation. The structural fiscal reforms aim to improve the effectiveness of public administration, public healthcare, and tax collection – the first priority being the fight against tax evasion – and to secure the viability of the pension scheme. The aim of the growth-enhancing structural reforms is to improve the supply-side conditions of the economy, and increase internal competition and external competitiveness (DG ECFIN, 2011a: 32-41; DG ECFIN, 2012: 21-43). In particular:

(a) Expenditure control for increased cost-effectiveness via reforms that will strengthen public expenditure monitoring and increase public administration efficiency.[103] Moreover, healthcare and pension reforms are also crucial since they are the main foundations of fiscal consolidation.
(b) Tax reforms and policies that will strengthen revenue administration and the fight against tax evasion.
(c) The target of collecting €50 billion in privatisation receipts until 2015.
(d) The short-term freezing of minimum wages set by collective agreements and the special firm-level collective agreements are a step towards making the wage setting system more adequate to

[102] For a discussion on Greek debt restructuring see DG ECFIN (2011b: 7-8). Although the "haircut" was put forward by the joint EC/IMF/ECB "rescue" mission as a prerequisite for the extension of the bailout, several voices question its effectiveness for two reasons. Firstly, the debt relief – on a trajectory to reach 120% of GDP by 2020 – will be at best as it was two years earlier, when Greece required for international financial assistance. Secondly, the exchange of Greek-law regulated titles with new debt instruments issued under English law guarantees that the Greek government will not be able to perform a future "haircut", or convert it in case Greece is forced to return to a national currency.

[103] Cost reduction entails lay-offs and merging of public administration units.

reflect the current economic conditions of both the public sector and the business environment. In addition, by relaxing the strictness of employment protection, it is expected that the size of youth and long-term unemployment would decrease.

(e) The deregulation of closed professions is expected to increase competition and enhance growth. In addition, the liberalisation of the wholesale electricity market and transport sector – freight, tourism, urban transport – has a great growth-enhancing potential.

(f) An incentive framework – put forward by the "National Strategic Reference Framework" – for general entrepreneurship, technological development, and large-scale investments aiming to support private investment is expected to contribute to regional cohesion and the adoption of new technologies (absorption of structural funds). Other growth oriented policies include fast-track licensing[104] and methods to increase the R&D intensity of the economy.

(g) The development of a national export strategy that entails the formation of a national brand, an improved information network for exporters, removal of bureaucratic procedures, etc., is expected to increase the share of Greek exports globally and assist to the country's development as an outward looking economy.

The economic adjustment programme has been supported by various reports that aim to designate a new economic model that will be able to bring Greece back on the growth track. In particular, the Foundation of Economic and Industrial Research (2011: 8) – the most popular think tank of Greek business circles – points out that "the new model of economic development should be characterized by export orientation, meritocracy in the public sector, competition, competitiveness, fiscal discipline through limitation of expenditure, liberalization of restricted markets and professions, higher private and public investment, privatization, development of the extensive but idle public assets, emphasis on the knowledge triangle: education, research and development, innovation." With regard to the role of the public sector, earlier arguments (see inter alia Angelopoulos and Philippopoulos, 2007) that a smaller government share in GDP, a reallocation of funds away from the wage bill to public investment, and an improvement in government quality/efficiency, which can become engines of long-term growth, are among the top priorities of the economic adjustment programme.

---

[104] Further policies beyond the acceleration of start-up procedures are considered – that would limit/speed up the procedures to enforce contracts, register property, etc. – in order to exploit the Greeks' high propensity towards entrepreneurship.

The success of the economic adjustment programme is in the generation of extra revenue that will ensure the repayment of the Greek sovereign debt and will be the result of privatizations, primary surpluses and GDP growth. The reports in support of the appropriateness of the economic adjustment programme (see inter alia report published in Greek; IOBE, 2011β) indicate that:

(a) there are several unexploited sources of growth – particularly from the supply side[105] – which are able to contribute significantly to government revenue.
(b) cuts in defense spending, and in particular, the reduction of public expenditures on health through the primary care system reform, and the introduction of accounting books and information systems in public hospitals, are able to minimize the size of the budget deficit.
(c) the size of sovereign debt can be reduced through privatization.

7.1 The Case against the Programme

The main argument about the policy measures adopted or put forward by the Greek government (i.e. the economic adjustment programme) concern the dilemma of:

(a) remaining in the euro-area with the prospect of rebuilding the economy, or
(b) abolishing the euro despite the possibility that this option could mean the experience of economic and social catastrophe.

Those in favor of choosing to remain in the euro-area recognize the severe costs to the economy in terms of suffering fiscal austerity measures during a depression, yet continue to be optimistic not only because finance is secured and the necessary reforms – otherwise neglected – will be accomplished, but also because an "aggressive" response to the euro-area debt crisis is anticipated from the ECB through monetary expansion and eurobonds issuance. These expectations are shaped by the growing consensus that Greece was a pretext for the outbreak of the crisis and not the cause.[106]

---

[105] The realization of policies fostering the liberalization of the labour market – i.e. termination of closed professions in non-tradable sectors (services) – would result in a medium-term GDP growth of 10%.

[106] There are several views in the literature leading to the conclusion that EU should be reconstructed with a new pact of solidarity measures that would be able

The case against the economic adjustment programme is rooted in the deflationary spiral caused by the combination of fiscal austerity and output contraction.[107] Deficit reduction via contraction of government spending – both in wages and amount of benefits and public services – and increase in taxes continuously postpone the expectations for economic growth and have resulted in the formulation of a growing anti-euro coalition. The historically unprecedented postwar contraction of the Greek economy, which is currently expected to persist until 2013, justifies the concern about the Greek economy's future development within the euro-area, as:

(a) Austerity measures taken to reduce fiscal deficits amid depression have a significant social impact in terms of greater inequality and increased poverty (Matsaganis and Leventi, 2011).[108]
(b) Horizontal austerity measures amplify existing disparities and spatial imbalances (Monastiriotis, 2011).
(c) Although higher tax rates raise additional tax revenue, the economic costs of higher distortionary taxation in terms of output contraction are substantial (Vogel, 2012).
(d) The deflationary spiral endangers sovereign debt sustainability. Tax increases and fiscal austerity measures aiming to generate a balanced budget, boost unemployment and output contraction, which in turn reduce government receipts and as a result, further tax increases and fiscal austerity measures are required. Moreover, the failure to generate a balanced budget expands the level of sovereign debt.

---

to establish an enduring social model (see Petit, 2012). Furthermore, a blueprint for an EU treasury is put forward, which would benefit both fiscally strong and weak members and would halt the crisis (Matziorinis, 2012).

[107] Unfortunately, the expectations for a severe unprojected impact of the economic adjustment programme are fulfilled. Fiscal adjustment is projected by the IMF (2013: 13) to have a larger impact – than before – on domestic demand and economic growth, as several factors were wrongly considered unrelated to fiscal developments. The impact of these "unrelated" factors – such as the political crisis and rising euro exit fears – on confidence in Greece has resulted to the endurance of a deeper recession and tighter liquidity.

[108] The failure to address tax evasion requires for measures whose impact has been unevenly and severely felt by workers, pensioners and honest tax-paying citizens (Lanara-Tzotze, 2012).

Box 3 – An exit from the euro.

An exit from the euro-area would involve positive and negative economic impacts for Greece via several channels (IMF, 2012: 46-47).

Positive:

(a) Competitiveness gains from nominal exchange rate depreciation. However, this would be temporary due to fiscal and external imbalances, i.e. currency depreciation and monetary financing of deficit spending could lead to a surge in inflation.

(b) Trade deficit would diminish as imports would concern only primary goods.

(c) Inflation would reduce the size of private debt converted to national currency and issued domestically at a fixed rate.

Negative:

(a) Inflation consequent on devaluation would reduce the real value of savings.

(b) The payment system would be disrupted, and uncertainty would reign about contracts.

(c) Liquidity and credit (especially from abroad) would dry up. The banking sector would require for bailout.

(d) External debt burden would soar – sovereign debt issued under foreign law will not be exposed to a haircut resulting by the inflated national currency – thus announcing a default would be inevitable.

(e) Dramatic decrease in living standards and lack of primary goods.

All the above may insinuate the ineffectiveness – so far – of the strategy adopted to lead to recovery, but they cannot justify the option to exit from the euro-area. The adoption of a national currency would imply more negative consequences than positive ones (see *Box 3*). However, even in the case that Greece's exit from the euro-area would take place due to the failure of implementing the economic adjustment programme – or due to the programme's failure to deliver results within a socially tolerable timeframe – the adoption of a national currency requires for extreme organization and discipline (since the Greek economy depends heavily on imports), and huge financial support to prevent the banking system from collapsing. As a result, the case against the policy measures adopted should only be an argument for a renegotiation of the economic adjustment programme[109] – i.e. by including fiscal injections that would

[109] Arguments for a renegotiation of the economic adjustment programme appeared with Greece's agreement to the "Memorandum of Understanding on Specific Economic Policy Conditionality." Earlier arguments were build around the notion that since Greek sovereign debt is primarily owned by French, German – and of

re-ignite economic growth and reverse gloomy prospects – and to urge an ECB "aggressive" response to the euro-area debt crisis.

7.2 Is Internal Devaluation the Cure for Competitiveness?

The generation of a surplus may be difficult for a country grappling with excessive debt – and thus, reduced access to finance – but it gets even more difficult when that country is unable to use the exchange rate as a policy tool and as a result, has to undergo an internal devaluation to restore competitiveness. While "countries with outright exchange rate devaluations usually recover faster," "restoring competitiveness by way of internal devaluation has proved to be a difficult undertaking with very few successes" as "country experience suggests several factors are needed for internal devaluation to work" – i.e. open economy with high factor mobility and a high degree of wage and price flexibility (IMF, 2012: 48).

The reduction of labour costs in the tradable sector is prioritised by several reports at an international level (see inter alia Marzinotto et al., 2011) as Greece needs to export more goods and services. A recent study by DG ECFIN (2011d) indicates that a tax shift from employers' social security contributions towards consumption taxes and public-sector wage moderation – with spillovers to private-sector wages – have a long-lasting impact (real effective depreciation) on production costs contrary to permanent nominal exchange rate devaluation.

Evidence in support of the twin deficits hypothesis – the notion that an economy's fiscal and current account balances move in the same direction – indicate that, especially for the euro-area, internal devaluation enhances the effort of reducing the twin deficits. Fiscal consolidation is required for the reduction of current account deficits and contraction in investment and real exchange rate depreciation play a key role in this adjustment process (Bluedorn and Leigh, 2011). Since the two deficits are also found to be positively linked in the Greek case, policymakers expect that improvement in competitiveness will be attained by (see Kalou and Paleologou, 2012):

(a) limiting price and wage rises in order to increase competitiveness in the short-run, and
(b) focusing on technological change and quality improvement in the long-run.

---

course Greek – and to a lesser extent British banks, if Greece defaults not only these banks would face default but also the EU and the euro-area financial system would be at risk (Mylonas, 2011).

Ever since the adoption of the euro, most of the deterioration in Greece's competitiveness took place in the agricultural and industrial sector, not in the service sector, which represents approximately 4/5 of the private economy. Therefore, since relative wage costs decline due to depression – which, combined with higher labor market flexibility and a weaker euro, will help to restore competitiveness over the next few years – the need for internal devaluation is not as large as markets seem to discount (Malliaropulos, 2010).

Nevertheless, irrespectively of whether internal devaluation is appropriate or not for the Greek case – with respect to the circumstances and alternative policies – "with Germany's reluctance to raise spending, a cash-strapped Greece has no alternative but to deflate" (Eichengreen and Temin, 2010: 382). The economic adjustment programme aims to improve Greek competitiveness through internal devaluation and the direct measures focus on the reduction of minimum wage and non-wage labor costs in order to make collective bargaining more effective (and reduce rent sharing). Further measures such as the liberalization of services are also in the agenda to improve competitiveness (IMF, 2012).

However, is internal devaluation the cure for the competitiveness of Greek firms? If not policymakers should focus "immediately" on – the second part of the measures highlighted above (Kalou and Paleologou, 2012) – technological change and quality improvement of the business environment. From a general point of view, a recent literature survey indicates that productivity is determined by factors other than labour cost – i.e. quality of inputs and external business environment (Syverson, 2011). This general rule is also applied in the Greek case, where labour costs are not primarily responsible for the country's mediocre rank in the "Ease of Doing Business" index (see World Bank and International Finance Corporation, 2012).

Recovery through FDI inflows is falsely perceived to be hindered by labour costs, since excessive wages (i.e. wages that do not follow labour productivity developments) do not affect the return on capital; profits are responses to changes in the economic, political and institutional environment and there should not be a priori statement for a negative relationship between them (Katsimi et al., 2012).

The inadequacy of the approach to improve competitiveness via reducing labour cost in euro-area member states suffering by the crisis is denoted by the Kaldor's paradox: the positive correlation observed between the international competitiveness of several countries and their relative unit labour costs.[110] This apparent contradiction was explained by the 'non-price' factors of competitiveness, such as R&D and innovation.[111] *Table 6* indicates that in 2011 Greece tops the six countries that decreased their real unit labour costs with respect to 2005 – i.e. labour's contribution to output increased at the same time as its reward decreased. Reduction of real unit labour cost in Greece has also been higher than the respective average reduction of the euro-area throughout the 2000s. Nevertheless, despite the improvement on labour productivity, economic growth, the business climate and expectations in general, have been continuously deteriorating after the eruption of the crisis.[112]

The preceded discussion denotes that investment propensity in Greece is primarily affected by the institutional setting and that in order for progress in competitiveness to take place, advancement of technological change and quality improvement of the business environment are deemed necessary.

---

[110] For a discussion about the need to reduce unit labour costs in euro-area periphery see Felipe and Kumar (2011). For the causes behind real unit labor costs growth differentials in the euro-area see Lebrun and Perez (2011).

[111] For example, an increase of the relative export prices of developed high-income economies is accompanied by improvements on other quality factors that offset the negative effect of price increase (Ortiz-Villajos, 2004). A rise in labour costs higher than the rise in labour productivity may be a threat to an economy's cost competitiveness only if other costs are not adjusted in compensation.

[112] Bulgaria, whose most important driver for inward FDI is the combination of production costs and EU membership, exhibits an increasing real unit labour cost (see ***Table 6***) and has significantly lower gross national income per capita than Greece (see World Bank statistics online at http://data.worldbank.org). Despite the rise of real unit labour cost, Bulgaria enjoyed a continuous increase in inward FDI stock during the 2000s, which finally reached 100% of GDP in 2010 (see UNCTAD statistics online at http://www.unctad.org/en/Pages/Statistics.aspx). This observation implies that the size of real unit labour costs should be seen comparatively only between countries with similar levels of income. For example, FDI directed to Greece was primarily market-seeking; reduction of real unit labour cost will attract efficiency-seeking FDI in Greece only if the country's gross national income per capita will deteriorate to Bulgaria's levels. Therefore, policymakers should first decide whether the model for recovery in Greece entails the country's placement as an advanced economy, and in case it does they should promote the advancement of technological change and quality improvement of the business environment.

Table 6 – Real unit labour cost in the euro-area and Bulgaria (Index 2005=100).

Country/Year	2000	2001	2002	2003	2004	2005	2006	2007	2008	2009	2010	2011
Greece	97.7	94.5	100.6	98.3	97.6	100	95.4	95.5	97.6	101.8	98.4	93.9
Cyprus	96.7	94.8	98.2	102.7	101.4	100	97.6	94.6	92.1	98.1	95.3	95.3
Portugal	99.9	100.2	99.7	100.5	99	100	98.2	96.6	98.4	100.6	98	96.6
Spain	106.3	105.2	103.9	102.5	101	100	99	99.9	102.2	103.4	100.3	97.1
Luxembourg	101.2	107.7	107.8	103.1	102.5	100	94.9	93	94.6	102.6	99.4	98
Malta	96.8	102.1	100	102.6	103.3	100	101.9	99.6	99.8	102.9	99.5	98.3
Germany	104.8	104.1	103.3	103.1	101.5	100	97.7	95.4	96.8	100.9	99.1	99.7
Euro-area	102.4	102.2	102	101.9	100.7	100	98.9	98	99.6	102.7	101.2	100.8
Austria	104.8	103.8	102.9	102.9	100.9	100	99.3	98.5	100.5	103.9	102.1	100.8
Italy	98.7	98.7	98.9	99.8	99.5	100	100.2	99.5	101.4	103.3	102.4	102.1
France	99.5	99.9	100.7	100.7	100	100	99.7	98.8	99.4	102.3	101.9	102.2
Netherlands	102.2	102.1	103.1	103.4	102.9	100	98.9	98.7	99.5	105.1	102.9	102.7
Belgium	102.2	104.4	104.7	103.8	100.9	100	99.7	99.5	101.6	104.3	102.4	103
Slovakia	104.9	102.6	102.9	101.6	98.5	100	98.8	98.1	99.7	107.8	105.9	103.5
Finland	97.3	97.9	97.4	98.9	98.3	100	99.5	97.1	100.7	108.1	106	104.6
Slovenia	102.2	102.5	101	99.9	100.2	100	99	97.5	99.4	105	106.4	106
Estonia	103.4	101	100.2	101.1	102.1	100	100.3	105.4	114.1	116.9	109.2	106.1
Bulgaria	105.9	107.8	104.5	103.8	101.7	100	96.5	96.6	100.1	108.2	111.2	107.1
Ireland	100	99.3	95.3	95.8	97.6	100	100.5	103.4	113.8	115.8	110.5	-

Source: Eurostat (http://epp.eurostat.ec.europa.eu/portal/page/portal/statistics/search_database, as accessed 10 July 2012).

* Unit labour cost compares remuneration (compensation per employee in current prices) and productivity (GDP in current prices per employment) to show how the remuneration of employees is related to the productivity of their labour. It is the relationship between how much each "worker" is paid (numerator) and the value he/she produces by their work (denominator).

** Euro-area(11) for 2000, euro-area(12) for 2006, euro-area(13) for 2007, euro-area(15) for 2008, euro-area(16) for 2010, euro-area(17) for 2011

- Not available.

7.3 The Critical Significance of Corruption and the Shadow Economy

An issue neglected so far or not considered of top priority by the economic adjustment programme is that of corruption and the shadow economy. The requirement to face these two phenomena as a single issue is rooted to the fact that the size of the shadow economy is greatly affected by the sizes of corruption and bureaucracy – i.e. the "inability to exercise control on" or the "ability to influence" underground economic activities (see earlier discussions on clientelism, rent-seeking behaviour, poor rankings on business indexes, etc.).

Several studies (see inter alia Schneider et al., 2010[113]) converge on the view that the size of the Greek shadow economy – and the consequent level of tax evasion – is over 25% of GDP, which is more than the size of the budget deficit of general government (see the difference between total general government revenue and expenditure in *Table 2*). A reduction of the size of the shadow economy – and its transfer to the formal economy – could significantly assist the Greek government in achieving its fiscal targets without adopting such severe measures during depression, by either reducing the tax burden, or containing fiscal austerity measures, or even allowing a combination of both.

The General Secretariat for Information Systems generates statistical reports (statistical databases and reports in Greek are available at http://www.gsis.gr/ggps/statistika/statistika.html) that can give a thorough background to Greece's high levels of undeclared economic activities. The following indicators are an example for 2007, the year the financial crisis was triggered – but still the Greek economy was growing – and for which the latest estimates for the size of the Greek shadow economy are available (see Schneider et al., 2010). Firstly, 90% of individuals' personal income was less than €30 thousand, had an average tax rate of 4% and paid 25% of total personal income tax. As a result, 75% of total personal income tax was paid by 10% of taxpayers. Furthermore, only 2% of Greek households declared annual revenues in excess of €60 thousand, and paid 34% of total tax levied on the income of individuals. Moreover, employees and retirees declared 74% of total personal income, while self-employed only 4%.

[113] Schneider et al. (2010) provide estimates of the shadow economy for 162 countries for the period of 1999-2007. The estimated size of the Greek shadow economy is 26.5% of GDP in 2007, and the average estimated size for 1999-2007 is 27.5% of GDP. The respective averages of other euro-area member states – except for Italy which exerts an almost identical level of 27% of GDP – ranges from 23% of GDP in Portugal to 9.8% of GDP in Austria.

Secondly, 99.5% of enterprises were SMEs with up to 5 employees and paid an average annual tax of €6.1 thousand, which was relevant to the tax levied on the income of an individual declaring €24 thousand. Finally, the largest Greek enterprises – counting 1,500 in 2007 and with 350 employees on average – paid 72.2% of total corporate income tax.

Turning to dated evidence, a recent survey (OECD, 2011: 83-86) indicates that inefficient tax collection and the size of tax evasion are – partly due to bribery and corruption and – the outcome of activities in the realm of the shadow economy, which result in losses of fiscal resources between 2-4% of GDP per annum. An increase in tax revenues, which requires a great deal of progress both in the efficiency of collection and in combating tax evasion, is necessary for the consolidation needed to place the public finances on a sustainable path. The progress required is explicitly related to personal income tax – e.g. the self-employed declare incomes near the minimum taxable threshold. Of equal importance is also the problem in collecting the value added tax and social security contributions. The – lately annual – practice of tax amnesties adopted by Greek governments is likely to have encouraged people not to pay taxes when due as the expected penalties are low.

To successfully fight the shadow economy it has proven important to increase tax morale[114] and to benefit from electronic means of payments (Jensen and Wohlbier, 2012), and unfortunately there is still much needed to be done in Greece for both aspects to date. The influence of the main determinants – i.e. clientelism and rent-seeking behaviour (see earlier discussion) – of the ex post facto "interlocked" phenomena of corruption, bureaucracy and shadow economic activities on tax morale, is signified by a relationship of mutual mistrust between the Greek state and its citizens. Low tax morale contributes to higher tax evasion and for high tax morale, institutional and cultural factors (i.e. bureaucracy, corruption and individual factors such as age, sex, marital status and employment status) are at least as important as economic incentives (see Frey and Torgler, 2007; Torgler and Schneider, 2009).

Corruption and bureaucratic inefficiency amount to a tax on all firms that operate in Greece's formal sector (Romer, 2010). If corruption, bureaucracy, and the shadow economy will continue to remain uncontained, and fit into each other as parts of the Greek economy, all efforts to reform the labour market and deregulate closed professions will

[114] The willingness to pay taxes depends greatly on whether taxation is morally justified or not.

not be able to enhance productivity and competitiveness as much as expected (in the best case scenario).

8. Conclusions

Typically, after a period of recession, growth is recovering rapidly and the economy covers the lost ground. That is not true this time, at least so far. Once Greece's current sovereign debt problems were revealed – by government officials who hided the size of the nation's debt and exposure to risky assets from their foreign creditors – the Greek economy began an endless downward spiral. Greek politicians inflated the public sector not only as a substitute for a network of social welfare but also as a field for their patronage. The escalating crisis of the Greek political scene is primarily responsible for the eruption and progression of the Greek sovereign debt crisis.[115] The lack of political consensus for the development of a common front hinders the efforts for international sympathy and support and moreover, delays the reforms put forward through the economic adjustment programme. Furthermore, the lack of political consensus on a plan to exit the crisis fuels uncertainty and deteriorates the credibility of the Greek state. These forms of instability along with the contraction of domestic demand due to the enduring depression worsen further the business climate in Greece and postpone the necessary injections of private investment that will assist the Greek economy to recover.

The escalation of the Greek sovereign debt crisis since late 2009 is the result of an unfavourable shift in country-specific market expectations, which concern mainly the importance of restoring confidence. The perils that the Greek economy faces and will face, for as long as this situation persists, can be easily depicted by the fact that even the possibility to erase part of sovereign debt would not improve the country's fiscal space. Gradual improvement of the fiscal space will eventually grant the country access to international financial markets and depends on the latter's expectations for Greek recovery.[116]

---

[115] For the political leadership in Greece during the crisis see Smith (2011). For the "enforcement" of the economic adjustment programme see Panayotakis (2011).

[116] An improvement in a country's structural characteristics – which define the size and nature of economic linkages between productive sectors and household income – or economic growth rate raises its debt limit, while the occurrence (or recognition of the possibility) of a negative shock could push an otherwise sustainable debt level to the unsustainable territory. Current facts along with the findings of a recent study (Ghosh et al., 2011) indicate that there is limited or no

The failures of the economic policy since the eruption of the crisis have not only been contracting Greece's fiscal space, but have also had tremendous impact on economic activity. The continuous contraction of real wages and the slow progression of structural reforms have led to depression and gigantic unemployment levels. The reasons that the economic policy adapted to date has limited the prospects and expectations for economic growth – which will eventually lead to an exit from the crisis – can be summed up into four general points:

(a) The decrease of public investments (see *Table 2*) was accompanied by a decrease in private investment (see *Table 5*).
(b) Although wages decreased significantly since 2010, inflation is still well above the euro-area average[117] due to tax increases, oligopolistic markets and "closed-shop" practices.
(c) The failure to battle bureaucracy, corruption and the shadow economy, and the inability to support a cash-strapped market with reduced access to finance have had a major negative impact to private investment. As already stated, Greece is ranked 100 out of 183 economies in the "Ease of Doing Business" index (see World Bank and International Finance Corporation, 2012).
(d) Tax rates increased more than the decrease in government expenditure, raising questions on the efficiency of fund allocation, which in conjunction with all the above have led to even gloomiest prospects for recovery.

The failure to generate a growth enhancing impact on the Greek economy within the given time constraints requires for urgent action that would redefine and rebuilt the Greek business environment, so as to re-ignite the engine of economic growth. This strategy should focus on:

(a) improving competitiveness without further labour cost reduction,
(b) increasing the levels of productive public expenditure, and
(c) incorporating part of the shadow economy to the formal one by reducing the levels of bureaucracy and corruption – and consequently tax evasion.

---

available fiscal space – the difference between projected debt ratios and debt limits – for Greece.

[117] The annual average rate of change of the "Harmonised Indices of Consumer Prices" was 4.7% in 2010 and 3.1% in 2011 in Greece, at the same time that it was 1.6% in 2010 and 2.7% in 2011 in the euro-area.

The inappropriateness – as already discussed in subsection 7.2 – and inability of internal devaluation to enhance Greek competitiveness to date indicate the requirement for institutional reforms. Improvement in competitiveness through reduction of labour cost is not a panacea; Greece already suffers from depression and further deflation will further aggravate the situation rather than providing an exit from it. In order to exit depression, it is preferable that deflation be achieved only through a downward adjustment of non-competitively set prices, especially in state-regulated sectors (Christodoulakis, 2010). Price adjustment should take place by making firms behave more competitively, rather than through lower incomes. This form of price adjustment has to be the outcome of a deteriorating domestic demand within a liberalized market of firms that do not engage with the shadow economy. The government can assist this situation through the liberalization of "closed-shop" practices and administrative price-setting in several sectors – from transportation lorries to lawyers' fees – and by increasing the efficiency of state's firms and institutions through the reduction of corruption and bureaucracy.

Furthermore, productive public expenditure is vital for the recovery of economic growth and debt sustainability. While there is a number of seemingly contradictory findings in the empirical literature, there is some consensus on the importance of differentiating between "productive" and "unproductive" public expenditure, with the former positively correlated with growth and the latter either displaying no relationship or indicating a slightly negative one (Braunstein, 2012: 32).[118] A recent paper – that extends the previous theoretical literature – indicates that productive public capital maximises the welfare of decentralized economies (Kalaitzidakis and Tzouvelekas, 2011).[119]

Although it is generally observed that public investment crowds-out private investment (Afonso and Aubyn, 2010; Cavallo and Daude, 2011), the crowding-out effect dominates in countries with weak institutions and restricted access to financing, and is reversed in countries that have good institutions, open to trade and financial flows. Hence, public policies should focus on the quality of public investment and the selection, evaluation and monitoring of investments, rather than just quantitative targets (Cavallo and Daude, 2011).

---

[118] Productive expenditures include physical capital expenditures as well as spending aimed at generating human capital (including education, housing and health), and unproductive expenditures tend toward current public consumption, including spending on social insurance and wages (Braunstein, 2012: 32).

[119] For empirical support of this notion see inter alia Creel and Poilon (2008).

Simulations of the Greek situation indicate that the expectations for recovery and debt sustainability will be met only when contraction on public spending will be accompanied by privatizations and fiscal expansion – for example through EU funds (Christodoulakis, 2011). Moreover, the reduction in public consumption should be compensated by targeted increases in public investment with the aid of EU funds and revenue-generating efforts that concentrate more on tackling tax evasion and increasing tax progressivity (Monastiriotis, 2011).

In a nutshell, the Greek government should appeal for an alternative more realistic economic adjustment programme, in order to plan for a pragmatic exit from depression. Recent research (Ball, 2009; Bagaria et al., 2012) – that emerged across continents since the eruption of the crisis – indicates that fiscal tightening and deflationary measures are dangerous amid recessions and have severe impacts on output and employment. Productive public expenditure or at least a halt on fiscal austerity and the recent tax storm are necessary for re-igniting economic growth. A reduction of the size of the shadow economy could significantly assist the Greek government in achieving its fiscal targets without adopting such severe measures during depression. All at once, the Greek government should also focus on reducing the bureaucracy and corruption of the public sector, in order to improve the ease of doing business and eventually, attract FDI. These directions would alter domestic expectations and prospects, re-ignite economic growth and stimulate consumption expenditure, put forward the prolonged privatization plans from a positive growth/value-enhancing perspective, and ultimately, promote the Greek business environment as an attractive market to invest.

References

English

Abbritti, M. and Fahr, S. (2011). Macroeconomic implications of downward wage rigidities. *ECB Working Papers No. 1321*. Frankfurt: European Central Bank.

Adams, C. and Park, D. (2009). Causes and consequences of global imbalances: Perspective from developing Asia. *Asian Development Review*, 26 (1): 19-47.

Afonso, A. and Aubyn, M.S. (2010). Public and private investment rates of return: Evidence for industrialized countries. *Applied Economics Letters*, 17 (9): 839-843.

Aguiar-Conraria, L. and Soares, M.J. (2011). Business cycle synchronization and the Euro: A wavelet analysis. *Journal of Macroeconomics*, 33 (3): 477-489.

Akerlof, G.A. and Shiller, R.J. (2009). *Animal Spirits: How Human Psychology Drives the Economy and why it Matters for the Global Economy*. Princeton: Princeton University Press.

Albers, R., Dionyssopoulou, F. and Van Hooydonk, C. (2004). How could Greece engineer a soft landing? *ECFIN Country Focus*, 1 (2): 1-5.

Alessi, L. and Detken, C. (2009). Global liquidity as an early warning indicator for asset price boom/bust cycles. *ECB Research Bulletin*, 8: 7-9.

Alexiou, C. and Tsaliki, P.V. (2007). Foreign direct investment-led growth hypothesis: Evidence from the Greek economy. *Zagreb International Review of Economics & Business*, 10 (1): 85-97.

Altissimo, F., Benigno, P. and Palenzuela, D.R. (2011). Inflation differentials in a currency area: Facts, explanations and policy. *Open Economies Review*, 22 (2): 189-233.

Alvarez, M. (2010). *Working document no. 5 on European economic governance and EU tools for economic and social recovery*. Brussels: European Parliament; Special Committee on the Financial, Economic and Social Crisis.

Anastassopoulos, G., Filippaios, F. And Phillips, P. (2009). An eclectic investigation of tourism multinationals: Evidence from Greece. *International Journal of Hospitality Management*, 28 (2): 185-194.

Andres, J., Ortega, E. and Valles, J. (2008). Competition and inflation differentials in EMU. *Journal of Economic Dynamics and Control*, 32 (3): 848-874.

Angeloni, I. and Ehrmann, M. (2007). Euro area inflation differentials. *The B.E. Journal of Macroeconomics*, 7 (1): Article 24.

Angelopoulos, K. and Philippopoulos, A. (2007). The growth effects of fiscal policy in Greece 1960-2000. *Public Choice*, 131 (1): 157-175.

Angelopoulos, K., Dimeli, S., Philippopoulos, A. and Vassilatos, V. (2010). Rent-seeking competition from state coffers in Greece: A calibrated DSGE model. *Bank of Greece Working Papers No. 120*. Athens: Bank of Greece.

Angelopoulos, K., Philippopoulos, A. and Vassilatos, V. (2011). Rent-seeking competition from state coffers: A calibrated DSGE model of the Euro area. *CESifo Working Papers No. 1644*. Munich: Ifo Institute for Economic Research.

Antonopoulos, G.A., Hobbs, D. and Hornsby, R. (2011). Soundtrack to (illegal) entrepreneurship: Pirated CD/DVD selling in a Greek provincial city. *British Journal of Criminology*, 51 (5): 804-822.

Apergis, N. and Pekka-Economou, V. (2010). Incentives and female entrepreneurial activity: Evidence from panel firm level data. *International Advances in Economic Research*, 16 (4): 371-387.

Apergis, N., Mamatzakis, E., Staikuras, C. (2011). Testing for regime changes in Greek sovereign debt crisis. *International Advances in Economic Research*, 17 (3): 258-273.

Apospori, E., Papalexandris, N. and Galanaki, E. (2005). Entrepreneurial and professional CEOs: Differences in motive and responsibility profile. *Leadership & Organization Development Journal*, 26 (2): 141-162.

Arghyrou, M.G. (2009). Monetary policy before and after the euro: evidence from Greece. *Empirical Economics*, 36 (3): 621-643.

Arghyrou, M.G. and Kontonikas, A. (2011). The EMU sovereign-debt crisis: Fundamentals, expectations and contagion. *European Economy Economic Papers No. 436*. Brussels: European Commission, DG ECFIN.

Arghyrou, M.G. and Tsoukalas, J.D. (2011). The Greek debt crisis: Likely causes, mechanics and outcomes. *World Economy*, 34 (2): 173-191.

Aspachs-Bracons, O. and Rabanal, P. (2011). The Effects of Housing Prices and Monetary Policy in a Currency Union. *International Journal of Central Banking*, 7 (1): 225-274.

Athanasoglou, P.P., Backinezos, C. and Georgiou, E.A. (2010). Export performance, competitiveness and commodity composition. *Bank of Greece Working Papers No. 114*. Athens: Bank of Greece.

Athanassiou, E. (2007). Prospects for household borrowing in Greece and their importance for growth. *South-Eastern Europe Journal of Economics*, 5 (1): 89-101.

—. (2009). Fiscal policy and the recession: The case of Greece. *Intereconomics*, 44 (6): 364-372.

Attinasi, M.G., Checherita, C. and Nickel, C. (2010). Euro area fiscal policies and the crisis: The reaction of financial markets. In van Riet A. (ed.), Euro area fiscal policies and the crisis. *ECB Occasional Papers No. 109*. Frankfurt: European Central Bank.

Azis, I.J. (2010). Predicting a recovery date from the economic crisis of 2008. *Socio-Economic Planning Sciences*, 44 (3): 122-129.

Babecky, J., Du Caju, P., Kosma, T., Lawless, M., Messina, J. and Room, T. (2010). Downward nominal and real wage rigidity: Survey evidence from European firms. *Bank of Greece Working Papers No. 110*. Athens: Bank of Greece.

Backus, D., Henriksen, E.R., Lambert, F. and Telmer, C. (2009). Current account fact and fiction. *NBER Working Papers No. 15525*. Cambridge (Massachusetts): National Bureau of Economic Research.

Bagaria, N., Holland, D. and Van Reenen, J. (2012). Fiscal consolidation during a depression. *National Institute Economic Review*, 221 (1): F42-F54.

Baldwin, R., DiNino, V., Fontagne, L., De Santis, R.A. and Taglioni, D. (2008). Study on the impact of the euro on trade and foreign direct investment. *European Economy Economic Papers No. 321*. Brussels: European Commission, DG ECFIN.

Ball, L.M. (2009). Hysteresis in unemployment: Old and new evidence. *NBER Working Papers No. 14818*. Cambridge (Massachusetts): National Bureau of Economic Research.

Balli, F., Basher, S.A. and Ozer-Balli, H. (2010). From home bias to Euro bias: Disentangling the effects of monetary union on the European financial markets. *Journal of Economics and Business*, 62 (5): 347-366.

Barbosa, N. and Louri, H. (2002). On the determinants of multinationals' ownership preferences: Evidence from Greece and Portugal. *International Journal of Industrial Organization*, 20 (4): 493-515.

Barrel, R., Gottschalk, S., Holland, D., Khoman, E., Liadze, I. and Pomerantz1, O. (2008). The impact of EMU on growth and employment. *European Economy Economic Papers No. 318*. Brussels: European Commission, DG ECFIN.

Barrios, S. and Fargnoli, R. (2010). Discretionary measures and tax revenues in the run-up to the financial crisis. *European Economy Economic Papers No. 419*. Brussels: European Commission, DG ECFIN.

Barrios, S., Deroose, S., Langedijk, S. and Pench, L. (2010a). Introduction. In Barrios, S., Deroose, S., Langedijk, S. and Pench, L. (eds.), External imbalances and public finances in the EU. *European Economy Occasional Papers No. 66*. Brussels: European Commission, DG ECFIN.

Barrios, S., Langedijk, S. and Pench, L. (2010b). EU fiscal consolidation after the financial crisis: Lessons from past experiences. *European Economy Economic Papers No. 418*. Brussels: European Commission, DG ECFIN.

Bastos, R. (2010). *Working document no. 8 on economic exit strategies: Financial and monetary aspects, SMEs, innovation and new opportunities for sustainable growth*. Brussels: European Parliament; Special Committee on the Financial, Economic and Social Crisis.

Belke, A. (2010). Euro area crisis management framework: Consequences and institutional follow-ups. *Crisis Management Framework: What follows after the EFSF and the EFSM expire in 3 years time? (Monetary dialogue with the ECB 2010)*. Brussels: European Parliament; Committee on Economic and Monetary Affairs.

Bennett, H., Escolano, J., Fabrizio, S., Gutierrez, E., Ivaschenko, I., Lissovolik, B., Moreno-Badia, M., Schule, W., Tokarick, S., Xiao, Y. and Zarnic, Z. (2008). Competitiveness in the Southern euro area: France, Greece, Italy, Portugal, and Spain. *IMF Working Papers No. 08/112*. Washington DC: IMF.

Bilbow, J. (2008). The international monetary (non-)order and the "global capital flows paradox". *Levy Economics Institute Working Papers No. 531*. New York: The Levy Economics Institute of Bard College.

Biroli, P., Mourre, G. and Turrini, A. (2010). Adjustment in the euro area and regulation of product and labour markets: An empirical assessment. *European Economy Economic Papers No. 428*. Brussels: European Commission, DG ECFIN.

Bitzenis, A. and Vlachos, V.A. (2011). Outward FDI from Greece and its policy context. In Sauvant, K.P., Mallampaly, P., Davies, K. and Poveda-Garces, A.M. (eds.), *Columbia FDI Profiles*. New York: Vale Columbia Center on Sustainable International Investment.

Bitzenis, A., (2006). Determinants of Greek FDI outflows in the Balkan region: The case of Greek entrepreneurs in Bulgaria. *Eastern European Economics*, 44 (3): 79-96.

Bitzenis, A., Tsitouras, A. and Vlachos, V.A. (2007). Motives for FDI in a small EMU member state: The case of Greece. *East-West Journal of Economics and Business*, 10 (2): 11-42.

—. (2009). Decisive FDI obstacles as an explanatory reason for limited FDI inflows in an EMU member state: The case of Greece. *Journal of Socio-Economics*, 38 (4): 691-704.

Blanchard, O.J. and Milesi-Ferretti, G.M. (2010). Global imbalances: In midstream? *CEPR Discussion Papers No. 7693*. London: Centre for Economic Policy Research.

Blonigen, B.A., Davies, R.B., Waddell, G.R. and Naughton, H.T. (2007). FDI in space: Spatial autoregressive relationships in foreign direct investment. *European Economic Review*, 51 (5): 1303-325.

Bluedorn, J. and Leigh, D. (2011). Revisiting the twin deficits hypothesis: The effect of fiscal consolidation on the current account. *IMF Economic Review*, 59 (4): 582-602.

Blundell-Wignall, A. and Slovik, P. (2011). A market perspective on the European sovereign debt and banking crisis. *OECD Journal: Financial Market Trends*, 2010 (2): 85-112.

Botsiou, K.E. and Klapsis, A., eds. (2011). *Konstantinos Karamanlis Institute for Democracy Yearbook 2011: The Global Economic Crisis and the Case of Greece*. Berlin: Springer-Verlag.

Bracke, T., Boussiere, M., Fidora, M. and Straub, R. (2010). A framework for assessing global imbalances. *World Economy*, 33 (9): 1140-1174.

Braunstein, E. (2012). Neoliberal development macroeconomics: A consideration of its gendered employment effects. *Gender and Development Programme Paper No. 14*. Geneva: United Nations Research Institute for Social Development (UNRISD).

Bris, A., Koskinen, Y. and Nilsson, M. (2006). The real effects of the euro: Evidence from corporate investments. *Review of Finance*, 10 (1): 1-37

Brissimis, S.N., Hondroyiannis, G., Papazoglou, C., Tsaveas, N.T. and Vasardani, M.A. (2010). Current account determinants and external sustainability in periods of structural change. *Bank of Greece Working Papers No. 117*. Athens: Bank of Greece.

Bryant, R.C., Garganas, N.C. and Tavlas, G.S. (2001). Introduction. In Bryant, R.C., Garganas, N.C. and Tavlas, G.S. (eds.), *Greece's Economic Performance and Prospects*. Athens and Washington DC: Bank of Greece and the Brookings Institution.

Buhalis, D. (2001). Tourism in Greece: Strategic analysis and challenges. *Current Issues in Tourism*, 4 (5): 440-480.

Buiter, W. and Rabari, E. (2010). Greece and the fiscal crisis in the Eurozone. *CEPR Policy Insight No. 51*. London: Centre for Economic Policy Research.

Cavallo, E. and Daude, C. (2011). Public investment in developing countries: A blessing or a curse? *Journal of Comparative Economics*, 39 (1): 65-81.

Cecchetti, S.G.., Kohler, M. and Upper, C. (2009). Financial crises and economic activity. *NBER Working Papers No. 15379*. Cambridge (Massachusetts): National Bureau of Economic Research.

Chamley C.P. and Pinto B. (2011). Why official bailouts tend not to work: An example motivated by Greece 2010. *Economist's Voice*, 8 (1): Article 3.

Cholezas, I. and Tsakloglou, P. (2009). The economic impact of immigration in Greece: Taking stock of the existing evidence. *Southeast European and Black Sea Studies*, 9 (1-2): 77-104.

Chountis N. (2010). *Working document no. 2 on the social impact of the crisis: employment, demographic challenges and pension systems.* European Parliament; Special Committee on the Financial, Economic and Social Crisis.

Christodoulakis, N. (2010). Crisis, threats and ways out for the Greek economy. *Cyprus Economic Policy Review*, 4 (1): 89-96.

—. (2011). From indecision to fast-track privatizations: Can Greece still do it? In Monastiriotis, V. (ed.), *The Greek Crisis in Focus: Austerity, Recessions and Paths to Recovery*. London: Hellenic Observatory, London School of Economics.

Christoffel, K. (2011). What can the Diamond-Mortensen-Pissarides model tell us about the conduct of monetary policy in the euro area? *ECB Research Bulletin*, 12: 7-11.

Christoffel, K., Kuester, K. and Linzert, T. (2009). The role of labor markets for euro area monetary policy. *European Economic Review*, 53 (8): 908-936.

Christopoulos, D.K., Loizides, J. and Tsionas, E.G. (2005). The Abrams curve of government size and unemployment: Evidence from panel data. *Applied Economics*, 37 (10): 1193-1199.

Christopoulou, R. and Kosma, T. (2011). Skills and wage inequality in Greece: Evidence from matched employer-employee data, 1995-2002. *Bank of Greece Working Papers No. 123*. Athens: Bank of Greece.

Coenen, G., Kilponen, J. and Trabandt, M. (2010). When does fiscal stimulus work? *ECB Research Bulletin*, 10: 6-10.

Coenen, G., Mohr, M. and Straub, R. (2008). Fiscal consolidation in the euro area: Long-run benefits and short-run costs. *Economic Modelling*, 25 (5): 912-932.

Creel, J. and Poilon, G. (2008). Is public capital productive in Europe? *International Review of Applied Economics*, 22 (6): 673-691.

Danopoulos, C.P. and Znidaric, B. (2007). Informal economy, tax evasion, and poverty in a democratic setting: Greece. *Mediterranean Quarterly*, 18 (2): 67-84.

Daras, T. and Tyrowicz, J. (2011). Breeding one's own sub-prime crisis: The labour market effects on financial system stability. *Economic Systems*, 35 (2): 278-299.

Darvas, Z., Pisani-Ferry, J. and Sapir, A. (2011). A comprehensive approach to the euro-area debt crisis. *Bruegel Policy Briefs Issue 2011/2*. Brussels: Bruegel.

De Broeck, M. and Guscina, A. (2011). Government debt issuance in the euro area: The impact of the financial crisis. *IMF Working Papers No. 11/21*. Washington DC: IMF.

De Grauwe, P. (2011a). A less punishing, more forgiving approach to the debt crisis in the eurozone. *CEPS Policy Brief No. 230*. Brussels: Centre for European Policy Studies.

—. (2011b). Only a more active ECB can solve the euro crisis. *CEPS Policy Brief No. 250*. Brussels: Centre for European Policy Studies.

De la Dehesa, G. (2010). Global imbalancies, currency wars and the Euro. *The threat of "currency wars": Global imbalancies and their effects on currencies (Monetary dialogue with the ECB 2010)*. Brussels: European Parliament; Committee on Economic and Monetary Affairs.

De Mello, L., Padoan, P.C. and Rousova, L. (2011). The growth effects of current account reversals: The role of macroeconomic policies. *OECD Economics Department Working Papers No. 871*. Paris: Organization for Economic Co-operation and Development.

Dees, S. and Zorell, N. (2011). Business cycle sychronisation: Disentangling trade and financial linkages. *ECB Working Papers No. 1322*. Frankfurt: European Central Bank.

Dellas, H. and Tavlas, G.S. (2009). An optimum-currency-area odyssey. *Journal of International Money and Finance*, 28 (7): 1117-1137.

Demos, A., Filippaios, F. and Papanastassiou, M. (2004). An event study analysis of outward foreign direct investment: The case of Greece. *International Journal of the Economics of Business*, 11 (3): 329-348.

DG ECFIN (2008). *EMU@10: Successes and Challenges after 10 years of Economic and Monetary Union (European Economy 2/2008)*. Luxembourg: Office for Official Publications of the European Communities.

DG ECFIN (2009a). *Economic Crisis in Europe: Causes, Consequences and Responses (European Economy 7/2009)*. Luxembourg: Office for Official Publications of the European Communities.

—. (2009b). Impact of the current economic and financial crisis on potential output. *European Economy Occasional Papers No. 49*. Brussels: European Commission, DG ECFIN.

—. (2010a). *Surveillance of Intra-Euro-Area Competitiveness and Imbalances (European Economy 1/2010)*. Luxembourg: Publications Office of the European Union.

—. (2010b). *Public finances in EMU – 2010 (European Economy 4/2010)*. Luxembourg: Office for Official Publications of the European Communities.

—. (2010c). *Monitoring tax revenues and tax reforms in EU Member States – 2010 (European Economy 6/2010)*. Luxembourg: Office for Official Publications of the European Communities.

—. (2010d). The economic adjustment programme for Greece. *European Economy Occasional Papers No. 61*. Brussels: European Commission, DG ECFIN.

—. (2010e). The economic adjustment programme for Greece: First review – summer 2010. *European Economy Occasional Papers No. 68*. Brussels: European Commission, DG ECFIN.

—. (2011a). The economic adjustment programme for Greece: Third review – winter 2011. *European Economy Occasional Papers No. 77*. Brussels: European Commission, DG ECFIN.

—. (2011b). The economic adjustment programme for Greece: Fourth review – spring 2011. *European Economy Occasional Papers No. 82*. Brussels: European Commission, DG ECFIN.

—. (2011c). The economic adjustment programme for Greece: Fifth review – October 2011. *European Economy Occasional Papers No. 87*. Brussels: European Commission, DG ECFIN.

—. (2011d). Internal devaluation and external imbalances: A model-based analysis. *Quarterly Report on the Euro Area*, 10 (3): 22-27.

—. (2012). The second economic adjustment programme for Greece. *European Economy Occasional Papers No. 94*. Brussels: European Commission, DG ECFIN.

Dritsakis, N. (2004). Tourism as a long-run economic growth factor: An empirical investigation for Greece using causality analysis. *Tourism Economics*, 10 (3): 305-316.

Dritsakis, N. and Adamopopoulos, A. (2004). A causal relationship between government spending and economic development: An empirical examination of the Greek economy. *Applied Economics*, 36 (5): 457-464.

Du Caju, P., Katay, G., Lamo, A., Nicolitsas, D. and Poelhekke, S. (2010). Inter-industry wage differentials in EU countries: What do cross-country time varying data add to the picture? *Journal of the European Economic Association*, 8 (2-3): 478-486.

Dunaway, S. (2009). Global imbalances and the financial crisis. *CFR Special Report No. 44*. New York: Council on Foreign Relations.

Duran, J. and Ubeda, F. (2001). The investment development path: A new empirical approach and some theoretical issues. *Transnational Corporations*, 10 (2): 1-34.

Easterly, W., Irwin, T. and Serven, L. (2008). Walking up the down escalator: Public investment and fiscal stability. *World Bank Research Observer*, 23 (1): 37-56.

Egert, B. (2011). Catching-up and inflation in Europe: Balassa-Samuelson, Engel's law and other culprits. *Economic Systems*, 35 (2): 208-229.

Eichengreen, B. and Temin, P. (2010). Fetters of gold and paper. *Oxford Review of Economic Policy*, 26 (3): 370-384.

Eijffinger, S.C.W. (2010). Policy implications of increasing debt and deficits. *Briefing Papers by Monetary Experts Panel: Policy Implications of Increased Debt and Deficits (Monetary dialogue with the ECB 2010)*. Brussels: European Parliament; Committee on Economic and Monetary Affairs.

Enste, D.H. (2010). Shadow economy - The impact of regulation in OECD-countries. *International Economic Journal*, 24 (4): 555-571.

Escolano, J. (2008). Competitiveness of the Southern euro area. In Bennett, H., Escolano, J., Fabrizio, S., Gutierrez, E., Ivaschenko, I., Lissovolik, B., Moreno-Badia, M., Schule, W., Tokarick, S., Xiao, Y. and Zarnic, Z., "Competitiveness in the Southern euro area: France, Greece, Italy, Portugal, and Spain". *IMF Working Papers No. 08/112*. Washington DC: IMF.

Estrin, S. and Mickiewicz, T. (2010). Shadow economy and entrepreneurial entry. *IZA Discussion Papers No. 5053*. Bonn: Institute for the Study of Labor.

European Economic Advisory Group at CESifo (2011). *The EEAG Report on the European Economy, 2011*. Munich: Ifo Institute for Economic Research.

Featherstone, K. (2003) Greece and EMU: Between external empowerment and domestic vulnerability. *Journal of common market studies*, 41 (5): 923-940.

—. (2008). Varieties of Capitalism' and the Greek case: Explaining the constraints on domestic reform? *GreeSE – Hellenic Observatory Papers on Greece and Southeast Europe No. 11*. London: Hellenic Observatory, London School of Economics.

—. (2011). The Greek sovereign debt crisis and EMU: A failing state in a skewed regime. *Journal of Common Market Studies*, 49 (2): 193-217.

Feldstein, M.S. (2008). Resolving the global imbalance: The dollar and the U.S. saving rate. *Journal of Economic Perspectives*, 22 (3): 113-125.

Felipe, J. and Kumar, U. (2011). Unit labor costs in the eurozone: The competitiveness debate again. *Levy Economics Institute Working Papers No. 651*. New York: The Levy Economics Institute of Bard College.

Foundation for Economic Industrial Research (2011). *The Greek Economy 4/11 (Quartely Bulletin No. 66)*. Athens: Foundation for Economic Industrial Research.

Freedman, C., Kumhof, M., Laxton, D. and Muirb, D. (2010). Policies to rebalance the global economy after the financial crisis. *International Journal of Central Banking*, 6 (1): 215-252.

Freund, C. (2009). The trade response to global downturns: Historical evidence. *World Bank Policy Research Working Papers No. 5015*. Washington DC: World Bank.

Frey, B. and Torgler, B. (2007). Tax morale and conditional cooperation. *Journal of Comparative Economics*, 35 (1): 136-159.

Furceri, D. and Mourougane, A. (2010). The effects of fiscal policy on output: A DSGE analysis. *OECD Economics Department Working Papers No. 770*. Paris: OECD.

Ganelli, G. (2010). The international effects of government spending composition. *Economic Modelling*, 27 (3): 631-640.

Ganelli, G. and Tervala, J. (2009). Can government spending increase private consumption? The role of complementarity. *Economics Letters*, 103 (1): 5-7.

Georgantopoulos, A.G. and Tsamis, A.D. (2011). The causal links between FDI and economic development: Evidence from Greece. *European Journal of Social Sciences*, 27 (1): 12-20.

Georgopoulos, A. and Preusse, H.G. (2006). European integration and the dynamic process of investments and divestments of foreign TNCs in Greece. *European Business Review*, 18 (1): 50-59.

—. (2009). Cross-border acquisitions vs. greenfield investment: A comparative performance analysis in Greece. *International Business Review*, 18 (6): 592-605.

Gerlach, S. (2010). The Greek sovereign debt crisis and ECB policy. *Meeting documents: Update on exit strategies (Monetary dialogue with the ECB 2010)*. Brussels: European Parliament; Committee on Economic and Monetary Affairs.

Ghosh, A.R., Kim, J.I., Mendoza, E., Ostry, J.D. and Qureshi, M.S. (2011). Fiscal fatigue, fiscal space and debt sustainability in advanced economies. *NBER Working Papers No. 16782*. Cambridge (Massachusetts): National Bureau of Economic Research.

Giannone, D. and Lenza, M. (2009). Business cycles in the euro area. *ECB Research Bulletin*, 8: 5-7.

Giannone, D., Lenza, M. and Reichlin, L. (2010). Market freedom and the global recession. *CEPR Discussion Papers No. 7884*. London: Centre for Economic Policy Research.

Gibson, H.D. and Malley, J. (2008). The contribution of sectoral productivity differentials to inflation in Greece. *Open Economies Review*, 19 (5): 629-650.

Gibson, H.D., Hall, S.G. and Tavlas, G.S. (2011). The Greek financial crisis: Growing imbalances and sovereign spreads. *Bank of Greece Working Papers No. 124*. Athens: Bank of Greece.

Gomes, P. (2011). Fiscal policy and the labour market: The effects of public sector employment and wages. *European Economy Economic Papers No. 439*. Brussels: European Commission, DG ECFIN.

Gorg, H., Hanley, A., and Strobl, E. (2008), Productivity effects of international outsourcing: Evidence from plant level data. *Canadian Journal of Economics*, 41 (2): 670-688.

Gregoriou, A., Kontonikas, A. and Montagnoli, A. (2011). Euro area inflation differentials: Unit roots and nonlinear adjustment. *Journal of Common Market Studies*, 49 (3): 525-540.

Gross, D. (2010). Fiscal policy coordination and competitiveness surveillance: What solutions to what problems? *Ideas on the Multilateral Surveillance Regulation under Article 121 (6) of the Treaty (Monetary dialogue with the ECB 2010)*. Brussels: European Parliament – Committee on Economic and Monetary Affairs (ECON).

Hatziprokopiou, P. (2008). Migrant entrepreneurship in Greece. *Migrações*, 3 : 73-84.

Havranek, T. (2010). Rose effect and the euro: Is the magic gone? *Review of World Economics*, 146 (2): 241-261.

Hofmann, B. and Remsperger, H. (2005). Inflation differentials among the Euro area countries: Potential causes and consequences. *Journal of Asian Economics*, 16 (3): 403-419.

Hubner, D. (2010). *Working document no. 4 on the contribution of cohesion policy to the economic recovery: linking crisis exit policy with long term growth and structural change*. Brussels: European Parliament; Special Committee on the Financial, Economic and Social Crisis.

Iakovidou, O., Koutsou, S. and Partalidou, M. (2009). Women entrepreneurs in the Greek countryside: A typology according to motives and business characteristics. *Journal of Developmental Entrepreneurship*, 14 (2): 165-179.

Iara, A. and Wolff, G.B. (2010). Rules and risk in the euro area: Does rules-based national fiscal governance contain sovereign bond spreads? *European Economy Economic Papers No. 433*. Brussels: European Commission, DG ECFIN.

Ierapetritis, D.G., Lagos, D. and Balomenou, C.K. (2010). Outlining the determinants of youth entrepreneurship in the Greek periphery. *International Journal of Entrepreneurship and Small Business*, 11 (2): 205-217.

Ietto-Gillies, G. (2010). The current economic crisis and international business: Can we say anything meaningful about future scenarios? *Futures*, 42 (9): 910-919.

IMF (2012). *Greece: Request for Extended Arrangement under the Extended Fund Facility*. Washington DC: IMF.

—. (2013). Greece: First and second reviews under the extended arrangement under the extended fund facility, request for waiver of applicability, modification of performance criteria, and rephasing of access. *IMF Country Report No. 13/20*. Washington DC: IMF.

Invest in Greece Agency (2010). *Greek Companies in Foreign Markets 2004-2008*. Athens: Invest in Greece Agency.

Ivaschenko, I. (2008). Southern euro area five countries: Trends in value added. In Bennett, H., Escolano, J., Fabrizio, S., Gutierrez, E., Ivaschenko, I., Lissovolik, B., Moreno-Badia, M., Schule, W., Tokarick, S., Xiao, Y. and Zarnic, Z., "Competitiveness in the Southern euro area: France, Greece, Italy, Portugal, and Spain". *IMF Working Papers No. 08/112*. Washington DC: IMF.

Jensen, J. and Wohlbier, F. (2012). Improving tax governance in EU Member States: Criteria for successful policies. *European Economy Occasional Papers No. 114*. Brussels: European Commission, DG ECFIN.

Kalaitzidakis, P. and Tzouvelekas, V. (2011). On the growth and welfare maximizing allocation of public investment. *Journal of Economics*, 104 (2): 127-137.

Kalogeresis, A. and Labrianidis, L. (2010). From spectator to walk-on to actor: An exploratory study of the internationalisation of Greek firms since 1989. *European Journal of Comparative Economics*, 7 (1): 121-143.

Kalou, S. and Paleologou, S.M. (2012). Twin deficit hypothesis: Revisiting an EMU country. *Journal of Policy Modeling*, 34 (2): 230-241.

Kaplanoglou, G. and Rapanos, V.T. (2011). The Greek fiscal crisis and the role of fiscal governance. *GreeSE – Hellenic Observatory Papers on Greece and Southeast Europe No. 48*. London: Hellenic Observatory, London School of Economics.

Kaplanoglou, G. and Rapanos, V.T. (2013). Tax and trust: The fiscal crisis in Greece. *South European Society and Politics*, forthcoming.

Kapopoulos, P. and Siokis, F. (2005). Stock and real estate prices in Greece: Wealth versus 'credit-price' effect. *Applied Economics Letters*, 12 (2): 125-128.

Karagianni, S. and Labrianidis, L. (2001). The pros and cons of SMEs going international: Greek companies in Bulgaria. *Eastern European Economics*, 39 (2): 5-28.

Karamessini, M. (2010). Transition strategies and labour market integration of Greek university graduates. *GreeSE – Hellenic Observatory Papers on Greece and Southeast Europe No. 32*. London: Hellenic Observatory, London School of Economics.

Kasimati, E. (2011). Did the climb on the Greek sovereign spreads cause the devaluation of euro? *Applied Economics Letters*, 18 (9): 851-854.

Katsaitis, O. and Doulos, D. (2009). The impact of EU structural funds on FDI. *Kyklos*, 62 (4): 563-578.

Katsimi, M. and Moutos, T. (2010). EMU and the Greek crisis: The political-economy perspective. *European Journal of Political Economy*, 26 (4): 568-576.

Katsimi, M., Kalyvitis, S. and Moutos T. (2012). Excessive wages and the return on capital. *Cambridge Journal of Economics*, 36 (2): 435-461.

Katsios, S. (2006). The shadow economy and corruption in Greece. *South-Eastern Europe Journal of Economics*, 4 (1): 61-80.

Kelley, D.J., Bosma, N. and Amoros, J.E. (2011). *Global Entrepreneurship Monitor 2010 Global Report*. London: Global Entrepreneurship Research Association.

Kenen, P.B. (1969). The theory of optimum currency areas: An eclectic view. In Mundell, R.A. and Swoboda, A.K. (eds.), *Monetary Problems of the International Economy*. Chicago: University of Chicago Press.

Klyver, K., Hindle, K. and Meyer, D. (2008). Influence of social network structure on entrepreneurship participation – A study of 20 national cultures. *International Entrepreneurship and Management Journal*, 4 (3): 331-347.

Konstantinou, P. and Tagkalakis, A. (2010). Boosting confidence: Is there a role for fiscal policy? *Bank of Greece Working Papers No. 113*. Athens: Bank of Greece.

Kratsa-Tsagaropoulou, R. (2010). *Report on the contribution of EU regional policy towards fighting the financial and economic crisis, with a special reference to Objective 2*. Brussels: European Parliament; Committee on Regional Development.

Labrianidis, L. and Hatziprokopiou, P. (2010). Migrant Entrepreneurship in Greece: Diversity of Pathways for Emerging Ethnic Business Communities in Thessaloniki. *Journal of International Migration and Integration*, 11 (2): 193-217.

Labrianidis, L., Lyberaki, A., Tinios, P. and Hatziprokopiou, P. (2004). Inflow of migrants and outflow of investment: Aspects of interdependence between Greece and the Balkans. *Journal of Ethnic and Migration Studies*, 30 (6): 1-26.

Lamartina, S. and Zaghini, A. (2011). Increasing public expenditure: Wagner's law in OECD countries. *German Economic Review*, 12 (2): 149-164.

Lamo, A. and Smets, F. (2010). Wage dynamics in Europe: Some new findings. *ECB Research Bulletin*, 10: 2-5.

Lanara-Tzotze, Z. (2012). *The Impact of Anti-Crisis Measures, and the Social and Employment Situation in Greece*. Brussels: European Economic and Social Committee.

Landmann, O. (2012). Rotating slumps in a monetary union. *Open Economies Review*, 23 (2): 303-317.

Larch, M. (2010). Fiscal performance and income inequality: Are unequal societies more deficit-prone? Some cross-country evidence. *European Economy Economic Papers No. 414*. Brussels: European Commission, DG ECFIN.

Larch, M., Van den Noord, P. and Jonung, L. (2010). The Stability and Growth Pact: Lessons from the great recession. *European Economy Economic Papers No. 429*. Brussels: European Commission, DG ECFIN.

Lazaridis, G. and Koumandraki, M. (2003). Survival ethnic entrepreneurs in Greece: A mosaic of informal and formal business activities. *Sociological Research Online*, 8 (2).

Lebrun, I. and Perez, E. (2011). Real unit labor costs differentials in EMU: How big, how benign and how reversible? *IMF Working Papers No. 11/109*. Washington DC: IMF.

Leitao, N.C. (2010). Localization factors and inward foreign direct investment in Greece. *Theoretical and Applied Economics*, 17 (6): 17-26.

Liddle, J. (2009). Regeneration and economic development in Greece: De-industrialisation and uneven development. *Local Government Studies*, 35 (3): 335-354.

Linnemann, L. and Schabert, A. (2010). Debt non-neutrality, policy interactions, and macroeconomic stability. *International Economic Review*, 51 (2): 461-474.

Lipsey, R.E. (2004). Home- and host-country effects of foreign direct investment. In Baldwin, R.E. and Winters, L.A. (eds.), *Challenges to Globalization: Analyzing the Economics*. Chicago: University of Chicago Press.

Livanos, I. (2007). The incidence of long-term unemployment: Evidence from Greece. *Applied Economic Letters*, 14 (6): 405-408.

—. (2009a). What determines self-employment? A comparative study. *Applied Economic Letters*, 16 (3): 227-232.

—. (2009b). Modelling the incidence of unemployment: The case of Greece. *Applied Economic Letters*, 16 (6): 1607-1611.

Lommatzsch, K. and Tober, S. (2006). Euro-area inflation: Does the Balassa-Samuelson effect matter? *International Economics and Economic Policy*, 3 (2): 105-136.

Lynn, M. (2011). *Bust: Greece, the Euro and the Sovereign Debt Crisis*. New Jersey: John Wiley & Sons.

Lyrintzis, C. (2011). Greek Politics in the era of economic crisis: Reassessing causes and effects. *GreeSE – Hellenic Observatory Papers on Greece and Southeast Europe No. 45*. London: Hellenic Observatory, London School of Economics.

Malliaropulos, D. (2010). How much did competitiveness of the Greek economy decline since EMU entry? *Eurobank Research: Economy & Markets*, 5 (4): 1-16.

Mamadouh, V. and Van Der Wusten, H. (2011). Financial, monetary and governance crisis: An outlook on the euro(zone). *Tijdschrift voor economische en sociale geografie*, 102 (1): 111-118.

Manolopoulos, J. (2011). *Greece's 'Odious' Debt: The Looting of the Hellenic Republic by the Euro, the Political Elite and the Investment Community*. London: Anthem Press.

Marzinotto, B., Pissany-Ferry, J. and Wolff, G. (2011). An action plan for Europe's leaders. *Bruegel Policy Contribution No. 2011/9*. Brussels: Bruegel.

Mathieu, C. and Sterdyniak, H. (2010). European debt crisis and fiscal exit strategies. *Documents de Travail de l' OFCE 2010/11*. Paris: Observatoire Francais des Conjonctures Economiques.

Matsaganis, M. and Flevotomou, M. (2010). Distributional implications of tax evasion in Greece. *GreeSE – Hellenic Observatory Papers on Greece and Southeast Europe No. 31*. London: Hellenic Observatory, London School of Economics.

Matsaganis, M. and Leventi, C. (2011). The distributional impact of the crisis in Greece. In Monastiriotis, V. (ed.), *The Greek Crisis in Focus: Austerity, Recessions and Paths to Recovery*. London: Hellenic Observatory, London School of Economics.

Matthes, J. (2009). Ten years EMU – Reality test for the OCA endogeneity hypothesis, economic divergences and future challenges. *Intereconomics*, 44 (2): 114-128.

Matziorinis, K.N. (2012). Is the 'Euro Bond' the answer to the euro sovereign debt crisis? What outcome can investors expect out of Europe? *Journal of Wealth Management*, 14 (4): 11-21.

Merkl, C. and Snower, D. (2009). Monetary persistence, imperfect competition, and staggering complementarities. *Macroeconomic Dynamics*, 13 (1): 81-106.

Merler, S. and Pisani-Ferry, J. (2012). Sudden stops in the euro area. *Bruegel Policy Contribution Issue 2012/6*. Brussels: Bruegel.

Mitrakos, T.M. and Zonzilos, N. (2006). The impact of exogenous shocks on the dynamics and persistence of inflation: A macroeconomic model-based approach for Greece. *Economic Bulletin (Bank of Greece)*, 26: 37-57.

Mitsopoulos, M. and Pelagidis T. (2007). Does staffing affect the time to dispose cases in Greek courts? *International Review of Law and Economics*, 27 (2): 219-244.

—. (2009a). Vikings in Greece: Kleptocratic interest groups in a closed, rent-seeking economy. *Cato Journal*, 29 (3): 399-416.

—. (2009b). Economic and social turbulence in Greece: The product markets are a no-brainer, the labour market is not. *Intereconomics*, 44 (4): 246-254.

—. (2010). *Understanding the Crisis in Greece: From Boom to Bust*. Basingstoke: Palgrave MacMillan.

—. (2011). The real cause of Greek debt: Taxation and labour market distortions in Greece. *Intereconomics*, 46 (2): 112-120.

Monastiriotis, V. (2011). Making geographical sense of the Greek austerity measures: Compositional effects and long-run implications. *Cambridge Journal of Regions, Economy and Society*, 4 (3): 323-337.

Monastiriotis, V. and Jordaan, J. (2010). Does FDI promote regional development? Evidence from local and regional productivity spillovers in Greece. *Eastern Journal of European Studies*, 1 (2): 139-164.

—. (2011). Regional distribution and spatial impact of FDI in Greece: Evidence from firm-level data. *GreeSE – Hellenic Observatory Papers on Greece and Southeast Europe No. 44*. London: Hellenic Observatory, London School of Economics.

Monokroussos, P. (2010). Assessing fiscal policy with the use of sustainability indicators: The case of Greece. *Eurobank Research: Economy & Markets*, 5 (6): 1-22.

Montoya, L.A. and Dohring, B. (2011). The improbable renaissance of the Phillips curve: The crisis and euro area inflation dynamics. *European Economy Economic Papers No. 446*. Brussels: European Commission, DG ECFIN.

Moreno-Badia, M. (2008). Are the Southern euro area's exports moving to markets with less competition? In Bennett, H., Escolano, J., Fabrizio, S., Gutierrez, E., Ivaschenko, I., Lissovolik, B., Moreno-Badia, M., Schule, W., Tokarick, S., Xiao, Y. and Zarnic, Z., "Competitiveness in the Southern euro area: France, Greece, Italy, Portugal, and Spain". *IMF Working Papers No. 08/112*. Washington DC: IMF.

Moschovis, G. and Servera, M.C. (2009). External imbalances of the Greek economy: The role of fiscal and structural policies. *ECFIN Country Focus*, 6 (6): 1-6.

Mylonas, H. (2011). Is Greece a failing developed state? Causes and socio-economic consequences of the financial crisis. In Botsiou K.E. and Klapsis A. (eds.), *The Konstantinos Karamanlis Institute for Democracy Yearbook 2011: The Global Economic Crisis and the Case of Greece*. Athens: The Konstantinos Karamanlis Institute for Democracy.

Nelson, R.M., Belkin, P. and Mix, D.E. (2010). *Congressional Research Service Report – Greece's debt crisis: Overview, policy responses, and implications*. Washington DC: Penny Hill Press.

Nobili, A. (2007). Assessing the predictive power of financial spreads in the euro area: does parameters instability matter? *Empirical Economics*, 33 (1): 177-195.

Nye, J.S. (1967). Corruption and political development: A cost-benefit analysis. *American Political Science Review*, 61 (2): 417-427.

Obstfeld, M. and Rogoff, K. (2009). Global imbalances and the financial crisis: Products of common causes. *CEPR Discussion Papers No. 7606*. London: Centre for Economic Policy Research.

OECD (2005). *OECD Economic Surveys: Greece 2005*. Paris: OECD.

—. (2007). *OECD Economic Surveys: Greece 2007*. Paris: OECD.

—. (2010a). *OECD Economic Surveys: Euro Area 2010*. Paris: OECD.

—. (2010b). *Jobs for Youth: Greece*. Paris: OECD.

—. (2011). *OECD Economic Surveys: Greece 2011*. Paris: OECD.

Ortiz-Villajos, J.M. (2004). Kaldor paradox. In Segura, J. and Braun, C.R. (eds.), *An Eponymous Dictionary of Economics: A Guide to Laws and Theorems Named after Economists*. Cheltenham: Edward Elgar.

O'Sullivan, K.P.V. (2010). Supervision in Ireland. Where to now? In Kinsella, S. and Leddin, A. (eds.), *Understanding Ireland's Economic Crisis Prospects for Recovery*. Dublin: Blackhall.

Pagoulatos, G. and Triantopoulos, C. (2009). The return of the Greek patient: Greece and the 2008 global financial crisis. *South European Society and Politics*, 14 (1): 35-54.

Panayotakis, C. (2011). Democracy and the capitalist crisis: The case of Greece. *International Journal of Pluralism and Economics Education*, 2 (2): 216-222.

Panizza, U., Sturzenegger, F. and Zettelmeyer, J. (2010). International government debt. *UNCTAD Discussion Papers No. 199*. Geneva: United Nations Conference on Trade and Development.

Pantelidis, P. and Nikolopoulos, E. (2008). FDI attractiveness in Greece. *International Advances in Economic Research*, 14 (1): 90-100.

Papageorgiou, D. (2009). Macroeconomic implications of alternative tax regimes: The case of Greece. *Bank of Greece Working Papers No. 97*. Athens: Bank of Greece.

Papageorgiou, G. (2008). The human dimension of tourism supply-side perspectives. *Annals of Tourism Research*, 35 (1): 211-232.

Papageorgiou, T., Michaelides, P.G. and Milios, J.G. (2010). Business cycles synchronization and clustering in Europe (1960-2009). *Journal of Economics and Business*, 62 (5): 419-70.

Pelagidis, T. (2010). The Greek paradox of falling competitiveness and weak institutions in a high GDP growth rate context (1995-2008). *GreeSE – Hellenic Observatory Papers on Greece and Southeast Europe No. 38*. London: Hellenic Observatory, London School of Economics.

Pelagidis, T. and Taun, T. (2007). Expensive living: The Greek experience under the Euro. *Intereconomics*, 42 (3): 167-176.

Petit, P. (2012). Building faith in a common currency: can the eurozone get beyond the Common Market logic? *Cambridge Journal of Economics*, 36 (1): 271-281.

Petroulas, P. (2007). The effect of the euro on foreign direct investment. *European Economic Review*, 51 (6): 1468-91.

—. (2008). Foreign direct investment in Greece: Productivity and spillover effects. *Economic Bulletin (Bank of Greece)*, 31: 31-48.

Piperopoulos, P. and Piperopoulos, G. (2010). Is Greece finally on the right path toward entrepreneurship, innovation, and business clusters? *International Journal of Public Administration*, 33 (1): 55-59.

Pisani-Ferry, J. (2012). The euro crisis and the new impossible trinity. *Bruegel Policy Contribution Issue 2012/1*. Brussels: Bruegel.

Portes, R. (2009). Global imbalances. In Dewatripont M., Freixas, X. and Portes, R. (eds.), *Macroeconomic Stability and Financial Regulation: Key Issues for the G20*. London: Centre for Economic Policy Research.

Posner, R.A. (2010). *The Crisis of Capitalist Democracy*. Cambridge (Massachusetts): Harvard University Press.

Price, R. (2010). The political economy of fiscal consolidation. *OECD Economics Department Working Papers No. 776*. Paris: Organization for Economic Co-operation and Development.

Reinhart, C.M. and Rogoff, K.S. (2010). Growth in a time of debt. *American Economic Review*, 100 (2): 573-578.

—. (2011). From financial crash to debt crisis. *American Economic Review*, 101 (5): 1676-1706.

Rodokanakis, S. and Vlachos, V.A. (forthcoming). Unemployment in the Greek regions of Attica and Central Macedonia: Comparative econometric analysis between the 2nd and the 3rd CSFs. *International Journal of Economics and Business Research*.

Roeger, W. and in 't Veld, J. (2010). Fiscal stimulus and exit strategies in the EU: A model-based analysis. *European Economy Economic Papers No. 426*. Brussels: European Commission, DG ECFIN.

Romer, P. (2010). Cutting the corruption tax in Greece. *SIEPR Policy Brief August 2010*. Stanford: Stanford Institute for Economic Policy Research.

Rose, A.K. (2000). One money, one market: Estimating the effect of common currencies on trade. *Economic Policy*, 15 (30): 9-45.

Rose, A.K. and Spiegel, M.M. (2011). Cross-country causes and consequences of the crisis: An update. *European Economic Review*, 55 (3): 309-324.

Rossi, V. and Aguilera, R.D. (2010). No painless solution to Greece's debt crisis. *International Economics Programme Papers 2010/03*. London: Chatham House.

Sancak, C., Liu L.Q. and Nakata, T. (2011). Canada: A success story. In Mauro, P. (ed.), *Chipping Away at Public Debt: Sources of Failure and Keys to Success in Fiscal Adjustment*. Hoboken (New Jersey): John Wiley & Sons.

Sarri, K. and Trihopoulou, K. (2005). Female entrepreneurs' personal characteristics and motivation: A review of the Greek situation. *Women in Management Review*, 20 (1): 24-36.

Sauer, C. and Scheide, J. (1995). Money, interest rate spreads, and economic activity. *Review of World Economics*, 131 (4): 708-722.

Schalck, C. (2011). The European fiscal framework: What lessons can we learn from the crisis? *Economics Bulletin*, 31 (1): 358-366.

Schmitt-Grohe, S. and Uribe, M. (2004). Optimal fiscal and monetary policy under imperfect competition. *Journal of Macroeconomics*, 26 (2): 183-209.

Schneider, F., Buehn, A. and Montenegro, C. (2010). Shadow economies all over the world: New estimates for 162 countries from 1999 to 2007.

Policy Research Working Papers Series No. 5356. Washington DC: The World Bank.

Schule, W. (2008). The role of imports – structural shifts and economic benefits. In Bennett, H., Escolano, J., Fabrizio, S., Gutierrez, E., Ivaschenko, I., Lissovolik, B., Moreno-Badia, M., Schule, W., Tokarick, S., Xiao, Y. and Zarnic, Z., "Competitiveness in the Southern euro area: France, Greece, Italy, Portugal, and Spain". *IMF Working Papers No. 08/112*. Washington DC: IMF.

Serven, L. and Nguyen, H. (2010). Global imbalances before and after the global crisis. *World Bank Policy Research Working Papers No. 5354*. Washington DC: World Bank.

Servera, M.C. and Moschovis, G. (2008). Tax shortfalls in Greece. *ECFIN Country Focus*, 5 (5): 1-6.

Sibert, A. (2010). Global imbalances and the financial crisis. *Briefing Papers by Monetary Experts Panel: Future Development of Global Imbalances (Monetary dialogue with the ECB 2010)*. Brussels: European Parliament; Committee on Economic and Monetary Affairs.

Smith, M.L. (2011). Political leadership in Greece in times of crisis. In Botsiou K.E. and Klapsis A. (eds.), *The Konstantinos Karamanlis Institute for Democracy Yearbook 2011: The Global Economic Crisis and the Case of Greece*. Athens: The Konstantinos Karamanlis Institute for Democracy.

Souitaris, V. (2002). Firm-specific competencies determining technological innovation: A survey in Greece. *R&D Management*, 32 (1): 61-77.

Stein, J.L. (2011). The diversity of debt crises in Europe. *Cato Journal*, 31 (2): 199-215.

Stockhammer, E., Onaran, O. and Ederer, S. (2009). Functional income distribution and aggregate demand in the Euro area. *Cambridge Journal of Economics*, 33 (1): 139-159.

Stoian, C.R. and Filippaios, F. (2008). Dunning's eclectic paradigm: A holistic, yet context specific framework for analysing the determinants of outward FDI: Evidence from international Greek investments. *International Business Review*, 17 (3): 349-367.

Stolz, S.M. and Wedow M. (2010). Extraordinary measures in extraordinary times: Public measures in support of the financial sector in the EU and the United States. *ECB Occasional Papers No. 117*. Frankfurt: European Central Bank.

Sturgess, B. (2010). Greek economic statistics: A decade of deceit. *World Economics*, 11 (2): 67-99.

Swinburne, K. (2010). *Working document no. 7 on global governance, international monetary policy and tackling global imbalances (incl. the issue on tax havens).* Brussels: European Parliament; Special Committee on the Financial, Economic and Social Crisis.

Syverson, C. (2011). What determines productivity? *Journal of Economic Literature*, 49 (2): 326-365.

Tagkalakis, A. (2009). Fiscal adjustments: Do labor and product market institutions matter? *Public Choice*, 139 (3-4): 389-411.

Task Force of the Monetary Policy Committee of the European System of Central Banks (2005). Competitiveness and the export performance of the euro area. *Occasional Papers Series No. 30*. Frankfurt: European Central Bank.

Taylor, J.B. (2009). The financial crisis and the policy responses: An empirical analysis of what went wrong. *NBER Working Papers No. 14631*. Cambridge (Massachusetts): National Bureau of Economic Research.

Torgler, B. and Schneider, F. (2009). The impact of tax morale and institutional quality on the shadow economy. *Journal of Economic Psychology*, 30 (2): 228-245.

Turrini, A. (2012). Fiscal consolidation in reformed and unreformed labour markets: A look at EU countries. *European Economy Economic Papers No. 462*. Brussels: European Commission, DG ECFIN.

UNCTAD (2009). *The Global Economic Crisis: Systemic Failures and Multilateral Remedies*. New York and Geneva: United Nations.

—. (2010). *Trade and Development Report, 2010*. New York and Geneva: United Nations.

United Nations (2010). *World Economic and Social Survey 2010: Retooling Global Development*. New York: United Nations.

—. (2011). *World Economic Situation and Prospects 2011*. New York: United Nations.

Valiante, D. (2011). The eurozone debt crisis: From its origins to a way forward. *CEPS Policy Brief No. 251*. Brussels: Centre for European Policy Studies.

Van Bergeijk, P.A.G. (2009). *Economic Diplomacy and the Geography of International Trade*. Cheltenham: Edward Elgar.

Vogel, L. (2011). Structural reforms and external rebalancing in the euro area: A model-based analysis. *European Economy Economic Papers No. 443*. Brussels: European Commission, DG ECFIN.

—. (2012). Tax avoidance and fiscal limits: Laffer curves in an economy with informal sector. *European Economy Economic Papers No. 448*. Brussels: European Commission, DG ECFIN.

Von Hagen, J. and Hofmann, B. (2004). Macroeconomic implications of low inflation in the euro area. *North American Journal of Economics and Finance*, 15 (1): 5-23.

Wagner, J. (2011). Offshoring and firm performance: Self-selection, effects on performance, or both? *Review of World Economics*, 147 (2): 217-247.

Whelan, K. (2010). Global imbalances and the financial crisis. *Briefing Papers by Monetary Experts Panel: Future Development of Global Imbalances (Monetary dialogue with the ECB 2010)*. Brussels: European Parliament; Committee on Economic and Monetary Affairs.

World Bank and International Finance Corporation (2011). *Doing Business 2012: Doing Business in a Transparent World*. Washington DC: International Bank for Reconstruction and Development / World Bank.

Wyplosz, C. (2010a). The debt crisis and the treaty. *How to use the Treaty for more effective economic coordination in the euro area? (Monetary dialogue with the ECB 2010)*. Brussels: European Parliament; Committee on Economic and Monetary Affairs.

—. (2010b). High deficits and debts: What to do about them? *Briefing Papers by Monetary Experts Panel: Policy Implications of Increased Debt and Deficits (Monetary dialogue with the ECB 2010)*. Brussels: European Parliament; Committee on Economic and Monetary Affairs.

Xiao, Y. (2008). Role of foreign direct investment in boosting productivity and exports in the Southern euro area economies. In Bennett, H., Escolano, J., Fabrizio, S., Gutierrez, E., Ivaschenko, I., Lissovolik, B., Moreno-Badia, M., Schule, W., Tokarick, S., Xiao, Y. and Zarnic, Z., "Competitiveness in the Southern euro area: France, Greece, Italy, Portugal, and Spain". *IMF Working Papers No. 08/112*. Washington DC: IMF.

Yue, V.Z. (2010). Sovereign default and debt renegotiation. *Journal of International Economics*, 80 (2): 176-187.

Zemanek, H., Belke, A. and Schnabl, G. (2010). Current account balances and structural adjustment in the Euro area. *International Economics and Economic Policy*, 7 (1): 83-127.

Greek

Γιαννακόπουλος, Ν., Λαλιώτης, Ι., Νταούλη, Ι. και Ντεμούσης, Μ. (2010). Διερεύνηση της σχέσης μεγέθους επιχείρησης και μισθών στην Ελλάδα. Μελέτη από τα πρακτικά της ημερίδας της Τράπεζας της

Ελλάδος: *Η Ελληνική Αγορά Εργασίας: Χαρακτηριστικά, Εξελίξεις και Προκλήσεις*. Αθήνα: Τράπεζα της Ελλάδος.

ΙΟΒΕ (2010α). *Δελτίο Αποτελεσμάτων Έρευνας Επενδύσεων στη Βιομηχανία: 2η Έρευνα 2009*. Αθήνα: Ίδρυμα Οικονομικών & Βιομηχανικών Ερευνών.

—. (2010β). *Η Ελληνική Οικονομία 3/10*. Αθήνα: Ίδρυμα Οικονομικών & Βιομηχανικών Ερευνών.

—. (2010γ). *Δελτίο Αποτελεσμάτων Έρευνας Επενδύσεων στη Βιομηχανία: 2η Έρευνα 2010*. Αθήνα: Ίδρυμα Οικονομικών & Βιομηχανικών Ερευνών.

—. (2011α). *Τριμηνιαίο Δελτίο Οικονομικής Συγκυρίας στον Τομέα Τηλεπικοινωνιών και Πληροφορικής: Α' Τρίμηνο 2011*. Αθήνα: Ίδρυμα Οικονομικών & Βιομηχανικών Ερευνών.

—. (2011β). *Η Ελληνική Οικονομία 1/11*. Αθήνα: Ίδρυμα Οικονομικών & Βιομηχανικών Ερευνών.

—. (2011γ). *Η Ελληνική Οικονομία 2/11*. Αθήνα: Ίδρυμα Οικονομικών & Βιομηχανικών Ερευνών.

—. (2011δ). *Δελτίο Αποτελεσμάτων Έρευνας Επενδύσεων στη Βιομηχανία: 1η Έρευνα 2011*. Αθήνα: Ίδρυμα Οικονομικών & Βιομηχανικών Ερευνών.

Ιωαννίδης, Σ., Τσακανίκας, Α. και Χατζηχρήστου, Σ. (2009). *Η Επιχειρηματικότητα στα Πρόθυρα της Κρίσης: Η Έρευνα του GEM 2008-2009*. Αθήνα: Ίδρυμα Οικονομικών & Βιομηχανικών Ερευνών.

—. (2010). *Η Επιχειρηματικότητα στα Πρόθυρα της Κρίσης: Η Έρευνα του GEM 2009-2010*. Αθήνα: Ίδρυμα Οικονομικών & Βιομηχανικών Ερευνών.

Κέντρο Διεθνούς Πολιτικής Οικονομίας (2010). *Η Ελληνική Οικονομική Κρίση στον Διεθνή Τύπο*. Αθήνα: Ινστιτούτο Διεθνών Σχέσεων.

Παπαναστασίου, Μ. (2009). *Οι Θυγατρικές των Ελληνικών Πολυεθνικών Επιχειρήσεων και Στρατηγικές Διεθνοποίησης*. Αθήνα: Ίδρυμα Οικονομικών & Βιομηχανικών Ερευνών.

Τράπεζα της Ελλάδος (2010). *Έκθεση του Διοικητή για το Έτος 2009*. Αθήνα: Τράπεζα της Ελλάδος.

—. (2011). *Έκθεση του Διοικητή για το Έτος 2010*. Αθήνα: Τράπεζα της Ελλάδος.

CHAPTER FIVE

MYTHS AND FACTS OF THE GREEK SOVEREIGN DEBT CRISIS WITHIN AN EXTENSIVE SHADOW ECONOMIC ENVIRONMENT

ARISTIDIS BITZENIS AND VASILEIOS A. VLACHOS

1. Introduction

The sovereign debt crisis that initially appeared in Greece developed into a crisis of the euro-area. There is no doubt that the major responsibility for the eruption of the Greek sovereign debt crisis rests with Greek authorities who mismanaged their economy and deceived everybody about the true nature of their budgetary problems. However, the responsibility for letting this crisis to transform into a systemic crisis of the euro-area rests with the institutions of Economic and Monetary Union (EMU) of the European Union (EU), as the reasons behind the escalating size of sovereign debt may be different across economies – eventually hit by the sovereign debt crisis – but the criteria that these economies have to meet in order to regain access to international financial markets are the same.

The mutation of the financial into an economic and eventually a sovereign debt crisis has been influenced by the hesitation and ambiguities of euro-area governments and the European Central Bank (ECB). Euro-area governments failed to give a clear signal about their readiness to support Greece and other economies with deteriorating macroeconomic fundamentals, such as Italy and Spain. The failure of euro-area governments and EMU institutions to provide a plan for the worst scenario has led to downgradings from rating agencies and fuels uncertainty in international financial markets.

Moreover, the suitability of the economic adjustment programme that accompanies the bailouts received by the Greek government is in question, since the country has entered a vicious deflationary spiral that sinks further into depression. Accordingly, reforms aiming to restrain bureaucracy, corruption, and tax evasion, and thus, to make the public sector more productive and efficient, should immediately be the main priority of government policy. Such reforms would reduce the levels of corruption and transfer a part of the shadow economy in the Greek formal economy and, ultimately, assist the Greek government in achieving its fiscal targets without adopting severe measures of fiscal austerity during depression.

This chapter discusses the development of the euro-area sovereign debt crisis[1] – underlining the role and nature of the Stability and Growth Pact (SGP) – and the causes of the Greek sovereign debt crisis in order to indicate that there is a distortion of reality on major issues concerning the Greek situation to date. The second – and next – section gives an overview of EU, EMU and the role of SGP in order to discuss the events that contributed to the development of the euro-area sovereign debt crisis. The third section firstly presents Greece's accession in EU and EMU and then discusses the causes that led to the states' sovereign debt crisis. The fourth section presents the distortion of reality with regard to the causes of drying up of credit and liquidity, the reality behind the option to default, and the main weaknesses of the economy that postpone recovery.

2. The Euro-area Sovereign Debt Crisis

The discussion in this section begins with an overview of EU and EMU in order to turn on the crucial role of the SGP. The SGP is the official regulator of fiscal policy in EMU and as a result, compliance to its rules – through fiscal consolidation in order to reduce government expenditure and bring government debt to sustainable levels – generates expectations for the termination of the sovereign debt crisis. However, several critics question not only its appropriateness as a measure against the spread and climax of the sovereign debt crisis, but also its ability to safeguard the sense of fiscal balance and stability within EMU.

[1] Although the crisis of sovereign debt is usually termed "European" in the literature, it exclusively concerns the euro-area fundamentals.

2.1 A Brief Overview of EU and EMU

The EU is an economic and political partnership built on the idea of a single market, which extends to EMU (also termed "eurozone/euro-area/euroland") that promotes integration further, with the adoption of the euro as a common currency, and a common monetary policy (see http://europa.eu/about-eu/basic-information/index_en.htm). Prior to joining the EU a country must meet the Copenhagen criteria, which are mainly political, social and administrative, and to a lesser degree economic. If a country wishes to join the EMU, it must primarily be a member of EU and then meet the Maastricht criteria (see ***Box 1***), which are solely economic. EMU accession requires from the member state to conform to the rules outlined in the SGP.

Box 1: Maastricht convergence criteria

The Maastricht convergence criteria are presented in Article 121(1) of the European Community (EC) Treaty. Each EU member state must satisfy all of the following criteria in order to be able to participate in EMU (see http://europa.eu/abc/eurojargon/index_en.htm):

- With respect to price stability, the inflation rate should not exceed more than 1.5% of the average of the three lower respective rates of EU member states indicated in the preceding year.
- With respect to interest rates, the nominal long-term interest rate should not exceed more than 2% of the average of the three EU member states with the lower inflation rates in the preceding year.
- The ratio of the annual government deficit to gross domestic product (GDP) must not exceed 3% at the end of the financial year.
- The ratio of gross government debt to GDP must not exceed 60% at the end of the financial year. Higher debt levels are acceptable provided that debt is decreasing at a steady rate.
- The national currency's exchange rate should stay within certain margins of fluctuation – set by the Exchange Rate Mechanism (ERM) II – for two years.
- Each candidate state has to ensure compatibility of their national legislation with that of Articles 108 and 109 of the Treaty and the Statute of the European System of Central Banks.

Furthermore, prior to joining the euro-area, an EU member state must participate in the ERM II.[2] Latvia and Lithuania from 1 January 2009, and Denmark from 1 January 1999 are the EU member states that currently participate in ERM II. The remaining EU currencies are expected to follow as soon as they meet the Maastricht criteria though no target date has been declared. Denmark and the United Kingdom obtained special opt-outs from the original Maastricht Treaty. Both countries are legally exempt from joining the euro-area unless their governments decide otherwise, either by parliamentary vote or referendum.

The EU currently consists of 27 member states, of which only 17 (Austria, Belgium, Cyprus, Estonia, Finland, France, Germany, Greece, Ireland, Italy, Luxembourg, Malta, the Netherlands, Portugal, Slovakia, Slovenia, and Spain) are members of EMU. The 10 EU member states yet to join the EMU are Bulgaria, the Czech Republic, Denmark, Hungary, Latvia, Lithuania, Poland, Romania, Sweden, and the United Kingdom. Three European microstates – Monaco, San Marino and the Vatican – have concluded agreements with the EU, which allows them the use of the euro as their official currency and to mint coins. However, these microstates are neither formally part of the euro-area nor are they represented on the board of the ECB.[3]

Physical coins and banknotes (circulation) of the euro were introduced in 12 member states of EMU on 1 January 2002. Five states entered the euro-area after 2006. Slovenia qualified in 2006 and was admitted on 1 January 2007. Cyprus and Malta qualified in 2007 and were admitted on 1 January 2008. Slovakia qualified in 2008 and joined on 1 January 2009. Estonia joined the euro-area on 1 January 2011.

2.2 The Role of SGP

The economic importance of the SGP in EMU is fourfold (Heipertz and Verdun, 2004):

i. Firstly, the SGP stresses the need for consolidation, i.e. sets limits on welfare-state expansion in order to prevent the sacrifice of government revenue in debt servicing and maintains low inflation

---

[2] ERM II is a system designed to avoid excessive exchange-rate fluctuations between the participating currencies and the euro that might disrupt economic stability within the single market (see http://ec.europa.eu/economy_finance/euro/adoption/index_en.htm).

[3] Montenegro is using the euro as well, as the country does not issue any currency. Montenegro has initiated the EU accession process in 2010.

and interest rates that contribute to the generation of a favourite economic climate for private investment.

ii. Secondly, the SGP prevents externalities that would occur from increased debt servicing by member states – i.e. strict budgetary discipline prevents member states from excessive bond issuance that would fuel inflationary pressures and subsequently, and forces the ECB to increase interest rates, which would in turn depress investment and consumption.
iii. Thirdly, the SGP fosters a fiscal regime that prevents excessive deficits from undermining the independence of ECB.
iv. Fourthly, the SGP fosters economic policy co-ordination between member states by adjusting according to demands of changes in the general economic conditions – i.e. the flexibility reform in 2005, and the so-called "six-pack" of legislation on economic governance (four of these laws were used to reform the SGP by enforcing a stricter application of fiscal rules) that passed in 2011.

The SGP is the concrete EU answer to concerns on the continuation of budgetary discipline in EMU. Political agreement on the pact was reached at the Dublin European Council in December 1996. During initial negotiations leading up to the establishment of the pact, Germany was the main driving force pushing for rigid rules and strict regulations. The European Council called on the Council of Ministers to draw up a resolution on the SGP, which was adopted by the Amsterdam European Council on 17 June 1997. The SGP strengthened the EC Treaty provisions on fiscal discipline in the EMU foreseen in Articles 99 and 104 (the amendments were adopted in 1993 in Maastricht). The full provisions took effect when the euro was launched in the third stage of EMU in 1 January 1999. The SGP was built on the convergence criteria, which member states have to fulfil in order to join the single Euro currency. In more detail, the SGP was put forward by:

i. The Resolution of the Amsterdam European Council on the Stability and Growth Pact of 17 June 1997; Regulation (EC) No. 1466/97 on the surveillance of budgetary positions and the coordination of economic policies (prevention aspect);
ii. Regulation (EC) No. 1467/97 on the implementation of the excessive deficit procedure (EDP) whenever a Member State exceeds the reference value, i.e. a deficit of more than 3% of GDP (punitive aspect).

The SGP established a system for the coordination and surveillance of national budgetary policies. The countries adopting the single currency were required to submit an annual stability programme. All central government deficits could not exceed the 3% of GDP threshold. A relatively broad margin was given to a member state to adjust its budgetary policy in accordance with its economic climate.

The member states undertake to abide to the medium-term budgetary objective of positions close to balance or in surplus. In addition, they are required to make public, on their own initiative, the Amsterdam European Council recommendations made to them; to commit themselves to take the corrective budgetary action they deem necessary to meet the objectives of their stability or convergence programmes; to launch the corrective budgetary adjustments they deem necessary without delay upon receiving information indicating the risk of an excessive deficit; to correct excessive deficits as quickly as possible after their emergence; and finally, to undertake not to invoke the exceptional nature of a deficit linked to an annual fall in the GDP of less than 2%, unless they are in severe recession (annual fall in real GDP of at least 0.75%). The Economic and Financial Affairs – ECOFIN – Council is committed to rigorous and timely implementation of all provisions of the SGP within its competence. In addition, it is urged to regard the deadlines for the application of the EDP as upper limits and it is requested to impose sanctions if a participating member state fails to take the necessary steps to bring the excessive deficit situation to an end and to apply rigorously the whole range of sanctions, which for this circumstance are provided. Lastly, it must state in writing the reasons that justify a decision not to be acted.[4]

There have been several criticisms on the appropriateness of the SGP, questioning even the conformity of member states' governments to its enforcement. ***Table 1*** indicates that five out of the seventeen member states conformed to the debt threshold in 2011 and that only six exhibited a budgetary position that does not exceed the deficit/GDP 3% ratio threshold. ***Table 1*** also indicates that the issue of conforming to SGP rules has been in question since the formation of EMU, since only Estonia, Finland, Luxembourg, Slovakia and Slovenia seem to have been able to – partly – comply with the Maastricht thresholds until 2011. Moreover, the prospects to conform to the SGP framework amid slowdown/recession and the spread of the sovereign debt crisis is not realistic, as the primary balances of several countries deteriorate – from Cyprus, that also required

[4] For an overview of ongoing EDPs see
http://ec.europa.eu/economy_finance/economic_governance/sgp/deficit/index_en.htm.

a bailout, to the Netherlands, which are placed in the economically sound core of the euro-area.

Early criticisms on the appropriateness of the SGP prior to the flexibility reform in 2005 were on the flexibility required by governments to balance their budgets (Buti et al., 2003). After the flexibility reform in 2005, arguments concerned the future of EMU, i.e. that, instead of cohesion, it would foster collusion (Buti, 2006; Beetsma and Debrun, 2007; Bonatti and Christini, 2007). Recent developments ("six-pack") fuel criticism based on the fact that the new rules do not take account of the flexibility that governments require in order to balance their budgets across economic cycles (for the deviation from balanced budgets see ***Table 1***).[5] As a result, euro-area members have to meet the targets at an annual basis, starting from a period characterized by weak growth (even recession) and amid the perils of European sovereign debt crisis.

The criticism on the appropriateness of SGP concerns the set of rules that comprise it. For example, with regard to the soundness of relaxing the government debt threshold, research indicates that the relationship between government debt and real GDP growth is weak for debt/GDP ratios below a threshold of 90% of GDP, while above 90%, median growth rates fall by 1%, and average growth falls considerably more (Reinhart and Rogoff, 2010). Furthermore, the appropriateness of SGP to substitute for a unique fiscal policy is in question because the theory of optimum-currency-areas indicates the necessity for fiscal integration (Kenen, 1969; Dellas and Tavlas, 2009).

Finally, critics of the SGP question its ability to restore the lost credibility of EMU, which is responsible for the persisting rise of bond yields' spreads across member states as the sovereign debt crisis climaxes. Commitment to SGP is a source of uncertainty with negative implications for recovery and exit from the sovereign debt crisis (Ferre, 2012), which requires for alternatives such as strengthening the institutional framework of EMU and increasing the transparency of the decision-making process (Wyplosz, 2011; Muscatelli et al., 2012). "As long as the SGP is not adhered to and effectively monitored, it cannot serve as a substitute for a European fiscal authority" (Candelon and Palm, 2011: 389).

[5] See inter alia Mathieu and Sterdyniak (2010) who argue that strengthening the SGP would be dangerous if it deprived member states of policy tools proven to be helpful during the economic crisis.

Table 1 - Government debt and deficit in the Eurozone (% of GDP)

State	Indicator/Time	1995	1999	2002	2003	2004	2005	2006	2007	2008	2009	2010	2011
Austria	Gross debt	68.2	66.8	66.2	65.3	64.7	64.2	62.3	60.2	63.8	69.5	71.9	72.2
	Net lending/borrowing	-5.8	**-2.3**	**-0.7**	**-1.5**	-4.4	**-1.7**	**-1.5**	**-0.9**	**-0.9**	-4.1	-4.5	**-2.6**
	Primary balance	-1.8	1.1	2.4	1.4	-1.6	1.2	1.2	1.9	1.7	-1.3	-1.8	0.0
Belgium	Gross debt	130.2	113.6	103.4	98.4	94.0	92.0	88.0	84.1	89.3	95.8	96.0	98.0
	Net lending/borrowing	-4.5	**-0.6**	**-0.1**	**-0.1**	**-0.1**	**-2.5**	**0.4**	**-0.1**	**-1.0**	-5.6	-3.8	-3.7
	Primary balance	4.3	6.2	5.6	5.1	4.5	1.7	4.3	3.8	2.8	-2.0	-0.4	-0.4
Cyprus	Gross debt	**51.8**	**59.3**	65.1	69.7	70.9	69.4	64.7	**58.8**	**48.9**	**58.5**	61.5	71.6
	Net lending/borrowing	**-0.9**	-4.3	-4.4	-6.6	-4.1	**-2.4**	**-1.2**	**3.5**	**0.9**	-6.1	-5.3	-6.3
	Primary balance	1.2	-1.3	-1.2	-3.0	-0.8	1.1	2.1	6.5	3.8	-3.6	-3.1	-3.8
Estonia	Gross debt	**8.2**	**6.5**	**5.7**	**5.6**	**5.0**	**4.6**	**4.4**	**3.7**	**4.5**	**7.2**	**6.7**	**6.0**
	Net lending/borrowing	**1.1**	-3.5	**0.3**	**1.7**	**1.6**	**1.6**	**2.5**	**2.4**	**-2.9**	**-2.0**	**0.2**	**1.0**
	Primary balance	1.6	-3.2	0.5	1.9	1.9	1.8	2.6	2.6	-2.7	-1.8	0.4	1.1
Finland	Gross debt	**56.6**	**45.7**	**41.5**	**44.5**	**44.4**	**41.7**	**39.6**	**35.2**	**33.9**	**43.5**	**48.4**	**48.6**
	Net lending/borrowing	-6.1	**1.7**	**4.1**	**2.6**	**2.5**	**2.8**	**4.1**	**5.3**	**4.3**	**-2.5**	**-2.5**	**-0.5**
	Primary balance	-2.2	4.7	6.2	4.3	4.0	4.3	5.6	6.8	5.7	-1.3	-1.5	0.6
France	Gross debt	**55.5**	**58.9**	**58.8**	62.9	64.9	66.4	63.7	64.2	68.2	79.2	82.3	85.8
	Net lending/borrowing	-5.5	**-1.8**	-3.1	-4.1	-3.6	**-2.9**	**-2.3**	**-2.7**	-3.3	-7.5	-7.1	-5.2
	Primary balance	-2.0	1.2	-0.2	-1.3	-0.9	-0.3	0.3	0.0	-0.4	-5.1	-4.7	-2.6
Germany	Gross debt	**55.6**	61.3	60.7	64.4	66.3	68.6	68.1	65.2	66.7	74.4	83.0	81.2
	Net lending/borrowing	-9.5	-1.6	-3.8	-4.2	-3.8	-3.3	**-1.6**	**0.2**	**-0.1**	-3.2	-4.3	**-1.0**
	Primary balance	-6.0	1.6	-0.9	-1.1	-0.9	-0.5	1.2	3.0	2.7	-0.5	-1.8	1.6

Greece	Gross debt	97.0	94.0	101.7	97.4	98.6	100.0	106.1	107.4	113.0	129.4	145.0	165.3
	Net lending/borrowing	-	-	-4.8	-5.6	-7.5	-5.2	-5.7	-6.5	-9.8	-15.6	-10.3	-9.1
	Primary balance	-	-	0.7	-0.7	-2.6	-0.7	-1.4	-2.0	-4.8	-10.4	-4.7	-2.2
Ireland	Gross debt	80.2	**46.6**	**31.9**	**30.7**	**29.4**	**27.2**	**24.5**	**24.8**	**44.2**	65.1	92.5	108.2
	Net lending/borrowing	**-2.0**	**2.7**	**-0.4**	**0.4**	**1.4**	**1.7**	**2.9**	**0.1**	-7.3	-14.0	-31.2	-13.1
	Primary balance	3.2	5.0	1.0	1.6	2.5	2.7	3.9	1.1	-6.0	-12.0	-28.0	-9.7
Italy	Gross debt	120.9	113.0	105.1	103.9	103.4	105.4	106.1	103.1	105.7	116.0	118.6	120.1
	Net lending/borrowing	-7.4	**-1.9**	-3.1	-3.6	-3.5	-4.4	-3.4	**-1.6**	**-2.7**	-5.4	-4.6	-3.9
	Primary balance	4.1	4.6	2.5	1.5	1.2	0.2	1.2	3.4	2.5	-0.8	0.0	1.0
Luxembourg	Gross debt	**7.4**	**6.4**	**6.3**	**6.1**	**6.3**	**6.1**	**6.7**	**6.7**	**13.7**	**14.8**	**19.1**	**18.2**
	Net lending/borrowing	**2.4**	**3.4**	**2.1**	**0.5**	**-1.1**	**0.0**	**1.4**	**3.7**	**3.0**	**-0.8**	**-0.9**	**-0.6**
	Primary balance	2.8	3.7	2.4	0.7	-0.9	0.2	1.5	3.9	3.3	-0.4	-0.4	-0.1
Malta	Gross debt	**35.3**	**57.1**	**59.1**	67.6	71.7	69.7	64.4	62.3	62.3	68.1	69.4	72.0
	Net lending/borrowing	-4.2	-7.7	-5.8	-9.2	-4.7	**-2.9**	**-2.8**	**-2.4**	-4.6	-3.8	-3.7	**-2.7**
	Primary balance	-2.2	-4.0	-2.1	-5.6	-1.1	0.7	0.8	1.0	-1.4	-0.6	-0.7	0.4
Netherlands	Gross debt	76.1	61.1	50.5	52.0	52.4	51.8	47.4	45.3	58.5	60.8	62.9	65.2
	Net lending/borrowing	-9.2	0.4	-2.1	-3.1	-1.7	-0.3	0.5	0.2	0.5	-5.6	-5.1	-4.7
	Primary balance	-3.6	4.7	0.7	-0.6	0.7	2.1	2.7	2.4	2.7	-3.4	-3.1	-2.6
Portugal	Gross debt	**59.2**	**51.4**	**56.6**	**59.2**	61.9	67.7	69.3	68.3	71.6	83.1	93.3	107.8
	Net lending/borrowing	-5.4	-3.1	-3.4	-3.7	-4.0	-6.5	-4.6	-3.1	-3.6	-10.2	-9.8	-4.2
	Primary balance	0.2	-0.2	-0.6	-1.0	-1.4	-4.0	-1.8	-0.2	-0.6	-7.3	-7.0	-0.4

Slovakia	Gross debt	**22.1**	**47.8**	**43.4**	**42.4**	**41.5**	**34.2**	**30.5**	**29.6**	**27.9**	**35.6**	**41.1**	**43.3**
	Net lending/borrowing	-3.4	-7.4	-8.2	**-2.8**	**-2.4**	**-2.8**	-3.2	**-1.8**	**-2.1**	-8.0	-7.7	-4.8
	Primary balance	-1.0	-4.0	-4.7	-0.3	-0.2	-1.1	-1.7	-0.4	-0.8	-6.6	-6.3	-3.2
Slovenia	Gross debt	**18.6**	**24.1**	**27.8**	**27.2**	**27.3**	**26.7**	**26.4**	**23.1**	**21.9**	**35.3**	**38.8**	**47.6**
	Net lending/borrowing	-8.3	-3.0	**-2.4**	**-2.7**	**-2.3**	**-1.5**	**-1.4**	**0.0**	**-1.9**	-6.1	-6.0	-6.4
	Primary balance	-6.2	-0.7	-0.3	-0.7	-0.6	0.1	0.0	1.2	-0.7	-4.7	-4.4	-4.5
Spain	Gross debt	63.3	62.4	**52.6**	**48.8**	**46.3**	**43.2**	**39.7**	**36.3**	**40.2**	**53.9**	61.2	68.5
	Net lending/borrowing	-7.2	**-1.2**	**-0.2**	**-0.3**	**-0.1**	**1.3**	**2.4**	**1.9**	-4.5	-11.2	-9.3	-8.5
	Primary balance	-2.1	2.3	2.5	2.0	1.9	3.1	4.0	3.5	-2.9	-9.4	-7.4	-6.1

Source: Eurostat
(http://epp.eurostat.ec.europa.eu/portal/page/portal/statistics/search_database, as accessed 31 July 2012).
Notes to Table 1
1. Dash implies that data is not available.
2. Gross debt refers to "government consolidated gross debt" ("Maastricht debt"), which is the sum of government liabilities as defined in the European System of Accounts (ESA) 95 in: a) currency and deposits, b) securities other than shares, excluding financial derivatives and c) loans outstanding at the end of the year, measured at nominal value and consolidated.
3. Net lending/ borrowing refers to "government surplus/deficit under EDP, which is net lending (+)/net borrowing (-) of "general government" (as defined in ESA95), plus net streams of interest payments resulting from swaps arrangements and forward rate agreements.
4. Primary balance is government net borrowing or net lending, excluding interest payments on consolidated government liabilities.
5. Figures in bold for "gross debt" and "net lending/borrowing" meet the thresholds set by the Maastricht criteria.

2.3 Causes and Facts of the Euro-area Sovereign Debt Crisis

The main (direct) indicator of a debt crisis is the ratio of government debt/GDP, which in case it moves beyond a certain threshold, the state would face rising financing costs. Nevertheless, even if the particular ratio is a simple indicator, it neglects the cost of debt: i.e. the size of debt should not always be conceived as an indicator of its sustainability, as in some cases, it is better to have a high government debt/GDP ratio at a low cost (rate of interest) than a low level of debt at a high rate. Therefore, the government deficit/GDP ratio – another straightforward indicator – is used in conjunction with the government debt/GDP for the formulation of a direct evaluation about the sustainability of a state's debt. Both of these indicators appear on ***Table 1*** and constitute the essence of the SGP.

The rapid build-up of government debt in an environment of financial instability and low growth have increased the importance of government debt sustainability (***Box 2*** indicates briefly the notion of debt sustainability). ***Table 1*** indicates that the debt and deficit ratios which are well over the euro-area average – i.e. approximately over 100% of debt/GDP and 8% of deficit/GDP – question the sustainability of debt servicing. As a result, the state has to pay a higher risk premium for financing its debt and faces a sovereign debt crisis.[7]

Empirical findings indicate that there is a link between the financial/banking crisis and the sovereign debt crisis. The banking crises precede sovereign debt crises – hence can be used as predictors – as they increase significantly the stock of public debt and push up the risk of default (Reinhart and Rogoff, 2011). ***Table 1*** indicates that debt growth rates have been increasing in the euro-area since 2008.

The financial crisis originated in the explosion of the real estate bubble in the US in 2007. The bankruptcy of Lehman Brothers, a year later, caused havoc on stock markets. The inter-banking market stopped functioning and governments were forced to intervene in order to stabilize the banking sector. Moreover, governments used the sovereign bond markets not only to support the banking sector, but also to finance the recessionary real effects implied by the banking crisis.[8]

---

[7] Fiscal austerity remains the only remedy for containing the increases of risk premiums since the ECB cannot directly finance the fiscal expansion of member states.

[8] For the causes and mutation of the financial crisis into sovereign debt crisis see Candelon and Palm (2010) and Arghyrou and Kontonikas (2011). The precursors of the sovereign debt crisis – i.e. the persistent global imbalances, the subprime mortgage crisis, and the volatile oil prices that followed it – were tightly

Box 2: Debt sustainability

The volume of a government debt is sustainable when it can be serviced at any point in time. Short to long-term government debt sustainability requires from governments to be both liquid and solvent (ECB, 2012: 59-60):

- "*Liquidity* is a short-term concept and refers to a government's ability to maintain access to financial markets, ensuring its ability to service all upcoming obligations in the short-term.
- *Solvency* is a medium to long-term concept and requires that the government's net present value budget constraint is fulfilled, stipulating that the net present value of the government's future primary balances must be at least as high as the net present value of outstanding government debt."

The financial crisis increased the levels of global risk and consequently, markets started to scrutinize macro-fundamentals and fled to quality. The turning point for spreads (risk premiums) took place a year before the outbreak of the financial crisis and the subsequent increases in government debt/GDP ratio, as markets integrate quickly and even anticipate news (i.e. the transformation of banking risk into sovereign risk through bank-bailouts). Until the financial crisis, the spread of 10- years government bond yields against Germany were very low, despite deteriorating fundamentals in many EMU member states. The differences in spread increases that followed across EMU member states are explained by their heterogeneous fundamentals and their interaction with international risk. Greek spreads have been much higher than those of other peripheral member states because Greek authorities did not recognise market signals and did not commit to bold action as early as they should have.

Although during the decade after the launch of the euro (1999-2008) spreads between the sovereign debts of Germany and the rest of the euro-area have consistently been below 50 basis points, since the last quarter of 2009 spreads have widened dramatically, resembling the pre-euro era. Three member states – namely Greece, Portugal and Ireland[9] – have

---

interconnected. The run-up of oil prices in 2007-2008 were not caused by the Organisation of the Petroleum Exporting Countries – OPEC – oligopoly (Khan, 2009) and had significant effects on overall consumption spending (Hamilton, 2009). "Speculation on the future price of oil led to both overshooting of spot prices in the first half of 2008 and undershooting in the second half of the year" (Hudson and Maioli, 2010: 59). The sharp rise in oil prices following the subprime mortgage crisis was the result of a speculative response to the financial crisis itself, in an attempt to rebuild asset supply (Caballero et al., 2009).

[9] The Irish government has managed to co-finance its budget through the bond markets since late 2012.

currently no access to private financing on a medium to long-term basis (but can only issue bills) and have had to be bailed out by an EC/International Monetary Fund (IMF)/ECB rescue mission. Other member states – namely Spain, Italy and Belgium – have been indirectly financed through purchases of their bonds by the ECB on secondary debt markets. Spain also received financial assistance for the recapitalisation and restructuring of its banking sector – with the aim of restoring access to the markets on affordable terms – which had suffered as a result of the real estate bubble and subsequent economic recession.

The spread of the sovereign debt crisis across euro-area member states and the ECB's stance of restraining the leverage that would immediately appease the demand of international financial markets for debt sustainability have fueled a crisis of confidence and uncertainty.[10] The crisis of confidence and uncertainty persists due to the unrealistic expectations that fiscal austerity does not pin down economic growth.

3. The Greek Sovereign Debt Crisis

This section presents the path leading to what has recently developed into a sovereign debt crisis. The discussion begins with a presentation of the key events regarding Greece's integration with the European institutions until EMU accession. The discussion then focuses on the deterioration of Greece's macroeconomic fundamentals and on the institutions that fueled the climax of the state's sovereign debt crisis.

3.1 Milestones in Greece's EU and EMU Accession

Greece was the first country to sign an Association Agreement with the European Economic Community (EEC). Greece's path towards united Europe began on 8 June 1959, when an application was lodged for association with the EEC. The application was approved by EEC Foreign Ministers on 27 July 1959 and on 10 September 1959 negotiations commenced between representatives of Greece and the EEC. The negotiations eventually led to the signing of the Association Agreement in the Hellenic Parliament in Athens on 9 July 1961. The Association Agreement came into force on 2 November 1961.

However, Greece's path towards united Europe was suspended on 21 April 1967 due to the abolition of democratic institutions by a military

[10] For a review on the mechanisms for achieving sovereign debt sustainability see Hileman (2012).

junta. On 14 August 1974 – a few days after the restoration of democracy in Greece – the country witnessed the second wave of the Turkish invasion of Cyprus. The decision taken by former Prime Minister Constantine Karamanlis was not to respond with war but to exert political and economic pressure on Turkey. At the same time, a particularly costly programme to bolster Greek military capacity in order to achieve and maintain a credible balance of power so as to deter the intense Turkish aggression was implemented. If – in the particular period of 1974-1975 – Greece's Prime Minister had opted to unleash a retaliatory war against Turkey, regardless of its outcome, Greece and Turkey would have been drawn into an extended period of conflict and as a result, the accession of Greece to EEC would have been postponed or aborted and the impact on Greek political institutions would have been extremely destabilising.

The government of national unity led by Constantine Karamanlis lodged a memorandum with the president of the EC Council of Ministers on 22 August 1974, requesting immediate reactivation of the Association Agreement. The request was accepted, allowing Karamanlis' government one year later to lodge an application for Greece's accession as a full member of the EC. The Council of Ministers requested on 9 February 1976 that the procedure for Greece's full accession should be continued, despite the reservations on the part of the Commission, which requested a pre-accession period. A few months later, on 27 July 1976 negotiations began between Greece and the EC which were successfully concluded on 21 December 1978. On 28 May 1979, the Treaty on Greece's accession to the EC was signed in Athens in the Zappeion Hall, followed on 28 June 1979 by ratification of the Accession Treaty by the Hellenic Parliament. Two years later, on 1 January 1981, the Accession Treaty came into force.

The years of preparation for accession (1974-1980) and the first thirteen years of EC membership (1981-1993) were periods of slow but continuous maturation of Greek society's economy and institutions. The set of restrictive policies and/or stabilization programs implemented in 1979-81, 1983, 1985-1987 and 1991-1993 did not yield permanent gains, although they managed to avert to some degree a further deterioration of the economic situation. The economic climate changed in the early 1990s and specifically since 1994, when the new "1994-1999 Convergence Program of the Greek Economy" was adopted, marking a qualitative shift in economic policies. The steady improvement in the economic situation meant that sacrifices had not been wasted. The ailing economy soon found itself on the road to recovery. Moreover, since the improvement was visible, not only was the credibility of the reform policies increased, but the adoption of a moderate stance with regard to wages and prices was made easier for social partners.

Box 3: Euro-area's statistical irregularities

It appears that the Greek government accounts had been "falsified" (although Eurostat diplomatically avoids this word), chiefly by having "postponed" to account for huge military expenditures from 1997 onwards. Calculations based on the "corrected" deficits employed by the ESA95 methodology indicate that Greece would not be able to meet the required criteria for joining EMU. However, according to the ESA79 methodology – the methodology employed to calculate the deficits of the first 12 euro-area members at the time of their applications – Greece met the deficit criterion for the reference year of 1999. Thus, since the remaining criteria had also been met, Greece was rightly accepted into the euro-area.

In March 2002, Eurostat refused to validate the data transmitted by the Greek government. In reaction, the National Statistical Service of Greece revised the debt level by several percentage points. In September 2002, Eurostat again refused to validate the data. The debt was revised upwards once again, and the government balance, which the Greek government had presented as a surplus, appeared to be a deficit. As a result, in March 2004, Eurostat continued to refuse again to validate the Greek numbers. All this had occurred shortly before Greek elections and a new government (New Democracy, a conservative party) was to be inaugurated. When New Democracy won the March 7 elections in 2004, it claimed it would launch an objective financial audit of the government accounts. Thus, the newly formed government produced new estimates after investigating the fiscal years 1997-2003. The new data was given to Eurostat, which in turn published a report http://epp.eurostat.cec.eu.int/cache/ITY_PUBLIC/GREECE/EN/GREECE-EN.PDF).

"Irregularities" (the word falsification was never officially used, as mentioned before) in deficit reporting had also been practised by other euro-area members, chiefly by Italy and Portugal. Moreover, there were arguments about massive "creative accounting" employed by many countries in order to meet the deficit criterion to enable their entrance to the euro-area. The practice of temporary measures adopted by several states has also been criticised, since in several cases, their deficits rose again over 3% soon after the reference year. At the same time, big economies like Germany and France seem to have made it a practise of defying the SGP rules.

Greece entered the ERM I on 16 March 1998. At that time, the central parity was 357 Greek Drachmas (GRD) against the European Currency Unit (ECU) and the fluctuation band +/-15%. However, the ERM II replaced the ERM I in January 1999 and the euro replaced the ECU. Greece became part of ERM II and the GRD was valued at a central rate of 353,109 GRD against the euro. On 9 March 2000 Greece applied for EMU accession and on 19 June 2000 the application was successfully approved. On 1 January 2001 the central rate of the Greek drachma was locked at 340.75 GRD against the euro, and euro notes and coins entered circulation in the following year.

Greece failed for 2 consecutive years to meet the criteria for EMU accession. Greece had recorded very high deficits for several years prior to 1995 – over 10% of GDP – which then melted down miraculously (for a brief discussion of statistical issues in the euro-area see ***Box 3***). In 2000, with a deficit below 3% of GDP, Greece was accepted as the 12th member of the EMU.

3.2 The Causes of the Greek Sovereign Debt Crisis

Since the end of 2009 Greece has been experiencing a crisis unprecedented in the state's modern history. Although the Greek sovereign debt crisis has not been predicted neither anticipated – despite early alarming signals by the Organisation for Economic Co-operation and Development – OECD – dating back to 2005 about fiscal unsustainability and issues in competitiveness – it has captured global attention and has developed into a threat to EMU by revealing its weaknesses. The escalating economic and sovereign debt crises in Greece are the result of (Arghyrou and Tsoukalas, 2011):

i. steadily deteriorating macroeconomic fundamentals over the previous decade to levels inconsistent with long-term EMU participation (i.e. external competitiveness deficit and unsustainable fiscal finances), and
ii. negative market expectations.

The latter shaped an unfavourable external environment and in fact deemed the joint EC/IMF/ECB rescue mission necessary to act as a guarantee of Greek fiscal liabilities, in order for Greece to promote all necessary reforms so as to regain the markets' confidence and remain in EMU.[10]

---

[10] However, the appropriateness of the economic adjustment programme put forward by the joint EC/IMF/ECB rescue mission has been in doubt, not only because recovery for Greece still seems afar, but also due to bidirectional effects with third parties. For example, although the mid-2010 bailout appears to be potentially consistent with Pareto optimality – i.e. no alternative deals would have made the interested parties better-off – the mid-2011 bailout is not inside the

"The Greek sovereign debt crisis of 2010 exposed the weaknesses of governance of both the euro area and of Greece." (Featherstone, 2011: 193). On the one hand, Greek governments failed successively to overcome low competitiveness, trade and investment imbalances, and fiscal mismanagement, thus placing the economy in a vulnerable international position. On the other hand, the denial of agency and resources that might limit the obligation of states to rescue an errant peer, have fostered a negative economic climate both within and outside Greek borders, and have made the recession immutable to all efforts for reform that promote development and growth.

The literature on the Greek sovereign debt crisis posits its roots in the expansion of the public sector – via excessive borrowing – that the phenomenon of clientelism has nurtured. It is argued that clientelism and rent-seeking behavior have contributed to the climax of the Greek political and economic crisis and that the Greek paradox of rapid growth in the previous decade – until 2008 – was the outcome of rent-seeking groups. These groups control and distort product and labour markets in a manner that had led Greece to match the prosperity of advanced countries at the same time as the quality of governance and social cohesion has been closer to that of a developing country (see Mitsopoulos and Pelagidis, 2009; Katsimi and Moutos, 2010; Lyrintzis, 2011; Manolopoulos, 2011). Clientelism and rent-seeking behavior have been held responsible in the literature for issues such as the corrupt political system, uncompetitive economy, and inefficient public sector, which in turn block all reforms put forward by the economic adjustment programme and considered necessary for restoring competitiveness and bringing back Greece on the path to recovery.

4. Myths on the Greek Sovereign Debt Crisis

This section presents how several major issues concerning the Greek sovereign debt crisis have been ill-conceived and have consequently led to a neglect of facts. Namely, the issues discussed are the causes of drying up credit and liquidity, the reality behind the option to default, and the main weaknesses of the economy that hold back all efforts to recover. However, before discussing these myths, it is important to highlight the importance

---

Pareto frontier. This notion is put forward by Ardagna and Caselli (2012), who imply that if the Greek government had not negotiated a reduction in the value of its outstanding debt to private creditors, and had instead followed more lenient austerity measures, all interested parties would be better-off.

of public expenditure on the domestic demand of the Greek economy, and the requirement to recapitalize and to secure the solvency of the Greek banking system.

Firstly, government expenditure via borrowing was a significant fraction of Greek GDP.[11] Its growth rate substantially exceeded that of GDP in 2009 – a year before the adoption of fiscal consolidation (austerity) – and the Greek economy entered into depression by the time productive public expenditure froze in 2010 due to the adoption of austerity measures. An accommodating increase in private sector debt would only substitute for the public debt that boosted domestic demand. Nevertheless, the size of private sector debt and risk perceptions did not allow for such an expansion, although the Greek economy is placed in the second cluster of euro-area states according to its private debt ratio to GDP (see ***Table 2***). Only Slovakia exhibits a private debt ratio that is less than 100% of GDP, while Ireland maintains a private debt ratio that is over 300% of GDP.

Furthermore, ***Table 3*** indicates that Greece's external debt/GDP ratio is similar to, or lower than, many stronger economies. This implies that the issue of debt sustainability for the Greek case concerns to a greater extent the corrupt political system, the uncompetitive economic structure and practices, and the inefficient public sector and to a lesser extent the size of government expenditure. Since the picture presented in ***Table 3*** was similar before the outbreak of the sovereign debt crisis, it is the effect of the variables already stated – which characterize the sustainability of larger external debts – that has to be altered in the equation, in the course of successful reforms.[12]

[11] For a theoretical background see the "financial instability hypothesis" (see Minsky, 1994; Keen, 1995), which emphasizes the importance of debt in the economy and asserts it as a key determinant of economic growth.

[12] As with all debt ratios, external debt ratios should be considered in conjunction with key economic and financial variables, such as growth and interest rates in order to determine their trend in medium-term scenarios. In addition, further information on the composition of external debt – such as external income, external assets, financial derivatives, and the economy's creditors – contribute on the analysis of its sustainability (IMF, 2003: 171-183).

Table 2 - Private debt in the Eurozone (percentage of GDP)

State/Time	1995	2000	2005	2008	2009	2010	2011
Slovakia	55.6	47.1	48.5	62.2	68.8	69.0	-
Greece	37.4	58.2	90.2	119.3	122.7	125.2	125.0
Italy	71.5	79.5	101.0	119.3	125.6	126.4	-
Slovenia	-	-	85.2	117.3	127.4	128.8	130.6
Germany	113.0	131.5	128.4	123.7	130.6	128.2	-
France	105.5	117.2	131.6	149.9	156.8	159.8	-
Austria	102.7	125.0	132.3	156.5	161.4	165.7	-
Finland	108.2	129.3	141.6	168.9	178.3	177.7	-
Estonia	35.7	67.4	122.8	167.5	190.6	176.7	-
Malta	-	-	180.6	202.3	214.7	212.0	-
Netherlands	145.3	189.5	210.5	211.0	225.5	225.3	224.6
Spain	77.1	122.3	176.6	220.5	226.9	226.6	216.1
Belgium	117.4	168.5	185.0	217.3	228.6	233.3	236.8
Portugal	83.4	170.7	200.4	240.4	252.5	250.2	249.1
Cyprus	126.4	164.6	203.9	241.9	261.7	278.1	287.5
Luxembourg	-	-	:	353.6	317.8	253.9	-
Ireland	-	-	192.3	284.0	336.1	341.3	-

Source: Eurostat (http://epp.eurostat.ec.europa.eu/portal/page/portal/statistics/search_database, as accessed 31 July 2012).
1. Dash implies that data is not available.

Secondly, the solvency of the banking system has to be secured, as it is vital for securing that the economic system will not collapse. Due to leverage practices, the cost of securing the solvency of the banking system is a lot smaller than the cost of allowing it to become insolvent (i.e. the example of Lehman Brothers). For example, assuming a leverage rate on deposits of 10 to 1 for Greek banks, their bankruptcy would cost over €1 trillion.[14]

[14] Authors' calculations based on Bank of Greece data available at http://www.bankofgreece.gr/Pages/el/Statistics/monetary/deposits.aspx).

Table 3 - Gross external debt positions (percentage of GDP)

Eurozone	2011	OECD	2011
Luxembourg	3675.9	United Kingdom	419.8
Ireland	1019.0	Australia	97.6
Malta	511.6	Canada	69.9
Netherlands	304.7	United States	102.6
Belgium	277.1	Japan	52.2
Finland	219.1	Switzerland	210.3
Portugal	213.3	Turkey	41.2
Austria	196.1		
France	187.6		
Greece	173.5		
Germany	161.9		
Spain	159.5		
Cyprus	129,0*		
Slovenia	114.1		
Italy	114.0		
Estonia	95.5		
Slovakia	73.6		

Source: Authors' calculations from World Bank data.
* Value for Cyprus regards 2008.

4.1 The Myth about Cash-strapped Greece

The first myth concerns the reasons behind the liquidity problems of the Greek economy, as there is a false general belief – projected by the media – that funds do not exist domestically (i.e. by individuals and enterprises). A recent report published in Greek (Τράπεζα της Ελλάδος, 2012: 33) indicates that the issue is not whether there are funds available but why these funds do not circulate in the economy and, moreover, why they are not invested. Deposits of Greek enterprises and households in domestic financial institutions were approximately €126 billion in December 2001 – right before the introduction of the euro – and peaked at approximately €238 billion in September 2009, when elections and the necessity of austerity measures due to the budgetary difficulties were announced (see Bank of Greece data, op. cit.). This enormous generation of wealth has been influenced by the stability and growth prospects of the euro. Accordingly, austerity measures and the deflationary spiral of income shrinking, output contraction and unemployment have decreased the size of these deposits in June 2012 to approximately €151 billion. M1 and M2 have deteriorated further in 2011 due to money transfers abroad or purchases of gold, and deposits of Greek enterprises and households in domestic financial institutions decreased by approximately €38 billion from June 2011 to June 2012, and by approximately €7 billion from May to June 2012 due to the Greek elections.[15] Consequently, the decrease of gross fixed capital formation from approximately 24% of GDP in 2007 to 14% of GDP in 2011 (see Eurostat[16]) indicates that the issue at hand concerns the prospects and expectations for growth of the Greek economy and the credibility of the state. As a result, the myth of cash-strapped Greece is the misconception of unwillingness to invest domestic savings due to psychological reasons – i.e. increased perception of risk – and lack of growth prospects imposed by the sovereign debt crisis.

Furthermore, the size of domestic demand is also a hint that liquidity problems primarily concern investment and not consumption. The contraction of domestic output has been greater than domestic demand (see Eurostat[17]): GDP at market prices in Purchasing Power Standards – PPS –decreased (until 2008 this figure was increasing) over 10% for 2008-2011; domestic demand in PPS has been well over GDP in PPS until 2011 (latest data is 107.5% of GDP) and decreased by approximately 8% for 2008-2011 (this figure was also increasing until 2008). In order to sustain such a size of domestic demand – since loanable funds have been tremendously diminished – cash is required. However, these "available" funds have not been invested since the state's credibility is at stake and future prospects of the economy are gloomy and, moreover, they have been consumed by continuously rising taxes. These funds have been transferred in 2010-2011 away from domestic banks, abroad or to personal safes.

---

[15] However, their position is expected to improve since the elections in June 2012 have resulted in a more co-operative and stable government that will put forward the economic adjustment programme and is eventually expected to stabilize the economy and generate prospects for recovery. Furthermore, the ratio of Greek deposits to GDP has been more or less similar to that of other euro-area member states. For example, the ratio of Greek deposits to GDP was 1.6 in 2010 and 1.4 in 2011, at the same time as Italy's ratios were 1.3 and 1.4 respectively, and only three states have a ratio that is over 2, namely Luxembourg, Ireland and Spain (authors' calculations based on data from Eurostat statistics database at http://epp.eurostat.ec.europa.eu/portal/page/portal/statistics/search_database).

[16] Eurostat statistics database, op. cit.

[17] Eurostat statistics database, op. cit.

4.2 Debt Sustainability and Default

The second major disorientation of public opinion concerns the issues of debt sustainability and default. There is a general belief that since the Greek sovereign debt crisis has systemic consequences for the euro-area, there should be a better negotiation of the economic adjustment programme and the bailout terms, under the threat of default. Indeed, the assistance of fellow member states for the containment of the Greek sovereign debt crisis is rooted in the fact that a potential default would have – without doubt – systemic consequences for the euro-area. However, although the ability of the euro-area to overcome without great sacrifices a potential Greek default is debatable, the case of default would have dramatic consequences for the Greek economy. In effect, the Greek state has two options.

The first option concerns the choice to remain in the euro-area, which requires from the Greek economy to endure austerity measures during depression. Nevertheless, finance is secured both for the state's obligations and the banking system, all necessary reforms – otherwise neglected – will eventually be accomplished, and, ultimately, sovereign debt levels will be sustainable so that Greece will be able to access again international financial markets. Furthermore, an "aggressive" response to the euro-area's debt crisis is anticipated from the ECB through monetary expansion and eurobonds issuance, as the sovereign debt crisis spreads across member states even more rapidly than anticipated, and since there is a growing consensus that Greece was a pretext for the outbreak of the crisis and not the cause.

The second option regards the choice of adopting a national currency. The growing urge for this option is rooted in the deflationary spiral caused by the combination of austerity and rising levels of unemployment, income shrinking and output contraction. Deficit cuts via contraction of government spending – both in wages and amount of benefits and public services – and tax increases continuously postpone the expectations for economic growth and have resulted in the formulation of a growing anti-euro coalition. Nevertheless, the ineffectiveness of the strategy adopted to lead to recovery cannot justify the option to exit the euro-area, since the adoption of a national currency would imply more negative consequences than positive ones:

i. Positive: competitiveness gains and contraction of trade deficit induced by nominal exchange rate depreciation, haircut on private debt issued domestically at a steady rate due to inflation.

ii. Negative: credit and liquidity would dry up, inflation and devaluation would reduce the real value of savings, the burden of external debt issued under foreign law would soar, institutional quality would plunge, living standards would decrease dramatically and there would be lack of primary goods.

Furthermore, the adoption of a national currency would require for extreme organization and discipline regarding the allocation of resources – since the Greek economy depends heavily on imports – and huge financial support to prevent the banking system from collapsing. The public administration of the Greek state has not exhibited such organizational skills – since the state suffers greatly from bureaucracy and corruption – and an alternate provision of finance for potential bailouts required under the adoption of a national currency is not available.

4.3 The Path to Recovery

The third major myth concerns the roots of Greece's low competitiveness and the role of the public sector in fiscal adjustment. Both of these issues are part of the process of internal devaluation in terms of cost reduction. The economic adjustment programme for Greece is based on evidence of the twin deficit hypothesis. Specifically, improvement in Greece's competitiveness will be attained by (see Kalou and Paleologou, 2012):

i. limiting price and wage raises in order to increase competitiveness in the short-run and
ii. focusing on technological change and quality improvement in the long-run.

However, there is a contradiction in these two directions. Firstly, improvement in competitiveness of member states suffering by the crisis via labour cost reduction is challenged by Kaldor's paradox (Felipe and Kumar 2011), i.e. the positive correlation observed between the international competitiveness of several countries and their relative unit labour costs and hence reduction of the latter does not imply improvement of the former. Secondly, recent research indicates that the volumes of foreign direct investment (FDI) inflows do not always decrease due to rising labour costs. Katsimi et al. (2012) indicate that wages that do not follow labour productivity developments do not affect the return on capital, and that profits are responses to changes in the economic, political and institutional environment. As a result, the hesitation of investors is mainly due to gloomy growth prospects and the improper institutional setting. Thirdly, Greece's decrease of real unit labour costs with respect to 2005 tops the euro-area in 2011 (see Eurostat[18]). Real unit labour cost reduction in Greece has also been higher than the respective average efforts of the euro-area during the 2000s. Nevertheless, economic growth, the business climate and expectations in general, have been continuously deteriorating in Greece after the eruption of the financial crisis – and its subsequent mutation in a sovereign debt crisis – despite the relative improvements on labour productivity. An explanation for this irregularity is that the size of real unit labour costs should be seen comparatively, only between countries with similar levels of income. For example, as Greece's FDI inflows have been primarily market-seeking, subsequent reductions of real unit labour cost will attract efficiency-seeking FDI in Greece only if the country's gross national income per capita will deteriorate to that of a less developed country – i.e. Bulgaria's levels.[19]

The Greek investment climate is primarily affected by the institutional setting – namely bureaucracy and corruption – and therefore, reforms should focus in the improvement of institutional quality and the advancement of technological change. Contraction of labour costs raises questions whether the model for recovery in Greece will sustain the country's placement as an advanced economy.

With regard to the size of the Greek public sector, Greek government expenditure as a percentage of GDP has been less or similar to the respective levels of the EU and the euro-area in the previous decade. Nonetheless, at the same time as Greek government expenditure as a percentage of GDP has been analogous to that of the euro-area, Greek government revenue was 5% less of the last decade's average annual euro-area receipts (see Eurostat[20]). It seems that the underperformance in the collection of government revenue – despite the tremendous tax storm of 2010-2012 that had a significant impact on inflation (see report published in Greek; Τράπεζα της Ελλάδος, 2011: 98-101) – is countered by a contraction in expenditure in order to meet the requirements of generating a balanced budget. As a result, the main priority should be the reforms that have to be undertaken in order to restrain bureaucracy, corruption, and tax evasion, and moreover, to make the public sector more productive and efficient.

---

[18] Eurostat statistics database, op. cit.

[19] Bulgaria's most important drivers for inward FDI are production costs – despite exhibiting an increasing real unit labour cost (see Eurostat statistics database, op. cit.) – and EU membership.

[20] Eurostat statistics database, op. cit.

Nevertheless, irrespectively of whether internal devaluation, contraction in government expenditure and reduction of the public sector are appropriate or not for the Greek case – with respect to the circumstances and alternate proposals for recovery – "with Germany's reluctance to raise spending, a cash-strapped Greece has no alternative but to deflate" (Eichengreen and Temin, 2010: 382). Greece must endure the difficulties and proceed with all necessary adjustments that will improve public administration efficiency. This effort will not only improve the country's competitiveness, but will also assist in regaining lost credibility and, ultimately, remaining in the euro-area until the time that the inevitable ECB monetary expansion through eurobonds issuance will occur.

5. Conclusions

The European sovereign debt crisis has exposed euro-area's structural problems, i.e. – as analyzed in several papers to date – the imbalance between full centralization of monetary policy and the maintenance of almost all economic policy instruments at the national level. As long as euro-area governments and EMU institutions continue to hesitate and fail to provide a plan or mechanism for the worst case scenario:

i. there will be voices that a sustainable EMU would occur only if it is embedded in a political union,
ii. rating agencies will carry on downgrading and fueling uncertainty in international financial markets,
iii. and the sovereign debt crises of member states will persist.

Nevertheless, there is no doubt that the major responsibility of the Greek sovereign debt crisis rests with the Greek authorities, who mismanaged their economy and deceived everybody about the true nature of their budgetary problems. The escalation of the Greek sovereign debt crisis since November 2009 is the result of an unfavourable shift in country-specific market expectations, which concern mainly the importance of restoring confidence.[21] The escalating economic and sovereign debt crises in Greece are the by-products of steadily deteriorating macroeconomic fundamentals over the previous decade to levels inconsistent with long-term EMU participation, and negative market expectations caused by the

[21] Any attempt to estimate the time of recovery highlights the importance of restoring confidence, making thus the other predicting factors less important (Azis, 2010).

uncertainty for Greece's sovereign debt sustainability. The roots of deteriorating macroeconomic fundamentals are:

i. in the expansion of the public sector through excessive borrowing that has nurtured the phenomenon of clientelism, which in turn favored the development of rent-seeking behaviour, and
ii. in the underperformance of government revenue generation (i.e. tax evasion).

Overall uncertainty – which has reached previously unmet levels – the pessimistic prospects and expectations for growth of the Greek economy, and the questioning credibility of the state have deteriorated further the available amounts of credit and liquidity to the Greek business environment. The process of internal devaluation and austerity measures adopted as parts of the economic adjustment programme – and put forward as competitiveness enhancing techniques – fuel the deflationary spiral of output contraction and unemployment and endanger the goals of government revenue and recovery. In addition, the progress of real unit labour cost in Greece and the comparative size of Greek government expenditure levels to the respective of the euro-area indicate that:

i. adjustments in competitiveness could threaten Greece's placement as an advanced economy, and
ii. instead of reducing the public sector and fueling the deflationary spiral, there should be attempts in increasing the efficient use of resources and reducing the levels of corruption.

Nevertheless, the difficulty of the efforts in making the level of Greece's sovereign debt sustainable should not reinforce the arguments welcoming the option to exit the euro-area. The option to exit may indicate competitiveness gains and contraction of trade deficit induced by nominal exchange rate depreciation as realistic targets, however, no more than the requirement for alternate provision of finance for the bailouts (i.e. for the banking sector) required under the adoption of a national currency and the enormous burden of external debt issued under foreign law – which are merely two of the negative consequences – indicate the dramatic consequences of a tremendous, under the current circumstances, endeavor.

The lack of consensus among the EMU member states about the necessity to adopt an option of last resort, while the European sovereign debt crisis spreads and escalates, should not disorient the Greek effort to comply with the economic adjustment programme. However, the effort should be redirected from the severe exercise of internal devaluation to increasing the efficient use of resources in the public sector, battling corruption and minimizing tax evasion, and improving competiveness through institutional reforms: i.e. liberalization of "closed-shop" practices and administrative price-setting in several sectors – from transportation lorries to lawyers' fees – and by increasing the efficiency of state firms and institutions through the reduction of corruption and bureaucracy. Such an effort would primarily signify the prolonged improvement of the business environment that has not been achieved, regardless of the EU directions and the assistance of the community support frameworks. Moreover, these necessary reforms will eventually restore confidence in international markets and re-ignite the engine of economic growth by attracting sufficient levels of private investment.[22]

Although all efforts to date have not put an end to the Greek sovereign debt crisis, hope should not be abandoned, as a more uniform European approach seems to be soon materializing. At the same time as the necessary reforms demand for further sacrifices, and the fears that austerity will keep sustaining the deflationary spiral of output contraction and unemployment – endangering thus the goals of government revenue and recovery – are not unfounded, the climax of the debt crisis across the euro-area requires for an alternative approach than the one adopted to date. The growing consensus that Greece was a pretext for the outbreak of the crisis and not its cause, and the inappropriateness of the SGP to contain the spread of the debt crisis across member states and to appease markets fuels the expectations for an "aggressive" response from the ECB through monetary expansion and eurobonds issuance. Such a response would not only improve sovereign debt solvency, but would also take the form of fiscal injections that substitute for the absence of productive public expenditure (i.e. physical capital expenditures and spending aimed at generating human capital). Moreover, further positive developments can also take place if the ECB would demand the market value – as at time purchased – for the bonds it purchased since 2009 (an approximate total of €30-35 billion) at their maturity, and not their face value. Such an action would significantly reduce the size of Greece's sovereign debt.

Perhaps many more positive future unexpected developments will occur, and very well seem to be underway. An "aggressive" response from the ECB would appease international markets, strengthen the euro against the US dollar and energy products (i.e. oil), and decrease the cost of

[22] The profound necessity of structural, competitiveness-inducing reforms is highlighted as the primary tool that is able to generate favourable country-specific market expectations (Arghyrou and Kontonikas, 2011).

borrowing in euro-area members suffering from austerity.[23] However, until the time of such positive externalities, Greece has to secure a stable political environment that will focus on performing the necessary institutional reforms, which will secure EMU membership, and will eventually generate an attractive business environment.

References

Greek

Τράπεζα της Ελλάδος (2011). *Έκθεση του Διοικητή για το Έτος 2010*. Αθήνα: Τράπεζα της Ελλάδος.

Τράπεζα της Ελλάδος (2012). *Νομισματική Πολιτική 2011-2012*. Αθήνα: Τράπεζα της Ελλάδος.

English

Ardagna, S. and Caselli, C. (2012). The political economy of the Greek debt crisis: A tale of two bailouts. *CEP Special Paper No. 25*. London: Centre for Economic Performance (London School of Economics and Political Science).

Arghyrou, M.G. and Kontonikas, A. (2011). The EMU sovereign-debt crisis: Fundamentals, expectations and contagion. *European Economy Economic Papers No. 436*. Brussels: European Commission, DG ECFIN.

Arghyrou, M.G. and Tsoukalas, J.D. (2011). The Greek debt crisis: Likely causes, mechanics and outcomes. *World Economy*, 34 (2): 173-191.

Azis, I.J. (2010). Predicting a recovery date from the economic crisis of 2008. *Socio-Economic Planning Sciences*, 44 (3): 122-129.

Beetsma, R.M.W.J. and Debrun, X. (2007). The new stability and growth pact: A first assessment. *European Economic Review*, 51 (2): 453-477.

Bonatti, L. And Christini, A. (2007). Breaking the stability pact: Was it predictable? *Journal of Policy Modeling*, 30 (5): 793-810.

Buti, M. (2006). Will the new stability and growth pact succeed? An economic and political perspective. *European Economy Economic Papers No. 241*. Brussels: European Commission, DG ECFIN.

---

[23] However, an appreciation of the euro would threaten the competitiveness of EU exports.

Buti, M., Eijffinger, S. and Franco, D. (2003). Revisiting EMU's stability pact: A pragmatic way forward. *Oxford Review of Economic Policy*, 19 (1): 100-111.

Caballero, R.J., Farhi, E. and Gourinchas, P.O. (2009). Financial Crash, Commodity Prices and Global Imbalances. *NBER Working Paper No. 14521*. Cambridge (Massachusetts): National Bureau of Economic Research.

Candelon, B. and Palm, F. (2010). Banking and debt crises in Europe: The dangerous liaisons? *De Economist*, 158 (1): 81-99.

—. (2011). From banking to sovereign debt crisis in Europe. In Kolb, R.W. (ed.), *Sovereign Debt: From Safety to Default*. Hoboken (NJ): John Wiley & Sons.

Dellas, H. and Tavlas, G.S. (2009). An optimum-currency-area odyssey. *Journal of International Money and Finance*, 28 (7): 1117-1137.

ECB (2012). Analysing government debt sustainability in the euro area. *ECB Monthly Bulletin*, April 2012: 55-70.

Eichengreen, B. and Temin, P. (2010). Fetters of gold and paper. *Oxford Review of Economic Policy*, 26 (3): 370-384.

Featherstone, K. (2011). The Greek sovereign debt crisis and EMU: A failing state in a skewed regime. *Journal of Common Market Studies*, 49 (2): 193-217.

Felipe, J. and Kumar, U. (2011). Unit labor costs in the eurozone: The competitiveness debate again. *Levy Economics Institute Working Papers No. 651*. New York: The Levy Economics Institute of Bard College.

Ferre, M. (2012). The effects of uncertainty about countries' compliance with the stability and growth pact. *Journal of Policy Modeling*, 34 (5): 660-674.

Hamilton, J.D. (2009). Causes and consequences of the oil shock of 2007-08. *NBER Working Paper No. 15002*. Cambridge (Massachusetts): National Bureau of Economic Research.

Heipertz, M. and Verdun, A. (2004). The dog that would never bite? What we can learn from the origins of the stability and growth pact. *Journal of European Public Policy*, 11 (5): 765-780.

Hileman, G. (2012). The seven mechanisms for achieving sovereign debt sustainability. *LSE Department of Economic History Working Paper No. 162/12*. London: London School of Economics and Political Sciences.

Hudson, R. and Maioli, S. (2010). A response to "Reflections on a global financial crisis". *Critical Perspectives on International Business*, 6 (1): 53-71.

IMF (2003). *External Debt Statistics: Guide for Compilers and Users*. Washington, DC: International Monetary Fund.

Kalou, S. and Paleologou, S.M. (2012). Twin deficit hypothesis: Revisiting an EMU country. *Journal of Policy Modeling*, 34 (2): 230-241.

Katsimi, M., Kalyvitis, S. and Moutos T. (2012). Excessive wages and the return on capital. *Cambridge Journal of Economics*, 36 (2): 435-461.

Katsimi, M. and Moutos, T. (2010). EMU and the Greek crisis: The political-economy perspective. *European Journal of Political Economy*, 26 (4): 568-576.

Keen, S. (1995). Finance and economic breakdown: Modelling Minsky's financial instability hypothesis. *Journal of Post Keynesian Economics*, 17 (4): 607-635.

Kenen, P.B. (1969). The theory of optimum currency areas: An eclectic view. In Mundell, R.A. and Swoboda, A.K. (eds.), *Monetary Problems of the International Economy*. Chicago: University of Chicago Press.

Khan, M.S. (2009). The 2008 oil price "bubble". *Policy Brief 09-19*. Washington, DC: Peterson Institute for International Economics.

Lyrintzis, C. (2011). Greek Politics in the era of economic crisis: Reassessing causes and effects. *GreeSE – Hellenic Observatory Papers on Greece and Southeast Europe No. 45*. London: Hellenic Observatory, London School of Economics.

Manolopoulos, J. (2011). *Greece's 'Odious' Debt: The Looting of the Hellenic Republic by the Euro, the Political Elite and the Investment Community*. London: Anthem Press.

Mathieu, C. and Sterdyniak, H. (2010). European debt crisis and fiscal exit strategies. *Documents de Travail de l' OFCE 2010/11*. Paris: Observatoire Francais des Conjonctures Economiques.

Minsky, H.P. (1994). The financial instability hypothesis. In Arestis, P. and Saywer, M.C. (eds.), *The Elgar Companion to Radical Political Economy*. Aldershot: Edward Elgar.

Mitsopoulos, M. and Pelagidis T. (2009). Vikings in Greece: Kleptocratic interest groups in a closed, rent-seeking economy. *Cato Journal*, 29 (3): 399-416.

Muscatelli, V.A., Natale, P. and Tirellli, P. (2012). A simple and flexible alternative to stability and growth pact deficit ceilings. Is it at hand? *European Journal of Political Economy*, 28 (1): 14-26.

OECD (2005). *OECD Economic Surveys: Greece 2005*. Paris: Organisation for Economic Co-operation and Development.

Reinhart, C.M. and Rogoff, K.S. (2011). From financial crash to debt crisis. *American Economic Review*, 101 (5): 1676-1706.

—. (2010). Growth in a time of debt. *American Economic Review*, 100 (2): 573-578.

Wyplosz, C. (2011). Fiscal discipline: Rules rather than institutions. *National Institute Economic Review*, 217 (1): R19-R30.

CHAPTER SIX

THE SHADOW ECONOMY IN GREECE AND THE OTHER OECD-COUNTRIES

FRIEDRICH SCHNEIDER[1]

1. Introduction

Since the worldwide economic crisis affected the real economy of many Organisation for Economic Co-operation and Development (OECD) countries, among them Germany, the German official gross domestic products (GDP) declined by 5 percent in 2009 and unemployment increased too. The economic crisis that developed into a sovereign debt crisis has had a negative impact on the levels of economic growth of European economies and the world, in general. More specifically, the negative impact of austerity measures adopted by euro-area member states hit by the sovereign debt crisis, on their economic prosperity – i.e. on economic growth or unemployment or both – may have been largely a European issue, however, the continent's problems have slowed down the world's other advanced economies. Against this background, the extent of the shadow economy in Greece and other OECD countries are once again the subject of an intense debate, as many people will attempt to make up for loss of income in the official economy through greater participation in the shadow economy. Furthermore, policy-makers are also considering how shadow economy activities can be transferred into the official economy.

This Chapter reports on the development of the shadow economy in Germany, Greece and further in 19 OECD countries since 1990 and provides first and preliminary calculations for 2010, taking the continuing economic crisis into account. For as long as the eurozone debt crisis holds

---

[1] Due to recent developments the author suggests the reader to consider the findings of this chapter only for the period that the data sample refers to.

back economic growth on a global scale all OECD countries are expected to experience rising levels of the shadow economy (first time in 2009).

The estimates of the size of the shadow economy are based on a combination of the cash (currency demand) approach with the Multiple Indicators Multiple Causes (MIMIC) method.[2] The basic idea behind the currency demand approach is that goods and services performed in the shadow economy are paid for in cash and that, using a cash demand function, it is possible to estimate such goods and services performed in return for cash and thus to calculate the volume of the shadow economy.

The MIMIC approach is based on the idea that the shadow economy is not a directly observable figure, but that it is possible to approximate it using quantitatively measurable causes of working in the underground economy (such as the tax burden and amount of regulation), and using indicators (such as cash, official working hours, etc.), in which shadow economic activities are reflected.[3] As the MIMIC method only enables relative orders of magnitude of the underground economy of individual countries to be calculated, some values that were calculated with the help of the cash approach are necessary to convert the shadow economy quantities into absolute values (in percentage of official GDP or in billions of euros).

2. Development of the Shadow Economy over Time up to 2010

Table 2.1 shows the development of the shadow economy figures for Germany, Austria and Switzerland over the period 1975 to 2010.

---

[2] Compare e.g. Feld and Schneider (2010), Schneider, Buehn and Montenegro (2010), Schneider and Enste (2000, 2006), Schneider (2005), and Dell'Anno and Schneider (2009).

[3] These methods (among others) are presented in detail and subjected to critical assessment in the following books: Schneider (2004), and Schneider and Enste (2002).

Table 2.1: Size of the shadow economy in Germany, Austria, and Switzerland in the period 1975 to 2010 – calculated using the currency demand approach and the MIMIC method

Size of the shadow economy (in percent of official GDP)						
Year	Germany		Austria		Switzerland	
	In %	EUR billion	In %	EUR billion	In %	SFR billion
1975	5.75	29.6	2.04	0.9	3.20	12
1980	10.80	80.2	2.69	2.0	4.90	14
1985	11.20	102.3	3.92	3.9	4.60	17
1990	12.20	147.9	5.47	7.2	6.20	22
1995	13.90	241.1 [1)]	7.32	12.4	6.89	25
1996	14.50	257.6 [1)]	8.32	14.6	7.51	27
1997	15.00	274.7 [1)]	8.93	16.0	8.04	29
1998	14.80	280.7 [1)]	9.09	16.9	7.98	30
1999	15.51	301.8 [1)]	9.56	18.2	8.34	32
2000	16.03	322.3 [1)]	10.07	19.8	8.87	35
2001	16.02	329.8 [1)]	10.52	21.1	9.28	37.5
2002	16.59	350.4 [1)]	10.69	21.8	9.48	38.7
2003	17.10	370.0 [1)]	10.86	22.5	9.52	39.4
2004	16.12	356.1 [1)]	11.00	23.0	9.43	39.5
2005	15.41	346.2 [1)]	10.27	22.0	9.05	38.7
2006	15.00	345.5 [1)]	9.51	21.20	8.48	37.0
2007	14.74	349.0[1)]	9.06	20.80	8.23	36.8
2008	14.22	346.8 [1)]	8.07	19.92	7.96	35.4
2009 [2)]	14.57	351.8 [1)]	8.47	20.50	8.28	36.4
2010 [2)]	14.65	359.2 [1)]	8.67	21.32	8.34	37.2

Source: Own calculations (2010).

1) From 1995 figures for the *whole* of Germany.

2) Provisional estimates.

Development of the Shadow Economy in Germany from 1975 to 2010

Turning first to the development of the underground economy in **Germany**, it did sharply rise up to the beginning of this decade, but then there was a decline from EUR 370 billion in 2003 to EUR 345.5 billion in 2006. In 2007, for the first time in three years, there was once again a rise in the underground economy compared with the previous year calculated at EUR 3.5 billion or 1 percent to EUR 349 billion; one important reason for this was the increase in the Value Added Tax (VAT) rate from 16% to 19%. However, as the official economy grew by just under 3 percent in nominal terms more than the shadow economy, the ratio of the shadow to the official economy continued to improve further even in 2007. While the value of the shadow economy in relation to the official GDP was still 17.1 percent in 2003 and 15.0 percent in 2006, this ratio, at just under 14.7 percent, even returned to below the level of 1998 for the first time.

In 2008, thanks to the healthy "official" economic environment, the shadow economy shrank again by EUR 2.2 billion. However, a renewed rise took place in the shadow economy in 2009 and is expected to continue as long as the eurozone sovereign debt crisis contracts economic activity. The detailed results are set out in table 2.2 for 2010.

Table 2.2: Effects of the global economic crisis/recession and some economic policy measures of the CDU/CSU/FDP government on the shadow economy in 2010

(Policy) Measures in 2010	Increase (+) / decrease (-) of the underground economy and [] average value
(1) Economic crisis: GDP rise in unemployment by 600,000 to 4.100 Mio.	+ 7.600 to + 10.100 [8.850] million €
(2) Decrease in health insurance contribution rate by 0.6 percentage points to 14.9%.	- 500 to - 800 [- 650] million €
(3) Various tax deductions	- 900 to - 1.400 [- 1.150] million €
(4) Introduction of minimum wages in the fields of painting, garbage collection and mining.	+ 200 to + 400 [+ 300] million €
Net effect for 2010	+ 6.400 to 8.300 [7.350] million €

Source: Own calculations.

This table shows, based on the assumption of a rise in the unemployment rate of up to 500.000, that the economic crisis led to an increase in the shadow economy of between EUR 7.6 billion and EUR 10.1 billion. The shadow economy is also expected to fall slightly due to the 0.6 percentage point decrease in the health care insurance contribution rate. Against this, the introduction of minimum wages in some further areas have a positive impact on the development of the shadow economy in an amount of between EUR 200 million and EUR 400 million. A new law of tax deductions (Bürgerentlastungsgesetz) reduced the shadow economy between EUR 900 and EUR 1.150 million. The net effect of all these measures is a rise in the shadow economy of between EUR 6.4 billion and EUR 8.3 billion.[4]

Shadow Economy in Austria and Switzerland

In **Austria** the shadow economy had grown from EUR 22.5 billion in 2003 to EUR 23.0 billion in 2004, a rise of 2.2 percent. One fundamental cause of the increase in the shadow economy in 2004 was the continuously high burden of taxation and social contributions following the restructuring of budget revenues in Austria in recent years. In 2005, the shadow economy in Austria was only EUR 22.0 billion, that is, it declined for the first time and fell by about EUR 1 billion, a drop of 4.35 percent compared with the previous year. The main cause of this decline was the reduction in direct tax rates that came into effect at the beginning of 2005. For 2007 and 2008, the figures for Austria again show a slight reduction in the shadow economy from EUR 20.80 billion (2007) to EUR 19.9 billion (2008). Due to the worldwide recession a renewed rise in the shadow economy to EUR 20.5 billion or 8.5 percent of official GDP took place in 2009. For 2010, a further increase of the shadow economy by 4.0% to EUR 21.32 billion took place due to the continuing economic crisis.

In **Switzerland,** as in Austria, a decline in the shadow economy was observed for the first time; it decreased from SFR 39.5 billion in 2004 to SFR 38.7 billion in 2005, or a good 9 percent of GDP, and it dropped further to EUR 37 billion, or 8.5 percent of GDP in 2006. Among the reasons for the decline were stricter legal measures to combat the shadow economy and in part a more attractive treatment of domestic services in the official economy. In 2007 and 2008, the shadow economy shrank due to the healthy economic conditions and a package of measures from the Swiss federal government against moonlighting; in 2007 it fell to SFR 36.8 billion and in 2008 to SFR 35.4 billion. As in Germany and Austria, due to the world economic crisis, the shadow economy grew to SFR 36.4 billion or 8.3 percent of official GDP in 2009, and increased further by 2.2% to SFR 37.2 or 8.34% in 2010.

---

[4] It must be clearly pointed out that, based on the information available as of March 2010, it is still extraordinarily difficult to estimate the full extent of the economic crisis in Germany but also the effect of the new law of tax deductions (*Bürgerentlastungsgesetz*).

Shadow Economy in Greece

In figure 2.1 the size and development of the Greek shadow economy and the average size of the shadow economy of the 21 OECD countries are presented. It clearly shows that from 1990 the Greek shadow economy rose from 22.6% of the official GDP to 28.2% in 2004.

Figure 2.1: The Size and Development of the Greek Shadow Economy and the Average one of 21 OECD countries over 1990 to 2010

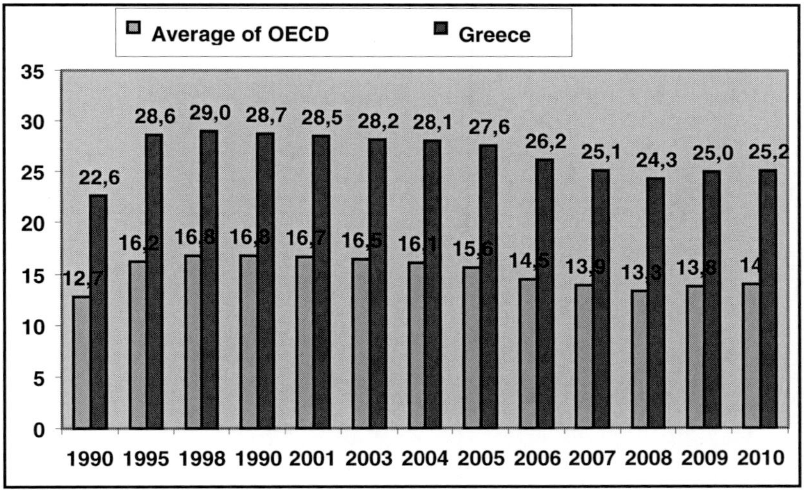

After 2004, it declined to 24.3% of official GDP up to 2008 due to a booming official economy. In 2009, it rose again to 25.0% due to the economic crisis and continued to rise in 2010 to 25.2%.

In figure 2.2 a comparison of the size of the shadow economies is made for 2010 for the 21 OECD countries. It clearly demonstrates that the Greek one is the highest with 25.2% followed by Italy with 22.2% and Spain with 19.8%. At the lower end are the U.S. with 7.8% and Switzerland with 8.3%.

Figure 2.2: The Size of the Shadow Economies of 21 OECD countries in 2010 (Projection); method: MIMIC and currency demand functions

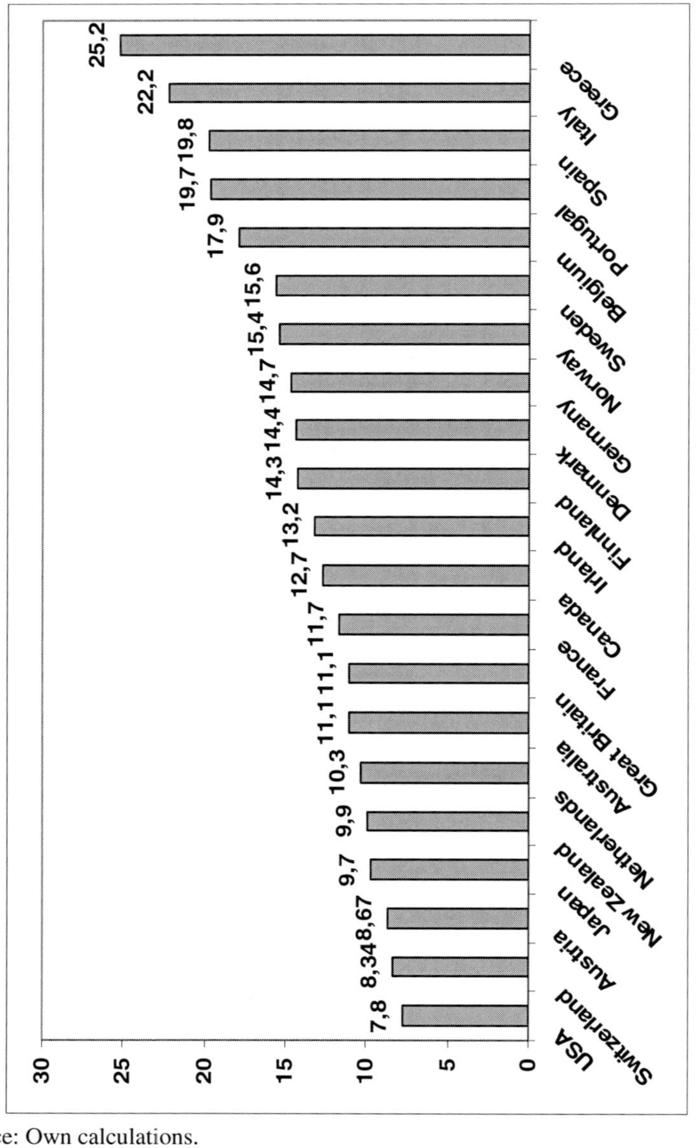

Source: Own calculations.

In table 2.3 the breakdown of the shadow economy into economic and service sectors in Greece is shown. The largest shadow economy sector is a service sector (tourism), hotels, restaurants, catering, etc. with 22.0% and a size of 14.19 billion €, followed by the entertainment and leisure sector of 21,0% and a value of 13.55 billion € in 2008/2009. Then the household shadow economy sector has a magnitude of 18.0% (out of 100% total shadow economy) and a value of 11.61 billion €.

In table 2.4 a further breakdown of the construction sector is shown. In the main construction trade the share is 35% (out of 100% of the total construction sector) and a value of 4.31 billion €. Miscellaneous repairs have a share of 21% and a value of 2.58 billion €. Finally, considering the construction related trade sub-sector, its share is 26% and has a value of 3.20 billion €.

Table 2.3: Breakdown of the shadow economy into economic and service sectors in Greece over 2008/2009 [1)]

Sector	Breakdown of shadow economy Greece 2008/2009	
	In %	EUR billion
Construction sector and skilled manual trades (including repairs)	20%	12.30
Other trades and industries (motor vehicles, machines, etc.)	19%	11.69
Services (Hotels, restaurants, etc.)	22%	14.19
Entertainment and leisure sector	21%	13.55
Miscellaneous trades and domestic services (private tuition, hairdressing, babysitting)	18%	11.61
Total underground economy	100%	61.5

1) Source: Own calculations (2010).

Table 2.4: Breakdown of the shadow economy in the construction trade and skilled manual trades in Greece over 2008/2009

Sector	Breakdown of shadow economy in construction trade and skilled manual trades Greece 2008/2009	
	In %	EUR billion
Main construction trade	35%	4.31
Construction-related trades	26%	3.20
Skilled manual trades in the construction sector	18%	2.21
Miscellaneous repairs (televisions, electric appliances, domestic appliances)	21%	2.58
TOTAL Construction trade and skilled manual trades (including repairs)	100 %	12.30

International Comparison of the Extent of the Shadow Economy

In order to make an international comparison of the size of the shadow economy with other OECD countries, table 2.5 presents the shadow economy of 21 OECD countries up to 2010.

Table 2.5 clearly shows that the shadow economy declined in most OECD countries from the end of the 1990s to 2008. The unweighted average of the shadow economy in the 21 OECD countries in 1999/2000 was 16.8 percent and was reduced to 13.3 percent in 2008, that is, a drop of fully 3.5 percentage points! Taking 1997/98 as the peak year for the shadow economy in most OECD countries, the shadow economy has declined continuously in 18 OECD countries. Only in Germany, Austria, and Switzerland did the growth in the shadow economy persist somewhat longer and did not fall until 2003, or 2004, respectively. The decline in the shadow economy from 1997/98 to 2009 measured as a proportion of GDP was greatest in Italy, with a drop of 5.3 percentage points, in Finland and Belgium with a fall of 4.7 percentage points, and in Sweden with 4.5 percentage points of GDP.

The continuous decline of the shadow economy in the OECD countries from 1997 to 2008 came to an end in 2009. With the beginning of the global economic crisis the shadow economy grew in all 21 OECD countries. On average it amounted to 13.8 percent – a rise of 0.5 percentage points compared with 13.3 percent in 2008 – thus almost returning to the level of 2007. In 2010 we had a further increase of all 21 OECD countries between 0.1 percentage points (Denmark, Ireland, etc.) and 0.3 percentage points (in Spain); the average was 14.0% in 2010!

The size of Germany's shadow economy places it in the mid-range for the OECD, while Austria and Switzerland are in the lower bottom third. The southern European countries (hence Greece, too) have shadow economies that measure between 20 and 25 percent of official GDP and continue to be among the frontrunners. The Scandinavian countries are next, with shadow economies measuring between 15 and 16 percent.

Table 2.5: Size of the shadow economy in 21 OECD countries from 1989/90 to 2010 (in % of official GDP) using the cash approach and the MIMIC method

OECD countries	Average 1989/90	Average1994/95	Average 1997/98	Average 1999/00	Average 2001/02	2003	2004	2005	2006	2007	2008	2009	2010[1]
1. Australia	10.1	13.5	14.0	14.3	14.1	13.7	13.2	12.6	11.4	11.7	10.6	10.9	11.1
2. Belgium	19.3	21.5	22.5	22.2	22.0	21.4	20.7	20.1	19.2	18.3	17.5	17.8	17.9
3. Canada	12.8	14.8	16.2	16.0	15.8	15.3	15.1	14.3	13.2	12.6	12.0	12.6	12.7
4. Denmark	10.8	17.8	18.3	18.0	17.9	17.4	17.1	16.5	15.4	14.8	13.9	14.3	14.4
5. Germany	11.8	13.5	14.9	16.0	16.3	17.1	16.1	15.4	15.0	14.7	14.2	14.6	14.7
6. Finland	13.4	18.2	18.9	18.1	18.0	17.6	17.2	16.6	15.3	14.5	13.8	14.2	14.3
7. France	9.0	14.5	14.9	15.2	15.0	14.7	14.3	13.8	12.4	11.8	11.1	11.6	11.7
8. Greece	22.6	28.6	29.0	28.7	28.5	28.2	28.1	27.6	26.2	25.1	24.3	25.0	25.2
9. United Kingdom	9.6	12.5	13.0	12.7	12.5	12.2	12.3	12.0	11.1	10.6	10.1	10.9	11.1
10. Ireland	11.0	15.4	16.2	15.9	15.7	15.4	15.2	14.8	13.4	12.7	12.2	13.1	13.2
11. Italy	22.8	26.0	27.3	27.1	27.0	26.1	25.2	24.4	23.2	22.3	21.4	22.0	22.2
12. Japan	8.8	10.6	11.1	11.2	11.1	11.0	10.7	10.3	9.4	9.0	8.8	9.5	9.7
13. Netherlands	11.9	13.7	13.5	13.1	13.0	12.7	12.5	12.0	10.9	10.1	9.6	10.2	10.3
14. New Zealand	9.2	11.3	11.9	12.8	12.6	12.3	12.2	11.7	10.4	9.8	9.4	9.9	9.9
15. Norway	14.8	18.2	19.6	19.1	19.0	18.6	18.2	17.6	16.1	15.4	14.7	15.3	15.4

16. Austria	6.9	8.6	9.0	9.8	10.6	10.8	11.0	10.3	9.7	9.4	8.1	8.47	8.67
17. Portugal	15.9	22.1	23.1	22.7	22.5	22.2	21.7	21.2	20.1	19.2	18.7	19.5	19.7
18. Sweden	15.8	19.5	19.9	19.2	19.1	18.6	18.1	17.5	16.2	15.6	14.9	15.4	15.6
19. Switzerland	6.7	7.8	8.1	8.6	9.4	9.5	9.4	9.0	8.5	8.2	7.9	8.3	8.34
20. Spain	16.1	22.4	23.1	22.7	22.5	22.2	21.9	21.3	20.2	19.3	18.7	19.5	19.8
21. U.S.A.	6.7	8.8	8.9	8.7	8.7	8.5	8.4	8.2	7.5	7.2	7.0	7.6	7.8
Unweighted average of 21 OECD countries	12.7	16.2	16.8	16.8	16.7	16.5	16.1	15.6	14.5	13.9	13.3	13.8	14.0

→ Source: Own calculations, 2010, (Prof. Dr. Friedrich Schneider, University of Linz, Altenbergerstraße 69, A-4040 Linz/Auhof).

1) Provisional figures.

3. Sector Breakdown of the Shadow Economy for Germany and Austria

A breakdown of the shadow economy into economic and service sectors is given for Austria and Germany in table 3.1.

Table 3.1: Breakdown of the shadow economy into economic and service sectors in Austria and Germany[1)]

Sector	Breakdown of shadow economy Austria 2010		Breakdown of shadow economy Germany 2010	
	In %	EUR billion	In %	EUR billion
Construction sector and skilled manual trades (including repairs)	39%	8.2	38%	136.5
Other trades and industries (motor vehicles, machines, etc.)	16%	3.3	17%	61.1
Services (hotels, restaurants, etc.)	16%	3.3	17%	61.1
Entertainment and leisure sector	12%	2.5	13%	47.0
Miscellaneous trades and domestic services (private tuition, hairdressing, babysitting)	17%	3.6	15%	53.5
Total underground economy	100%	20.9	100%	351.8

This shows that in 2010, the construction sector and skilled manual trades account for about 38 percent of the volume of the shadow economy (39% for Austria), followed by other trades and industries (e.g. car services) and services (hotels, restaurants, etc.), with 17 percent each (16 percent). Miscellaneous trades and domestic services (such as private tuition, hairdressing, or babysitting, for example) account for 15 percent (17 percent) of volume of the underground economy; the entertainment and leisure sector represents a further 13 percent (12 percent). Table 3.2 provides a further breakdown of the results of estimates for the largest sector, that of the construction trade and skilled manual trades.

This shows that in Germany about 47.8 billion € in shadow economic volume applies to the main construction sector. Construction-related sectors represent 35.5 billion €. Skilled manual trades in the construction sector generate EUR 24.6 billion in shadow activities and miscellaneous repairs (televisions, domestic appliances, etc.) generate EUR 28.6 billion in shadow activity.

Table 3.2: Breakdown of the underground economy in the construction trade and skilled manual trades[1)]

Sector	Breakdown of shadow economy in construction trade and skilled manual trades Austria 2010		Breakdown of shadow economy in construction trade and skilled manual trades Germany 2010	
	In %	EUR billion	In %	EUR billion
Main construction trade	41%	3.4	35%	47.8
Construction-related trades	30%	2.5	26%	35.5
Skilled manual trades in the construction sector	16%	1.3	18%	24.6
Miscellaneous repairs (televisions, electric appliances, domestic appliances)	13%	1.0	21%	28.6
TOTAL Construction trade and skilled manual trades (including repairs)	100 %	8.2	100 %	136.5

4. Calculation of the Number of Moonlighters in Austria, Germany and Switzerland

Table 4.1 shows the results of an estimate of the development of full-time non-foreign moonlighters and of the illegal foreign workers (only as it relates to shadow economic activities) in Germany, Austria, and Switzerland for the period 1995-2010.[5]

[5] **Non-foreign full-time moonlighters** are **an artificial quantity** calculated from the billions of hours worked in the shadow economy. Illegal foreign workers represent an initial estimate of foreigners working illegally (**only with respect to shadow economic activities**). It must be clearly pointed out that two thirds of the added value in the shadow economy is generated by Germans, Austrians, or Swiss citizens or by foreigners legally resident in those countries and all having a good job (part-time or full-time) in the official economy, so that the calculation of the development of full-time non-foreign moonlighters only demonstrates the volume of moonlighting by full-time workers. Compare also Feld and Schneider (2010).

Table 4.1: Development of full-time non-foreign moonlighters and illegal foreign workers in Germany, Austria, and Switzerland in the period 1995 to 2010[1)]

Year	Development of full-time non-foreign moonlighters and illegal foreign workers in thousands of people					
	Germany		Austria		Switzerland	
	Full-time non-foreign moonlighters	Illegal foreign workers	Full-time non-foreign moonlighters	Illegal foreign workers	Full-time non-foreign moonlighters	Illegal foreign workers
1995	7,320	878	575	75	391	55
1996	7,636	939	617	83	426	61
1997	7,899	987	623	86	456	67
1998	8,240	1,039	634	89	462	69
1999	8,524	1,074	667	93	484	74
2000	8,621	1,103	703	99	517	79
2001	8,909	1,149	734	104	543	84
2002	9,182	1,194	746	109	556	88
2003	9,420	1,225	769	112	565	90
2004	9,023	1,103	789	114	560	89
2005	8,549	1,002	750	104	520	82
2006	8,124	952	716	98	493	78
2007	8,206	961	709	97	490	77
2008	8,154	955	679	93	471	74
2009[2)]	8,272	968	713	98	484	76
2010[2)]	8,677	1,022	741	102	495	78

Source: Own calculations (2010).
1) Please note: **Non-foreign full-time moonlighters are an artificial quantity**, calculated from the billions of hours worked in the shadow economy. The illegal foreign workers represent an initial estimate of foreigners working illegally (in underground economic activities).
2) Provisional figures.

In Germany, the national figure of full-time non-foreign moonlighters in 1995 totaled 7.3 million people and increased by 2010 to 8.67 million people. However, the number of illegal foreign workers in Germany is also not negligible; while this figure was 878,000 people in 1995, it increased to 1.020.000 people by 2010.

The rise in the number of full-time non-foreign moonlighters or full-day moonlighters in Austria is also substantial; while this figure was 575,000 people in 1995, it increased to 741.000 people by 2010. The number of illegal workers was 75.000 people in 1995 and rose to 102.000 people in 2010.[6]

5. The Financial Crisis and the Greek Shadow Economy

It is obvious that the "bad" official figures (e.g. high current budget deficit, and high overall debt), but also the high unemployment rates and in general the rather "weak" official economy contributed to a high extent to the financial and economic crisis that Greece is going through. In this context, I would like to point to a quite important problem that was not discussed when the official figures were used to force the Greek government to undertake substantial budget cuts, tax rate increases and other measures in order to reduce the deficit. The size and development of the Greek shadow economy fluctuated between 25 and 24 percent of the official GDP during the last five years. This means that we had a shadow economy of roughly 60 billion euro. Now using the macro approaches, some double counting occurs, so that it is not possible to add the total Greek shadow economy value to the official one. However, if one would be very, very conservative and add only half of the Greek shadow economy to the official Greek GDP, the new total GDP would be at least by 30 up to 35 billion euro higher. This would mean that the current public deficit (in % of GDP) would be considerably reduced and also the total overall debt, measured in GDP! Also the unemployment figure may not be correct and in general, the purchasing power of the Greek population is, if one includes only half of the size of the Greek shadow economy, much higher than the officially calculated one. For me as a scientist, I do not understand why no efforts have been undertaken in order to at least partly include the size and development of the Greek shadow economy into the official figures, like the Italian statistical office does, so that the official figures could be somewhat corrected. Obviously, these figures are not correct if one completely leaves out the shadow economy. Hence, the policy conclusion from this would be that in Greece, probably with the help of the European Union and other experts, one should make an attempt to estimate the real extra value produced in the Greek shadow economy and add this to the official GDP.

---

[6] The term "illegal workers" refers here solely to those who mostly "only" carry out moonlighting, and not, for example, to those who pursue traditionally criminal activities.

Conclusions: Incentive-oriented Policy Measures to Reduce the Shadow Economy

Every government, including the Greek one, faces the challenge to undertake incentive-oriented policy measures to reduce the shadow economy and to have shadow economy activities transformed into the official one. Hence, the first and maybe most important question is whether a decrease in size of the shadow economy is a blessing or a curse. If one assumes that two thirds of all activities in the shadow economy complement those in the official sector (i.e. those goods and services would not be produced in the official economy), the development of the shadow economy can lead to higher value-added figures; with this I mean that the total GDP, which consists of the shadow economy GDP and the official GDP, is always higher than the official GDP. Hence, a decline of the shadow economy will increase the social welfare and the total welfare in a country (here Greece) only if almost all of it is transferred to the official economy. Therefore, it is necessary to choose such economic and fiscal measures that strongly increase incentives to move the production from the unofficial (shadow) economy sector to the official sector (official economy). Only then the decline of the shadow economy will be a blessing for the entire economy.

In sum, the regulation of most Western European labor markets and the high tax and social security contribution burdens are the two most important causes of the relatively large shadow economy in most European OECD (including Greece) countries compared to the U.S. or to some Asian countries (Japan, Singapore, etc.). Hence, a first measure would be to reduce non-wage labor costs, but such a reduction is in most cases and for most countries only moderately successful because a reduction without compensation of the finance loss leads to a huge public deficit which is not tolerable any more.

To reduce the shadow economy, the following policy measures could be used:

First, one policy measure is to reimburse the VAT on labor intensive services (the so-called Luxemburg Model) in order to strengthen the incentive to supply those services in the official economy.

Second, other household investments (e.g. in Germany 1200 Euro per household per year) could be tax deductible, hence if you need a bill, you cannot do it in the shadow economy.[7]

[7] Compare also Schneider and Enste (2006).

Third, only to use the policy instruments with increased punishment and detection rates can be successful in special areas like in those ones where the shadow economy activities are connected with organized crime (e.g. the case of prostitution).

What type of policy conclusions can we now draw?

1. The first is that shadow economy activities are a complex phenomenon, presented to an important extent in all types of economies. People engage in shadow economy activities for a variety of reasons, like government actions, most notably taxation and regulation and the non-functioning of public institutions.[8]
2. The second is that a government aiming to decrease shadow economy activities has to first and foremost analyze the complex relationships between the official and shadow economy as well as – even more importantly – the consequences of its own policy decisions.
3. Considering a public choice perspective, a third conclusion is that a government may not have a great interest to reduce the shadow economy due to the following reasons:
   i. Income earned in the shadow economy increases the standard of living of roughly one third of the working population.
   ii. Between 40 and 50 percent of the shadow economy activities have a complementary character, which means that additional value added is created and this increases the overall (official and unofficial) GDP.
   iii. Tax losses may be moderate, as at least two thirds of the income earned in the shadow economy is immediately spent in the official economy.
   iv. People who work in the shadow economy have less time for other things like going on demonstrations, etc.

If we consider these policy conclusions, it is obvious that there are two big policy challenges for every government: The first is to undertake incentive oriented policy measures in order to make work less (more) attractive in the shadow (official) economy. The second is to have policy institutions which work efficiently and as a constraint for selfish politicians.

For the Greek economy, but also for the Greek population, it would be very important to undertake a serious micro-founded calculation of the

---

[8] Compare Dreher and Schneider (2010), and Dreher, Kotsogiannis and McCorriston (2009).

Greek shadow economy so that one would know how much extra value added (or GDP) is produced, so that the country comes to a bit more realistic figures of the state of the economy (official and unofficial). This would certainly help to overcome the current financial and economic crisis the country is facing.

References

Dell'Anno, R. and F. Schneider (2009): A Complex Approach to Estimate Shadow Economy: The Structural Equation Modelling, in: M. Faggnini and T. Looks (eds.): Coping with the Complexity of Economics, Berlin: Springer, pp. 1110-130.

Dreher, A., C. Kotsogiannis and S. McCorriston (2007): Corruption around the World: Evidence from a Structural Model, Journal of Comparative Economics 35, pp. 443-466.

—. (2009): How Do Institutions Affect Corruption and the Shadow Economy?, International Tax and Public Finance 16, pp. 773-796.

Dreher, A. and Schneider, F. (2010): Corruption and the shadow economy: an empirical analysis, Public Choice 144(1), pp. 215-238

Feld, L.P. and F. Schneider (2010): Survey on the Shadow Economy and Undeclared Earnings in OECD Countries, German Economic Review 11(2), pp. 109-149.

Schneider, F. (2005): Shadow Economies around the World: What Do We Really Know?, European Journal of Political Economy 21, pp. 598-642.

—. (2004). Arbeit im Schatten: Eine Wachstumsmaschine für Deutschland? Wiesbaden: Gabler Verlag.

Schneider, F., Buehn, A. and C. Montenegro (2010): Shadow Economies All over the World: New Estimates for 162 Countries from 1999 to 2007, Policy Research Paper 5356, WPS5356, Washington, D.C.: The World Bank, July 2010.

Schneider, F. and D. Enste (2000): Shadow Economies: Size, Causes and Consequences, Journal of Economic Literature 38, pp. 73-110.

—. (2002): The Shadow Economy: Theoretical Approaches, Empirical Studies, and Political Implications. Cambridge (UK): Cambridge University Press.

—. (eds.) (2006): Jahrbuch Schattenwirtschaft 2006/07. Zum Spannungsfeld von Politik und Ökonomie. Berlin: LIT Verlag.

CHAPTER SEVEN

THE GREEK DEBT CRISIS: LEGAL ASPECTS OF THE SUPPORT MECHANISM FOR THE GREEK ECONOMY BY EUROZONE MEMBER STATES AND THE INTERNATIONAL MONETARY FUND"

KOSTAS C. CHRYSSOGONOS AND GEORGIOS D. PAVLIDIS

A. An Introduction to the Theoretical Discussion on a Statutory Sovereign Bankruptcy Framework

The global financial crisis (2007-2012) has gradually morphed into an international debt crisis, more specifically into a First World debt crisis[1]. Financial support to the banks in the developed countries, in the form of generous liquidity injections, debt guarantees, banking safety net, and purchases of assets, has effectively transferred the colossal losses and massive costs of the recent crisis to the states. The menacing mutation of the financial crisis into a debt crisis has renewed the theoretical discussion on the establishment of bankruptcy procedures for sovereign states. This question emerges every time a major economic crisis recurs[2].

---

[1] A. Pettifor (2006), The Coming First World Debt Crisis, Palgrave Macmillan; see also C. Reinhart / K. Rogoff (2009), This Time Is Different. Eight Centuries of Financial Folly, Princeton, p. 81 ff.; R. Wade (2008), The First-World Debt Crisis of 2007-2010 in Global Perspective, Challenge, vol. 51, no. 4, July-August 2008, p. 23 ff., p. 37; A. Haldane / P. Alessandri (2009), Banking on the State, BIS Review 139/2009, p. 11.

[2] K. Rogoff / J. Zettelmeyer (2002), Bankruptcy Procedures for Sovereigns : A History of Ideas, 1976-2001, IMF Staff Papers, vol. 49, no. 3, p. 470 ff.

As early as 1776, Adam Smith identified the need to establish an international bankruptcy law for those sovereign states that face the spectre of insolvency[3]. Since then, there have been several major default cycles in the international economic history[4]. The sovereign debt crisis of the 1930s left us the legacy of classical theoretical works[5] and the proposal of the League of Nations (1939)[6], favouring the creation of an "*International Loans Tribunal*". Unfortunately, that plan was pushed aside, as countries and blocs were moving hastily towards World War II.

The idea of a bankruptcy procedure for sovereign states was rediscovered in the 1980s and 1990s, as a remedy to the growing and threatening public debt crisis. The idea was discussed in several studies[7], although the analysis was often superficial and did not go into the legal details. Compared to these studies, the Krueger proposal on a Sovereign Debt Restructuring Mechanism (2001)[8] was definitely the most comprehensive and came closer to fruition. In the aftermath of the crisis in Argentina, the project was studied in detail by the International Monetary

---

[3] A. Smith (1776), An Inquiry into the Nature and Causes of the Wealth of Nations, Book V, chapter III ("*When it becomes necessary for a state to declare itself bankrupt, in the same manner as when it becomes necessary for an individual to do so, a fair, open, and avowed bankruptcy is always the measure which is both the least dishonourable to the debtor, and least hurtful to the creditor*").

[4] C. Reinhart / K. Rogoff (2009), This Time Is Different. Eight Centuries of Financial Folly, Princeton, p. 81 ff.

[5] Such as the lecture of G. Jèze at The Hague Academy of International Law; G. Jèze (1935), Les défaillances d'Etat, Académie de Droit International, Recueil des Cours, 1935, p. 381 ff.

[6] League of Nations (1939), Report of the Committee on International Loan Contracts, League of Nations Publication, II. Economic and Financial, 1939.II. A.10 (document C.145.M.93.1939.1I.A).

[7] G-77 Ministerial meeting, Arusha, February 1979; C. Oechsli (1981), Procedural Guidelines for Renegotiating LDC Debts: An Analogy to Chapter 11 of the U.S. Bankruptcy Reform Act, Virginia Journal of International Law, vol. 21, no. 2, p. 305 ff.; B. Barnett / S. Galvis / G. Gouraige (1984), On Third World Debt, Harvard International Law Journal, vol. 25, p. 83 ff.; International Monetary Fund (1995), Note on an International Debt Adjustment Facility, IMF Legal Department, May 1995; A. Pettifor (2002), Chapter 9/11? Resolving International Debt Crises: the Jubilee Framework for International Insolvency, New Economics Foundation, NEF Report, London, 2002; J. Stiglitz (2003), Dealing with Debt: How to Reform the Global Financial System, Harvard International Review, vol. 25, no. 1, p. 54 ff.

[8] A. Krueger (2001), A New Approach to Sovereign Debt Restructuring, American Enterprise Institute, Washington D.C., 26.11.2001.

Fund (2002)[9], but met very strong (and effective) opposition from the international capital markets and the United States (U.S.) Treasury. The proposal was formally rejected in 2003.

There is an important and generally admitted fact: when sovereign debt is not restructured in a timely, equitable and orderly manner, all implicated parties suffer considerable financial losses. Nowadays, collective action and negotiation in the context of a debt crisis are complicated due to the multiplication of investors in the bond markets (banks, pension funds, mutual funds, retail investors) and because of the increase in the number of international bond issues.

In the management of a sovereign insolvency crisis, policy makers need to address serious problems and systemic weaknesses, such as the moral hazard, the bondholders' collective action problem and the possibility of legal complications (see Pravin Banker case and Eliot Associates case). These issues continue to preoccupy the economic and legal theory[10]. The two existing institutions (Paris Club and London Club) are not sufficient in the era of bond finance[11]. The contractual approach, based on the introduction of collective action clauses in international bond contracts, has its limits too.

These observations confirm the need for a new international mechanism for sovereign debt restructuring. Such a legal framework would balance the conflicting interests of the state and its creditors; it would facilitate creditors' coordination, assure the equitable treatment of all parties and provide for dispute resolution mechanisms. The recent Greek debt crisis has given valuable lessons and pushed the debate about

---

[9] International Monetary Fund (2002), A Sovereign Debt Restructuring Mechanism: Further Reflections and Future Work, IMF publication, Washington D.C., 14.02.2002.

[10] See B. Eichengreen (2000), Can the moral hazard of IMF bailouts be reduced? Geneva Reports on the World Economy, Special Report 1/2000, p. 17 ff.; K. Kletzer (2003), Sovereign Bond Restructuring: Collective Action Clauses and Official Crisis Intervention, IMF working paper, no. WP/03/134, Washington D.C., June 2003; International Monetary Fund (2003), Collective Action Clauses: Recent Developments And Issues, IMF International Capital Markets, Legal and Policy Development and Review Departments, Washington D.C., 25.03.2003, etc.

[11] The Paris Club is an informal forum for the renegotiation of bilateral intergovernmental loans. The London Club is also an informal forum for the renegotiation of syndicated bank loans. See G. Pavlidis (2006), La défaillance d'Etat, Athens, p. 154 ff., p. 168 ff. See also R. Olivares-Caminal (2009), Is There a Need for an International Insolvency Regime in the Context of Sovereign Debt? A Case for the Use of Corporate Debt Restructuring Techniques, Journal of International Banking Law and Regulation, vol. 24(1), p. 21 ff.

reform. This need is clearer in times of crisis, when the system is threatened with a domino of government bankruptcies. The Greek insolvency is a part of the global problem and the time is suitable for seeking a new systemic approach.

B. The Greek Debt Crisis and the EU/IMF Rescue Mechanism

In the aftermath of the recent debt crisis, constitutional theory[12] in Greece faces an intriguing challenge, concerning the interpretation and implementation of two controversial legislative instruments: The Law 3845/2010 (Official Gazette A 65/06.05.2010), entitled "*Measures for the implementation of the support mechanism for the Greek economy by eurozone Member States and the International Monetary Fund*" (hereinafter: IMF) and the Bill ratifying the Loan Facility Agreement, which was concluded on 08.05.2010 between Greece, on the one hand, and the other eurozone Member States and the IMF, on the other hand. The content and structure of these instruments raise the issue of their compatibility with specific provisions of the Greek Constitution (hereinafter: Const.)[13], the European Union (EU) law and the European Convention for the Protection of Human Rights and Fundamental Freedoms (hereinafter: ECHR). In addition to this legal issue, there is also a political one: the path from the elections of 2009 to the Law 3845/2010 is, indeed, suggestive of the quality and reality of democracy in Greece.

The reasons that led to the creation of the "*support mechanism*" are described in the Council Decision 2010/320/EU[14] and in paragraphs 1 to 3 of the article 1 of the Law 3845/2010. Greek gross public debt at the end of 2009 stood at 115 % of GDP, a debt ratio among the highest in the EU (the reference value of the Treaty is 60 % of GDP). Market confidence in

---

[12] K. Chryssogonos, The Lost Honour of the Greek Democracy, Nomiko Vima, vol. 58, p. 1354 ff (published in Greek); P. Glavinis (2010), The Memorandum of Greece in the European, International and National Legal Order, Sakkoulas editions, Athens Thessaloniki (published in Greek); G. Katrougalos (2010), Memoranda Sunt Servanda?, Journal of Administrative Law, issue 2/2010, p. 151 ff (published in Greek).

[13] The Greek Constitution has been translated in English by the Directorate of Studies of the Hellenic Parliament (2004).

[14] Council Decision 2010/320/EU of 10 May 2010 addressed to Greece with a view to reinforcing and deepening fiscal surveillance and giving notice to Greece to take measures for the deficit reduction judged necessary to remedy the situation of excessive deficit, OJ L 145 of 11.06.2010, p. 6 ff.

the ability of the Greek government to service its debt had been rapidly undermined by several factors, such as the excessive budget deficits and the questionable quality of the Greek statistics; one should also mention a chronically unsustainable fiscal policy, a consistently higher inflation than the European average, a shift in market expectations about Greek participation to the Eurozone and about implicit fiscal guarantees from Eurozone countries[15]. As a result, in May 2010, Greek/German bond yield spread scaled more than 1000 basis points[16], prohibiting essentially access to the bond markets. At the time, there was no legal framework allowing the EU to deal with the financial difficulties or failure of a member state[17].

B. 1. A Look into Pre-crisis Greek Politics

As already hinted earlier, an important dimension of the Greek debt crisis is the political one. Undoubtedly, the parliamentary elections of 2009 were different from all the previous ones. Before that date, the government used to call election earlier than scheduled, by invoking article 41 par. 2 Const. ("problem of extraordinary national importance"), only when the ruling party had a near-certain prospect of prevailing[18].

The snap election of October 2009, based on article 41 par. 2 Const., took place five months after the painful defeat that the ruling conservative party ("*New Democracy*") suffered in the elections to the European Parliament. In addition, the election polls were unfavourable for the ruling party, whose leader opted for early elections anyhow. This politically suicidal decision could qualify as a deliberate transition of power from the

---

[15] M. Arghyrou / J. Tsoukalas (2010), The Greek Debt Crisis: Likely Causes, Mechanics and Outcomes, Cardiff Business School, Cardiff Economics Working Papers, E2010/3, p. 5 ff.

[16] A. Sibert (2010), The Greek Sovereign Debt Crisis and the Eurosystem, European Parliament, Policy Department: Economic and Scientific Policies, 5 June 2010. There was also a considerable increase in Credit Default Swaps (CDS) spreads.

[17] D. Gros / T. Mayer (2010), How to Deal with Sovereign Default in Europe: Create the European Monetary Fund now!, CEPS Policy Brief, No. 202/February 2010, p. 6; K. Featherstone (2011), The Greek Sovereign Debt Crisis and EMU: A Failing State in a Skewed Regime, Journal of Common Market Studies, 2011, p. 18 ff.

[18] This has happened in 1977, 1985, 1996, 2000 and 2007, leading to renewed popular mandate. Only the 1993 early elections brought the change of government, but then behind the reasons invoked as pretext there was a special one, namely the loss of parliamentary majority from the "*New Democracy*" party.

government to the opposition, a desperate means to disclaim responsibility for the imminent default[19].

In the electoral campaign, the ruling conservative party warned that Greece was headed down a dangerous path, so austerity measures were indispensable to prevent the worst. This warning was certainly tantamount to an admission of guilt, an implicit acknowledgment that government policies had failed miserably. In contrast, the socialist party ("*PASOK*") promised that it would mobilise financial resources, ensure the well-being of workers, increase wages and revive the economy. Soon after his election victory, the socialist Prime Minister had to retract, mugged by reality. Harsh economic policies were announced, not unlike the policies advocated by the previous government before the election. Later, the situation deteriorated and things led to the EU/IMF rescue package and the signature of Memoranda.

As far as internal party democracy is concerned, there was no participation of socialist party members in the decision-making and the resolution of this matter. The key political decisions were taken by the leader of the party, the Prime Minister. The activation of the rescue mechanism and its conditionality were not brought for vote, either in the party's extraordinary congress, or in the supreme party organ, namely the National Council (Article 36 of PASOK Statute, as in force in 2008) or the socialist parliamentary group. This practice can be considered as a violation of the principle of party democracy, as the latter derives from article 29 par. 1 Const[20].

The relative autonomy of governments from the organization of the governing parties is a problem common, to some degree, in many democracies of our time[21]. However, the Greek case is exceptional, not only because of the almost complete lack of internal party democracy, but also because of other features of the Greek political system, such as the

---

[19] Past economic performance is not always the key element for remaining in office; J. A. Cheibub / A. Przeworski (1999), Democracy, Elections, and Accountability for Economic Outcomes, in: A. Przeworski/ S. Stokes/ B. Manin (eds.), Democracy, Accountability, and Representation, New York: Cambridge University Press, p. 239.

[20] P. Spyropoulos, T. Fortsakis (2009), Constitutional Law in Greece, Kluwer/ Sakkoulas, p. 121 ff; K. Kerameus, P. Kozyris (1993), Introduction to Greek Law, Kluwer/Sakkoulas editions, p. 31.

[21] J. Blondel / M. Cotta (1996), Party and Government: An Inquiry into the Relationship between Governments and Supporting Parties in Liberal Democracies, London, Macmillan, p. 249 ff.

strong presence of political dynasties, the absence of any effective control of private subsidies to parties and politicians, etc.[22]

In addition to the political questions, there are some important legal aspects to consider when examining the Greek debt crisis. The following provides a brief analysis of the Law 3845/2010 and the Loan Facility Agreement, focusing on their effect in the national legal order.

B. 2. The Establishment of the EU/IMF Rescue Mechanism and the De Facto Transfer of Economic Sovereignty

As initially enacted, article 1, par. 4 of the Law 3845/2010 authorized the Minister of Finance to sign memoranda, agreements and conventions on the mechanism, adding that these instruments would be submitted in Parliament for ratification. This would be the right approach, since these conventions fall, due to their purpose, into the scope of article 36, par. 2 Const[23]. However, only five days after the publication of the Law 3845/2010, a new law was introduced; in par. 9 of its sole article, the new Law 3847/2010 (Government Gazette A 67/11.5.2010) determines that these understandings, agreements and conventions shall be submitted in Parliament not for ratification, but for "*discussion and information*," a rather peculiar wording for Greek parliamentary practice. According to the same provision, these instruments shall be "*valid with effect from the time of their signature*."

Article 1 par. 9 of the Law 3847/2010 violates not only article 36 par. 2 Const., but also article 36 par. 1 Const[24]. For such international instruments, the State is internationally represented by the President of the Republic, not by the Minister of Finance. The law implicitly repeals the condition that these contracts should be signed by the President, as

[22] See also C. Lyrintzis (1984), Political Parties in Post-Junta Greece: A Case of Bureaucratic Clientelism? West European Politics, vol. 7, no. 2, p. 99 ff.

[23] "Conventions on trade, taxation, economic cooperation and participation in international organizations or unions and all others containing concessions for which, according to other provisions of this Constitution, no provision can be made without a statute, or which may burden the Greeks individually, shall not be operative without ratification by a statute voted by the Parliament."

[24] "The President of the Republic, complying absolutely with the provisions of article 35 paragraph 1, shall represent the State internationally, declare war, conclude treaties of peace, alliance, economic cooperation and participation in international organizations or unions and he shall announce them to the Parliament with the necessary clarifications, whenever the interest and the security of the State thus allow."

condition of their validity. In the same way, the Law 3847/2010 violates article 35 par. 1 Const.[25], which is explicitly referred to by article 36 par. 1 Const. Finally, the law violates article 36 par. 4 Const.[26] because it effectively authorizes the Minister of Finance to sign and ratify international treaties.

Article 1 par. 3 of the Law 3845/2010 makes reference to three annexed documents, i.e. the Declaration made on 25.03.2010 by the Heads of State and Government of the eurozone, the Statement of the Eurogroup of 11.04.2010 and the Draft Plan agreed to by the Ministry of Finance, on the one hand, and the European Commission, the European Central Bank (hereinafter: ECB) and the IMF, on the other. The Draft Plan consists of two Memoranda: the Memorandum of Economic and Financial Policies and the Memorandum of Understanding on Specific Economic Policy Conditionality.

The aforementioned program and statements have not become binding rules of law, within the Greek legal order, by virtue of article 1 par. 3 of the Law 3845/2010. These documents are merely annexed to the Law 3845/2010, which does not make any explicit reference to their legal force. They mainly present historical findings and general quantitative objectives for the future, without any specification as to the exact means of their legal implementation. It could be argued that the program and the statements serve a purpose that is analogous to the function of explanatory reports in ordinary law making.

Article 2, par. 1, let. A of the Law 3845/2010 confers statutory authority for the adoption of secondary/delegated legislation (Presidential Decrees[27]), particularly on the fiscal policy measures that are necessary for achieving the objectives of the program. Article 2, par. 2 and 3, of the Law 3845/2010 confers authority for the adoption of emergency measures to protect the weaker economic classes and vulnerable social groups, as well

---

[25] "No act of the President of the Republic shall be valid nor be executed unless it has been countersigned by the competent Minister who, by his signature alone shall be rendered responsible, and unless it has been published in the Government Gazette. If the Cabinet has been relieved of its duties as provided by article 38 paragraph 1, and the Prime Minister fails to counter- sign the relative decree, this shall be signed by the President of the Republic alone."

[26] "The ratification of international treaties may not be the object of delegation of legislative power as specified in article 43 paragraphs 2 and 4."

[27] P. Spyropoulos, T. Fortsakis (2009), Constitutional law in Greece, Kluwer/Sakkoulas, p. 73 ff; K. Kerameus, P. Kozyris (1993), Introduction to Greek law, Kluwer/Sakkoulas editions, p. 13.

as to support the real economy, strengthen small businesses, etc. during the implementation of the program set in article 1.

Therefore, Law 3845/2010 is an enabling Act, a framework law in the sense of article 43, par. 4, 2nd phrase, Const., according to which "*these statutes shall set out the general principles and directives of the regulation to be followed and shall set time-limits within which the delegation must be used.*" In this case, it could be argued that the general principles and guidelines are included in the draft plan, i.e. mainly Annexes III and IV of the Law.

There is, however, a legal impediment. As explained above, the Annexes (in other words the two Memoranda) contain quantitative targets without always specifying the ways to achieve them. For example, for the years 2013-2014, the Annexes (Table 1 of the Memorandum of Economic and Financial Policies) provide "*unspecified measures*" of nearly ten billion Euros (!) without any further explanation. Such a provision runs the risk of disrupting the notion of separation of powers: if the Minister of Finance and the respective co-competent Minister can exercise legislative powers through the issuance of Presidential Decrees on public spending or revenue up to a limit of ten billion Euros, then all existing legislation for those years is wiped out, based on article 2 par. 1 of the Law 3845/2010. This would no longer constitute a delegation of authority, but a state of emergency. Hence, the Parliament has exceeded its authority in delegating these powers to the administration.

Even if one admits that the delegation is legitimized by the existence of general principles and guidelines within the Law 3845/2010, there is no reference to the duration of validity of such delegation either in the law itself or in its annexes. For example, in Annex III (Memorandum of Economic and Financial Policies), chapter III, par. 7, there is a reference to the year 2020, the year when primary annual fiscal surpluses of over 5% of GDP must be achieved. In Chapter V, par. 25 of the same Annex, specific fiscal targets are set until the year 2014, while on other occasions targets are set for shorter periods. So, even if one accepts with the premise that, within the meaning of article 43 par. 4, 2nd phrase Const.[28], general principles and guidelines can be set in an Annex to the framework law and not in the actual legislative text, there is a solid basis for challenging the

[28] "By virtue of statutes passed by the Plenum of the Parliament, delegation may be given for the issuance of general regulatory decrees for the regulation of matters specified by such statutes in a broad framework. These statutes shall set out the general principles and directives of the regulation to be followed and shall set time-limits within which the delegation must be used."

constitutionality of the Presidential Decrees to be issued, since the law fails to define the time limits for the use of such authority.

However, it could be argued that article 2, par. 1 of the Law 3845/2010 is not a framework law pursuant to article 43, par. 4 Const. but according to article 78 par. 5 Const. ("*It shall, exceptionally, be permitted to impose by means of delegation granted in framework by statute, balancing or counteractive charges or duties, and to impose, within the framework of the country's international relations to economic organizations, economic measures or measures concerning the safeguarding of the country's foreign exchange position*").

Under this interpretation, the question is whether the conditions under the latter provision are identical to the ones stated in article 43 par. 4 Const. or whether another type of framework law is introduced, whereby authority can be delegated without time limits and not just to the President of the Republic, but to other organs of the executive as well. In Greek constitutional theory, diametrically opposed answers have been given to this. However, the thesis that article 78 par. 5 Const. introduces an entirely different form of framework laws, free from the restrictions of article 43 par. 4 Const., can lead to excessive (in view of the fundamental principles of articles 1[29] and 26[30] of the Constitution) transfer of powers from the legislature to the government. The formal law does not cease to be accompanied by major democratic guarantees compared to the normative acts of the administration. The issue goes beyond the scope of this study; nevertheless, it seems more plausible to assert that the exception of article 78 par. 5 Const. refers to the rule of par. 4 of the same article (the exclusion of legislative delegation in tax matters) and not to article 43 par. 4 Const.

The remaining part of article 2 of the Law 3845/2010 contains other special mandates for issuing decrees and presidential decrees on the census of civil servants and public entities and on emergency measures to tackle the adverse consequences of the program. The Law 3845/2010 provides

---

[29] "1. The form of government of Greece is that of a parliamentary republic.
2. Popular sovereignty is the foundation of government.
3. All powers derive from the People and exist for the People and the Nation; they shall be exercised as specified by the Constitution."

[30] "1. The legislative powers shall be exercised by the Parliament and the Presidents of the Republic.
2. The executive powers shall be exercised by the President of the Republic and the Government.
3. The judicial powers shall be exercised by courts of law, the decisions of which shall be executed in the name of the Greek People."

for salaries and pensions cuts (article 3), permanent tax increases (article 4), special levy on profits of legal persons and a special tax on television advertisements (article 5), organizational measures of the Ministry of Finance (article 6) and, finally, the time of entry into force of the law (article 7).

The provisions of the Law 3845/2010, in particular article 3, have raised concerns in terms of their compatibility with social rights guaranteed by the Greek Constitution (e.g. article 22 par. 1[31] and article 22 par. 4 Const.[32]) and the protection of property in article 1 of the First Protocol to the ECHR[33]. In fact, the concept of property may, in accordance with the relevant ECHR jurisprudence, encompass social security benefits[34]. Moreover, there are recent examples of Constitutional court decisions in Eastern Europe, which have declared unconstitutional laws for drastic cuts in pensions, which were voted by the parliaments of these countries in order to comply with IMF programs (see below, section B.4.).

The Memorandum of Economic and Financial Policies of 3 May 2010 (Annex III) is the most comprehensive among the texts attached as annexes to the Law 3845/2010. After a summary of recent economic developments and key objectives of the program, (Chapters I and II respectively), the Memorandum states the economic policies that Greece is bound to follow for a period not determined exactly, but still bound to last several years (Chapter III). From their part, the other member states of the eurozone and the IMF promise to accord to Greece loans amounting to 110 billion euros (Chapter IV). As one would expect, the Memorandum also provides for monitoring mechanisms and follow-up dates of the program

---

[31] "Work constitutes a right and shall enjoy the protection of the State, which shall seek to create conditions of employment for all citizens and shall pursue the moral and material advancement of the rural and urban working population."

[32] "The State shall care for the social security of the working people, as specified by law."

[33] "Every natural or legal person is entitled to the peaceful enjoyment of his possessions. No one shall be deprived of his possessions except in the public interest and subject to the conditions provided for by law and by the general principles of international law. The preceding provisions shall not, however, in any way impair the right of a State to enforce such laws as it deems necessary to control the use of property in accordance with the general interest or to secure the payment of taxes or other contributions or penalties."

[34] See ECHR, Stec and Others v. United Kingdom (decision as to the admissibility)[GC], nos. 65731/01 and 65900/01, παρ.51, ECHR 2005-X. In general, the Court in Strasbourg has found that an agreement with the IMF can not deny protection under the ECHR. See Capital Bank AD v. Bulgaria, no. 49429/99, par.110-111, ECHR 2005-XII, 24.11.2005.

and quantifies its objectives through a series of tables (Chapter V). The first Memorandum is completed by a second one, the Memorandum of Understanding on Specific Economic Policy Conditionality, which documents fiscal actions, various reforms, and schedules for monitoring by the European Commission, the ECB and the IMF (Annex IV of the Law 3845/2010). These two Memoranda determine a priori the economic, fiscal and social policy in the country in the long run. They bring the implementation of these policies under the constant and relentless surveillance of the European and international "*troika*" (European Commission, ECB, and IMF).

As to their legal nature, the Memoranda may not be considered as international conventions within the meaning of article 28 par. 1 Const. Therefore, they have no legal force superior to the formal (statutory) law. They can only qualify as "*agreements in simplified form*" in the light of article V of the Articles of Agreement of the IMF, in conjunction with the decision "*Guidelines on Conditionality*" n° 12864 - (02/102) of 25.9.2002, as amended by Decision n° 13814-(06/98) of 15.11.2006 of the IMF[35].

An eventual enactment of laws or regulations, whose content contradicts the objectives of memoranda, does not imply in any case that these laws or regulations are invalid or unenforceable. No such provision is contained in the understandings. Also, all acts required for the implementation of the Memoranda are issued by the Greek authorities; there is no transfer of powers to the bodies of international organizations within the meaning of article 28 par. 2 Const.[36]

Legally, there does not seem to be any commitment and restriction of sovereignty within the meaning of Article 28 par. 3 Const.[37] The Greek Government has signed the Memoranda voluntarily; moreover, Greece is not legally unable to withdraw from their application, even if such a

[35] The Constitutional Court of Thailand has examined the legal nature of Memoranda in the context of an IMF program and has found that these documents do not constitute international treaties, but unilateral statements of the Government of Thailand. See Ruling No. 11/2542 [1999] THCC 11 (25 May 1999).

[36] "Authorities provided by the Constitution may by treaty or agreement be vested in agencies of international organizations, when this serves an important national interest and promotes cooperation with other States. A majority of three-fifths of the total number of Members of Parliament shall be necessary to vote the law anctioning the treaty or agreement."

[37] "Greece shall freely proceed by law passed by an absolute majority of the total number of Members of Parliament to limit the exercise of national sovereignty, insofar as this is dictated by an important national interest, does not infringe upon the rights of man and the foundations of democratic government and is effected on the basis of the principles of equality and under the condition of reciprocity."

decision would lead to substantial economic losses. The national government remains the focal point of authority, as it is often the case in international law[38].

In reality, of course, the Memoranda imply an assignment to the "*troika*" of the responsibility for defining and implementing economic, financial and social policy. There is, therefore, a *de facto* transfer of the economic sovereignty for the (undetermined) period of the program. The Greek government and parliament are under the direct control on these issues, since a refusal to comply will result in failure to collect the next instalment of the loan and thus in the cessation of payments by the Greek government. There is also a triangular relationship between the "*troika*," the Greek government and the (supposedly) sovereign people, whereby the national government seems more like a retailer, who tries to convince the final consumer of the need for compliance. In this context, there are abundant historical examples of countries that have lost their political independence and turned into protectorates, as a result of their bankruptcy[39].

B. 3. The Scope and Limits of Greece's Waiver of Immunity from Enforcement

One should distinguish the legal nature of the Memorandum from the legal nature of the Loan Facility Agreement that was concluded on 08.05.2010 between the Hellenic Republic, as Borrower, and the other Member States of the eurozone and the Kreditanstalt fuer Wiederaufbau (hereinafter: KfW), as Lenders. KfW is a German financial institution, subject to the instructions of, guaranteed by and acting in the public interest of the Federal Republic of Germany[40]. This is clearly an international agreement, which was submitted to Parliament for ratification.

---

[38] C. Schreuer (1993), The Waning of the Sovereign State: Towards a New Paradigm for International Law? European Journal of International Law, vol. 4, p. 447 ff., p. 470; P. Tangney (1996), The New Internationalism: The Cession of Sovereign Competences to Supranational Organizations and Constitutional Change in the United States and Germany, Yale Journal of International Law, vol. 21, p. 395 ff.

[39] See C. Reinhart / K. Rogoff (2009), This Time Is Different. Eight Centuries of Financial Folly, Princeton, p. 81 ff. See also U. Panizza / F. Sturzenegger / J. Zettelmeyer (2009), The Economics and Law of Sovereign Debt and Default, Journal of Economic Literature, vol. 47:3, p. 1 ff.

[40] The Federal Government of Germany has mandated KfW, pursuant to §2 par. 4 of the KfW Law (Zuweisungsgeschäft) to participate in the loan facility granted to

According to article 3 par. 4 (a) of the Loan Facility Agreement, administration and disbursement of the loan are subject to the submission of "*legal opinions*" (essentially prefabricated statements) from the legal advisers at the Ministries of Justice and Finance, while article 4 par.1 (b) adds that the borrower (i.e., Greece) represents and warrants that the "*opinions*" are true and correct.

Section 12 of the "*opinions*", whose content is pre-determined in Annex 4 of the Loan Facility Agreement assures the lenders (i.e. the other member states of the zone) that "*[n]either the Borrower nor any of its property are immune on the grounds of sovereignty or otherwise from jurisdiction, attachment – whether before or after judgement – or execution in respect of any action or proceeding relating to the Agreement*".

Under article 14 par. 5 "*[t]he Borrower hereby irrevocably and unconditionally waives all immunity to which it is or may become entitled, in respect of itself or its assets, from legal proceedings in relation to this Agreement, including, without limitation, immunity from suit, judgement or other order, from attachment, arrest or injunction prior to judgement, and from execution and enforcement against its assets to the extent not prohibited by mandatory law*".

It is generally accepted that the state-borrower may waive its immunity from execution with an express act[41]. The aforementioned article 14 par. 5 of the Loan Facility Agreement and section 12 of the Legal Opinions seem to be such a waiver. It should be noted that the law applicable to the agreement in accordance with its article 14 par. 1 is English law and that the Court of Justice of the European Union in Luxembourg (hereinafter: ECJ) has exclusive jurisdiction for any dispute arising from the agreement, in accordance with its article 14 par. 2. For that reason, it is important to examine how sovereign immunity is viewed in the English legal system.

In English law, articles 13 (2) to 13 (4) of the State Immunity Act 1978 (hereinafter: SIA)[42] allow for the execution against foreign states only for "*property in use or intended for use for commercial purposes*" (*iure gestionis*). Contrary to French law, which prohibits enforcement against non-commercial property regardless of the waiver, section 13(3) SIA allows enforcement against non-commercial property, where there is a

---

Greece. KfW's commitment to participate amounts to EUR 22.3 billion. The German Federal Parliament (Bundestag) has authorized the Government to guarantee this loan.

[41] See A. Reinisch (2006), European Court Practice Concerning State Immunity from Enforcement Measures, European Journal of International Law, vol.17, p. 816 ff.

[42] State Immunity Act 1978 c. 33 (UK), 17 ILM (1978) 1123, as amended.

waiver, because "*that provision would be redundant if the award could only be enforced against commercial property because the claimant would simply rely on section 13(4)*"[43]. So, if the requirements of section 13(3) SIA are met, enforcement against non-commercial property of the foreign state is possible. The scope of this provision is limited by jurisprudence, which takes into consideration immunities derived from consular or diplomatic law[44]; thus, even if there is a waiver of immunity from enforcement, there can be no enforcement against the property of a diplomatic mission or the private property of a diplomatic agent (see articles 22 and 30 of the Vienna Convention on Diplomatic Relations). It is generally accepted that central bank assets, such as international reserves, are typically immune from attachment, although there are still concerns about the attachment of these assets in some European jurisdictions[45].

Furthermore, the applicable English law gives the state-borrower few defences for failure to perform. In cases of unilateral termination or deferment of debt, the application of the Act of State Doctrine is restricted by jurisprudence, which further recognizes that "*the circumstances in which this defence is available are very ill defined*"[46]. A state's actions within its own territory may not be challenged in the courts of another nation; nevertheless, the courts have adopted a commercial exception to the Act of State. Although « *it is difficult to discern the precise scope of the commercial act exception* »[47], the international loan transactions and the suspension of external debt payments clearly fall within it. The

[43] A. Rooney / R. Kennell (2010), The State Immunity Act 1978 and Article 28(6) of the ICC Rules: A Missed Opportunity, Arbitration, 76(1), p. 181, pp. 184-185.

[44] A Co. Ltd v. Republic of X, QBD, 21 Dec. 1989, [1990] 2 Lloyds Rep. 520, 87 ILR 412.

[45] U. Panizza / F. Sturzenegger / J. Zettelmeyer (2009), The Economics and Law of Sovereign Debt and Default, Journal of Economic Literature, vol. 47:3, p. 4; see M. Singh (2003), Recovery Rates from Distressed Debt—Empirical Evidence from Chapter 11 Filings, International Litigation, and Recent Sovereign Debt Restructurings, International Monetary Fund Working Paper no. 03/161

[46] Buttes Gas & Oil Co. v. Hammer [1975] 1 Q.B. 573; see also M. Singer (1981), The Act of State Doctrine of the United Kingdom: An Analysis, with Comparisons to United States Practice, The American Journal of International Law, vol. 75, p. 283 ff.; C. Barker (1998), State Immunity, Diplomatic Immunity and Act of State: A Triple Protection Against Legal Action? International & Comparative Law Quarterly, vol. 47, issue 4, p. 950 ff.

[47] Alfred Dunhill of London, Inc. v. Republic of Cuba , 425 U.S. 682 (1976) at 728.

common law "*doctrine of champerty*" is another defense[48], which could protect sovereign debtors against vulture funds' litigation; however, this defense, which prohibits litigation in cases where a claim was acquired with the sole intent of pursuing litigation, was formally rejected in English case law[49].

There is, however, a last part in the waiver clause in the Loan Facility Agreement: immunity from enforcement is waived "*to the extent not prohibited by mandatory law.*" It is rather unclear of what this mandatory law consists. The notion could refer to local mandatory rules ("*lois de police*") in Greece or in another place of execution. It could also refer to mandatory rules of international law, overriding the governing law and the law of the place of execution. More specifically:

1. If the assets to be attached are located in Greece, one should examine whether there are local mandatory rules in the Greek legal system, limiting the scope of the waiver and excluding execution. Article 4 par. 1 let. a of the Law 3068/2002, an executive statute implementing the article 94 par. 4 *in fine* Const., allows execution to be directed only against private property of the government, the local administration and public entities, to the exclusion of public property. In principle, when the Loan Agreement is ratified, it will acquire legal force under article 28 par. 1 Const. and therefore will supersede the Law 3068/2002. It is obvious that there are un-attachable public assets necessary to ensure the existence and status of a sovereign state (e.g. the weapons and facilities of the armed forces and security forces, the buildings where direct state organs operate, cash requirements for salaries of staff). One can argue that Greece cannot derogate from article 4 par. 1 let. a of the Law 3068/2002, by choosing the English law as applicable in the Loan Facility Agreement. In addition to this, in view of the fundamental provisions of articles 1 and 26 Const., the jurisprudence of the Greek supreme administrative court holds that State may not delegate the exercise of certain powers, connected predominantly to public authority and viewed as an expression of sovereignty[50]. This is the equivalent of the "*non-delegation doctrine*," applied in many legal systems, which restricts the ability of the national parliament to delegate powers reserved by the Constitution for specific branches of the

---

48 R. Cohen/ R. Schwartz (2003) Champerty and Claims Trading, American Bankruptcy Institute Law Review, vol. 11, p. 197 ff.

49 Camdex International Ltd. v Bank of Zambia, Court of Appeals (1996), 3 All ER 431. See also P. Bedford / A. Penalver / C. Salmon (2005), Resolving Sovereign Debt Crises: The Market-Based Approach and the Role of the IMF, Bank of England - Financial Stability Review, June 2005, p. 96.

50 Hellenic Council of State (ΣτΕ) decision 1934/1998 (plenary session).

government. Subsequently, the State may not be deprived of the material resources that are essential for the exercise of its sovereignty.

Therefore, the Bill ratifying the Loan Agreement would be unconstitutional, since the extent of the waiver of immunity from enforcement goes too far. Such a provision could not have been legitimately adopted even by means of article 28 par. 2 and 3 Const., because it clearly undermines Greek sovereignty. For the same reason, it could not have been legitimately adopted by means of a constitutional revision under Article 110 Const. However, as stated, the ECJ has exclusive jurisdiction over any differences which arise from the Loan Agreement. It can now be inferred that the Court (consisting of a majority of judges from the lender member-states) will be guided by article 27 of the Vienna Convention of 1969 on the Law of Treaties, prohibiting states from invoking the provisions of national law (including the national Constitution) to avoid their international obligations.

2. If the assets to be attached are located in other countries, there may be local mandatory rules, limiting the scope of execution against a foreign state. In many legal systems, a waiver of immunity from enforcement can only cover property that is used for commercial purposes[51]. For instance, under U.S. law, even when a foreign state completely waives its immunity from execution, courts in the U.S. may execute only against property that meets the two statutory criteria of Foreign Sovereign Immunities Act of 1976 (hereinafter: FSIA)[52], i.e., property located in the United States and used for a commercial activity in the United States. U.S. courts must also determine the location of each form of property at the time of issuance of the garnishment order to ensure that it governs property located in the United States[53]. In the litigation associated with Argentina's default, some creditors obtained judgments in their favour, but their requests to attach assets in the U.S. have been denied[54]; plaintiffs sought unsuccessfully to attach "*the representation office of the province of Buenos Aires in New York, diplomatic facilities,*

---

[51] G. Robin (2002), Enforcement Immunities in the Domain of International Commercial Transactions, International Business Law Journal 2002/1, p. 7 ff.

[52] 28 U.S.C. § 1610(a)(1); Connecticut Bank of Commerce v. Republic of Congo, United States Court of Appeals, Fifth Circuit, July 17, 2002, 309 F.3d 247; Af-Cap Inc. v. The Republic of Congo, United States Court of Appeals, Fifth Circuit, September 17, 2004, 383 F.3d 361.

[53] Em Ltd v. Republic of Argentina, 473 F.3d at 481 n.19; cf. FG Hemisphere Assocs., LLC v. République du Congo, 455 F.3d 575, 594 (5th Cir. 2006)

[54] For example, Aurelius Capital Partners, LP v. Republic of Argentina, 584 F.3d 120 (2nd Cir. 2009).

U.S. accounts of Correo Argentino S.A. (the renationalized postal service), and—most significantly—$ 105 million in reserves held by the Central Bank of Argentina in New York"[55].

3. Mandatory rules of international law may also limit the scope of the waiver. There is some evidence in favour of the view that international customary law prohibits attachment of state assets destined for public purposes (iure imperii)[56]. There are numerous international and national instruments that form the two elements necessary to prove the existence of a customary rule (state practice and opinio juris). For instance, the ILA Draft Articles for a Convention on State Immunity provide for exceptions to the rule of immunity from enforcement, when there is a waiver and the property is used for commercial purposes[57]. The same approach is adopted by the 2004 United Nations Convention on Jurisdictional Immunities of States and Their Property (based on the 1991 ILC Draft Articles) and the European Convention on State Immunity, which has been though ratified by only 8 states. The distinction between assets destined for purposes iure gestionis and iure imperii exists in national legislation in many common law countries[58] and in jurisprudence in civil law countries, such as France[59], Germany[60], the Netherlands[61], etc.

[55] U. Panizza / F. Sturzenegger / J. Zettelmeyer (2009), The Economics and Law of Sovereign Debt and Default, Journal of Economic Literature, vol. 47:3, p. 8, footnote 4 .

[56] See the judgement of the Landgericht Stuttgart, on the case Spanish Consular Bank Accounts (1971), International Law Reports vol.65 (1971), p. 114 ff., p. 117.

[57] International Law Association, Draft Articles for a Convention on State Immunity 1982 (ILA Draft Convention), 22 ILM (1983) 287; see also the Revised Draft Articles for a Convention on State Immunity, ILA Report (1994) 21.

[58] USA (Foreign Sovereign Immunities Act of 1976), Canada (State Immunity Act 1982), Australia (State Immunity Act 1986), Singapore (State Immunity Act of 1979), South Africa (Foreign States Immunities Act 1981), Pakistan (State Immunity Ordinance of 1981).

[59] Cour de cassation (1re chambre civile), Société Eurodif contre République islamique d'Iran,14 mars 1984, Revue critique de droit international privé, 1984, p. 644 ff.; Cour d'appel de Paris (1re chambre), Société Creighton Limited contre ministère des finances et le ministère des affaires municipales et de l'agriculture du gouvernement de l'Etat du Qatar, 12 décembre 2001, Revue de l'arbitrage, avril 2003, n° 2, p. 417 ff.; Cour de cassation (1re chambre civile), Société Sonatrach contre Migeon, 1er octobre 1985, Revue critique de droit international privé, 1986, p. 527 ff.

[60] BVerfGE 15, 25 (Jugoslawische Militärmission) BVerfGE 16, 27 (Iranische Botschaft) BVerfGE 46, 342 (Philippinische Botschaft) BVerfGE 64, 1 (National Iranian Oil Company).

It is interesting to note that common law countries have enacted statutes on sovereign immunities, while civil law countries rely on jurisprudence to deal with the same issues. All these provisions point towards the existence of an overriding mandatory rule of customary international law, which prohibits execution against state assets destined for purposes iure imperii.

B. 4. The Compatibility of Salary and Pension Cuts with National and International Law

Article 3 of the Law 3845/2010 imposes the reduction of the salaries of civil servants and of staff employed under private law. This is clearly a limitation of collective autonomy, which is guaranteed by article 22 par. 2 Const.[62] The constitutionality of a statute that repeals or amends a collective bargaining agreement is questionable[63]. In addition to this, the limits imposed on collective bargaining violate several instruments of international labour law. For example, article 8 of the International Labour Convention no 151 of 1978 states that "*[t]he settlement of disputes arising in connection with the determination of terms and conditions of employment shall be sought [...] through negotiation between the parties or through independent and impartial machinery*". According to article 5 of the International Labour Convention no 154 of 1981, "*[m]easures adapted to national conditions shall be taken to promote collective bargaining*". From its part, Council of Europe's European Social Charter of 1961 (revised in 1996) refers to the right to bargain collectively (article 6) and to the right to social security (article 12)

One could also argue that salary cuts violate article 1 of the First Additional Protocol of the ECHR, which guarantees the protection of property rights. This concept also includes rights of pecuniary nature and acquired economic interests and legitimate claims expectations[64]. This is the case of the claims of the employee arising from the employment

---

[61] Court of Appeals at The Hague, N. V. Cabolent v. National Iranian Oil Co., 28.11.1968, Netherlands Yearbook of International Law, vol. 1970, p. 225

[62] "General working conditions shall be determined by law, supplemented by collective labour agreements contracted through free negotiations and, in case of the failure of such, by rules determined by arbitration."

[63] Hellenic Council of State (ΣτΕ), decision 632/1978.

[64] See Hellenic Supreme Court of Civil and Penal law, decisions 40/1998 and 33/2002.

relationship and from the collective agreement[65]. According to a variant of the principle "*lex non cogit ad impossibilia*" (the law does not compel the impossible), constitutional interpretation could not force the Greek government to maintain the same salary policy regardless of the absolute budgetary impossibility.

From a comparative law point of view, the issue of the constitutionality of pension cuts has also been raised in the jurisprudence of national constitutional courts. In Latvia, the Constitutional Court has declared unconstitutional the national law that imposed massive cuts in pensions[66], demanded by the EU/IMF program. According to this decision, the rights to receive pension disbursements are deemed as property rights in the meaning of article 105 of the Latvian Constitution. Moreover, the Latvian Court stated that the agreement with the IMF and the international commitments assumed by the government cannot by themselves serve as an argument for the restriction of the fundamental rights established by the Constitution. In Romania, the Constitutional Court has ruled that the law to cut pensions by 15% is unconstitutional[67]. Pursuant to that decision, the IMF announced that the next instalment of the loan to Romania would delay, until equivalent measures were adopted. In Hungary, the constitutional court struck down as unconstitutional a retroactive 98% tax on severance payments above a capped amount in the civil service[68]. The ruling suggested that there might be constitutional issues with the proposed reform on pension-fund contributions. Shortly afterwards, a constitutional amendment was passed in the Hungarian Parliament, curtailing the powers of the Hungarian Constitutional Court, which can no longer annul the budget, tax laws and import duties; it can only declare such laws unconstitutional, without having the powers to annul[69]. In France, a country that is not under IMF surveillance, the Constitutional

---

[65] Van der Mussele v. Belgium, of 23 November 1983, Series A no. 70, par. 48, Pine Valley Developments v. Ireland, of 29 November 1991, Series A no. 222, par. 51.

[66] Decision 2009-43-01 of 21.12.2009, available in English at the website of the Latvian Constitutional Court:
http://www.satv.tiesa.gov.lv/upload/judg__2009_43_01.htm

[67] Decision no. 873 of June 25, 2010, on the objection of unconstitutionality of the provisions of the Law on the establishment of measures related to pensions, Official Gazette, Part I, no. 433 of June 28, 2010 (in Romanian), available at: http://www.monitoruloficial.ro/

[68] Decision 184/2010 of 26 October 2010, available at the website of the Court (in Hungarian): http://mkab.hu/index.php?id=hatarozatkereso

[69] Financial Times (2010), Hungary curbs constitutional court's powers, November 16, 2010.

Council examined President Nicolas Sarkozy's pension bill (Loi portant réforme des retraites) in November 2010 and held that it was not contrary to the Constitution[70]. The law imposed a raise of the retirement age by two years, but there were no pension cuts.

In the Greek legal system, the Greek supreme administrative court (Council of State)[71] reviewed the constitutionality of the Memoranda. According to the report of the two judges-rapporteurs, the Memorandum itself contains no rule of law and therefore has no legal effect. Furthermore, the Memorandum is not an international treaty within the meaning of the Vienna Convention on the Law of Treaties. The Law 3845/2010 needs not to be approved pursuant to article 28 par. 2 Const. (qualified majority of 3/5), because the Memorandum is not an international agreement. Moreover, the Law 3845/2010 did not transfer powers to international organizations, limiting the exercise of national sovereignty. As far as article 1 of the Protocol to the ECHR is concerned, the right to pension and salary is protected as a property right; however, the limitation of that right (cuts pursuant to the Law 3833/2010 and the Law 3845/2010) is justified by reasons of public interest, i.e. the need to reduce the excessive budget deficit and the external debt. Finally, the contested regulation is not found contrary to the principle of proportionality.

B. 5. The EU/IMF Rescue Mechanism as an Asymmetric Bankruptcy Framework

The loss of the creditworthiness of the Greek government at the beginning of 2010 was the triggering event for the creation of the mechanism to support the Greek economy in the spring of 2010. The state faces a huge public debt, the servicing of which (without new loans) would absorb almost all tax revenue. The national economy as a whole faces an even bigger foreign debt and continuing massive deficits in the balance account. In essence, Greece is a quasi-bankrupt country with a negative past record[72]. The question is who will manage the bankruptcy, how it will be done, and who shall bear most of its consequences.

---

[70] Décision n° 2010-617 du 09 novembre 2010, Journal officiel du 10 novembre 2010, p. 20056 ff.

[71] See Council of State (ΣτΕ) Press Release of 19.11.2010 on the cases concerning the Memorandum [Cases 6192/2010 and 6770/2015].

[72] See C. Reinhart / K. Rogoff, This Time Is Different, op. cit. p. 99 ff. According to these authors, Greece, Ecuador and Honduras are among the few countries that have spent more than half of their existence in a state of sovereign bankruptcy or debt restructuring. According to the same study (p. 121), from 1827 to 2003,

The mechanism "*to support the Greek economy*," as the Law 3845/2010 is entitled, is a misnomer. It is in fact a support mechanism for foreign financial institutions that were unreasonably lending money to the Greek government in the past and now see their balance sheets weakened for that reason. Through this mechanism, Greece temporarily ensured repayment of those loans that would expire until the middle of 2011, despite the failure of Greece to borrow from capital markets. In other words, through the support mechanism, private creditors of the Greek state, banks and other financial institutions were substituted by member states of the eurozone and the IMF. Thus, foreign banks were exempted from the risk they had towards them as a sovereign debtor country (the so-called sovereign risk), and the latter would henceforth be faced with other states, for much part of its debt.

Obviously, a failure to meet legal obligations according to the Loan Agreement would be incomparably more difficult than a standstill and a restructuring of debt owed to private creditors. In this case, the heavily indebted Greek government will have to deal with other sovereign states and with the IMF. The situation would be diplomatically delicate and perplexing, even if it were not for the "*leonine*" conditions of the Loan Facility Agreement that have already been discussed (see above, II).

The EU/IMF mechanism is intended, therefore, to the asymmetric repayment of creditors of the (de facto) bankrupt Greek government. This is a bewildering complete reversal of the principle of equitable treatment / "symmetric" recovery that determines the institution of commercial bankruptcy. The lenders are satisfied in full (principal and interest), at least in the case of loans maturing in the near future. On the contrary, the lenders in kind, i.e. those who have credited the state with their labour force (civil servants and workers) or their social security contributions (retired) and forced contributors, i.e. the taxpayers, bear the entire burden of the fiscal adjustment. The paradox is that these are all voters, in contrast with most creditors that get preferential treatment (since the overwhelming majority of the debt is due, directly or indirectly, to foreign creditors). This paradox is an indication of the quality of the Greek democracy, i.e., how limited is the real influence of the electorate in making key political decisions.

A restructuring could be a means to achieve a minimally equitable sharing of the burden of fiscal adjustment among the Greek people and the

---

European countries in default had a ratio of public debt to public revenues of 4:1. In Latin American states the ratio was 5:1. In 2009, Greek public revenues (excluding loans) amounted to 50 billion euros; external debt was about 300 billion. Thus, the ratio debt to revenues was at least 6:1.

creditors of the Greek government. The fact that the EU/IMF mechanism attributed all the consequences of the debt crisis to the Greek people was primarily unjust and unequal. Responsibility does not lie solely on the Greek voters who vote their rulers, who borrowed irresponsibly and thoughtlessly in recent decades. Responsibility also lies with shareholders of foreign financial institutions, who voted their administrations, who lent money in an equally irresponsible manner and contrary to the Keynesian concept of sound banking[73]. The expression "*moral hazard*" describes such a distortion of incentives, whereby there are no consequences (p. ex. write-offs of loans, reduction of net present value, etc.) for risky investment decisions[74].

B. 6. Towards a Greek Debt Restructuring with Bond "*Haircut*"

The restructuring of the Greek debt ultimately proved to be unavoidable due to the financial distress of the Greek state[75]. In fact, "*even if the IMF programme were to be implemented to the letter, the Greek debt-to-GDP ratio is projected to rise to 150% by 2013. Assuming an interest rate of 5%, Greece would have to pay every year 7.5% of its GDP to bond holders. With over 80% of creditors being foreign by then, the country would transfer over 6% of its GDP abroad*"[76].

---

[73] J. M. Keynes (1931), The Consequences to the Banks of the Collapse of Money Values, Essays in Persuasion, Macmillan Publishers, pp. 176-178.

[74] See among others B. Eichengreen (2000), Can the Moral Hazard of IMF Bailouts be Reduced?, Geneva Reports on the World Economy, Special Report 1/2000, p. 17; H. Scott (2003), A Bankruptcy Procedure for Sovereign Debtors? Symposium: International Company and Securities Law, International Lawyer, vol. 37, p. 113 ff.

[75] The principle of "*fiscal impossibility*" as a ground for non-payment of foreign loans in international law is questionable; see BVerfGE vol.118, p. 124 ff. As far as "*force majeure*" is concerned, there are no cases in international debt litigation where its restrictive conditions are considered to have been met; see T. Walde (2004), The Sanctity of Debt and Insolvent Countries : Defense of Debtors in International Loan Agreements, Transnational Dispute Management, vol. 1, issue 2 , p. 142 ff. ; J. Perillo (1996), Hardship and its Impact on Contractual Obligations : A Comparative Analysis, Centro di Studi e Ricerche di Diritto Comparato e Straniero, no. 20, p. 9.

[76] D. Gros / T. Mayer (2010), How to Deal with Sovereign Default in Europe: Create the European Monetary Fund now!, CEPS Policy Brief, No. 202/February 2010, p. 1.

Restructuring may take the form of a rescheduling (longer maturities) or a reduction of the principal amounts (haircut) or of the interest rate[77]. Given the seniority status of multilateral official debt (IMF, World Bank, multilateral development banks), the risk of restructuring mainly affects the bondholders[78]. In practice, a restructuring is generally sought on a consensual basis and bondholders compromise in order to secure the payment of interest on their bonds[79]. For instance, in the case of Argentina, bondholders accepted a haircut of 73% in the exchange offer 2005, followed by a haircut of 66.3% in the exchange offer of 2010[80]. Such a restructuring is a consensual modification of the initial terms of the loan, where the existing debt instruments are exchanged for the newly issued, modified ones. If the bonds contain collective action clauses (as in the case of Greek debt), the approval of the restructuring by a qualified majority of bondholders is appreciably facilitated[81].

The question is whether restructuring could also be applied by unilateral government action. From a contractual point of view, similar unilateral measures would constitute breaches of the loan contract. Unilateral action imposing a haircut would also be contrary to article 1 of the First Protocol to the ECHR. In any event, the debt holders would not stay passive, but would doubtless take legal action against the debtor (litigation/arbitration)[82], according to the terms of the loan. Clearly, the

---

[77] On restructuring mechanisms see G. Pavlidis (2006), La défaillance d'Etat, Athens, p. 124 ff.

[78] R. Monteros (1995), *Les dettes publiques des Etats à l'égard des organisations internationales*, in: D. Carreau / M. Shaw [ed.], *La dette extérieure / The external debt*, The Hague Academy of International Law, Recueil des Cours - Colloques, vol. 17, Martinus Nijhoff Publishers, The Hague, p. 260 and 270.

[79] D. Carreau (1985), Le rééchelonnement de la dette extérieure des Etats, Journal du Droit International, tome 112 (1985) p. 5 ff.

[80] R. Buckley (2010), The Bankruptcy of Nations: Let the Law Reflect Reality, Banking and Financial Services Policy Report, vol. 29, no. 6, p. 1 ff.; G. Gomez-Giglio (2005), A New Chapter in the Argentine Saga: The Restructuring of the Argentine Sovereign Debt, Journal of International Banking Law and Regulation, vol. 20(7), p. 345 ff.

[81] R. Olivares-Caminal (2009), Is There a Need for an International Insolvency Regime in the Context of Sovereign Debt? A Case for the Use of Corporate Debt Restructuring Techniques, Journal of International Banking Law and Regulation, vol. 24(1), p. 21 ff., p. 33.

[82] L. Palacios (2003), Argentina: EM Ltd. recent legal success is seen as increasing the likelihood of investors resorting to more litigation instead of negotiation, Japan Bank for International Cooperation: Latin American Update memorandums, September 2003, p. 2.

reputation risk, i.e. the risk of losing access to international capital markets, remains the decisive factor that discourages unilateral action from the part of the debtor[83].

In the case of Greece, there is an additional factor that hinders unilateral action in the future. By accepting English law as the applicable law of the Loan Facility Agreement, Greece casts off a valuable tool for an eventual debt restructuring. Indeed, a considerable part of Greek debt instruments (approximately 90%) are governed by Greek law. Consequently, in case of debt renegotiation, the Greek government would be able to change the national legal framework affecting the terms of repayment and the rights of the bondholders. This possibility would reinforce Greece's bargaining position and its legal arsenal in case of default, but it is no longer available under the EU/IMF support mechanism.

B. 7. Legal Implications of a Withdrawal (or Expulsion) from the Economic and Monetary Union

The Greek government has affirmed its commitment to maintain its EU Economic and Monetary Union (hereinafter: EMU) membership. Nevertheless, the severe debt crisis has questioned Greece's ability to remain in the eurozone. If the financial situation worsens, there are three scenarios that may occur: 1. a unilateral withdrawal from EMU, including the Stability and Growth Pact, 2. an *ad hoc* negotiated withdrawal or 3. an expulsion from the EMU. More specifically:

1. The primary law of the EU does not recognize a legal right of unilateral withdrawal from the EMU, although, in practice, this may be a matter of necessity. In exceptional cases sovereign states can adopt an "*actus contrarius*," repealing an agreement and reclaiming the conferred authority[84]. However, all the parties to the agreement should give their consent; otherwise, the principle of "*pacta sunt servanda*" would be violated. The unilateral withdrawal from the EMU, though inconsistent

[83] H. Grossman / J. van Huyck (1988), Sovereign Debt as a Contingent Claim: Excusable Default, Repudiation, and Reputation, American Economic Review, vol. 78, no. 5 (December 1988) p. 1088 ff, p. 1097.

[84] P. Karolewski, H. Kleger, M. Munke (2001), Europäische Verfassung Zum Stand der europäischen Demokratie im Zuge der Osterweiterung, LIT Verlag, Münster 2001, p. 439; K. Doehring (1993), Staat und Verfassung in einem zusammenwachsenden Europa, Zeitschrift für Rechtspolitik 1993, p. 98 ff, p. 99; R. Barents (2004), The Autonomy of Community Law, Kluwer Law International, p. 236 note 99, making a reference to Carl Schmitt's "Dezisionismus".

with the terms of the EU primary law, could also be based on public international law, in particular the Vienna Convention on the Law of Treaties. Under article 62 of the Vienna Convention ("*clausula rebus sic stantibus*"), a fundamental and unforeseen change of the circumstances, which were an essential basis of the parties' consent, can justify non-performance, if the change radically transforms the extent of the parties' obligations under the treaty. In the case of the Greek debt crisis, it seems that these conditions are met. Nevertheless, the main question is whether the "*sui generis*" nature of the EU would limit the role of the Vienna Convention in the EU legal order and, possibly, exclude the application of article 62.

2. The exit clause in the Lisbon Treaty (article 50 TEU[85]) deals with the negotiated secession of a member state, but does not provide for a withdrawal only from the EMU. Applying article 50 TEU by analogy could lead to a negotiated withdrawal from the EMU, although the legislative gap is undeniably too significant to be filled in this rather improvised manner. A negotiated withdrawal could also be possible via the "*actus contrarius*". Such a negotiated agreement would have to be followed by a Treaty amendment. A negotiated solution offers legal and practical advantages. For instance, Greece would disengage in an orderly manner from the financial and institutional structures of the EMU. The negotiations could address issues, such as Greece's subscription to the ECB's capital, its contribution to the foreign reserve assets of the Eurosystem, the termination of pending excessive deficit procedures for Greece, the termination of the open market and credit operations carried out by Greek central bank in the context of the Eurosystem, etc.

3. There is no treaty provision and no collective right of expulsion from the EMU. Nonetheless, some indirect avenues have been identified, in order to isolate the errant Member State, for example the extensive use of the enhanced co-operation procedure (article 20 TEU) and the radical

---

[85] According to article 50 par. 1 and 2 TEU, "*1. Any Member State may decide to withdraw from the Union in accordance with its own constitutional requirements. 2. A Member State which decides to withdraw shall notify the European Council of its intention. In the light of the guidelines provided by the European Council, the Union shall negotiate and conclude an agreement with that State, setting out the arrangements for its withdrawal, taking account of the framework for its future relationship with the Union. That agreement shall be negotiated in accordance with Article 218(3) of the Treaty on the Functioning of the European Union. It shall be concluded on behalf of the Union by the Council, acting by a qualified majority, after obtaining the consent of the European Parliament.*"

solution of a new (treaty-based) partnership "*outside the framework of the old EU*"[86].

A withdrawal from the EMU would have numerous legal and practical implications for Greece. First of all, a new domestic currency would have to be adopted, printed and put in circulation. The Greek central bank (Bank of Greece) would re-assume the responsibility of conducting monetary policy. A conversion rate would need to be fixed and the markets would immediately put it to the test. When a country opts for a flexible exchange rate regime, it always faces the risk of an output collapse and considerable depreciation of the exchange rate[87]. The (inescapable) devaluation of the new currency against the euro would provoke liquidity shortages and high lending interest rates, due to the devaluation of the assets of the Greek banking sector[88].

Another key issue associated with the adoption of a new currency is the re-denomination of contracts, including bond contracts. Debt instruments denominated in Euros and governed by the Greek law would be exposed to this risk. Debt instruments denominated in Euros and governed by foreign (non-Greek) law would not be affected, except if Greece introduces exchange controls. Hence, as far as the EU/IMF rescue package is concerned, Greece has to repay the loan in Euros, even if the country withdraws from the EMU and adopts a new national currency.

C. The Greek Debt Crisis Revisited: A Tragedy Without a Catharsis?

Undoubtedly, the coming issue in the management of financial crises will be the "*massive buildup of public debt*"[89]. The EU/IMF support mechanism is a temporary *ad hoc* solution, a limited response to the insolvency problem. Clearly, a new international mechanism for sovereign debt restructuring could offer more practical and equitable solutions, since the debt crisis constitutes a global and systemic problem. A new sovereign

---

[86] P. Athanassiou (2009), Withdrawal and Expulsion from the EU and EMU: Some Reflections, ECB, Legal Working Paper Series No. 10 / december 2009, p. 36.

[87] A. Asıcı (2010), Parametric and Non-Parametric Approaches to Exits from Fixed Exchange Rate Regimes, International Journal of Finance & Economics, vol. 15. p. 381 ff.

[88] M.G. Arghyrou / J. Tsoukalas (2010), The Greek Debt Crisis: Likely Causes, Mechanics and Outcomes, Cardiff Business School, Cardiff Economics Working Papers, E2010/3, p. 17.

[89] N. Roubini (2010), Greece Is Tip of Sovereign Debt Iceberg, The Evolving World Order, Summer 2010, p. 37 ff.

bankruptcy framework would be beneficial to the international financial system and to the debtor countries, including Greece[90].

As the Greek debt crisis unfolds, the effects of the Law 3845/2010 and the Loan Facility Agreement in the national legal order remain controversial. On the one hand, the Loan Facility Agreement seems to put in jeopardy the necessary instruments of Greek national sovereignty[91]; the scope of Greece's waiver of immunity exemplifies this risk. On the other hand, the compatibility of salary and pension cuts with the Greek Constitution and international law is questionable.

In practice, the EU/IMF support to Greece is an asymmetric bankruptcy mechanism, which temporarily ensures repayment of the loans that expire in medium-term. So, the Greek government and the (remaining) bondholders had to seek a negotiated solution, in a form of a consensual restructuring with a bond haircut. The success of such a restructuring always depends on the consensus of the implicated parties and, to a great extent, on the existence of collective action clauses in the bond contracts.

Greece also risks having to quit the EMU, if the rescue program fails and is discontinued. From a legal point of view, such a withdrawal is unprecedented and moves dangerously into uncharted waters. For the success of a withdrawal from the EMU, a negotiated solution would be indispensable, as in the case of the restructuring.

All these risks should not be underestimated by investors and policy makers. The recession may deepen, as the service of the Greek debt rapidly drains more and more financial resources, creating a vicious circle. Furthermore, since social groups are rigid bodies, not susceptible to sudden changes, it is likely that drastic cuts in public expenditure will lead to social breakdown and ultimately to major social unrest and political instability[92]. The EU, facing the dilemma of being "*a monetary union but not a full-fledged economic and political union*," has to move towards

---

[90] H. Scott (2003), A Bankruptcy Procedure for Sovereign Debtors? Symposium: International Company and Securities Law, International Lawyer, vol. 37, p. 103 ff.

[91] The loan agreement should have probably clarified which types of property are used solely or principally for official purposes.

[92] P. Fallon / R. Lucas (2002), The Impact of Financial Crises on Labor Markets, Household Incomes, and Poverty, The World Bank Research Observer, vol. 17, no. 1, p. 21 ff.

stronger economic coordination[93], but it remains to be seen whether Greece will be able to keep up the pace.

The uncertainties remain and surround the implementation of the new program for Greece, according to the decisions of the Eurozone Summit held on 26.10.2011. This recent development has important implications. The Member States of the eurozone, the IMF and the private sector will try to cover the existing financing gap and help the Greek government meet its borrowing needs until mid-2014. The program provides for lower interest rates, extended maturities and a menu of options for the involvement of the private sector on a voluntary basis.

Nevertheless, the success of the new program depends on too many factors, external conditions and chance events. Internal conflicts within the EU, political uncertainties, recession deeper than expected in Greece, unforeseen delays in the implementation of the program, self-fulfilling market opinions and instability of the financial markets may hamper Greece's chances of coming out of the crisis. It is still unclear whether the EU policy response and the measures undertaken by the Greek government can alleviate all these risks, in order for Greece to overcome this unprecedented debt crisis.

---

[93] J. Pisani-Ferry / A. Sapir (2009), Weathering the Storm: Fair Weather versus Stormy-Weather Governance in the Euro Area, Bruegel Policy Contributions, no. 286, p. 5 ff.; H. Van Rompuy (2010), Lessons from a Crisis: Reflections on Economic Governance for Europe, European View, vol. 9 p. 133 ff, p. 138.

PART 3:

CRITICAL HISTORICAL DEVELOPMENTS

CHAPTER EIGHT

THE STABILITY AND GROWTH PACT

BITZENIS P. ARISTIDIS
AND MAKEDOS IOANNIS

Introduction

It is significant to note that at present, of the 27 member states of the European Union (EU) only 17 (Austria, Belgium, Cyprus, Finland, France, Germany, Greece, Ireland, Italy, Luxembourg, Malta, the Netherlands, Portugal, Slovakia, Slovenia, Estonia and Spain) are members of the Economic and Monetary Union (EMU). Three European microstates (Monaco, San Marino and the Vatican City) have made agreements with the EU, which allows them to use euro as their official currency and to mint coins. However, they are neither formally part of the eurozone nor represented on the board of the European Central Bank. Physical coins and banknotes (real circulation of them) were introduced on 1 January 2002. Five states entered the eurozone after 2006. Slovenia qualified in 2006 and was admitted on 1 January 2007. Cyprus and Malta qualified in 2007 and were admitted on 1 January 2008. Slovakia qualified in 2008 and joined on 1 January 2009. Estonia joined the eurozone on 1.1.2011. These 17 member states bring 330 million people to the eurozone.

If a country wishes to join the EU, it must meet the Copenhagen criteria, which are mainly political, social and administrative, and to a lesser degree economic. If a country wishes to join the EMU, it must, first of all, be a member of EU and then meet the Maastricht criteria, which are solely economic. Below are quoted the 5 Maastricht criteria. The first two are financial, whereas the others are monetary. A member state of EMU (i.e. a member state of the EU that belongs to the eurozone) must obey the rules outlined in the Stability and Growth Pact (SGP).

Ten countries (Bulgaria, the Czech Republic, Denmark, Hungary, Latvia, Lithuania, Poland, Romania, Sweden, and the United Kingdom) are EU members, but do not use the euro. Prior to joining the eurozone, a state must participate two years in the European Exchange Rate Mechanism (ERM) II. Since 1 January 2009, the National Central Banks (NCBs) of Estonia, Latvia, Lithuania, and Denmark (from 1 January 1999) have been participating in ERM II. The remaining currencies are expected to follow as soon as they meet the criteria and no target date has been declared, with the exception of Estonia which joined the EMU on 1 January 2011, making it the 17th member country of the EMU. Denmark and the United Kingdom obtained special opt-outs from the original Maastricht Treaty. Both countries are legally exempt from joining the eurozone unless their governments decide otherwise, either by parliamentary vote or by referendum.

Short Description Regarding the Maastricht Criteria

As mentioned in Bitzenis (2009), the four Maastricht convergence criteria – or five, if we consider separately the budgetary discipline, thus the annual government deficit over gross domestic product (GDP) ratio and the ratio of gross government debt to GDP – are presented in Article 121(1) of the Treaty establishing the European Community (EC Treaty). They are set out in the Protocol on the convergence criteria referred to in Article 121 of the EC Treaty and reflect the degree of economic convergence that Member States must achieve. The Maastricht Treaty has been amended by the treaties of Amsterdam, Nice and Lisbon. The Lisbon Treaty was signed by the EU Member States on 13 December 2007 and entered into force on 1 December 2009. It amends the Maastricht Treaty and the Treaty establishing the European Community. Each Member State must satisfy all the criteria in order to be able to participate in the third stage of the EMU:

- The Treaty stipulates that the inflation rate of a given Member State must not have exceeded more than 1½% the average of the three best-performing Member States in terms of price stability during the year preceding the examination of the situation in that Member State.
- The nominal long-term interest rate must not have exceeded by more than 2% the average of the three best-performing Member States in terms of price stability. The period taken into consideration is the year preceding the examination of the situation in the Member State concerned.
- The ratio of the annual government deficit to GDP must not have exceeded 3% at the end of the preceding financial year. If this is not the case, the ratio must decline substantially and continuously and reach a level close to 3% (interpretation in trend terms

according to Article 104(2)) or alternatively, it must remain close to 3% while representing only an exceptional and temporary excess.

- The ratio of gross government debt to GDP must not have exceeded 60% at the end of the preceding financial year. If this is not the case, the ratio must sufficiently diminish and must approach the reference value at a satisfactory pace (interpretation in trend terms according to Article 104(2)).
- The Member State must have participated in the ERM of the European Monetary System (EMS) without any break during the two years preceding the examination of the situation and without severe tensions.
- Last but not least, each of the Member States should ensure compatibility of their national legislation with that of Articles 108 and 109 of the Treaty and the Statute of the European System of Central Banks (<http://europa.eu.int/scadplus/leg/en/lvb/l25014.htm>).

Table 1 presents the total government debt as percentage of GDP from 2000 up to 2010. Greece has the biggest debt in the eurozone from 2000 up to 2010 (108.9% in 2000 and 147.8% in 2010) and the second biggest in the Organisation of Economic Co-operation and Development (OECD) after Japan (183.5% in 2009). During these years (2000-2010), it seems that the Greek governments had not done anything to reduce the central government debt or they have done but they failed.

The Significance of SGP

As it has also been pointed out in Bitzenis (2009), the SGP is the concrete EU answer to concerns on the continuation of budgetary discipline in the EMU. Political agreement on the pact was reached at the Dublin European Council in December 1996. During initial negotiations leading up to the establishment of the pact, ironically enough, Germany was the main driving force pushing for rigid rules and strict regulations. The European Council called on the Council of Ministers to draw up a resolution on the SGP, which was adopted by the Amsterdam European Council on 17 June 1997. The SGP strengthened the European Community Treaty provisions on fiscal discipline in the EMU foreseen in Articles 99 and 104 (the amendments were adopted in 1993 in Maastricht). The full provisions took effect when the euro was launched in the third stage of the EMU on 1 January 1999 (Beetsma and Uhlig, 1997). The SGP was built on the convergence criteria, whose Member States have to fulfil in order to join the single Euro currency.

Table 1: Total Central Government Debt (% of GDP)

Dataset: Central Government Debt

Variable	Total central government debt % of GDP										
Type	Stocks: Outstanding amounts										
Unit	Percentage										
Frequency	Annual										
Time period	2000	2001	2002	2003	2004	2005	2006	2007	2008	2009	2010
Country											
Australia	11,361	9,552	8,576	7,549	6,716	6,312	5,76	5,181	4,922	8,195	10,966
Austria	61,188	60,659	60,401	60,882	62,242	62,116	60,434	57,829	59,319	64,916	65,754
Belgium	99,542	99,125	97,948	95,395	92,763	91,774	87,568	85,295	90,094	94,893	96,789
Canada	40,863	39,713	38,091	35,853	32,109	30,235	27,934	25,183	28,642	35,716	36,073
Chile	13,642	14,924	15,675	13,001	10,684	7,282	5,264	4,097	5,173	6,228	9,185
Czech Republic	13,216	14,669	16,064	19,137	21,064	23,164	24,904	25,24	27,102	32,496	36,625
Denmark	54,809	52,02	51,623	49,608	46,958	39,292	32,715	27,765	32,318	37,891	39,59
Estonia	3,336	2,925	3,555	3,141	2,634	2,091	1,836	1,319	1,761	3,55	3,227
Finland	48,017	44,368	41,279	43,544	41,925	38,17	35,561	31,201	29,452	37,549	41,683
France	47,417	48,346	49,941	51,88	52,561	53,275	52,131	52,118	53,406	61,231	67,418
Germany	38,357	36,452	37,164	38,48	39,862	40,832	41,232	39,55	39,55	44,205	44,403
Greece	108,926	109,684	109,199	105,777	108,624	110,572	107,675	105,674	110,617	127,022	147,839
Hungary	54,052	50,431	53,532	56,203	55,673	58,103	61,971	61,551	67,668	72,79	73,898
Iceland	33,83	39,238	35,26	33,327	28,179	19,378	24,807	23,237	44,175	87,473	81,257
Ireland	34,766	30,892	27,869	26,863	25,343	23,524	20,253	19,834	28,001	47,074	60,703
Israel	83,38	87,836	95,349	97,813	96,64	92,102	82,659	75,948	75,307	77,693	74,714
Italy	103,576	102,658	99,543	96,699	96,313	97,656	97,454	95,627	98,093	106,778	109,015
Japan	106,118	123,521	137,61	140,896	156,805	164,498	161,806	164,546	180,783	183,53	..
Korea	16,733	17,365	17,574	20,704	23,714	27,595	30,065	29,651	29,027	32,558	31,935
Luxembourg	3,17	3,092	2,678	1,686	1,428	0,821	1,458	1,419	8,153	8,489	12,578
Mexico	21,201	20,511	21,908	22,07	20,745	20,295	20,583	20,861	24,369	28,086	27,46
Netherlands	44,094	41,317	41,455	42,957	43,752	42,952	39,169	37,552	50,068	49,719	51,845
New Zealand	32,143	30,067	28,4	26,352	23,734	22,069	21,58	20,343	20,721	27,53	30,45
Norway	19,303	18,134	18,994	21,322	18,402	17,173	12,473	11,681	13,905	26,363	26,077
Poland	35,844	36,423	40,553	44,944	43,574	44,764	45,143	42,62	44,686	47,015	49,679
Portugal	52,103	54,012	56,71	58,299	60,97	66,194	67,732	66,622	68,88	78,73	87,962
Slovak Republic	23,875	36,009	35,031	35,069	38,405	33,103	29,164	28,108	26,342	33,749	39,078
Slovenia	..	..	..	26,871	27,063	26,9	25,782	23,207	21,188	33,628	36,023
Spain	49,872	46,274	43,942	40,68	39,268	36,36	32,965	30,019	33,695	46,026	51,693
Sweden	56,887	48,625	46,781	47,712	46,612	46,232	42,242	36,406	35,56	38,098	33,782
Switzerland	25,614	24,822	28,178	28,262	28,066	28,102	25,195	23,216	22,376	20,723	20,24
Turkey	38,184	74,06	69,239	62,185	56,621	51,087	45,498	39,551	40,011	46,35	42,851
United Kingdom	42,153	38,788	39,131	38,667	40,023	43,523	43,185	42,744	61,059	75,27	85,535
United States	33,896	32,408	33,204	34,865	36,044	36,149	36,039	35,703	40,183	53,573	61,274

data extracted on 29 Jul 2012 18:22 UTC (GMT) from OECD.Stat

Source: Total Central Government Debt (%) of GDP, OECD National Accounts Statistics (2012) (http://stats.oecd.org/Index.aspx?DatasetCode=GOV_DEBT)

The SGP established a system for the coordination and surveillance of national budgetary policies. The countries adopting the single currency were required to submit an annual stability programme. All public deficits (budgetary, social and those derived from local authority deficits) could not exceed the 3% of GDP threshold. A relatively broad margin was given to a member state to adjust its budgetary policy in accordance with its economic climate.

Initially, based on the old SGP rules, every EU member state should undertake to abide to the medium-term budgetary objective of positions close to balance or in surplus and to undertake not to invoke the exceptional nature of a deficit linked to an annual fall in the GDP of less than 2%, unless they are in severe recession (annual fall in real GDP of at least 0.75%). The council is committed to rigorous and timely implementation of all provisions of the SGP within its competence. In addition, it is urged to regard the deadlines for the application of the excessive deficit procedure (EDP) as upper limits; it is imperative that they impose sanctions if a participating member state fails to take the necessary steps to bring the excessive deficit situation to an end and to apply rigorously the whole range of sanctions provided for. However, we must state in writing the reasons that justify a decision not to be acted on.

Procedure of Sanctions According to the SGP

The Maastricht Treaty (Article 104) obliges Member States to avoid excessive budgetary deficits. In particular, Member States shall comply with budgetary discipline by meeting two criteria: a deficit to the GDP ratio must not exceed the reference value of 3% and a debt to the GDP ratio must not exceed the reference value of 60%, as it is defined in the Protocol of the EDP. The EDP is responsible for identifying and countering such excessive deficits, including the possibility to impose financial sanctions. For this to become a more effective deterrent, the SGP clarified and speeded up the excessive deficit procedure, in particular with Council Regulation 1467/97 (see also Bitzenis 2009).

Until March 2005 (after which decisive revisions to the SGP took place), the Commission was responsible for the surveillance procedure. It asked the Member States to provide it with the necessary information, analysed it and then submitted a report to the Economic and Financial Committee, which delivered its opinion. The Commission addressed a recommendation to the Ecofin Council, which then took a decision by a qualified majority vote. If a member state exceeded the 3% threshold, the Ecofin Council would address a recommendation to the Member State in breach of the EDP procedure. If this proved insufficient, sanctions adjusted to the State's national economy would be imposed. A recession above 2% of GDP would be recognized as an exceptional case and sanctions would not be imposed. The Ecofin Council would carry out an assessment for recessions of between 0.75% and 2%. In the case of recessions of less than 0.75%, the member state at fault would not be able to invoke exceptional circumstances and non-pecuniary sanctions would be imposed. The Ecofin Council may require the member state in question to do the following: publish additional information before issuing bonds and securities, ask the European Investment Bank to reconsider its lending policy towards the member state concerned, request the member state concerned to make a non-interest-bearing deposit until the excessive deficit has been corrected, and impose fines of an appropriate size.

When the Council decides that an excessive deficit does exist, it makes recommendations to the member state concerned and establishes a deadline of four months for effective corrective action to be taken. In the absence of special circumstances, such action is that which ensures completion of the correction of the excessive deficit in the year following its identification. If, after a progressive notice procedure, the member state fails to comply with the Council's decisions, the Council usually decides to impose sanctions, at the latest, ten to twelve months after the reporting of the data, indicating that an excessive deficit exists. Sanctions first take the form of a non-interest-bearing deposit to the Commission. The amount of this deposit comprises a fixed component equal to 0.2% of the GDP and a variable component linked to the size of the deficit. Each following year, the Council may decide to increase the sanctions by requiring an additional deposit, though the annual amount of deposits may not exceed the upper limit of 0.5% of the GDP.

A deposit as a rule is converted into a fine if, in the view of the Council, the excessive deficit has not been corrected after two years. The Council may decide to abrogate some or all of the sanctions, depending on the significance of the progress made by the participating Member State to correct the excessive deficit. The Council will abrogate all outstanding sanctions if the decision on the existence of an excessive deficit is itself abrogated. However, any fines already imposed are not reimbursable. Interest on the deposits lodge with the Commission, and the yield from fines is distributed among those Member States without an excessive deficit, in proportion to their share in the total GDP of eligible member states.

A Short Criticism of the SGP

A criticism for the implementation of the Maastricht Treaty and the SGP points to the unbalanced emphasis on the budget deficit. The term Excessive Deficit Procedure in fact illustrates that the second reference value, which keeps public debt below the limit of 60% of GDP, has been left completely in the shadow (Buti et al., 2003). A valid explanation is that had the debt criteria been omitted, it might have been that certain Member States at that time would have public debt levels far above the 60% threshold. The Commission and the Council possibly considered that any discussion whatsoever about the enormous divergence of the debt levels among member states and any attempts to find valid arguments to admit Belgium and Italy into the EMU, despite their debt level, would simply be too complicated to cope with for the political establishment. Consequently, the focus was put on the deficit and it was argued, somewhat against the spirit of the Treaty provisions, that Belgium and Italy were 'on track' to reduce the level of their debt (see also Bitzenis 2009).

Admittedly, while deficits are difficult to forecast and final data comes only with a considerable delay, forecasts for debt are even less reliable and subject to even more controversy. They are revised several times even after publication, to some extent due to revaluation of items of public debt, which are not directly influenced by the budget balance (Tamborini and Targetti, 2005).

More emphasis, however, on the debt criteria would also make it possible to take a more explicit account of cross-country differences with respect to the potential rate of growth. Countries with a higher potential rate of growth (notably low-income countries with a potential for reducing a productivity gap vis-à-vis the high income countries) could be allowed to run a higher budget deficit and yet respect the debt limit. For high income countries with a lower potential rate of growth of productivity and low growth of the labour force (notably, Germany), respecting the debt limit would involve keeping the budget deficit well below the limit of 3% fixed in the Maastricht protocol (Eichengreen et al., 1998).

The SGP treats all states the same without regard to their underlying fiscal institutions. The Pact should recognize explicitly that the debt-to-GDP ratio is more important than the deficit-to-GDP ratio and that the appropriate budgetary position will vary from country to country. Highly indebted countries should be required to balance their budgets or even run surpluses to reduce their debt ratios at a satisfactory pace. In determining the appropriate path for public debt, it is wise for policy-makers to take into account the need for higher public investment in some countries (especially in many of the new Member States), as well as future liabilities (in particular, as a result of aging populations). France and Germany may have breached the rules of the Pact, but fiscal policy has not been conducted irresponsibly. The rise in the euro area's budget deficit in the past years (2003–2006) has been largely due to the effects of the economic cycle. By allowing the automatic stabilizers to work to their fullest capacity, governments have helped to cushion the decrease in economic activity rather than exacerbate it.

Unlike the United States, France and Germany do not have 'twin deficit' (fiscal and current account) problems. If the deficit limit of 3% of the GDP had been strictly enforced, a much greater burden would have been placed on the European Central Bank to use monetary policy to support the economy. This would hardly have been sensible, since the interest rates are already at historic low levels. By requiring each country to achieve cyclically adjusted budgets 'close to balance or in surplus,' the Pact treats each country the same despite the very different ratios of government debt to GDP across the euro zone. The balanced budget rule implies a decline in debt ratios toward zero, which makes little economic sense and even less political sense. The rule takes no account of the fact that public investment can be added to a country's assets as well as to its debts. The Pact is asymmetric and therefore fails to make proper allowance for cyclical effects. Once the deficit breaches 3% of the GDP, Member States are expected to eliminate the 'excessive deficit' the year after it is identified, with little regard to the stage of its economic cycle. Conversely, the Pact is not forceful enough to require fiscal consolidation during good times.

It was recognized that the loss of the exchange rate instrument in the EMU would imply a greater role for automatic fiscal stabilizers at the national level in order to help economies adjust to asymmetric shocks and would make it 'necessary to ensure that national budgetary policies support stability oriented monetary policies.' This is the rationale behind the core commitment of the SGP, i.e. to set the "medium-term objective of budgetary positions close to balance or in surplus", which "will allow all Member States to deal with normal cyclical fluctuations while keeping the government deficit within the reference value of 3% of GDP" (Papademos, 2003).

Deductively, the SGP has been as widely criticized as acclaimed. Commission President Romano Prodi has called it "stupid, because it is rigid," while others believe that it is "one of the most remarkable pieces of policy coordination in world history." Most probably, the truth lies somewhere in between because if each country kept its budget in equilibrium, the aggregate budget position of the EMU would also be balanced. Automatic stabilizers could contribute to smooth down the business cycle and the European Central Bank (ECB) has sufficient margins for the fine-tuning of monetary policy. Calculations by the European Commission have shown that under normal conditions the 3% margin of avoiding excessive deficits was sufficient to ensure the unconstrained functioning of automatic stabilizers, provided that the structural budget objective was followed. However, in reality, the Eurozone's structural budget has never been in balance. With the exception of 1999 and 2000 (when it was lower), industrial balance has remained at an average deficit around 2.3%–2.8%. Countries such as Germany and France argued that the deterioration in the business climate after 2001 prevented them from fully implementing the consolidation of their budget positions and therefore the swings of automatic stabilizers should have allowed them to go above the required 3% limit.

There are many vulnerable points in the SGP. One especially is that the SGP establishes rules for the conduct of fiscal policy by individual EU Member States. It stipulates that countries of EU must ensure that budget deficits do not exceed 3% of the GDP and limit public debt to no more than 60% of it. "Internal" criticisms of this nature accept the purpose of the SGP is to make EU members practice fiscal policies consistent with the classical doctrine of "sound finance." On the other hand, "external" critics reject the purpose of the Pact. This is all very good if the level of economic activity is supply determined. They argue that meaningful reform of the Pact demands a reorientation of its ultimate purpose, toward that of functional finance (Setterfield 2009, 623-643).

It is a fact that there has been an increase of public debt in the euro zone since 2001, with a zone average of 79.8% of GDP in 2010. The slight improvement of fiscal balance during the post 2001 crisis recovery did not improve enough the level of public debt, leaving the euro zone member states in a problematic fiscal position during the 2008 crisis that could have been avoided. This means that the EU Member States did not diminish enough pro-cyclical fiscal policies during the 2004-2007 period, when they should have performed sound counter-cyclical fiscal policies to decrease public debt and to improve their fiscal discretionary policy capacities to anticipate the next economic crisis. The SGP did not reach its objectives. Because of these considerations, the SGP seems to clearly lack a sounder coercive tool to address this fiscal free rider issue (Sarrat de Tramezaigues, 2010).

Recent (2010, 2011 and 2012) criticisms reported that the measures of GDP were controversial, not only because of the closed way in which it was developed, but also for the goals that it postulated. The new "Euro Plus Pact" was designed as a more stringent successor to the SGP, which has not been implemented consistently (www.consilium.europa.eu/uedocs /cms_data/docs/pressdata/en/ecofin/119888.pdf).

The Pact had proved to be unenforceable against big countries such as France and Germany, which were its strongest promoters when it was created. These countries had run "excessive" deficits under the Pact definition for some years. The reasons that larger countries had not been punished include their influence and large number of votes on the Council of Ministers, which must approve sanctions; their greater resistance to "naming and shaming" tactics, since their electorates tended to be less concerned by their perceptions in the EU; their weaker commitment to the euro compared to smaller states; and the greater role of government spending in their larger and more enclosed economies (Bagus, 2010).

As a consequence, the aggregate fiscal stance should also be adjusted more flexibly to the business climate. This is a request for vertical budget flexibility. However, the argument is confusing. The business cycle should only affect the cyclical component of deficits, not their structural part. Theoretically, it would be possible to reduce structural deficits and simultaneously to increase cyclical deficits, if demand is insufficient. However, in reality, both Germany and France implemented tax reforms, which increased their structural deficits. Germany's structural deficit was below 1.6% of GDP in 1999 and 2000, but has stayed above the 3% rule in 2002-2005. In France, it rose from below 2% (1999-2001) to more than 3% in 2002-2005 (see also Table 2). In Germany, the deficits reflected a desperate attempt to redistribute the burden of transfers related to German unification, although that took place 15 years ago. In France, it was a direct consequence of the policy shift after the elections of 2002. Either way, the significance of the problem was not so much the business climate after a series of exogenous shocks (end of the Clinton-boom, 9/11 terrorism attack, Iraq war), but the management of domestic policy objectives. The economic issue was exactly what the Pact was intended to deal with – the difficulty of implementation was political.

On the other hand, even though it has been argued that an overall balanced budget position for the Eurozone might be desirable, 'one rule fits all,' this would be too restrictive. Horizontal flexibility is required. Why should some countries not be allowed to spread public investment over a period of several years? Especially if a country's debt/GDP ratio is low, higher deficits could be affordable. Yet, in the context of a *balanced or at least stable budget for the aggregate fiscal stance* this argument implies that some countries should be saving so that the others will be able to borrow. Otherwise, one country's deficits would increase interest rates for all. This idea of horizontal flexibility may be economically reasonable, but it crudely lacks political legitimacy. Who is responsible for deciding who saves and how much, and who is allowed to borrow?

Historical Points regarding Early Warnings of SGP to various Countries

Almost all member countries failed to follow the 3% rule during the years. Accordingly, since 2002, half of the Member States have been subjected to an 'early warning' (Ireland, Italy) or called on to take necessary steps to alleviate excessive government deficits (Portugal, the Netherlands, Greece, Italy, and six of the ten new Member States), some of which have now been repealed or suspended, in light of efforts made by the countries in question to control budgetary deficits. During the global crisis 2008-11 almost all the countries failed to follow the 3% rule (deficit rule) (see Table 2).

From Table 2 we can see the general government financial balances (surplus or deficit) as a percentage of nominal GDP from 1993 up to 2012. It is clear that Greece's deficit was decreased from -11.9% to -6.5%. But we know that the reality is completely different because the nominal GDP had big divergence from real GDP.

Following the audit carried out by the new Portuguese Government in 2002, the budgetary deficit for 2001 was revised upwards to 4.1% of the GDP, making Portugal the first Member State to exceed the reference value. After assisting the situation, in October 2002, the Commission initiated the excessive deficit procedure in accordance with the Treaty. The public deficit in Portugal fell back in 2002 and 2003 to below 3% of the GDP. Thus, the Commission recommended that the Council terminate the excessive deficit procedure against Portugal. In 2004, Portugal announced a deficit of 3.4% of the GDP, a 5.9% deficit in 2005, a 4.1% deficit in 2006 and remained above 3% for 2007 and 2008 (for further analysis, see Table 2).

In 2003, Germany and France were subjected to procedures for excessive government deficit (due to 2002-2003 excessive deficits for both countries). For example, Germany recorded a deficit of at least 3.7% in 2004. However, these procedures have been suspended. In November 2003, the Council refused to follow the recommendations, issued by the Commission that Germany and France return to deficit levels below the 3% reference value. The Commission filed a petition against this decision with the Court of Justice of the European Communities, which recognized in July 2003 that the Council was not required to follow the Commission's recommendations. Since that time, the Commission has not started any new procedures. In December 2004, it declared that 'no further steps are necessary at this point.' In addition to the institutional dispute that arose, this matter stressed the need to modernize the SGP, in particular with a view to look into the economic situation more seriously.

The Commission recommended that the Council address an early warning to Italy in view of the risk that its budget deficit would exceed the 3% threshold in 2004. However, during a meeting of finance ministers on 5 July 2004, the Council decided otherwise due to the promised additional budgetary commitments presented by Italy.

In June 2005, the Commission reported on Italian public finances, mentioning that the exceeding of the 3% threshold could be considered temporary. On the strength of this report, the Commission recommended that an excessive deficit procedure be initiated against Italy. Acting on the recommendation, the Council officially launched the excessive deficit procedure on 28 July 2005. In June 2004, the Commission had initiated the excessive deficit procedure in respect to the Netherlands. Following the reduction of the Dutch deficit from 3.2% in 2003 to less than 2.3% in 2004, the Commission recommended on 18 May 2005 that the procedure be suspended in view of the fact that the Netherlands was firmly back on the path of healthy fiscal consolidation.

As for Greece, the Council decided to initiate the excessive deficit procedure at a meeting of finance ministers on 5 July 2004. It called on the Greek Government to put an end to its excessive deficit situation by 2005, at the latest. In April 2005, the Commission assessed the Greek stability programme and came to the conclusion that, despite the Greek Government's efforts, the outlook for 2005 and beyond was uncertain and grim. It urgently called on Greece to implement the necessary permanent measures to correct its excessive deficit.

As for the United Kingdom (UK), the Council's recommendation gave the UK (although not a member of the EMU) six months to present corrective action and required its excessive deficit be brought to an end at the latest in the 2006-2007 financial year. The Council also called for an improvement of 0.5% of the GDP in the structural balance between the 2005-2006 and 2006-2007 financial years. In 2003-2004 and in 2004-2005, the UK deficit was 3.2% of GDP. The Commission's latest forecasts estimate that it will rise above the 3% ceiling in 2006-2007 (outdated). In reality, since the UK is not a member of the eurozone, Member States could only recommend that it reduce its deficit below the 3% ceiling, and not subject it to fines.

Table 2. General government financial balances

	1993	1994	1995	1996	1997	1998	1999	2000
Australia	-4,9	-4,7	-3,9	-2,6	-1,0	0,8	1,2	0,4
Austria	-4,4	-4,9	-5,9	-4,2	-2,0	-2,5	-2,4	-1,9
Belgium	-7,5	-5,2	-4,5	-4,0	-2,3	-1,0	-0,7	-0,1
Canada	-8,7	-6,7	-5,3	-2,8	0,2	0,1	1,6	2,9
Czech Republic	..	..	-13,4	-3,3	-3,8	-5,0	-3,7	-3,7
Denmark	-3,9	-3,4	-2,9	-2,0	-0,6	-0,1	1,3	2,2
Estonia	..	..	1,1	-0,3	2,2	-0,7	-3,5	-0,2
Finland	-8,3	-6,7	-6,2	-3,5	-1,4	1,5	1,6	6,8
France	-6,4	-5,5	-5,5	-4,0	-3,3	-2,6	-1,8	-1,5
Germany	-3,0	-2,3	-9,7	-3,3	-2,6	-2,2	-1,5	1,3
Greece	-11,9	-8,3	-9,1	-6,6	-5,9	-3,8	-3,1	-3,7
Hungary	..	..	-8,7	-4,6	-6,0	-7,9	-5,4	-3,0
Iceland	-4,5	-4,7	-3,0	-1,6	0,0	-0,4	1,1	1,7
Ireland	-2,7	-2,0	-2,1	-0,1	1,4	2,3	2,6	4,8
Israel	..	..	..	..	..	-8,0	-6,3	-4,0
Italy	-10,1	-9,1	-7,4	-7,0	-2,7	-3,1	-1,8	-0,9
Japan	-2,5	-3,8	-4,7	-5,1	-4,0	-11,2	-7,4	-7,6
Korea	1,7	2,3	3,5	3,2	3,0	1,3	2,4	5,4
Luxembourg	1,5	2,5	2,4	1,2	3,7	3,4	3,4	6,0
Netherlands	-2,8	-3,5	-9,2	-1,9	-1,2	-0,9	0,4	2,0
New Zealand	-0,4	2,7	2,5	2,5	0,9	0,0	-0,2	1,8
Norway	-1,4	0,3	3,2	6,3	7,6	3,3	6,0	15,4

Poland	..		-4,4	-4,9	-4,6	-4,3	-2,3	-3,0
Portugal	-7,5	-7,1	-5,0	-4,5	-3,4	-3,5	-2,7	-2,9
Slovak Republic	..	..	-3,4	-9,9	-6,3	-5,3	-7,4	-12,3
Slovenia	..	..	-8,4	-1,1	-2,4	-2,4	-3,0	-3,7
Spain	-7,3	-6,8	-6,5	-4,9	-3,4	-3,2	-1,4	-1,0
Sweden	-11,2	-9,1	-7,3	-3,3	-1,6	0,9	0,8	3,6
Switzerland	-3,5	-2,8	-2,0	-1,8	-2,8	-1,9	-0,5	0,1
Turkey	..	..	..	..	..	..	..	..
United Kingdom	-8,0	-6,8	-5,8	-4,2	-2,2	-0,1	0,9	3,7
United States	-5,1	-3,7	-3,3	-2,3	-0,9	0,3	0,7	1,5
Euro area	-5,8	-5,0	-7,5	-4,3	-2,7	-2,3	-1,4	-0,1
Total OECD	-5,1	-4,3	-4,8	-3,3	-1,9	-2,2	-1,0	0,1
Memorandum items								
General government financial balances excluding social security								
United States	-5,8	-4,5	-4,1	-3,2	-1,9	-0,9	-0,7	-0,1
Japan	-4,8	-5,8	-6,7	-6,9	-5,8	-12,5	-8,5	-8,2

Note: Financial balances include one-off factors, such as those resulting from the sale of the mobile telephone licenses, but exclude most financial transactions. As data are on a national accounts basis (SNA93/ESA95), the government financial balances may differ from the numbers reported to the European Commission under the Excessive Deficit Procedure for some EU countries. For more details, see footnotes to Annex Tables 25 and 26 and *OECD Economic Outlook* Sources and Methods (http://www.oecd.org/eco/sources-and-methods). *Source:* OECD Economic Outlook 89 database.

Table 3 presents the overview of ongoing excessive deficit procedures. Especially, the countries, the date of the Commission report (from 2004 up to 2010), the Council Decision on the existence of excessive deficit (from 2004 up to 2010) and the current deadline for correction (from 2011 up to 2015).

The rule of budgetary policy is that Member States should avoid excessive government deficits. Only an exceptional and temporary excess of the deficit could be exempt from being considered excessive. (http://www.ecb.int/mopo/eaec/html/excessive.en.html).

Table 3: Overview of ongoing excessive deficit procedures

Country	Date of the Commission report (Art.104.3/126.3)	Council Decision on existence of excessive deficit (Art.104.6/126.6)	Current deadline for correction
Bulgaria	12 May 2010	13 July 2010	2011
Denmark	12 May 2010	13 July 2010	2013
Cyprus	12 May 2010	13 July 2010	2012
Austria	7 October 2009	2 December 2009	2013
Belgium	7 October 2009	2 December 2009	2012
Czech Republic	7 October 2009	2 December 2009	2013
Germany	7 October 2009	2 December 2009	2013
Italy	7 October 2009	2 December 2009	2012
The Netherlands	7 October 2009	2 December 2009	2013
Portugal	7 October 2009	2 December 2009	2013
Slovenia	7 October 2009	2 December 2009	2013
Slovakia	7 October 2009	2 December 2009	2013
Poland	13 May 2009	7 July 2009	2012
Romania	13 May 2009	7 July 2009	2012
Lithuania	13 May 2009	7 July 2009	2012
Malta	13 May 2009	7 July 2009	2011
France	18 February 2009	27 April 2009	2013
Latvia	18 February 2009	7 July 2009	2012
Ireland	18 February 2009	27 April 2009	2015
Greece	18 February 2009	27 April 2009	2014
Spain	18 February 2009	27 April 2009	2013
UK	11 June 2008	8 July 2008	financial year 2014/15
Hungary	12 May 2004	5 July 2004	2012

Source: European Commission (2012)

Especially, the EDP sets out criteria, schedules and deadlines for the Council to reach a decision on the existence of an excessive deficit, which is taken within a fixed time period after the deadlines. If the Council decides that a deficit is excessive, it makes recommendations to the Member State concerned and establishes deadlines for effective corrective action to be taken. If the Member State fails to comply, the Council can decide to move to the next step, the ultimate possibility being to impose financial sanctions. (http://ec.europa.eu/economy_finance/economic_governance/sgp/deficit/index_en.htm).

Also from Table 3, we can point out that the date of the Commission report for Greece was on 18 February 2009, the Council Decision on existence of excessive deficit was on 27 April 2009, and the deadline for correction is up to 2014. In addition, we observe that between all the countries with ongoing excessive deficit procedures, Germany was also included with a deadline for correction up to 2013.

Table 4 presents the general government gross financial liabilities as a percentage of nominal GDP from 1994 up to 2012. We can see that Greece has the biggest percentage in the eurozone (159.3%) and the second in OECD, following Japan. Also, it has one of the biggest increased percentages (37%) in the time period from 1995 up to 2012 along with Portugal (42%) and Ireland (100%).

Table 4: General government gross financial liabilities per cent of nominal GDP

OECD Economic Outlook, Volume 2011 Issue 1 - No. 89 - © OECD 2011

Annex Table 32. General government gross financial liabilities

Version 1 - Last updated: 06-Jun-2011

Annex Table 32. **General government gross financial liabilities**

Per cent of nominal GDP

	1993	1994	1995	1996	1997	1998	1999	2000	2001	2002	2003	2004	2005	2006	2007	2008	2009	2010	2011	2012
Australia	30,3	39,6	41,3	38,6	37,0	32,0	| 27.6	24,6	21,8	19,8	18,3	16,5	16,1	15,3	14,2	13,6	19,4	25,3	29,3	30,9
Austria	62,1	65,4	69,7	70,2	66,7	68,4	71,2	71,1	72,1	73,0	71,2	70,8	70,9	66,6	63,1	67,3	72,6	78,6	80,0	81,6
Belgium[1]	140,7	137,8	135,4	133,4	128,0	123,2	119,7	113,7	112,0	108,4	103,5	98,5	95,9	91,7	88,1	93,3	100,5	100,7	100,7	100,4
Canada	96,3	98,0	101,6	101,7	96,3	95,2	91,4	82,1	82,7	80,6	76,6	72,6	71,6	70,3	66,5	71,3	83,4	84,2	85,9	88,0
Czech Republic	..	..	..	..	..	..	..	..	..	32,8	34,7	34,5	34,3	33,9	33,7	36,3	42,4	46,6	49,3	50,8
Denmark	92,4	85,8	81,7	79,1	74,8	72,4	67,1	60,4	58,4	58,2	56,6	54,0	45,9	41,2	34,3	42,6	52,4	55,5	57,1	60,0
Estonia	..	..	13,3	12,3	11,3	10,0	10,9	9,4	8,9	10,2	10,8	8,5	8,2	8,0	7,3	8,3	12,4	12,1	15,2	19,2
Finland	57,8	60,9	65,3	66,2	64,8	61,2	54,9	52,5	50,0	49,6	51,5	51,5	48,4	45,5	41,4	40,6	52,1	57,4	62,7	66,1
France	51,0	60,2	62,7	66	68,8	70,3	66,8	65,6	64,3	67,3	71,4	73,9	75,7	70,9	72,3	77,8	89,2	94,1	97,3	100,0
Germany[2]	46,2	46,5	55,7	58,8	60,3	62,2	61,5	60,4	59,8	62,2	65,4	68,8	71,2	69,3	65,3	69,3	76,4	87,0	87,3	86,9
Greece	..	..	101,1	103,1	100,0	97,7	101,5	115,3	118,1	117,6	112,3	114,8	121,2	115,6	112,9	116,1	131,6	147,3	157,1	159,3
Hungary	91,6	91,4	88,1	75,6	66,0	64,0	66,3	60,8	59,1	60,2	61,3	65,0	68,5	71,7	71,8	76,3	84,7	85,6	79,8	80,8
Iceland	..	..	..	..	..	77,3	73,6	72,9	75,0	72,0	71,0	64,5	52,6	57,4	53,3	102,0	120,0	120,2	121,0	120,2
Ireland	..	..	..	..	..	62,1	51,2	39,4	36,9	35,2	34,1	32,8	32,6	28,8	28,8	49,6	71,6	102,4	120,4	125,6
Israel	..	..	..	..	..	100,9	94,9	84,5	89,0	96,6	99,2	97,4	93,5	84,3	77,7	76,7	79,2	76,1	73,5	70,1
Italy	116,3	120,9	122,5	128,9	130,3	132,6	126,4	121,6	120,8	119,4	116,8	117,3	120,0	117,4	112,8	115,2	127,8	126,8	129,0	128,4
Japan[3]	73,9	79,0	86,2	93,8	100,5	113,2	127,0	135,4	143,7	152,3	158,0	165,5	175,3	172,1	167,0	174,1	194,1	199,7	212,7	218,7
Korea[4]	..	..	..	..	..	..	..	..	..	19,2	19,3	22,6	24,6	27,7	27,9	29,6	32,5	33,9	33,3	33,4
Luxembourg	..	..	9,5	10,1	10,2	11,2	10,0	9,2	8,2	8,4	7,9	8,6	7,6	12,1	11,7	16,4	14,7	19,7	20,5	23,9
Netherlands	96,5	86,7	89,6	88,1	82,2	80,8	71,6	63,9	59,4	60,3	61,4	61,9	60,7	54,5	51,5	64,5	67,6	71,4	74,3	75,2
New Zealand	..	56,8	50,7	44,3	41,7	41,6	39,0	36,9	34,9	33,0	30,9	28,2	26,9	26,6	25,7	28,9	34,5	38,7	45,8	52,0
Norway	37,8	34,6	37,9	33,6	29,7	28,0	29,1	32,7	31,6	38,8	48,2	51,0	47,9	59,4	57,4	54,9	48,0	49,5	56,1	51,2
Poland	..	..	51,6	51,5	48,4	44,0	46,8	45,4	43,7	55,0	55,3	54,8	54,7	55,2	51,7	54,5	58,4	62,4	65,6	66,3
Portugal	..	..	66,8	66,5	65,3	63,3	60,5	60,2	61,7	65,0	66,8	69,3	72,8	77,6	75,4	80,6	93,1	103,1	110,8	115,8
Slovak Republic	..	..	38,2	37,6	39,0	41,2	53,5	57,6	57,1	50,2	48,2	47,6	39,1	34,1	32,8	31,8	39,9	44,5	48,7	51,2
Slovenia	..	..	..	..	..	..	..	..	33,7	34,8	34,2	35,0	33,9	33,8	30,0	29,7	44,2	47,5	52,9	56,5
Spain	65,5	64,3	69,3	76,0	75,0	75,3	69,4	66,5	61,9	60,3	55,3	53,4	50,4	45,9	42,1	47,4	62,3	66,1	73,6	74,8
Sweden	78,2	82,5	81,1	84,4	83,0	82,0	73,2	64,3	62,7	60,2	59,3	60,0	60,8	53,9	49,3	49,6	52,0	49,1	45,4	41,1
Switzerland	42,9	45,5	47,7	50,1	52,1	54,8	51,9	52,4	51,2	57,2	57,0	57,9	56,4	50,2	46,8	43,7	41,5	40,2	38,7	37,0
United Kingdom	48,7	46,8	51,6	51,2	52,0	52,5	47,4	45,1	40,4	40,8	41,5	43,8	46,4	46,1	47,2	57,0	72,4	82,4	88,5	93,3
United States	71,9	71,1	70,7	69,9	67,4	64,2	60,5	54,5	54,4	56,8	60,2	61,2	61,4	60,8	62,0	71,0	84,3	93,6	101,1	107,0
Euro area	69,0	71,3	| 75.4	79,8	80,8	81,5	78,1	75,8	74,3	75,2	75,9	77,1	78,1	74,5	71,6	76,5	86,9	92,7	95,6	96,5
Total OECD	68,8	69,9	| 72.4	73,9	73,5	74,2	72,5	69,8	69,6	71,6	73,4	74,9	76,3	74,5	73,1	79,3	90,9	97,6	102,4	105,4

Note: Gross debt data are not always comparable across countries due to different definitions or treatment of debt components. Notably, they include the funded portion of government employee pension liabilities for some OECD countries, including Australia and the United States. The debt position of these countries is thus overstated relative to countries that have large unfunded liabilities for such pensions which according to ESA95/SNA93 are not counted in the debt figures, but rather as a memorandum item to the debt. Maastricht debt for European Union countries is shown in Annex Table 62. For more details, see *OECD Economic Outlook* Sources and Methods *(http://www.oecd.org/eco/sources-and-methods)*.

For euro area countries with unsustainable fiscal positions that have asked for assistance from the European Union and the IMF (Greece, Ireland and Portugal) the change in 2010 in government financial liabilities has been approximated by the change in government liabilities recorded for the Maastricht definition of general government debt (see Box 1.3 on policy and other assumptions in

1. Includes the debt of the Belgium National Railways Company (SNCB) from 2005 onwards.
2. Includes the debt of the Inherited Debt Fund from 1995 onwards.
3. Includes the debt of the Japan Railway Settlement Corporation and the National Forest Special Account from 1998 onwards.
4. Data are on a non-consolidated basis (SNA93).

Source: OECD Economic Outlook 89 database.

Possible Solutions for a Revision of the SGP

In view of the inability of Member States to adjust their government finances in 2003-2004 (due to poor financial growth) and to comply with the persistent pressures exerted on them by the Commission, the latter initiated a debate in the summer of 2004, with a view to revise the SGP more profoundly. After more than six months of vigorous negotiations between those countries in favour of minimal reform and other countries such as France and Germany, which supported a Pact that stressed more drastic measures to be taken to improve economic growth and employment, the Spring European Council (22-23 March 2005) adopted a reformed SGP that, because of its increased flexibility, would help to stimulate the economic growth of the Union. While maintaining stability related acquits, the reform would allow for economic cycles, future reforms (investments, structural reforms) and the specific needs of each Member State to be examined more thoroughly. Accordingly, the preventive component of the Pact would now take the specificities of each Member State into better consideration in defining the return to budget balance, while reinforcing budgetary discipline during favourable periods. As of spring 2003, on the Commission's initiative, the European Council adopted a more flexible interpretation of the SGP, emphasizing the need to consider structural – and not merely nominal – deficits. Through a better understanding of economic fluctuations, this approach should, to a certain extent, make counter-cyclical policies possible (Bitzenis 2009).

Thus, in September 2004, the Commission took strong action on the debate surrounding the SGP by clarifying the implementation of the SGP and promoting better communication among countries in order to strengthen economic governance. It proposed a series of improvements and focused particularly on the trend of economic factors in the Member States and the long-term sustainability of public finances.

In March 2005, the EU Council relaxed its rules in response to euro sceptic critics and to make the Pact more enforceable. To external observers of the Pact in countries where there is a movement to join the eurozone, such as the ones in the UK, the failure of the Pact to enforce its provisions on France and Germany was believed to have provided ammunition against joining the eurozone. This is cited as another major example of Franco-German 'bullying off' other Member States when it suits them. Most eurosceptic commentators assert that the Pact promotes neither stability nor growth, and correctly remarked that it has been applied inconsistently, since the Council of Ministers had failed to apply sanctions against France and Germany.

Three different proposals regarding the future of the SGP were put forward. The first referred to 'refrigeration,' 'hospitalisation' and 'death' of the SGP, three nouns the press used to describe the SGP on the eve of the historical Ecofin decision not to impose sanctions on the delinquent French and German fiscal stances. More to the point, when the Ecofin Council in November 2003 voted against proceeding with the EDP regarding Germany and France, many observers concluded that the SGP was dead or at least 'suspended.' There is no doubt that this decision violated the spirit of the SGP.

The fate of the SGP was settled in the early hours of 25 November 2003 in what was a true institutional crisis between the European Commission and the ECB who, on the one hand, demanded for the rules to be enforced, and the inter-governmentalist ensemble of the eurozone finance ministers, on the other hand, rejected the application of sanctions to the leading EU member states. The positions were clear: Romano Prodi, European Commission president and Jean-Claude Trichet, European Central Bank president, led demands for the rules to be enforced on France and Germany. Smaller countries, led by Gerrit Zalm, Dutch finance minister (1994-2002, 2003-2007), claimed in 2003 that Germany was exporting its excessive budget deficit to other countries through higher interest rates. Hans Eichel, the German finance minister (1999-2005), refused in 2003 to accept the Commission's recommendation, backed by the threat of sanctions, to make a further €6bn ($7bn, £4.2bn) of budget cuts in 2004.

France, overshooting the 3% deficit of the GDP rule for the second time in a row, supported Germany as Italy did, holder of the rotating EU presidency. The Italian EU presidency pushed through a political declaration asking France and Germany to bring their deficits within the 3% limit by 2005. However, it would never lift the threat of fines if both countries failed. Eventually, the Italian compromise proposal, put forward by Giulio Tremonti (1994-1995, 2001-2004, 2005-2006, 2008-2011), chairman of the meeting in 2003, was approved by the Ecofin. Only Austria, the Netherlands, Finland, and Spain voted against this political declaration of suspending the operations of the SGP for Germany and France. Gerrit Zalm, the Dutch finance minister (1994-2002, 2003-2007), who, along with his Austrian, Finnish and Spanish counterparts, voted in 25 November 2003 for the Commission proposals, protested that some small countries had been intimidated by France and Germany. He also predicted that all 12 members of the eurozone (in that time period, i.e. 2003) would pay the price of French and German fiscal incontinence.

Actually, there was no qualified majority at the Ecofin Council meeting of 25 November 2003 on the Commission recommendations under Articles 104(8) and 104(9) of the Treaty in respect to either France or Germany. Even so, most economists claimed that the euro area was still in dire need to find a way to persuade countries to control their budget deficits and debts. The problem would only become more acute, as most EU countries faced mounting fiscal burdens as their populations aged and both pension and health-care obligations increased. The fear was that without some common rules, countries that made painful reforms might be faced with higher interest rates caused by other countries' irresponsibility.

The second solution, which was the implementation and enforcement of SGP, failed. Actually the SGP failed with regard to the case of Portugal. Many economists had long argued that it would make no sense to force countries such as Germany and France, already struggling to come out of recession, to cut public spending at this point in the economic cycle. The consequences of such a policy were already on display in Portugal, which had breached the 3% limit in 2001. Since then, the economy has fallen into deep recession with budget deficits above 3% every year for almost a decade (see Table 2), tax revenues have fallen, and the budget deficit has, once again, soared out of control (for a critical analysis regarding SGP in that time period see also 'The death of the stability pact', 27 November 2003, *The Economist*, print edition).

The SGP came under attack when it became clear that if the EDP was to be applied, the French and the German government, for example, would be required to pursue 'pro-cyclical' policies, meaning that they would have to tax more and spend less in an economic downturn. On the other hand, an economic adviser would recommend that governments do exactly the opposite. As a result, the SGP was severely criticized. The clashing point came when France and Germany managed to hold the Pact in abeyance with the Ecofin Council's decision on 25 November 2003 not to move to the next stage of the excessive deficit procedure (there was no 'qualified majority' to carry through that decision). At this point, most newspapers declared the SGP died.

The third proposal was to revise or reform the SGP. Endless discussions took place in order to make the SGP more productive and respectful, possibly by examining the Golden Rule of finance or the question of whether deficits are being used to pay for investment rather than consumptive expenditures. Although these suggestions of reform have not been settled, various options are being considered. The "Golden Rule" of public finances is a solution that should not be taken lightly but the parameters by which it would be effective would have to be carefully agreed upon. Literally, the Golden Rule of public finances implies that the government can only borrow to finance investments and not for the current expenditures. In other words, by allowing a State to borrow in order to fund public capital formation, we have on the one hand, public capital formation (the so called 'good deficit') and on the other hand investments to finance public consumption ('the bad deficit').

The opponents of the Golden Rule, however, strongly criticize it because it might foster over investment, in the sense that investment decisions are usually taken by politicians who are only interested in the electoral cycle and often do not take into account the productivity effects of the investment, but rather its short term impact on voters. Accordingly, politicians are tempted to consider all investments as public capital formation investment and to have a rather expansionist use of fiscal policy, which ultimately could be damaging in the case of the EMU, as it would create inflation and a rise of interest rates. This, in turn, would result in lower investment, higher unemployment and consequently lower economic growth.

The main advantage of the Golden Rule is that it spreads the burden of capital projects over the different economic classes of taxpayers who benefit from these projects and avoids the efficiency loss caused by distortionary taxation if the tax rate fluctuates over time. The lack of this possibility may negatively affect capital spending. The problem is particularly acute in the initial transition period where current generations have to tax-finance new projects while they also have to pay interest on past debts. The Commission has already taken an important step by looking into the structural deficit rather than the nominal one which considers the effects of the business cycle. The reform of the SGP, however, should also include other variables, such as a better definition of public spending, namely a distinction between investment expenditure, current expenditure and revenues, and national debt levels.

Unfortunately, the SGP fails to carefully examine the causes that lead to a given deficit. For example, a country that has a deficit caused by high investment expenditure, due to increased investment in infrastructures and/or R&D, will under the current framework be regarded in the same way as a country that breached the threshold due to a rise in current expenditure and/or due to the use of pro-cyclical policies during an economic boom without the respective cuts in expenditure. Therefore, it is essential to distinguish 'productive' from 'non productive' spending.

Moreover, the sanction mechanism has lost its credibility and needs to be strengthened. This can only be accomplished through the strict reinforcement of the decision making procedure, which inevitably implies more powers to the European Commission rather than the reduction of sanctions. However, the best solution towards improvement of the sanction mechanism would be a smoother coordination of economic policies. This would necessarily imply that Member States would be less likely to be subject to any sanctions.

Nevertheless, the problem with the structure of the SGP is that sanctions arrive late in the process and thus the Council is unable to take the political responsibility to impose fines on one of its own peers. It would therefore be desirable to increase the political cost of not complying with the SGP, although it is far from evident how this could be done in practice.

Moreover , the euro zones' SGP has been under growing pressure from both European politicians and opinion-makers who maintain that the limitations imposed on budget deficits make it impossible for governments to pursue the so called 'expansionist' fiscal policies that would allegedly be appropriate for the current economic downturn (Beetsma, 1999).

To summarize, the debate concerning the SGP gathered momentum following a ruling on 13 July 2004 by the Court of Justice of the European Communities concerning the excessive deficit procedures initiated against Germany and France. Although, in November 2003, the Commission had sent to the Council recommendations for speeding up the excessive deficit procedure in both countries, the Council did not act on those recommendations and suspended the excessive deficit procedures. The Pact proved to be inapplicable against big countries such as France and Germany, which ironically were its biggest promoters when it was created. Indeed, these countries have run 'excessive' deficits under the Pact definition for 4 years (2002-5 see Table 2), however, the EU Council has not applied sanctions against them.

The experience with the "old" Pact was mixed, since it helped to exert some fiscal discipline, but many times implementation was poor. The first reform of the SGP in 2004 emphasised economic judgement at the expense of more simple rules and this presented an opportunity for Member States to renew their commitment to the Pact. But it also carried high risks that this increased room for judgement could be misused. A rigorous and consistent implementation of the new rules was considered essential (Gonzales-Peramo, 2005).

Also, the SGP has been criticised for being responsible for lower economic activity and higher unemployment or for imposing a strict constraint on short-run stabilization policies (Nello, 2009; Papaioannou, 2010).

The SGP Finally Revised Twice (2004 / 2011)

On 3 September 2004, the European Commission adopted a new proposal among countries in order to strengthen economic governance and clarify the implementation of the SGP. Sound management of public finances is essential for sustainable economic growth. The Treaty provisions which lay down the reference values for the government deficit and public debt (3% and 60% of GDP respectively) remain the centrepiece of the system in providing the budgetary framework with the necessary underpinning. Excessive deficits should be avoided and quickly corrected.

The Commission had put forward three suggestions for revising the SGP: clarifying and rendering operational the debt criterion, identifying country-specific medium-term budgetary objectives, and defining the adjustment path in the excessive deficit procedure, by looking into issues related to the sustainability of public finances. (http://europa.eu/legislation_summaries/other/l25067_en.htm)

As regards the debt criterion, the revised SGP could clarify the basis for assessing the 'satisfactory pace' of debt reduction provided for in Article 104(2)(b) of the Treaty. In defining this 'satisfactory pace,' the need to bring debt levels back down to prudent levels before demographic ageing has an impact on economic and social developments in member states should be taken into account. Member states' initial debt levels and their potential growth levels should also be considered. Annual assessments could be made relative to this reference pace of reduction, taking into account country-specific growth conditions. For instance, if a given member state growth is lower than its potential growth, the pact would allow for a slower rate of debt reduction.

Medium-term objectives were intended to provide sufficient room for manoeuvre to ensure that the government deficit does not exceed 3% of GDP during an economic slowdown without recourse to pro-cyclical fiscal policy. Also, medium-term objectives allowed Member States not only to reduce debt but to prepare for the budgetary impact of ageing populations as well.

The current SGP did not give an operational definition of the medium-term budgetary objective. Member states are currently supposed to present an annually balanced budget position throughout the economic cycle. The Commission stated that a medium-term objective could be based on current debt levels, taking into account their development over time. Furthermore, factors such as potential economic growth, inflation, the existing implicit liabilities related to ageing populations, the impact of structural reforms or the need for additional net investment should also be examined (http://europa.eu/legislation_summaries/other/l25067_en.htm).

As mentioned, the reference value for government deficit was 3% of GDP. A deficit exceeding this value was considered exceptional (Amending Act – Regulation (EC) No. 1056/2005 on 27 July 2005) when it results either from an unusual event outside the control of the Member State concerned and had a major impact on the financial position of the general government or from a severe economic downturn (if the excess over 3% of the GDP was the result of negative annual GDP growth or a cumulative fall in production over a prolonged period of very low annual growth). The scenario of slow but positive economic growth was not considered in the current regulatory framework. The Commission envisages a rethinking of the adjustment path once a country breaches the 3% deficit threshold and/or a redefinition of the 'exceptional circumstances clause.' A period of zero growth, bringing about deficits greater than 3%, would not at present trigger this clause so that the Member State would avoid being placed in an excessive deficit situation. Regulation (EC) No. 1467/97 sets out the exceptions to this. No EDP should be launched against a Member State experiencing negative growth or a prolonged period of low growth. Previously, the exception was for countries in a recession defined as 2% negative growth, something which has been virtually unheard among EU Member States. Member States recording a 'temporary' deficit or one close to the 3% reference value would be able to refer to a series of 'relevant factors' to avoid an excessive deficit procedure. Factors would include potential growth, the economic cycle, structural reforms (pensions, social security) and policies supporting research and development plus medium-term budgetary efforts (consolidating during good economic times, debt levels, public investment).

Countries would have two years (previously it was one) to correct an excessive deficit which might be extended in cases of 'unexpected and adverse economic events with major unfavourable budgetary effects occurring during the procedure.' To benefit from this, countries must provide evidence that they have adopted the correction measures recommended to them and make a commitment to use unexpected fiscal receipts during periods of strong growth to reduce their deficits and debt. Medium-term objectives should be tailored to individual member states based on their current debt ratio and potential growth. This would vary from 1% of GDP for low debt/high potential growth countries to balance or surplus for high debt/low growth countries. The Council wanted to strengthen Eurostat's resources, powers, independence and accountability.

As a reaction to the Greek under-reporting of statistics, the Council suggested that imposing sanctions on a Member State 'should be considered' when there was infringement of the obligations to duly report government data. Finally, the excess over the reference value was considered temporary if the Commission's budget forecasts stated that the deficit would fall below the reference value when the unusual circumstance or serious downturn is terminated.

The suspension of the SGP for two large European countries, France and Germany, which occurred in November 2003, determined the demise of its original form and the appearance of a "new" SGP after March 2005 (Holler and Reiss, 2012).

On 15 March 2011, following the 2010 European sovereign debt crisis, the EU Member States adopted a new SGP reform under the Open Method of Coordination, aiming at strengthening the rules in case of breaches of the deficit or the debt criteria. Four of the proposals deal with reform of the EU's SGP. They were aimed at enhancing the surveillance of fiscal policies, introducing provisions on national fiscal frameworks, and applying enforcement measures for non-compliant Member States more consistently and at an earlier stage. The other two proposals targeted macroeconomic imbalances within the EU.

The four broad strategic goals were: fostering competitiveness, fostering employment, contributing to the sustainability of public finances, reinforcing financial stability. An additional fifth issue was tax policy coordination. The European Fiscal Compact was a proposal for a treaty about fiscal integration described in a decision adopted on 9 December 2011 by the European Council. The participants were the Eurozone member states and all other EU members without the United Kingdom and Czech Republic.

It would be in line with and strengthen the existing economic governance in the EU, while providing added value. It will be consistent with and build on existing instruments (Europe 2020, European Semester, Integrated Guidelines, SGP and new macroeconomic surveillance framework). It will be focused, action oriented, and cover priority policy areas that are essential for fostering competitiveness and convergence. Each year, concrete national commitments will be undertaken by each Head of State or government. In doing so, Member States will take into account best practices and benchmark against the best performers, within Europe and vis-à-vis other strategic partners (http://www.consilium.europa.eu/uedocs/cms_data/docs/pressdata/en/ec/120296.pdf).

Thus, the reform package of SGP in 2010-11 included three elements: firstly, a reform of the SGP, secondly, an agreement on policy coordination to foster the competitiveness of eurozone member states and other EU countries called Euro Plus Pact, and thirdly, the creation of the European Stability Mechanism (ESM) (Fuest, 2011).

Generally, Europe's leaders have spent many years grappling with this challenge, beginning with the experience of the 1980s and the nascent plan to establish a monetary union. The founding fathers of EMU embedded fiscal rules in the Maastricht Treaty and the SGP in the early and mid-1990s. However, after two rounds of reforms in 2003-05 and 2010-11, scepticism prevailed. The latest reforms continued to reflect Member States' unwillingness to transfer the necessary degree of sovereignty over macro-fiscal objectives to the European level (ECB, 2011).

The Current Situation in 2010-2012

The fact that the preventive arm of the SGP has been strengthened — by introducing numerical benchmarks, making it easier to launch EDPs and introducing (symbolic) sanctions — can be considered a remarkable step, especially because the preventive arm aims at balancing out the procyclical effect that materializes when a country merely fulfills the requirements of the dissuasive arm. In light of the many exceptions, though, it remains highly questionable whether the debt rule will actually, as intended, impose stricter requirements on highly indebted countries. Despite the new voting procedure, which is designed to make sanctions more likely, we doubt that economically significant sanctions will be imposed in the foreseeable future. Still, it is expected that the new and earlier sanctions (interest-bearing deposits in case of noncompliance with the provisions of the preventive arm and noninterest-bearing deposits in case of breaches of the deficit criterion or the debt rule) will be imposed (Holler and Reiss, 2012).

As a consequence of the poor starting position, the deep economic downturn, fiscal expansion, public finances deteriorated significantly in the euro area. The average deficit increased by more than 5 percentage points, reaching 6.0% of GDP in 2010, as the dynamics of public expenditure failed to adjust to changes in the level and dynamics of output and public revenues. Ireland's record deficit of 32.4% dwarfed the next three largest deficits, which stood at around 10% of GDP. Average public debt reached 85% of GDP in the euro area, almost 20 percentage points above the pre-crisis level. Five countries had debt ratios approaching or exceeding 100%. In the case of Greece, misreporting of data on government finances aggravated concerns. Between autumn 2009 and spring 2011, access to liquidity in financial markets dried up first for Greece and then for Ireland and Portugal (Rother et al., 2011). These countries were forced to seek financial support. In order to establish an institutional framework for such operations, the European Financial

Stability Facility (EFSF) was set up in 2010 and tasked with providing emergency financing until 2013. Thereafter, the ESM is set to take over this role. The stimulus programmes generally failed to provide for credible exit strategies, leaving doubts about how and when sound public finance positions would be regained (Schuknecht, Moutot, Rother and Stark, 2011).

On the other hand, the objectives of the ECB should be reformulated to encourage higher employment and economic activity. This would call for the member-countries to encourage investment focusing on innovation. Specifically, higher employment and growth can be achieved through a less rigid SGP. In this way, we would allow higher flexibility in national fiscal policies, which is necessary to cope with the specific needs of the individual economies, like Greek economy. There is another way, the fully fledged EU policy on stimulating investment. This seems to be more desired for the viability of EMU, as national fiscal discipline has to be observed throughout the EU (Papaioannou, 2010).

The Extension of the Crisis in the Eurozone

The acceleration of globalization in the 1980s and 1990s stemmed from political developments and technological progress. In academic and applied economics, it was supported by the revival of neoclassical economics (Wojtyna 2008; Kowalski 2011). The monetary and fiscal criteria stipulated in the Treaty of Maastricht were not a reflection of the OCA criteria and are not easily justifiable according to theory lines (De Grauwe 2000) as they reflected some arbitrariness of political decisions that led to the establishment of the monetary union (Kowalski, Kowalski and Wihlborg, 2007, p. 60).

Analysis of the Maastricht criteria fulfillment, 1997 indicates the role played by political considerations in the establishment of EMU. Based on the European Commission (1998) synopsis of data, Greece was the only country from EU-12 that could not meet both the fiscal and monetary criteria in January 1997. Interestingly, the inflation criterion (the reference value of 2.7%) and the long term market interest rate (the reference value of 5.0%) were met by all aspiring economies (except Greece). This clearly signaled the scope of nominal convergence achieved. The ERM II criterion proved not to be difficult even for Greece.

The EMU countries retained their national control only of fiscal policy instruments, restricted by the SGP and other specific EU fiscal rules. The significant lack of national instruments of monetary policy, the regime of irrevocable exchange rates and the limitations imposed on national fiscal policies demonstrate the diminishing impact of the EMU states on the course of their domestic economic events (Kowalski 2011).

The current financial crisis is the result of the interplay of mistakes in economic policy, shifts in global real sphere, as well as technological advancements. These combined sectors led to sectoral disruptions and imbalances contaminated particular countries and finally hit cross-national integration groupings (such as the EMU) to cover the whole world economy in the end.

The ways particular EMU economies reacted to the global financial crisis that originated in the US depended on macroeconomic conditions, size and role of the financial intermediation sector in national economies and its scope and scale of international linkages and qualitative aspects of the EMU economies, as well as their adaptive ability at the micro and mezzo-levels (Kowalski, 2011).

Also, Greece was the only country that recorded the appreciation of its Real Effective Exchange Rate (REER) – on the basis of Consumer Price Indices – and thus lowered its position in international competitiveness. From 2007 up to 2011, we saw high relative changeability of real effective exchange rates. Comparing the REERs in January 2011 with the January 2007 level, the four economies deteriorated as far as their relative price and cost position is concerned (Greece 104.7%, Belgium 101.8%, and Luxembourg and Spain 100.6%). In the course of four years, the gap between the worst and best performers in EMU in terms of price and cost competitiveness reached over 9 percentage points, reflecting both structural differences and different abilities of the service and manufacturing sectors to react to the demand shock caused by the financial crisis (Setterfield, 2009).

But in 2010, most EMU economies recorded increases in industrial production. In January that year, as compared with January 2007, the best results were still the share of the Netherlands (108.6%). The difference between this country and Portugal (77.8%), the latter most affected by the slowdown, amounted to as much as 30.8 percentage points. This gives us some information on what yet another year of increasing divergence in the adjustment ability of the EMU industrial sectors was like. In January 2011, i.e. after four years, only four EMU economies witnessed a production growth: the Netherlands (108.3%), Austria (105.8%), Ireland (104.2%) and Germany (100.1%). The most difficult industrial sector situation was visible in Portugal (production at the level of 85.6% as compared with the level of January 2007), Luxembourg (85.9%), Italy (83.5%), Greece (82.6%), and Spain (79.6%). The gap between the best and the worst performer amounted to 28.7 percentage points in January. The scale and time arrangement of the EMU countries' industrial sector reaction to the external shock makes us aware of how extensive the recession-related phenomena might be. It also sheds light on the varying adjustment capabilities of respective economies as well as their structural efficiencies, especially in view of the lack of exchange rate adjustment instrument (Kowalski, 2012).

The economic crisis affected the General Government Financial Balances of the EMU countries in different ways. In the period of 2009-2010, it was at its peak, as all EMU members registered a deficit, with only Finland and Luxembourg not exceeding the 3% level. The gravest GGFB downturn took place in Ireland (32.4%), Greece (15.6%), Spain (11.1%), Portugal (10.9%) and France (7.5%).

In the 2010-2011 all the countries were sorting out their public finance condition. Greece does not fall into this category, having found itself on the verge of bankruptcy after the revised data became public. Part of the induced eurozone crisis was the result of an EMU-specific decision-making process and that the infection spread through the financial intermediation sector. The case of Ireland demanded special attention, as its banking sector was branded as the economy flagship. The sector's expansion transformed a model EU member as of 2008 into a country experiencing the most severe structural problems (Kowalski, Kowalski, and Wihlborg, 2007).

The European Financial Stabilisation Mechanism (EFSM), the European Financial Stability Facility (EFSF), and the ESM

The EFSF is a mechanism financed by EMU members in order to help the EMU countries with the European sovereign-debt crisis. It was agreed by the 27 EU Member States on 9 May 2010, with the objective of preserving financial stability in Europe by providing financial assistance to eurozone states in economic difficulty. The EFSF is authorized to borrow up to €440 billion, of which €250 billion remained available after the Greek, Irish and Portuguese bailout. The EFSF's mandate is to safeguard financial stability in Europe by providing financial assistance to euro area Member States. EFSF is authorised to use the following financial instruments (see also http://www.efsf.europa.eu/about/index.htm):

- Provide loans to countries in financial difficulties
- Intervene in the debt primary and secondary markets. Intervention in the secondary market will be only on the basis of an ECB analysis recognising the existence of exceptional financial market circumstances and risks to financial stability

- Act on the basis of a precautionary programme
- Finance recapitalisations of financial institutions through loans to governments

To fulfill its mission, EFSF issues bonds or other debt instruments on the capital markets. EFSF is backed by guarantee commitments from the euro area Member States for a total of €780 billion and has a lending capacity of €440 billion.

The EFSM is the mechanism that provides financial assistance to EU Member States in financial difficulties. The EFSM reproduces the basic mechanics for the 27 EU member countries of the existing Balance of Payments Regulation for non-euro area Member States. The European financial stabilisation mechanism provides assistance to Member States where:

- a Member State is experiencing, or is seriously threatened with, a severe financial disturbance;
- the financial disturbance or threat of financial disturbance is due to events beyond the control of the Member State concerned.

Under EFSM, the Commission is allowed to borrow up to a total of € 60 billion in financial markets on behalf of the EU under an implicit EU budget guarantee (see also
http://ec.europa.eu/economy_finance/eu_borrower/efsm/index_en.htm).
The EFSM has currently been activated for Ireland and Portugal, for a total amount up to € 48.5 billion (up to € 22.5 billion for Ireland and up to € 26 billion for Portugal), to be disbursed over 3 years.

The ESM is a proposed international organisation which will provide financial assistance to EMU members in financial difficulty. The ESM is intended to replace the existing temporarily funding programs of EFSF and EFSM. It is proposed that ESM be located in Luxembourg. The ESM will seek to operate jointly with the IMF, in order to have a higher overall level of available financial assistance. The ESM can grant financial assistance in the sense of loans to euro area member states which have financial difficulties, as in the cases of Greece, Ireland and Portugal, assistance is conditional on a macroeconomic adjustment program. Loans granted by the ESM will enjoy preferred creditor status relative to all other loans. But, it is unclear, whether this also applies to cases where the ESM purchases government bonds in the primary market (Fuest, 2011).

An innovative action of the ESM is that it specifies a set of provisions for the possible involvement of the private sector in cases where countries cannot fully repay their debt. These provisions include, firstly, the obligation for all Member States, since July 2013, to include collective action clauses in newly issued securities with maturities more than a year. Before financial assistance is granted, an assessment has to be made as to whether the public debt of the country seeking help is sustainable. If this assessment leads to the conclusion that, even with an adjustment programme, the country cannot realistically restore sustainability of its public debt, assistance will only be granted if the private sector creditors share the burden of reducing the debt to a sustainable level (Fuest, 2011).

Conclusions

In this Chapter we analyzed the role, the significance and the efficiency of the SGP. The Maastricht criteria were presented and analysed. Our argument is that the SGP promoted a system for coordination and surveillance of national budgetary policies but it failed. The countries adopting the single currency were required to submit an annual stability programme. On the other hand, the Maastricht Treaty obliges the states to avoid budgetary deficits, since they cannot have a deficit to GDP ratio above 3% and exceed the debt to GDP reference of 60%.

The SGP has been widely criticized as it has been acclaimed. Commission President R. Prodi has called it "stupid, because it is rigid," while others believe that it is "one of the most remarkable pieces of policy coordination in world history." Most probably, the truth lies somewhere in between because if each country kept its budget in equilibrium, the aggregate budget position of the EMU would also be balanced.

The Council decided to initiate the deficit procedure in 2004 and called the Greek government to put an end to the excessive deficit situation by 2005. But the situation in Greek numbers did not change in 2005, so the Commission called again the Greek government to correct its deficit.

On the other hand, we presented some solutions for a more productive SGP. One of these was the implementation and enforcement of the SGP, but it failed with regard to the case of Portugal. Also, the other solution was to revise or to reform the SGP. Many discussions and proposals took place to make the SGP more productive. In addition, the opponents of the "Golden Rule" strongly criticized it because it should have fostered other investments. In general, the SGP failed to examine the reasons that led to a given deficit.

After these economic facts, the SGP was finally revised. The countries could have two years to correct an excessive deficit that would possibly spill over to unexpected directions. As a reaction to the Greek under-reporting statistics, the Council suggested that imposing sanctions on a country like Greece "should be considered" in case of infringement of the obligations. On the other hand, the EMU countries accept their national control only by fiscal policy instruments.

In 2010-2011, all the countries were sorting out their public finance condition. Greece does not fall in this category, having found itself on the verge of bankruptcy after the revised data became public. Part of the induced eurozone crisis was the result of an EMU-specific decision-making process and that the infection spread through the financial intermediation sector.

The ESM will replace the EFSF and the EFSM in 2013 and can provide assistance to countries with financial difficulties.

References

Bagus, Phillipp. 2010, *Tragedy of the Euro,* Alabama: Ludwig von Mises Institute.

Beetsma, R.M.W.J. and Uhlig, H. (1997), *An Analysis of the 'Stability Pact'*, Centre for Economic Policy.

Beetsma, R.M.W.J. (1999), 'The Stability and Growth Pact in a Model with Politically Induced Deficit Biases', in A. Hughes Hallett, M.M. Hutchison and S.E. Hougaard Jensen (eds) *Fiscal Aspects of European Monetary Integration*, New York: Cambridge University Press, pp. 189–215

Bitzenis, A., (2009), *The Balkans: FDI and EU Accession*, Ashgate Publishing Ltd, UK, August 2009

De Grauwe, P. (2000), *Economics of Monetary Union,* fourth edition, Oxford: Oxford University Press.

Eichengreen, B. and Wyplosz, C. (1998), *Instability Pact? European Economic Perspectives,* London: Centre for Economic Policy Research (September).

European Central Bank (2011) The Stability and Growth Pact Crisis and Reform, in *Occasional Papers Series* 129.

European Commission (2012), "Excessive deficit procedure", http://ec.europa.eu/economy_finance/economic_governance/sgp/deficit /index_en.htm, [accessed 27/7/2012).

EU (2004), "Necessary improvement of the Stability and Growth Pact", http://europa.eu/legislation_summaries/other/l25067_en.htm, [accessed 28/7/2012].

European Council (2011), "European Council 24/25 March 2011, Conclusions", (www.consilium.europa.eu/uedocs/cms_data/docs/pressdata/en/ec/120296.pdf, [accessed 24/7/2012].

EU (2011), "Council reaches agreement on measures to strengthen economic governance", www.consilium.europa.eu/uedocs/cms_data/docs/pressdata/en/ecofin/119888.pdf, [accessed 24/7/2012].

European Central Bank (2006), "Monetary Policy", http://www.ecb.int/mopo/eaec/html/excessive.en.html, [accessed 27/7/2012].

European Financial Stability Facility (EFSF) (2012) http://www.efsf.europa.eu/about/index.htm [accessed 28/7/2012]

European Financial Stabilisation Mechanism (EFSM) (2012)
http://ec.europa.eu/economy_finance/eu_borrower/efsm/index_en.htm [accessed 28/7/2012]

Fuest, C. (2011) Will the reform of the institutional framework restore fiscal stability in the Eurozone? *Working paper presented at the CFS Research Conference 'The ECB and Its Watchers XIII'*, 10 June 2011, Frankfurt am Main, Germany.

Gonzales-Peramo, J.M. (2005) The reform of the Stability and Growth Pact: An assessment, *Executive Board of the ECB Conference on "New Perspectives on Fiscal Sustainability"*, 13 October 2005, Frankfurt, Germany.

Holler, J. and Reiss, L. (2012), What to Expect from the Latest Reform of the Stability and Growth Pact, *Monetary Policy and the Economy,* 4 (11), pp. 85-97.

Kowalski, P., Kowalski, T., Wihlborg, C. (2007), The EMU Entry Strategy vs. the Monetary Issues, *Poznan University of Economics Review,* 7 (2), pp. 59-88.

Kowalski, T. (2011), Economic Policy and the Financial and Economic Crisis. WP no. 01, FIBE, *Poznan University of Economics*, Poland, p. 15.

—. (2012), *The economic and monetary union countries vs. the global crisis. Poznan University of Economics*, MPRA Paper No 37942.

Nello, S. S. (2009), "The European Union: Economics, Policies and History", New York: Mc Graw Hill, Second Edition.

Papademos, L.D. (2003), 'The Stability and Growth Pact: An Asset Rather than a Liability', *CESifo Forum*, 4(2), pp. 73–77.

Papaioannou, G. (2010), Can the Stability and Growth Pact Criteria Lead to Sustainable Growth? *International Research Journal of Finance and Economics*, 50 (12), 151-156.

Sarrat de Tramezaigues, G.R. (2010), Assessing the 2005 Growth and Stability Pact Reform: A New Fiscal Policy Rule for the Euro Zone Is Required, *International Journal of Economics and Finance*, 2 (5), pp. 140-150.

Schuknecht, L., Moutot, P., Rother, P and Stark, J. (2011) The Stability and Growth Pact crisis and reform. *European Central Bank. Occasional Paper Series*. No 129.

Setterfield, Mark. 2009. "Fiscal and monetary policy interactions: lessons for revising the EU Stability and Growth Pact, *Journal of Post Keynesian Economics,* 31 (4): 623-643.

Tamborini, R. and F.Targetti, (2005) "The Crisis of the Stability Pact and a Proposal" in P. Arestis, J. Mc Combie and R. Vickerman (eds) "Growth and Economic Development, Essays in honour of A.P. Thirlwall, Edgard Elgar

The Economist (2003) "The death of the stability pact", 27 November 2003, print edition.

CHAPTER NINE

THE IMPORTANCE OF FISCAL AND BUDGETARY DISCIPLINE, AND THE CRISIS IN GREECE

PYRROS PAPADIMITRIOU
AND YIANNIS HADZIYIANNAKIS

Acknowledgments

The authors extend their appreciation to Maria Efthimiou and Irina Grigoryan for their invaluable contribution to the research of this paper.

Introduction

In 2009 Greece entered arguably the greatest fiscal crisis in its modern history. The international economic crisis has played its part in precipitating the Greek crisis but the underlying roots were firmly implanted in successive years of poor fiscal management and unruly public finances combined with an inherently uncompetitive economy. Sooner or later Greece would have come to this juncture, and whilst plenty of warning signals were ignored, it took a severe external shock to see the house of cards come crumbling down.

The purpose of this Chapter is to focus on two specific dimensions of the Greek crisis. The Chapter aims at unravelling some core elements of the poor budget management by looking at some very basic budgetary (expenditure) data and discussing the ineffectiveness (or complete absence altogether) of basic processes in public financial management. The Chapter also seeks to discuss how the architecture of the Eurozone may have contributed to fiscal unruliness by unwittingly creating a framework of perverse incentives for the members of the monetary union. The establishment of a monetary union of members with divergent ethics and capabilities in the management of public finances and uneven economic strength was bound to run into trouble under the Stability and Growth Pact

(SGP) regime of fiscal rules. The SGP has proven ineffective in restraining Eurozone member states from running excessive deficits and has not ensured stability.

The Chapter is composed of four sections: the first section looks at the data of the Greek budgets in the 2002-2008 period and compares actual expenditure outturn with the original budget appropriations. The purpose of this exercise is to examine aggregate fiscal discipline for the period under review and determine, to the extent that is possible, whether the fiscal meltdown was also due to unruliness in budget preparation and execution. This section also discusses certain qualitative aspects that have been obstacles to any attempt at instilling basic discipline in the Greek budgetary process.

The second section provides a brief review of the literature on the impact of the SGP to Eurozone governments' incentives in making budget and fiscal policy decisions. After more than a decade of research, there is consensus that the aggregate quantitative targets of the SGP have been largely ineffective in securing fiscal discipline in the Eurozone. Several economists had predicted the troubles that lay ahead in the absence of coordination in national fiscal and budgetary policies, including adherence to common fiscal principles and commonly agreed mechanisms for monitoring relevant processes. In the case of Greece, a weaker Eurozone member was given the opportunity to free ride on the collective credit worthiness of the Euro borrowing at rates that would have been unimaginable for the Drachma. A perverse incentive was created under the guise of keeping up appearances with the SGP fiscal deficit target. At the same time there was almost a disincentive to improve policies and systems needed to ensure discipline, and most importantly, to rationalise public spending and introduce some strategic focus; why change if all is well.

The third section discusses the proposals made by the European Commission in September 2010. The idea is to achieve a much broader policy co-ordination process by looking deeper than the annually reported deficit. The proposals also recommend adopting a system of automatic application of the penalty procedures, including the introduction of sanctions for the debt sustainability criterion. The question that looms is whether creating the right incentive structure for countries in the Eurozone to operate within a coordinated fiscal framework would require intrusive measures, and ultimately a trade-off in national economic policy independence.

The final section of the Chapter makes some key concluding remarks.

1. Greek Budgets in the Period 2002-2008

It is safe to say that in Greece the importance of the budget as one of the most critical policy instruments still eludes politicians, public servants or indeed the public. This is perhaps the most fundamental shortcoming of Greek public finances in relation to the most advanced Organisation of Economic Co-operation and Development (OECD) countries. There are ample cases documented in the Greek press where leading politicians have made statements that demonstrate a broad lack of understanding of the role and importance of the budget[1]. It is only very recently, and following the International Monetary Fund (IMF) – European Union (EU) rescue package, that intelligible commentary has managed to see the surface. The question therefore looms: how could Greece have had a credible budget and by consequence a reliable fiscal policy if there was arguably very little understanding of the importance of the budget?

It comes as no surprise that Greek budgets of the past were in effect not binding and characterised as indicative. In the years 2002-2008 examined by this paper there is evidence of a continuous practice of repetitive budgeting and of a perpetual struggle to balance the budget in December at the end of each fiscal year[2]. Moreover, it has now become clear that when expenditure outturns became uncontrollable in certain sectors, a practice of deferment of current liabilities to future fiscal years was deployed. These arrears were not duly authorised by or systematically recorded as liabilities and reported to the Ministry of Finance and the treasury.

Table 1 shows Greece's budget execution for the period 2002-2008 depicting the difference of actual expenditure outturns from the appropriated annual budgets (by administrative budget heading - vote) of the period under examination[3].

---

[1] A very characteristic example is a statement made by the former Prime Minister George Papandreou in a press conference on the 13th of January 2010 (www.primeminister.gov.gr/21010/01/13/601) stating that budgets are meant to be indicative. The statement was made a few months before Greece actually requested the bail-out package from the IMF and EU.

[2] The budget deficit for 2009 was revised by Eurostat in excess of 15% of gross domestic product (GDP) in November 2010.

[3] The analysis was made using performance indicators 1 and 2 from the Public Expenditure & Financial Accountability framework.

Table 1: Aggregate and composition expenditure outturns in relation to appropriated budgets 2002-2008 (in %)

Budget Institutions	2002	2003	2004	2005	2006*	2007*	2008*
Presidency of the Hellenic Republic	(3.1)	(6.8)	5.6	(4.4)	(1.9)	(3.1)	(4.9)
Parliament	3.0	(0.4)	8.5	(1.1)	(20.7)	1.7	(3.1)
Ministry of Interior, Public Administration & Decentralisation / *Note 1*	15.9	12.3	5.1	(2.2)	5.2	61.4	1.9
Ministry of Foreign Affairs	22.9	5.8	(7.8)	(2.9)	(3.0)	(8.4)	(8.1)
Ministry of National Defence	7.5	8.6	2.3	(6.5)	(2.7)	7.0	4.1
Ministry of Health	4.5	8.1	8.8	42.0	(11.3)	(7.9)	(11.0)
Ministry of Justice	0.2	0.5	0.5	(1.6)	(4.8)	(4.3)	20.5
Ministry of National Education & Religious Affairs	2.0	3.2	5.9	(0.6)	(3.5)	(2.7)	(1.2)
Ministry of Culture	8.5	6.1	8.0	3.7	13.1	13.9	15.9
Ministry of Economy & Finance excl. General Public Expenditures / *Note 2*	(2.6)	18.3	n.a.	n.a.	n.a.	n.a.	n.a.
Ministry of Economy & Finance – General Public Expenditures / *Note 2*	1.4	(7.0)	20.0	13.6	12.5	59.3	48.0
Ministry of Macedonia &Thrace / *Note 1*	(0.4)	18.5	(2.2)	(9.6)	(7.8)	(6.8)	0.4
Ministry of Aegean and Island Policy / *Note 3*	(0.5)	6.8	(3.3)	(11.2)	(12.8)	(100)	n.a.
Ministry of Agriculture	1.3	(2.0)	(18.7)	(12.1)	(4.7)	10.5	(9.2)
Ministry of Public Works, Spatial Planning & Environment	7.9	6.0	(15.9)	(21.2)	(1.5)	2.2	35.1

Ministry of Employment & Social Security	(2.8)	1.7	12.0	0.5	(0.2)	(3.1)	12.3
Ministry of Development	5.3	12.3	54.1	55.6	49.5	44.9	14.2
Ministry of Transport & Telecommunications	31.5	30.8	49.5	30.5	24.9	26.8	32.4
Ministry of Merchant Shipping / *Note 3*	0.5	9.6	24.7	5.2	6.5	11.7	9.2.
Ministry of Public Order / *Note 1*	3.5	2.6	19.8	(1.9)	(2.8)	(100)	n.a.
Minister of the Press & Media	4.7	18.7	61.7	17.9	13.3	(37.1)	(19.6)
Ministry of Tourism / *Note 4*	-	-	-	(16.9)	(9.4)	(11.6)	2.4
*Regions** / Note 5*	n.a.	n.a.	n.a.	*162.5*	*62.0*	*67.7*	*66.6*
Aggregate expenditure deviation (1)	2.6	1.5	11.4	8.6	5.9	33.0	28.3
Composition of expenditure variance (2)	3.1	6.7	17.1	13.3	9.7	40.7	30.3
Variance in excess of total deviation (2)-(1)	0.5	5.2	5.7	4.7	3.8	7.7	2.0

Source: *Annual budgets and the Budget Execution Bulletins (General Department of Treasury and Budget)*

* The information and data available on the Greek budget for public access are not always clear and/or consistent. This Chapter had to rely also on preliminary data for budget execution in years 2006, 2007 and 2008.

** The Regional Budget is included for indicative purposes only. It is not counted in the aggregate expenditure and composition of expenditure calculations because the funds are already included as part of central government fiscal transfers in the Ministry of Finance General Government Expenditures entry. There is no consistent data publically accessible for the Regional Budget in years 2002 to 2005

Box 1 – Explanatory Note to Table 1

This brief note is intended to help the reader put the financial data presented in Table 1 into a broader context. In particular, it is intended to highlight the continuous restructurings of government ministries which have not helped in the way of ensuring transparency in government affairs.

Note 1 – In 2007 the government of the day decided to disband the Ministry of Public Order and add its functions to the Ministry of Interior, Public Administration & Decentralisation. The overspending recorded in the expenditure outturn for the Ministry of Interior in 2007 can be largely attributed to the absorption of the expenditure of the Ministry of Public Order.

Note 2 – *General Public Expenditures* include the bulk of central government transfer payments in the form of entitlements, grants to local government and other devolved public entities, and debt repayment. Up until 2003 the Ministry of Finance administrative budget was shown in a separate budget head (vote). From 2004 onwards, the Ministry of Finance budget head covered both the administrative and general public expenditures' appropriations.

Note 3 – In 2007 the Ministry of Aegean was merged with the Ministry of Merchant Shipping, creating the Ministry of Merchant Shipping & Island Affairs. The expenditure outturn for the Ministry of Merchant Shipping in 2007 includes expenditure incurred by the Ministry of Aegean.

Note 4 – The Ministry of Tourism was created in 2005. Prior to this the Ministry of Development was responsible for tourism.

Note 5 – The Regional Budget included the deconcentrated functions of government until 2009. In 2010 under the new decentralisation law (*Kallikratis*) the Regions were transformed into self government entities with elected governors and councils amalgamating the hitherto smaller *Prefectures*.

In 2009 the newly elected government made another set of changes in the structure of government. A non-exhaustive list of changes undertaken in 2009 follows:

- The Ministry of Economy & Finance was split and the "Economy" part merged with the Ministry of Development. The new ministry included originally the functions of the Ministry of Merchant Shipping but in 2010 (under a further restructuring exercise) it was reinstated under the new name Ministry of Maritime Affairs, Islands & Fisheries. The Ministry of Development (now called Regional Development & Competitiveness) was also reinstated and the "Economy" functions returned to the Ministry of Finance.

- The Ministry of Public Order was reinstated, only this time entitled Ministry of Citizen Protection. This new ministry differed from its earlier form in that it included additional functions such as the Coast Guard, which had traditionally been under the Ministry of Merchant Shipping. The Ministry of Interior (entitled in 2009 Ministry of Interior, Decentralisation and Electronic Governance) would in turn absorb the functions of the Ministry of Macedonia & Thrace, which was disbanded.
- A new Ministry of Environment was created taking the function from the previous Ministry of Public Works, Spatial Planning & Environment.
- The functions of Public Works and Spatial Planning were merged with the Ministry of Transport & Telecommunications to form the Ministry of Infrastructure, Transport and Networks.
- The Ministry of Tourism was merged with the Ministry of Culture.

Table 1 reveals a very poor track record in aggregate budget discipline as shown by the "aggregate expenditure deviation" indicator. In 2007 and 2008 aggregate expenditure outturns were in excess of the budget appropriation by approximately 33 and 28 percentage points respectively. The picture is made grimmer knowing that there was a large amount of deferred liabilities and liabilities generated by discretionary (non-appropriated) funds[4] of line ministries over the same period.

To put the above into an overall fiscal context, total government spending rose from just over 60 billion euro in 2002 to an excess of 110 billion in 2008. Fiscal policy followed a pro-cyclical pattern for the most part of that period. According to data from IMF Article IV consultations, government payroll increased dramatically from 17.3 billion in 2002 to 27.2 billion in 2008. Social transfers (including entitlements and cash injections into ailing social insurance funds) almost doubled from 24.2 billion to 44.6 billion euro in the same period.

Similarly, the *composition of expenditure variance* indicator, which compares spending at sub-aggregate (ministry and other budget institution) level, shows considerable variance in expenditure outturns from the originally appropriated budgets of individual ministries. The variances recorded between the *composition of expenditure variance* and the *aggregate expenditure deviation* (*variance in excess of total deviation* indicator) are not as severe as one would expect, especially in 2007 and 2008, years when aggregate expenditure outturns seemed to have gone out

[4] According to an article of newspaper Kathimerini on the 26th of October 2006, the extra-budgetary funds amounted to 8 billion euro, the equivalent of about 10% of the total appropriated expenditure envelope in 2006.

of control. This is probably explained by the strict virement rules in force prohibiting large reallocations between budget heads.

The conclusion that can be readily drawn is that the Greek budget could not have been a credible instrument for maintaining basic discipline (hard budget constraint) in public spending, let alone being a useful statement of policy intent. Indeed, the fact that almost all newly elected governments in Greece have not resisted the temptation of applying novel ideas in search of the ideal structure of government has resulted in a perpetual reform process and very little managerial and administrative stability. The frequent restructuring of ministerial responsibilities and reshuffling of portfolios may have contributed considerably to the poor performance both in financial management and in terms of public service delivery – see Box 1.

Table 2 below provides a snapshot at a more detailed level in the Greek Regional Budget. The example is taken from the Regional Budget's expenditure on non-civil service employees. The table shows two specific economic classification items that make up the remuneration (fees and social contributions) of these employees. Table 3 illustrates the Ministry of Health programme for outsourcing social services (primarily for people in difficulty requiring specialised care) to non-governmental institutions and devolved public entities.

Table 2 manifests the inadequacies in planning human resource needs. There was no restraint in hiring contractual staff and no consideration that this practice was inflating liabilities by adding to an already overstaffed civil service[5] and disproportionately high government wage bill.

Table 3 shows the same pattern as above in what would be a programmatic expenditure item. It is not clear if some sort of budgeting (and cost analysis) did indeed take place when planning these services, but the data confirms a total absence of a hard budget constraint.

[5] According to the Hellenic National Statistical Service, the number of employees in general government increased by 18% in the period 2001 to 2009 bringing the overall number from 858,762 to over one million. The wage bill doubled in the same period from approximately 15 billion euro to 30 billion euro.

Table 2: Regional Budget; selected economic classification[6] lines (in euros)

Remuneration of staff employed under contracts of determined period[7] Code 0342			
Year	**Budget**	**Obligations**	**Payments**
2009	177,000.00	8,797,062.00	6,813,066.91
2008	214,100.00	12,559,912.00	10,752,449.70
2007	342,300.00	14,467,120.00	10,234,218.21
2006	249,500.00	8,463,449.00	7,566,314.69
Social insurance contributions for the above staff Code 0352			
Year	**Budget**	**Obligations**	**Payments**
2009	63,000.00	2,421,288.00	1,781,969.74
2008	71,000.00	3,466,210.00	2,814,224.94
2007	103,800.00	4,083,132.00	2,645,484.28
2006	75,000.00	2,359,860.00	1,943,959.47

Table 3: Ministry of Health; selected economic classification[8] lines (in euros)

Grants to mental health units Code 2544			
	Budget	**Obligations**	**Payments**
2009	40,000,000.00	70,907,000.00	82,760,244.85
2008	38,000,000.00	45,800,000.00	47,564,794.53
2007	23,000,000.00	45,017,735.00	54,247,485.00

Source: *Annual budgets and the Budget Execution Bulletins (General Department of Treasury and Budget)*

The information in the tables is indicative of the failure to draft credible budgets and demonstrates an inability to link policy intentions to properly planned expenditure decisions and reliable cost plans. These are not isolated cases. Our research has shown several examples of systematic

[6] The selected line is: 0300 "remuneration of employees under private law under contracts of a determined employment period and for special categories".
[7] Includes seasonal staff.
[8] The selected line is 2500 Grants to legal entities under private law.

budget overruns (as well as cases of gross overestimation) in a broad range of sectors – some of these examples are indicated in appendix.

In all the cases studied, some of the overspending may have been partly offset by savings in other budget lines, but this does not take away the fact that poor planning and budgeting appears to have been prevalent. The evidence suggests that due to poor budget preparation, operational shortcomings were addressed through ad hoc repetitive budgeting. Repetitive budgeting is very disruptive to financial and cash flow management and ultimately to maintaining budget discipline.

The norms, rules and systems governing the budget process in Greece are weak and there has been very little effort in improving things, let alone keeping up with innovation and developments in other OECD countries.

In January 2006, the IMF raised the alarm following the publication of its Report on the Observance of Standards and Codes (ROSC). The ROSC makes eleven key recommendations that practically point to severe problems in the whole spectrum of public financial management. Among other things the IMF stressed:

- The need to raise transparency of and public access to budget information.
- The importance of unifying the recurrent and investment budgets and provide full information on the activities of extra-budgetary funds, local governments, and other relevant public entities.
- The importance of providing estimates of contingent liabilities, especially those resulting from precarious government guarantees.
- The need to introduce a policy perspective and a medium term outlook to budget planning and formulation.
- The need for rationalising tax administration by introducing modern risk management, rationalising compliance and audit practices in order to curtail corrupt practices stemming from the combined problem of unclear regulations and unlimited discretion of tax officials.
- Strengthen the role of the supreme audit institution (*Elegktiko Sinedrio*).

The report was in many ways a stark warning about the state of Greece's fiscal and public financial management. There was need for urgent reform and for introducing modern systems and capabilities that were considered as given already for many years by most OECD countries.

The mix of poor public finances and an inherently uncompetitive economy left Greece very vulnerable to external shocks. The fact today is that Greece has one of the highest accumulated stocks of debt in the EU combined with a very high structural budget deficit that prohibits discretionary (counter-cyclical) spending. In addition, Greece faces an acute inter-temporal budget constraint as do many EU countries with ageing populations and comprehensive entitlements' schemes.

However, as much as Greece may have been incapable of a prudent fiscal policy, the SGP perverse incentive structure, confirmed by most research and analysis on the subject, made things worse.

2. The SGP: The Wrong Incentives

The Maastricht Treaty and the SGP (1997 and its reform in 2005) imposed the known deficit and public debt targets for the Eurozone. The SGP consisted of a commitment to a balanced or surplus general government[10] budget in the medium term, a binding budget 3% limit for the deficit to GDP ratio and a non-binding 60% limit for the debt to GDP ratio. The Pact in its original form combined ex-ante surveillance through a loose promise to discuss annual budget-fiscal frameworks of member countries and an ex-post warning system (with in-built sanctions) through the Excessive Deficit Procedure (EDP).

Track record, however, showed that the SGP framework did not guarantee compliance, which varied considerably among Eurozone members. The SGP very early became dysfunctional when it was made evident that the Council would not impose sanctions under the EDP. It was clear that SGP was ruled by political considerations and not by the formal fiscal rules. Even from the first years of its implementation the governments, including those of Germany and France, had started pushing for a reform of the SGP that would allow more ''flexibility.[11]''

There were plenty of warnings about the high risks involved with the SGP by economists well ahead of the launching of the Euro (Dafflon, B. and Rossi, S. 1998, Easterly, 1999). It was therefore apparent from very early that the impact of the SGP framework was to be less positive than originally anticipated by the politician-architects of the Economic and Monetary Union (EMU) of the EU.

---

[10] As defined by the European System of Integrated Economic Accounts (ESA). ESA 79 was replaced in 1999 by the updated ESA 95.

[11] Ironically, Germany, the very country that had pushed for tighter fiscal rules in EMU in the mid-1990s, was the second EMU country to violate the fiscal rules.

Economic theory teaches that a monetary union per se induces fiscal laxity. Specifically, the Mundell-Fleming model shows how under fixed exchange rates an expansionary fiscal policy can be effective in increasing output. In spite of the standing debate in the literature concerning the merits of expansionary fiscal policy involving continuous deficits, there is also evidence that fiscal consolidation may also have an expansionary impact on economic activity (Ferreiro et al., 2008). For many governments, the introduction of the Euro was a chance for more active fiscal policies in a context of relaxed fiscal constraints. The ability to borrow with low interest rates, the disappearance of the closed economy crowding out effect of expansionary fiscal policies and the removal of the threat of open economy exchange rate crises created wrong incentives to some governments.

In the period before 1999, when EMU membership was still not secured, Governments had more of an incentive to undertake discretionary fiscal consolidation even during election years. Voters were prepared to reward signals of fiscal discipline as these were clearly perceived as necessary for entrance in the Eurozone. Once EMU membership was secured, the old pattern of political opportunism in the budget cycles re-emerged in many countries. Koen and Noord (2005) and von Hagen and Wolff (2004) provided evidence that one-off measures[12] and creative accounting[13] have been used more frequently since the inception of EMU and showed that their probability was correlated with the level of the deficit.

The inauguration of the Euro saw many countries continuing using various techniques to reduce the deficit reported to Eurostat. Using "innovative" one-off transactions (e. g. SPVs – special purpose vehicles, public-private partnerships) that allowed spending without adding to the recorded deficit, deferring liabilities (e.g. maintenance of infrastructure) to future periods, and enforcing advances in tax payments were some of the weapons in the creative accounting arsenal of countries with governments with a short-termist agenda (Coeuré and Pisani-Ferry, 2005).

The SGP also produced disincentives to carry out productive public investments by treating all expenditures (the government deficit criterion does not qualify between current and capital expenditure) the same way. Ultimately, it is the share of discretionary spending directed to "productive"

[12] Fiscal decisions of a non-recurrent nature affecting temporarily government net lending/borrowing.

[13] The practice of producing accounts that suit a particular purpose which do not really show the *true and fair* view without, however, engaging in unlawful conduct.

expenditure (i.e. expenditure with multiplicative impact on the factors of production and productivity) that positively influences growth rates (Blanchard and Giavazzi, 2004, Coeuré and Pisani-Ferry, 2005, Heller 2005).

In addition, there have been outright disposals of public assets with the unique aim of showing a lower budget deficit and lowering gross debt. Many of these sales were controversial because, on the one hand, the disposal price of the public assets in question was more often than not considered particularly low, and, on the other, because most public asset sales were likely to have a negative impact on the net worth of the government concerned. A stratagem often used to show an improved situation in the current period was receiving immediate one-off inflows from privatisation (including public share offerings) of public enterprises whilst shouldering future pension liabilities. The first documented practice was during the partial privatisation of France Telecom in 1996. There is a large volume of evidence in the literature that includes several such asset disposals as part of many of the large-scale privatisation schemes across the EU. To mention but a few: the privatisation of EDF in France, of the postal services in Germany, and of the Italian, Portuguese or Greek telecoms (Dafflon and Rossi, 1998, Koen and Noord, 2005).

Milesi-Ferretti and Moriyama (2004), who investigated empirically the dynamics of EU governments' net worth, found that many became "poorer" after the establishment of the SGP. They compared changes in financial and non-financial assets with changes in financial liabilities and corrected for valuation effects. The research showed a sharp contrast between the periods 1992-1997 and 1997-2002. In the first period, increases in liabilities were matched by changes in assets and the net worth of governments was relatively stable. This was not the case in the second period. EU governments were worse off in 2002 than they were in 1997.

The above practices were attributed to the incentive structure created by the SGP. Many governments ignored sustainability and opted for current consumption and immediate political gains. Short-term considerations dominated long-term perspectives. Governments ignored the *inter-temporal budget constraint* (i.e. the discounted sum of a government's expected expenditures cannot exceed the discounted sum of its expected revenues) and did not consider making reference to today's balance sheet in relation to future revenues or liabilities.

The impact of the global economic crisis contributed to an increase of the Eurozone deficit from 1.6% in 1999 to 6.3% in 2009[14]. Today the debate can only be focused on learning the lessons of the past and on what comes next. There are those who call for seizing the moment to undertake a fundamental revision of the EU fiscal framework within the framework of the SGP, and others that advocate scrapping it altogether[15].

3. Reform Proposals: Introducing Preventive Mechanisms to the SGP

In September 2010, the European Commission presented proposals for the reform of economic governance in the EU[16]. The package contains six legislative proposals, including a second reform of the SGP and macro-economic coordination ("six-pack").

The proposed reforms aim at creating a framework for fiscal coordination, while at the same time introducing a stricter regime making the debt criterion operational by introducing sanctions and featuring a more automatic application (including the sanctions) of the EDP. The proposals therefore include a *preventive* component and an augmented *corrective* component for the revised SGP. There is as much controversy about the enforceability of the corrective component today as there was in the early days of EMU. The debate is centred on whether corrective measures can be realistically applied when sovereign nations are concerned[17]. This debate is beyond the scope of this Chapter. This section focuses primarily on the preventive part and looks at certain operational aspects of the Commission's proposals.

The preventive component rests on two elements; firstly, the creation of a harmonised budgetary framework for the EU member states, in particular for the countries of the Eurozone, and secondly, the enforcement

---

[14] In 2009 the largest government deficits in percentage of GDP in the EU were recorded by Ireland (-14.3%), Greece (-13.6%), the United Kingdom (-11.5%), Spain (-11.2%), Portugal (-9.4%), Latvia (-9.0%), Lithuania (-8.9%), Romania (-8.3%), France (-7.5%) and Poland (-7.1%).

[15] One such opinion was published in the Irish Examiner Thursday, May 27, 2010, entitled "Scrap the crazy EU stability and growth pact".

[16] See http://ec.europa.eu/economy_finance/articles/eu_economic_situation/2010-09-eu_economic_governance_proposals_en.htm

[17] Sceptics believe that the SGP has no real relevance because decisions on the application of the EDP are only made on political grounds – see article published by the Financial Times on October 24, 2010 "This stability pact obsession is not helpful".

of an ex ante system for budgetary and fiscal surveillance by member states and the Commission. The latter is supported by a proposal for a more automated system of sanctions to be imposed on Eurozone countries whose fiscal/budget consolidation process is making insufficient progress towards the SGP 3% of GDP government deficit target. The Commission believes that this approach will "provide incentives for prudent fiscal policy-making" and prevent the need of resorting to the corrective component foreseen by the EDP process.

What is particularly interesting in the new proposals is the first element of the preventive component. It articulates the way in which the Commission aspires to build upon the experience of the crisis and create a system of fiscal coordination.

According to the proposals, member states would need to operate under what the Commission calls a "new principle of fiscal policy making" including:

- Established and agreed (at the level of the Council) medium-term budgetary objective (MTOs) for a minimum period of three years;
- MTOs should support and justify national fiscal planning and provide a multi-annual fiscal perspective;
- National system of public sector accounting principles and standards adhering to GFS/ESA 95;
- National rules governing macroeconomic planning and the link with fiscal and budgetary planning – production of the most likely *macro-fiscal* scenario as well as alternative scenarios under different macroeconomic assumptions;
- National numerical fiscal rules in line with the MTOs and medium fiscal planning and in support of the SGP deficit and debt rules – the national systems should comprise clear monitoring systems, sanctions for non-compliance and escape clauses in the case of *force majeure*;
- Transparency of general government finances and budgetary framework and adequate public access to information, including extra-budgetary funds and operations that may entail large contingent liabilities.

All efforts made in the direction of improving fiscal and budgetary coordination are necessary. However, it is difficult to see how the Commission proposals (preventive or corrective) would work in practice without greater political union. The EU (and Eurozone) is made up of sovereign states that, unlike sub-national governments in a fiscally decentralised federal system, will be driven primarily by political considerations (incentives).

Moreover, experience so far confirms that the decision making process in the EU is not as straightforward in practice as envisaged by the EU Treaty and SGP. Fiscal and budgetary coordination can only happen at the discretion of national governments when it is commonly perceived (and accepted) that the cost of not conforming with the common budgetary and fiscal framework will be greater than the benefits – in other words, the extent to which countries such as Greece will indeed learn the lesson of the crisis.

On a technical and operational level, the type of policy coordination proposed by the Commission assumes the existence of adequate capabilities and systems within public administrations in all the member states concerned. It also assumes that the Commission is given an upgraded role (clear mandate and the necessary human resources and skills) to carry out the preventive role it has put forward. These assumptions would be for the most part precarious.

A member state like Greece, for instance, would have an insurmountable task ahead, under extremely adverse circumstances, in attaining an acceptable standard in public financial and fiscal management required to keep up with the "basic budgetary framework" proposed by the Commission.

In addition, the Commission proposals cover a number of technical issues that proved to be very hard challenges even to countries with advanced public services and public finance systems. For example, applying ESA95 involves unifying public sector accounting rules and being able to produce comprehensive balance sheets. This is easier said than done. Parry (2005) shows that New Zealand, a pioneer of public sector accounting reform, invested an estimated US$ 99 million in the 1980s on IT and administration systems alone (not covering the costs of training and developing of necessary skills and expertise) to ensure the transition to the new system of accounts. New Zealand is one of the wealthiest countries in the world with a small population, which means that corresponding necessary investment costs for countries like Greece may be prohibitive in the absence of fiscal space[18].

[18] Given the dire situation in Greece, even introducing basic techniques for the management of government non-financial assets can prove to be a great challenge. Non-financial government assets are commonly difficult to define and value. They are frequently non-marketable, and when they are, valuation methods are often very complex and expensive.

The above is not meant to serve as a critique of what the Commission has proposed. On the contrary, it is meant to draw on certain issues that require more detailed attention, in particular the commitment of EU financial and human resources to create and meaningfully support the SGP budgetary and fiscal framework of coordination and the corresponding surveillance mechanism. The Greek experience has clearly shown that the EU budget surveillance system has been dysfunctional. In the past, each member state was only obligated to provide information following the completion of the budget planning and formulation process. The reform proposals by the Commission, including the new principle of prudent fiscal policy making, will open the door for systematic consultations on member states' budgets before they are put forward for appropriation to Parliaments. Some may argue that this is tantamount to a loss in sovereignty, but others would say that this is a necessary evil for averting future crises and ultimately the survival of the Eurozone. It is possible that having to bring macro-fiscal policies and budgets before fellow EU members may be indeed a strong incentive to be prudent.

One important issue that is perhaps missing from the Commission's reform package is a closer consideration of the potential role of the supreme audit institutions (SAIs) of the EU and Eurozone. SAIs are independent institutions of the state and their primary mission is to oversee public accountability and scrutinise the operations of government. They operate under clear and rigorous principles and code of ethics governed by the original Lima Declaration and the workings of the International Organization of Supreme Audit Institutions (INTOSAI). INTOSAI (and the European subsidiary EUROSAI) have an undisputed reputation and track record that may serve the SGP well. INTOSAI also provides continuous methodological and technical support to national SAIs.

There is no apparent reason why all or certain more critical elements of the proposed preventive component for the SGP should not become a direct mandate for oversight by national SAIs. The involvement of SAIs could also dampen some of the public discontent and populism related to the perceived loss of sovereignty associated with external interventions to national budget and fiscal affairs. SAIs are national institutions, independent of government, and giving them a role in the surveillance process of the SGP would increase transparency and public awareness and arguably enhance overall effectiveness in monitoring enforcement.

4. Concluding Remarks

The new fiscal framework envisaged by the Commission is likely to face the same obstacles experienced before. As Murray and Wilkes (2009) point out about the UK, fiscal policy is ultimately about political decisions even when one country is concerned. Fiscal policy requires flexibility as much as it needs rules because its nature (and success) depends on pluralistic debate. Perhaps the most important step the Commission could take at this juncture would be to enhance transparency by pushing for greater cooperation in fiscal and budgetary matters among EU member states – thus the preventive component seems as the element of the reforms with the most realistic chance of achieving progress.

The problems of economic governance in Greece are deep-rooted and need to be addressed regardless of the on-going debate about reforming the SGP. Rebuilding governance in a credible way is a national matter. Greece would have to revisit the basics and master systems and capabilities that are taken as given in the OECD as well as in a great number of developing and transitioning countries. All this has to be done under extremely adverse economic circumstances and with Greece being in a debt trap situation. Regrettably, the good years were squandered due to policy-makers' short-termism, supported by voters' fiscal illusion,[19] which was translated to widespread inertia in the civil service and a general apathy to improvement or innovation.

Back to Basics

Whereas not all troubles in Eurozone countries are due to fiscal reasons, in the case of Greece problems are, to a very large extent, attributed to budgetary indiscipline. Greece would have to achieve basic financial compliance and budget discipline to support a credible fiscal policy. There is urgent need to restore basic financial management systems that ensure input control at a centralised level, starting with raising the capabilities of the central fiscal authority (ministry of finance) and ensuring it can indeed impose hard budget constraints over line ministries[20]. This should provide spending ministries, other budgetary

[19] For a theoretical analysis see Krogstrup and Wyplosz (2009).

[20] In 1992, an influential paper prepared by Jorgen von Hagen for the European Commission found that EU countries with dominant central fiscal authorities (combined with limited power by legislatures to amend the budget) had a strong positive impact on fiscal discipline in the countries concerned (Hagen, von, 1992). Fabrizio and Mody (2008) confirm "...that strong budget institutions are

institutions and local governments in Greece with an incentive to operate more efficiently and think about objectives more carefully.

The IMF 2006 ROSC provided a set of recommendations that is still valid today. Discretionary funds available should be prioritised for programmes that increase capabilities in modern public financial management, including macro-fiscal planning. These measures would be necessary also if Greece is to keep up with implementation of the proposals put forward by the Commission.

Fiscal Rules

Greece should consider enforcing a set of fiscal rules that would support compliance with SGP fiscal targets. Goodhart's law[21] teaches that it is best looking simultaneously at several indicators rather than relying on a single benchmark. One of these rules should be planning and executing a fiscal policy anchored on the Golden Rule. The rule requires maintaining a revenue (current) balance or surplus, which means that debt financing can only be used for capital expenditure. Fiscal rules of this nature are not a panacea, but would have significant potential value as rules of thumb in Greece that has long operated without fiscal restraint. Fiscal consolidation efforts are more likely to be successful when the starting position is difficult, such as in the case of Greece, as this heightens public awareness of the problem and makes the need of enforcing rules more palatable.

The immediate concern is to make the debt burden sustainable. This will happen when Greece achieves a primary balance and can pay the interest on outstanding debt without borrowing more. What the crisis should have taught decision makers in Greece is that the practice hitherto of running continuous revenue deficits by using protracted debt financing for basic government consumption is unsustainable – one of the main contributors to the present misfortunes.

Transparency and Public Access to Information

Another important challenge for Greece would be to achieve an acceptable level of transparency in its fiscal and budgetary systems and

---

associated with greater fiscal discipline even when the politics is unfavourable to such discipline".

[21] In 1975 Charles Goodhart first used this line of thinking, which became popular in the context of Margaret Thatcher's monetary policy in the UK.

information. The Open Budget Survey published in 2010 quotes Greece as an example to be avoided. The authors argue that the lack of transparency and effective oversight concerning the vulnerability of government debt and deficits to external shocks were also contributors to the present crisis.

The new role of the Commission, envisaged under the reforms, puts an increased emphasis on transparency. This is a critical element for Greece, which needs a lot of work in that direction, including increasing public access to information[22].

Capacity

Greece needs technical support in addition to financial support to exit the crisis in a way that reduces the risk of reverting to old practices. This means that Greece would need to build the necessary capabilities and invest in systems to comply with the reformed SGP, in particular the "basic budgetary framework" of the preventive component.

If the proposed reforms of the SGP are put in practice, the EU would need to upgrade the mandate and empower the European Commission to ensure that adequate human resources and skills are in place to handle the depth and volume of analysis required as well as to play an effective role as a coordinator. The Commission also needs to come forward by providing direct help to member states in need of technical and methodological support. Technical cooperation and coordination is a prerequisite for success in the implementation of the preventive mechanism in the SGP as presented in the reform proposals of September 2010.

References

Alesina, A. and Tabellini, G. (1990), A Positive Theory of Fiscal Deficits and Government Debt, *The Review of Economic Studies,* 57(3) (Jul. 1990), pp. 403–414.

Ayuso-i-Casals J., Deroose, S., Flores, E., Moulin, L. (2009) *Policy Instruments for Sound Fiscal Policies - Fiscal Rules and Institutions,* Palgrave Macmillan.

[22] In drafting this Chapter we encountered severe problems with accessing information. There is an obvious absence of consistency and reliability in the information made available on Greek government finances.

Baldwin, R., Gros, D. and Laeven, L. (2010), *Completing the Eurozone Rescue: What More Needs to Be Done,* Centre for Economic Policy Research.

Benoît, C. and Pisani-Ferry, J. (2005), Fiscal Policy in EMU: Towards a Sustainability and Growth Pact? Bruegel Working Paper n° 2005/01, December 2005.

Blanchard, O. J. and F. Giavazzi (2004), Improving the SGP through a Proper Accounting of Public Investment, CEPR Discussion Paper No. 4220.

Buiter, W.H. (2001), 'Notes on a "Code for Fiscal Stability", *Oxford Economic Papers*, 53(1): pp. 1–19.

Buiter, W., G. Corsetti, and N. Roubini (1993), "Excessive Deficits: Sense and Nonsense in the Treaty of Maastricht", *Economic Policy*, No 16, pp. 57-101.

Buiter, W and Grafe, C. (2002) Patching Up the Pact: Some Suggestions for Enhancing Fiscal Sustainability and Macroeconomic Stability in the Enlarged European Union, Discussion Paper No 3496, London, Centre for Economic Policy Research.

Buti, M. and Franco, D. (2005), Fiscal Policy in Economic and Monetary Union: Theory, Evidence and Institutions, Edward Elgar Publishing Limited

Caddy, J. and Vergez, C., (2001), Citizens as Partners: Information, Consultation and Public Participation in Policy-Making, Organisation for Economic Co-operation and Development: Paris, France.

Coeuré, B. and Pisani-Ferry, J. (2005) *Fiscal policy in EMU: Towards a Sustainability and Growth Pact?,* Bruegel Working Paper No 2005/01.

Dabla-Norris, E. et al. (2010) Budget Institutions and Fiscal Performance in Low-Income Countries, Working Paper 10/80, Strategy, Policy, and Review, and Fiscal Affairs Departments, IMF, Washington, March 2010.

Dafflon, B. and Rossi, S. (1998) Public accounting fudges towards EMU: A first empirical survey and some public choice considerations, *Public Choice* 101, pp. 59–84, Kluwer Academic Publishers.

De la Fuente, A. (1997), 'Fiscal Policy and Growth in the OECD', CEPR Discussion Papers, 1755.

Easterly, W. (1999), Fiscal Illusion: Taking the Bite Out of Budget Cuts, *Economic Policy,* April 1999.

Eichengreen, B. and Wyplosz, C. (1997), "The Stability Pact: Minor Nuisance, Major Diversion?" *Economic Policy*, 26, pp. 65-114.

European Commission (2004), 'Public Finances in EMU – 2004', *European Economy*, 3/2004.

—. (2006), 'Public Finances in EMU – 2006', *European Economy*, 3/2006

—. (2010), Directorate-General for Economic and Financial Affairs "The Economic Adjustment Programme for Greece, Second review – autumn 2010", *European Economy Occasional Papers* 72, December 2010.

Eurostat (2004), "Pensions: Eurostat Communication to the Advisory Expert Group", 2 December.

Fabrizio, S. and Mody, A. (2008), Breaking the Impediments to Budgetary Reforms: Evidence from Europe, Working Paper 08/82; European Department, IMF, Washington, March 2008.

Franco, D., Marino, M. R. and Zotteri, S. (2004), "Pension Expenditure Projections, Pension Liabilities and European Union Fiscal Rules", International workshop on the balance sheet of social security pensions, Tokyo, 1-2 November.

Feld, L. P. and Kirchgassner, G. (2004), On the Effectiveness of Debt Brakes: The Swiss Experience, paper presented at the CESifo-LBI Conference on Sustainability of Public Debt, Munich, October 22, 2004.

Ferreiro, J., Fontana, G. and Serrano, F. (2008), *Fiscal Policy in the European Union*, Palgrave Macmillan.

Gleich, H. (2003) Budget Institutions and Fiscal Performance in Cental and Eastern European Countries, ECB Working Paper, 215.

Gramberger, M.R. (2001), *Citizens as Partners: OECD Handbook on Information, Consultation and Public Participation in Policy-Making*, Organisation for Economic Co-operation and Development (OECD) Paris, France.

Hagen, von, J. (1992), Budgeting Procedures and Fiscal Performance in the European Communities, *European Economy Economic Papers*, 96, European Commission, Directorate-General for Economic and Financial Affairs.

Hagen von, J. and Harden, I. (1995), Budget Processes and Commitment to Fiscal Discipline, *European Economic Review*, 39 (3), pp. 771-779

Hagen von, J., and Wolff, G. (2004), "What do Deficits tell us about Debt? Empirical Evidence on Creative Accounting with Fiscal Rules in the EU", mimeo, Frankfurt, December.

Hagen von, J., Hallerberg, M. and Strauch, R. (2004), 'The Design of Fiscal Rules and Forms of Governance in European Union Countries', ECB Working Paper 419.

Heller, P. S. (2005) "Understanding Fiscal Space", IMF Policy Discussion Paper, Fiscal Affairs Department

Herzlinger, R. E. (1996) Can public trust in nonprofits and government be restored?, *Harvard Business Review*, 74 (2), pp. 97–107.

IMF (2006) Report on the Observance of Standards and Codes (ROSC) of Greece, Fiscal Affairs Department, Washington, March 2006.

—. (2010) Greece: First Review under the Stand-By Arrangement, Country Report No. 10/286, Washington, September 2010.

Koen, V. and van den Noord, P. (2005), "Fiscal Gimmickry in Europe: One-off Measures and Creative Accounting", Economics Department Working Paper, No 417, Paris: OECD.

Kopits, G. and Symanski, S. (1998), *'Fiscal Policy Rules'*, IMF Occasional Paper 162, Washington, July 1998.

Krogstrup, S. and Wyplosz, C. (2009), Dealing with the Deficit Bias: Principles and Policies, in *Policy Instruments for Sound Fiscal Policies - Fiscal Rules and Institutions, edited by* Ayuso-i-Casals, Deroose, Flores and Moulin, Palgrave Macmillan.

Lee, M. (2004), *Reporting: Strengthening Democratic Accountability*, IBM Centre for the Business of Government: Washington, DC.

—., (2005) Public Reporting, in *Encyclopedia of Public Administration and Public Policy*, edited by Jack Rabin, Taylor and Francis Group.

Marr, B. (2008), *Managing and Delivering Performance – How Government, Public Sector and Not For Profit Organisations Can Measure and Manage What Really Matters,* Elsevier

Milesi-Ferreti, G. M. and Moriyama, K. (2004), "Fiscal Adjustment in EMU Countries: a Balance Sheet Approach", Working Paper No. WP/04/143, Washington: International Monetary Fund.

Murray, A. and Wilkes, G. (2009) "Fiscal rules ok?" CentreForum.

Musgrave, R.A. (1939), "The Nature of Budgetary Balance and the Case for a Capital Budget", *American Economic Review*, 29: 260–71.

Oksanen, H. (2004), "Public Pensions in the National Accounts and Public Finance Targets", CESifo Working Paper, No 1214.

Open Budget Survey 2010, International Budget Partnership (IBP), http://internationalbudget.org

Parry, M. (2005), *Accrual Accounting for National Governments*, Public Fund Digest, vol.5 No 2 August 2005, Washington, International Consortium on Governmental Financial Management.

Poterba, J. and Rueben, K. (2001), Fiscal News, State Budget Rules, and Tax-Exempt Bond Yields, *Journal of Urban Economics*, 50, pp. 537–562.

Schiavo-Campo, S. and Tommasi, D. (1999), *Managing Government Expenditure*, Manila: Asian Development Bank (ADB).

Schick, A. (2003), 'The Role of Fiscal Rules in Budgeting', OECD Journal on Budgeting, Vol. 3, No. 3, pp. 7-34, OECD.

—. (2004), 'Fiscal Institutions Versus Political Will', in G. Kopits (ed.) *Rules-Based Fiscal Policy in Emerging Markets*, Basingstoke: Palgrave.

Steclebout-Orseau, E. and Hallerberg, M. (2009), Who Provides Signals to Voters about Government Competence on Fiscal Matters? The Importance of Independent Watchdogs, *edited by* Ayuso-i-Casals, Deroose, Flores, and Moulin, *Policy Instruments for Sound Fiscal Policies - Fiscal Rules and Institutions*, Palgrave Macmillan.

Wyplosz, C. (2002), 'Fiscal Policy: Institutions versus Rules', CEPR, Discussion Paper 3228.

—. (2002), *The Stability and Growth Pact: Time to Rethink*, Briefing Notes to the Committee for Monetary and Economic Affairs, European Parliament.

CHAPTER TEN

THE MANIPULATION OF GREEK STATISTICS AND THE GREEK ENTRANCE IN THE EMU: THE CASE OF ABSORPTION OF 9.6% OF SHADOW ECONOMY IN THE GREEK GDP

BITZENIS P. ARISTIDIS
AND MAKEDOS IOANNIS

1. Historical Points Regarding the Greek Entrance in the European Union (EU) and in the Economic and Monetary Union (EMU)

In recent decades the issue of relations between Greece and the European Economic Community (EEC) / EU has held a central position in the debate on the role of the country in the wider European family. The path of Greece towards a united Europe began on 8 June 1959, when an application was lodged for association with the EEC, which was approved by the EEC Foreign Ministers on 27 July 1959 and on 10 September 1959 negotiations commenced between representatives of Greece and the EEC. This led to the signing of the Association Agreement in the Trophy Hall of the Hellenic Parliament in Athens on 9 July 1961. The Association Agreement came into force on 2 November 1961 (actually on November 1962, after its ratification by the Hellenic Parliament on 28 February 1962). It is noteworthy that Greece was the first country to sign an Association Agreement with the newly established EEC (Bitzenis, 2009).

However, Greece's progress towards joining a united Europe was suspended on 21 April 1967 due to the abolition of democratic institutions by a military junta. On 14 August 1974, a few days after the restoration of democracy in Greece, the country witnessed the second wave of the Turkish invasion of Cyprus. The decision taken by Prime Minister Constantine Karamanlis was not to respond with war but to exert political and economic pressure on Turkey. At the same time, a particularly costly programme to bolster Greek military capacity in order to achieve and maintain a credible balance of power so as to deter the intense Turkish aggression was implemented. It is obvious that if during the period 1974-1975, Karamanlis had opted to unleash a retaliatory war against Turkey, regardless of its outcome, Greece and Turkey would have been drawn into an extended period of conflict. Consequently, the accession of Greece to the EEC would have been postponed or aborted and the impact on Greek political institutions would have been extremely destabilising (for further discussion see also Bitzenis, 2009).

On 22 August 1974, a government of national unity led by Constantine Karamanlis lodged a memorandum with the president of the European Community (EC) Council of Ministers requesting immediate reactivation of the Association Agreement. This request was accepted, allowing the Karamanlis' government one year later to lodge an application for Greece's accession as a full member of the EC. On 9 February 1976, the Council of Ministers requested that the procedure for Greece's full accession be continued, despite the reservations on the part of the Commission, which requested a pre-accession period. Thus, a few months later, on 27 July 1976, negotiations began between Greece and the EC, which were successfully concluded on 21 December 1978. On 28 May 1979, the Treaty on Greece's accession to the EC was signed in Athens in the Zappeion Hall, followed on 28 June 1979 by ratification of the Accession Treaty by the Hellenic Parliament. Two years later, on 1 January 1981, the Accession Treaty came into force (Bitzenis 2009, p. 258-9).

The years of preparation for accession (1974-1980), including the first thirteen years of EC membership (1981-1993), was a period of slow but continuous maturation of the Greek society, economy and institutions. It is revealing that restrictive policies and/or stabilization programs implemented in 1979-81, 1983, 1985-87 and 1991-93 did not yield permanent gains, although to some degree they averted a further deterioration of the economic situation. Things picked up pace in the early 1990s and more specifically since 1994, when the new "1994-1999 Convergence Program of the Greek Economy" was adopted, marking a qualitative shift in the economic policies. The steady improvement in the economic situation meant that sacrifices had not been wasted. The ailing economy soon found itself on the road to recovery. Moreover, since the improvement was visible, not only was the credibility of the reform policies increased, but the adoption of a moderate stance with regard to wages and prices was made easier for social partners (Bitzenis, 2009, p. 260).

2. The Greek membership into the EMU

The membership of Greece into the EU is a special case and worth mentioning (see also http://www.ecb.europa.eu/pub/pdf/conrep/cr2000 en.pdf) Commission of the European Communities, 2000, "European Central Bank (ECB) Convergence Report 2000 (prepared in accordance with Article 122 (2) of the Treaty)). Greece entered the Exchange Rate Mechanism (ERM) I on 16 March 1998. At that time, the central parity was 357 Greek Drachmas (GRD or GDR) against the European Currency Unit (ECU) and the fluctuation band +/-15%. However, the ERM II replaced the ERM I in January 1999 and the euro replaced the ECU - for further discussion see various Convergence reports of 1996-2012 (http://www.ecb.europa.eu/pub/convergence/html/index.en.html). After the conversion rate of the euro had been determined, the drachma was valued at a central rate of 353,109 GRD against the euro. On 17 January 2000, the central rate of the Greek drachma was re-valued at 340.75 GRD against the euro (see Table 1).

More specifically, the fluctuations during the two-year period before the entrance of Greece into the EMU were limited to the band of +-15%. For instance, between April – August 1998, an appreciation of 6% of the GRD against the Euro was recorded, which tightened the monetary policy to reduce inflation. In late January and early February 1999, it reached the highest level against the Euro (321 GDR to 1 Euro). Shortly afterwards, a gradual depreciation appeared and the Greek drachma reached 334.7 GRDs against the Euro on 31 March 2000. Thus, Greece, the ECB and the other member states agreed to a further depreciation of the Greek drachma against the Euro in order to reach the final official central rate of the Greek drachma against the Euro, which is 340.75, an appreciated rate compared to the initial central rate of 353.109 although depreciated compared to the rate existing at the time of decision (see Table 1).

Table 1: The fluctuation of exchange parity in 2000

JAN 2000	FEB 2000	MAR 2000	APR 2000	MAY 2000	JUN 2000	JUL 2000	AUG 2000	SEP 2000	OCT 2000	NOV 2000	DEC 2000
331.06	333.17	333.91	335.22	336.59	336.85	336.87	337.29	338.6	339.46	340.16	340.71

Source: EU

2.1 Manipulation of Greek Statistics: The Revision of the Greek Government Deficit and Debt Figures in 2004

Statistical issues in this field were debated with the Greek statistical authorities far more frequently than with any other Member State. Eurostat was forced to introduce several times footnotes about reservations on the quality of Greek debt and deficit figures. Decisions and interventions of Eurostat forced in 2002 the Greek statistical authorities, amongst others, to reclassify share convertible bonds and share exchangeable bonds in government debt, to treat some capital injections as capital transfers, to treat debt assumption by government as non financial operations, to classify DEKA (a state-owned company) inside general government, and to launch a new survey on social security funds.

More specifically, Eurostat had publicly expressed doubts on the debt and deficit figures transmitted by the Greek authorities since 2002 by the way of "footnotes" or specific comments in the press releases where these figures are published. Following these reserves, the Greek authorities transmitted in November 2002 a revised notification for years 2000 and 2001, published by Eurostat. This press release referred only to Greece. In 2002, the correction led to a deterioration of the Greek deficit by 1.0% of gross domestic product (GDP) for 2000 and 1.3% for 2001, while public debt increased by 1.5% and 1.9% of GDP respectively. The main reason for the increase of the public debt was the inclusion of information on share convertible bonds issued by special purpose vehicles in the context of securitisation operations undertaken by government.

Eurostat again maintained reservations on the data notified at the time of the notification of March 2004. Thus, Eurostat published on 7 May 2004 another specific press release on Greece (n° 62/2004), where the Greek deficit for 2003 was corrected from -1.7% to 3.2% of GDP, and the debt from 102.4% to 103.0% of GDP. According to Eurostat (2004), the increase in the Greek deficit was essentially due to a downwards revision of tax revenue estimates - mainly value added tax (VAT) - in public accounts, a downward revision of the payments received from the EU institutions in the context of certain structural fund programs, and the re-classification, as a financial transaction, of a payment from the Saving Postal Bank to government. Eurostat (2004) mentioned that it was not in a position to fully certify the debt and deficit figures for 2003 and asked the Greek authorities to make the necessary efforts to clarify all the outstanding issues. (Eurostat, 2004, p. 12).

Thus, in 2004 the Greek statistics had undergone a very large revision. In September of the same year was announced that the real government deficit for 2003 was 4.6% of GDP instead of 1.7% of GDP, which had been initially reported. Also, the government deficits for 1997-1999 and 2000-2002 were revised upwards at least two percentage points of GDP. Data revisions of such a scale rose questions about the reliability of the Greek statistics on public finances. The ECOFIN Council of 21 October 2004 took note of the Commission's information note on the fiscal notification of Greece and welcomed the Commission's initiative to present a detailed analysis of Greece's deficit and debt data back to 1997.

The information provided at the time of Eurostat's mission to Athens at the beginning of September 2004 made it possible to clarify with the Greek authorities some of the outstanding problems. Accordingly, based on Eurostat (2004, p.12), the data transmitted by Greece at the time of the notification of September 2004 and published by Eurostat on 23 September (press release n° 117/2004) made it possible to withdraw some of the reservations previously expressed on certain budgetary data from years 2000 to 2003. The Greek deficit passed, in relation to previously published data, from –2.0% of GDP to –4.1% for 2000, and from –1.4% to –3.7% for both of the years 2001 and 2002, and finally from –1.7% to –4.6% for 2003.

Following these revisions, which concerned data from 2000 up to 2003, a mission was sent to Athens on 12 October 2004 to check with the Greek authorities the debt and deficit data for the years before 2000. As this concerns historical data, the Greek authorities could not provide in place data concerning transactions undertaken in the period 1997 - 1999. Therefore Eurostat asked them to provide the relevant information by 18 October. This concerned, among other things, data on military expenditures, the recording of EU grants, and data on interest expenditures and capitalized interest, as well as methodological explanations on the recording of capital injections. Mr Kontopirakis, General Secretary of the National Statistical Service in Greece, addressed the response to Eurostat on 18 October 2004. This response was not complete and did not fully answer all the questions asked by Eurostat (http://epp.eurostat.ec.europa.eu/cache/ITY_PUBLIC/GREECE/EN/GREECE-EN.PDF).

Table 2 presents the main differences between the two notifications. The divergences due to the recording of military equipment account for 25% of the total revisions in 2003, 75% in 2002, 50% in 2001 and 90% in 2000. The Commission informed the ECOFIN Council on 21 October about the main reasons of the revisions.

Table 2: Main components of the revision of Greek data between the Figures reported in March 2004 and September 2004

(Revisions GREECE March 2004 / September 2004)

	2000	2001	2002	2003
DEFICIT	% GDP	% GDP	% GDP	% GSP
March 2004	*-2.0*	*-1.4*	*-1.4*	*-1.7*
Tax revenue				0.9
Payments of the EU				0.3
Reclassification of payments from the Postal Bank				0.2
Military expenditure	1.9	1.2	1.7	0.7
Surplus of social Security Funds	0.0	1.0	0.4	0.6
Under recording of interest	0.3	0.1	0.1	0.1
September 2004	*-4.1*	*-3.7*	*-3.7*	*-4.6*
DEBT				
March 2004	*106.1*	*106.6*	*104.6*	*102.6*
Capitalized Interest	4.5	4.2	3.9	3.4
Consolidating Assets of Social Security	3.2 0.1	3.8 0.1	3.8 0.2	3.7 0.1
September 2004	*114.0*	*114.7*	*112.5*	*109.9*

Source: Report by Eurostat (end 2004) on the revision of the Greek Government deficit and debt figures

Table 3 points out useful information on the development of Greek GDP, government debt and ratio, and Table 4 informs us on the development of Greek GDP, deficit and their ratio. So, we have a picture how these factors influenced the Greek economy from 2002-2006.

Table 3: The Greek general government consolidated gross debt level at nominal value extraordinary

Greece	GDP	DEBT	RATIO
2002	143482	158887	110.74%
2003	155543	167723	107.83%
2004	168417	182702	108.48%
2005	181088	194666	107.50%
2006	194458	202770	104.27%

Source: Eurostat, http://epp.eurostat.ec.europa.eu/cache/ITY_OFFPUB/KS-CD-06-001/EN/KS-CD-06-001-EN.PDF

Table 4: The Greek general government deficit

	GDP	DEFICIT	RATIO
2002	143,482	-7074	-4.93%
2003	155,543	-8965	-5.76%
2004	168,417	-11681	-6.94%
2005	181,088	-8222	-4.54%
2006	194,458	-5010	-2.58%

Source: Eurostat, http://epp.eurostat.ec.europa.eu/cache/ITY_OFFPUB/KS-CD-06-001/EN/KS-CD-06-001-EN.PDF

The big differences between the notifications in March 2004 and in September 2004 were a fact. The figures (from Table 2) show the information note presented by the Commission and explain the accounting rules and the contacts between Eurostat and Greek authorities. The Greek general government consolidated gross debt level at nominal value extraordinary was continuously increased and also the general government deficit was increased too.

2.2 The Debt and Deficit Accounts for the Greek Case Regarding the Years 1997, 1998 and 1999

Following the work of Eurostat during the period 1997-2003, the exchange of correspondence, and the final constructive discussion on the 10th November 2004 meeting, Eurostat and the Greek authorities came to concrete conclusions. The revised deficit figures during the period 1997-2003 are as follows:

1997: 6.6% of GDP instead of 4.0%; 1998: 4.3% of GDP instead of 2.5%; 1999: 3.4% of GDP instead of 1.8%; 2000: 4.1% of GDP instead of 2.0%; 2001: 3.7% of GDP instead of 1.4%; 2002: 3.7% of GDP instead of 1.4% 2003: 4.6% of GDP instead of 1.7%

On the other hand, the revised debt figures for the period 1997-2003 are of the following magnitude:

1997: 114.0% of GDP instead of 108.2%; 1998: 112.4% of GDP instead of 105.8%; 1999: 112.3% of GDP instead of 105.2%; 2000: 114% of GDP instead of 106.1% 2001: 114.7% of GDP instead of 106.6%; 2002: 112.5% of GDP instead of 104.6% 2003: 109.9% of GDP instead of 102.6%.

Bitzenis (2009, p.180) mentioned that the Greek budgetary statistics have undergone a great revision. The substantial increases, mentioned above, resulted from earlier actions undertaken by Eurostat as well as the initiatives taken by the new incoming Greek government to launch a thorough fiscal audit, in the spring of 2004. Revisions in statistics, and particularly in government deficit data, are not unusual. Since the publication of the first outcomes in March from the national statistical institutes, data are often revised as new information becomes available, or because errors are easily detected. However, the 2004 revision of the Greek budgetary data is exceptional. The reasons why these figures differ from the ones provided in previous notifications are essentially as follows:

- An increase of recording for military expenditures for equipment goods.
- Correct recording of capital injections and EU grants. It is important to underline, however, that in the case of Greece most capital injections in state-owned enterprises were mainly financed by EU grants earmarked for specific purposes. As a consequence, they should be treated as capital transfers (impacting the deficit)

and not as share capital increases (financial transaction without impact on the deficit).

Table 5: Figures for deficit and debt revised according to the information provided by the Greek authorities

	Mio €			*Percentage of GDP*		
	1997	1998	1999	1997	1998	1999
Government deficit (as it stands now)	3919	2605	1990	**4.03**	**2.46**	**1.77**
Corrections to be imputed in relation to:						
– Military expenditure (1)	149	70	974	0.15	0.07	0.86
– Debt assumptions (2)	124	140	97	0.13	0.13	0.09
– Capitalised interest (3)	990	282	108	1.02	0.27	0.10
– Capital injections (4)	822	1026	825	0.85	0.97	0.73
– Interest on convertible bonds (5)	0	12	38	0.00	0.01	0.03
– DEKA (6)	211	211	113	0.22	0.20	0.10
– EU grants (7)	202	179	-272	0.21	0.17	-0.24
– interest	0	0	0	0.00	0.00	0.00
Revised deficit (incl. the above corrections)	6417	4525	3873	**6.61**	**4.28**	**3.44**
GDP	97235	105773	112683			
	1997	**1998**	**1999**	**1997**	**1998**	**1999**
Government debt (as it stands now)	105186	111924	118583	**108.18**	**105.82**	**105.24**
Corrections to be imputed in relation to:						
– Capitalised interest (8)	4719	5001	5109	4.85	4.73	4.53
– Convertible bonds (9)	0	0	0	0.00	0.00	0.00
Consolidating assets of social security (10)	949	1972	2091	0.98	1.86	1.86
– share exchangeable bonds (11)	0	0	775	0.00	0.00	0.69
Revised debt (incl. the above corrections)	110854	118897	126558	**114.01**	**112.41**	**112.31**

Source: Eurostat (2004)
(http://epp.eurostat.ec.europa.eu/cache/ITY_PUBLIC/GREECE/EN/GREECE-EN.PDF)

The revision of figures for deficit and debt would be as shown in Table 5, according to the Greek authorities' information. We can see the development of government deficit from 1997-1999 and as percentage of GDP, as it stood then, and the equivalent revised deficit included the corrections. Also, Table 5 shows the government debt as it stood then and the revised debt including the equivalent corrections.

More specifically, the elements of Table 5 can be explained as:

Reasons for the *deficit* (see also Bitzenis (2009, p.180-1))**:**

- **Military expenditures** (military durables such as battleships, tanks, missiles, fighters, etc): data are as provided by the Greek authorities - on a cash basis in the absence of data on deliveries. Although Eurostat had demanded that Greek authorities provide figures according to the method of deliveries, the Greek authorities had answered that such data were not available. The discrepancies occurred because military equipment should be recorded as government expenditure at the moment of their delivery, irrespective of effective payments, which can take place when the equipment is ordered, during construction, upon delivery or even at a later stage. However, data on deliveries of military equipments is confidential or not presented in national accounts. As a consequence, national statistical institutes face difficulties in obtaining the necessary information to draw government accounts which are fully in line with the accounting rules. Although the method for recording expenditures was based on deliveries, in fact no information on deliveries has been given since 1997. Therefore, most military expenditures covered by borrowing have not been recorded in the specific time period (1997-2004) (Eurostat 2004). As information on deliveries cannot be obtained at present, "the Greek authorities have decided to record these amounts on a cash basis."

Thus, additional expenditure imputed in government accounts after revisions took place in September 2004: 0.2% of GDP burden of deficit in 1997, 0.1% of GDP burden of deficit in 1998, 0.9% of GDP burden of deficit in 1999, 1.9% of GDP burden of deficit in 2000, 1.2% of GDP burden of deficit in 2001, 1.7% of GDP burden of deficit in 2002, and 0.7% of GDP burden of deficit in 2003.

- **Debt assumptions**: Figures on previously notified debt assumptions were incomplete. Data available to the International Monetary Fund (IMF) were more detailed than the data reported to Eurostat. The Greek authorities explained that such differences are partly, due to different coverage of the notion of the public sector. Although the accounting rules on the recording of debt assumptions have been well established since at least 1995, they were one of the most frequently discussed issues between Eurostat and the Greek statistical authorities from 1996 to 2002. Although Eurostat has made clear the rules to be followed, such rules were not applied in a consistent way and data has frequently changed. It can be concluded that Eurostat's recommendations were not followed. The Greek authorities acknowledged that 217 millions of € of debt assumptions had taken place in 2000, and 494 millions of € in 2001, against the previously reported figures of 38 millions of € in 2000 and zero in 2001. Reports of 2004 included debt assumptions of 277 millions of € for 2002 and 168 millions of € for 2003. In 2003, Greece informed Eurostat that the 1997, 1998 and 1999 accounts need to be corrected to include 124, 140, and 97 billions of € of debt assumptions, respectively (see also Bitzenis (2009, p.181)).

- **Capitalised or capital interest**: Figures on previously notified capitalised or capital interest are incomplete. Once again, Eurostat had explicitly made it clear during the years 1996 to 1998 that capitalised interest should be properly recorded and accrued over time, deteriorating the deficit/surplus of government in those years in which the amounts had to be recorded. However, Greek authorities continued to misreport data. In spite of their explicit assurances pointing to the contrary, the rules on the recording of capitalised interest were not applied. The Greek authorities have informed Eurostat that capitalised interest for the years 1995 to 2000 is as follows:

1995: 1964 millions of €; 1996: 1765 millions of € ; 1997: 990 millions of € ;1998: 282 millions of € ; 1999: 108 millions of € ; 2000: 340 millions of €

It is recalled that in the first notification (before the revision), the amount of capitalised interest was 33 billions of GDR for 1997 (106 millions of €), 27 billions of GDR for 1998 (82 millions of €), and zero for 1999. It is also recalled that the Greek authorities notified in 2004 that in the year 2000 unrecorded capitalised interest amounted to 340 millions of €, an amount much bigger than the one recorded in 1999. However, the impact on the deficit/debt figures should still be limited (see also Bitzenis (2009, p.182)).

- **Capital injections**: Data once again was incomplete. Greece argued that all capital injections had been registered as financial transactions below the line without any impact on the government deficit because the beneficiaries of capital injections were "all quasi-corporations," "therefore, the amount received by them in order to finance infrastructure could be treated as a financial transaction. This, of course, would not have been possible in the case of corporations." The service sectors receiving capital injections, such as the Greek Electricity Company, and Greek Telecommunication Company, did have the legal status of a corporation and therefore could not be considered by accountants as quasi corporations. Moreover, some of the capital injections covered mainly past and consistent losses of state-owned enterprises that were highly indebted. Eurostat believes that capital injections from 2000 to 2003 have been correctly recorded in the Greek government accounts. This is also the case for the previous years 1997 to 1999, as a correction had been imputed according to the rules for the treatment of capital injections. Since Greece had agreed that several capital injections had not been properly recorded, the deficit for 2000 and 2001 was therefore revised upwards by 0.8% of GDP for 2000 and 0.9% for 2001. The reclassification of capital injections concerned a number of companies, notably OSE (the railways company), the Athens Metro, and EGNATIA (a motorway company). The Greek authorities seem to have correctly registered capital injections from 2000 onwards. However, the revision in the accounts of October 2002 was not extended back during the years before 2000. The Greek authorities informed Eurostat that capital injections amounted to 1,233 millions of € (1.27% of GDP) in 1997 and 1,415 millions of € (1.34% of GDP) in 1998, none of which had been registered as deficit increases. As regards 1999, Greece informed that capital injections amounted to 1,820 millions of € (1.61% of GDP) of which only 411 millions of € (or 0.36% of GDP) were imputed as capital transfers. Accordingly, they increased the deficit.

- **DEKA**: In 1997, the Greek government created a State-owned holding, known as DEKA. The government moved several enterprises to be privatised to the DEKA balance sheet. DEKA injected capital in some of the enterprises it controlled, sold others and paid dividends to the government. When the Greek government founded DEKA, the Greek authorities considered that it should be classified outside the government and that the dividends paid to the government could be recorded as deficit-reducing property income. Eurostat brought to the attention of the Greek statistical authorities the need to correct the sector classification of DEKA and/or the accounting treatment of its transaction immediately after DEKA's establishment in 1997. In 1999, Eurostat recommended that DEKA be classified within the government. However, the Greek authorities accepted to do so only in 2002. When Eurostat questioned whether the impact of the reclassification of DEKA has been properly assessed by the Greek authorities from 1997 to 2001, the Greek authorities, in a letter dated 27 October 2004 confirmed that this had not been the case. As a result, amounts previously classified as share capital increases equal to 211 millions of € both in 1997 and 1998, and to 113 millions of € in 1999, were reclassified as capital transfers, increasing the deficit. Data are now complete.

- **Interest on convertible bonds**: Eurostat requested shares from Greece that (unclear) convertible bonds had to be included in the reported government debt. Share-convertible bonds were finally included into government debt in September 2002 with a retroactive correction since 1998. The interest paid by the government was considered as government expenditure. As a consequence, the government deficit increased by 46 millions of € in 2000 and 82 millions of € in 2001. However, deficit figures before the year 2000 were not correct at that time. In 2003, Eurostat believed that share-convertible bonds had been correctly recorded in the accounts.

- **EU (structural funds) grants**: Data was provided by the Greek authorities during a meeting on 10 November 2004. The amounts correspond to projects co-financed by the European Union. On the basis of the information provided by the Greek statistical authorities, the figures for 1997-1999 have now been corrected to the following amounts: 1997: 202 millions of €; 1998: 179 millions of €; 1999: -272 millions of €.

The negative amount of the correction for the year 1999 is explained by the fact that the amounts to be added have been recorded under the heading "capital injections" due to national accounts classification practices in Greece. Finally, as far as structural funds are concerned, the deficit figure of 2003 was increased in the notification of September 2004 by an amount of 475 millions of € (equal to 0,3% of GDP), compared to the figure reported in the March 2003 notification, as a result of an error in public accounting, relative to the effective payments by EU institutions in 2003.

- **Interest**: The Greek authorities confirmed on 19 November 2004 that interest due to debt increase should not be added to government expenditures as it had already been previously incorporated in the Social Security Funds survey.

The *Debt*: It is asserted that between 2000 and 2003, amounts of approximately 5 billions of € per year were not included in the government debt due to a wrong consolidation done at a general government level of the government debt. For this reason, Eurostat asked the Greek authorities to record the amounts in order to be added to the government debt between 1997 and 1998. The Greek authorities confirmed on 19 November 2004 that the amount of debt that should be added to the general government debt for this issue was equal to 949 millions of € in 1997 and 1,972 millions of € in 1998. The debt of share exchangeable bonds which had been wrongly classified outside the government by the Greek authorities was added to the government debt in 1999. In order to correct the figure Eurostat used information it had previously received from the Greek authorities. Between March and September 2002, when the government debt increased from 1998 to 2001, due to the inclusion of share convertible bonds, previously excluded from government debt; between September and November 2002, when government debt increased again due to the inclusion of share exchangeable bonds into government debt (see also Bitzenis (2009, p.182-5)).

Table 6: Greece: Long-term interest rates *(percentages)*

	1998	1999	2000 Jan.	2000 Feb.	2000 Mar.	Apr. 1999 to Mar. 2000
Long-term interest rates	8.5	6.3	6.6	6.5	6.2	6.4
Reference value	6.6	6.8	-	-	-	7.2
Euro area average	4.7	4.6	5.7	5.7	5.5	5.0

***Source**: European Commission*

Note: The reference value is based on the best-performing Member States in terms of price (Austria, France and Sweden for the period from April 1999 to March 2000) plus 2 percentage points. The euro is included for information only.

From Tables 6 and 7 we can see that the Greek national legislation, including the statute of the national central bank, abides by the articles 108 and 109 of the treaty and the statute of the European System of Central Banks (ESCB). With regard to the fulfilment by Greece of the criteria of convergence, which are reported in the four cases of paragraph 1 of the article 121 of the Treaty in the year that expired in March 2000, the long-term interest-rate in Greece was, on average, 6.4%, that is less than the price of report. As far as the four criteria are concerned, Greece has achieved high degree of viable convergence. Consequently, Greece fulfilled the essential prerequisites for the adoption of single currency.

Table 7: Greece: Exchange rate stability

Membership of the ERM I/II	Yes	
Membership since	March 1998	
Devaluation of bilateral central rate on country's own initiative	No	
Maximum and minimum upward deviations from central rates in % (1)	Maximum upward deviations	Minimum upward deviations
From 1 April 1998 to 31 December 1998 (ERM currencies) (1)		
Belgian franc	8.0	3.2
Danish krone	7.9	3.2
Deutsche Mark	8.0	3.2
Spanish peseta	7.8	3.0
French franc	8.0	3.2
Irish pound	7.0	1.8
Italian lira	7.7	2.9
Dutch guilder	8.1	3.1
Austrian schilling	8.0	3.2
Portuguese escudo	7.9	3.1
Finnish markka	8.0	3.1
From *4 January 1999 to 31 March 2000 (ERM II currencies)*		
Euro (from 4 January 1999 to 16 January 2000)	9.0	5.9
Euro (from 17 January 1999 to 31 March 2000)	2.8	1.9
For information only		
Danish krone (4 January 1999 to 16 January 2000)	8.7	4.4
Danish krone (17 January 1999 to 31 March 2000)	2.6	1.7

***Source**: BIS and ECB calculations*

Note: ERM II replaced the ERM from the beginning of 1999. In effect from 17 January 2000 the central parity for Greece

(1) Daily data at business frequency; ten-day moving average

Table 8: GDP in US dollars at current prices and current PPPs (2011)

Economics: Key tables from OECD - ISSN 2074-384x - © OECD 2011

Gross domestic product in US dollars

At current prices and current PPPs

Billions of US dollars

	2003	2004	2005	2006	2007
Australia	642,1	678,7	721,3	774,5	831,0
Austria	252,3	266,3	274,8	299,9	313,8
Belgium	313,7	324,5	336,6	360,1	378,1
Canada	989,3	1 049,1	1 132,0	1 200,5	1 263,0
Chile	166,8	181,9	198,4	214,2	230,7
Czech Republic	183,5	197,0	208,4	229,5	253,7
Denmark	164,0	174,5	179,9	195,9	206,0
Estonia	18,1	19,9	22,3	25,7	28,5
Finland	143,8	156,1	161,0	174,3	191,2
France	1 692,4	1 761,9	1 860,7	1 991,0	2 114,4
Germany	2 357,3	2 466,8	2 586,5	2 776,8	2 930,5
Greece	250,3	266,5	272,8	302,1	316,2
Hungary	156,2	164,9	170,9	184,6	192,9
Iceland	8,9	9,9	10,4	10,9	11,6
Ireland	138,0	148,5	160,7	180,1	197,7
Israel (1)	149,0	161,0	162,1	176,1	190,9
Italy	1 563,2	1 594,9	1 649,4	1 781,5	1 893,9
Japan	3 509,9	3 708,5	3 872,8	4 071,4	4 290,2
Korea	965,8	1 039,1	1 096,7	1 173,0	1 269,1
Luxembourg	27,4	29,8	31,8	37,1	40,6
Mexico	1 108,7	1 186,6	1 293,8	1 432,2	1 540,9
Netherlands	514,3	540,5	572,9	622,0	667,3
New Zealand	94,8	100,4	104,6	113,4	121,2
Norway	174,8	194,0	218,7	248,4	259,0
Poland	457,8	496,9	526,1	574,6	638,9
Portugal	202,5	207,9	224,6	242,1	256,8
Slovak Republic	73,1	78,9	87,1	99,2	112,9
Slovenia	41,0	44,5	47,0	51,1	54,9
Spain	1 039,5	1 108,2	1 188,1	1 337,4	1 447,3
Sweden	272,5	292,4	295,3	324,0	352,1
Switzerland	246,3	257,4	266,1	295,6	325,7
Turkey	587,8	688,6	781,2	894,6	976,4
United Kingdom	1 777,7	1 902,6	1 971,3	2 118,7	2 178,4
United States	11 089,2	11 812,3	12 579,7	13 336,2	13 995,0
Euro area	..	..	..	..	..
OECD-Total	31 372,5	33 311,0	35 266,1	37 848,3	40 070,9

Last updated: 4 August 2011

Note: Data for Australia and New Zealand refer to fiscal year.

1 The statistical data for Israel are supplied by and under the responsibility of the relevant Israeli authorities. The use of such data by the OECD is without prejudice to the status of the Golan Hei

e Estimated value

Source: Annual national accounts: Gross domestic product, OECD National Accounts Statistics (database)

doi: 10.1787/2074384X-2011-table3

Source: Organisation for economic Co-operation and Development (OECD), 2011.

Table 8 presents the GDP in US dollars at current prices and current PPPs from 2003 up to 2010. We observe that Greece has 27.2% increased, but it started from 250.3 up to 318.7, one of the lowest numbers of eurozone. If we compare with the equivalent of Germany we'll see that it starts from 2357.3 up to 2974.7 (20.7%).

Table 9: Greece: General government financial position *(as a percentage of GDP)*

	1998	1999	2000(1)
General government surplus (+)/deficit (-)	-3.1	-1.6	-1.3
Reference value	-3	-3	-3
Surplus (+)/deficit (-) net of public investment expenditure (2)	0.6	2.7	2.9
General public debt	105.4	104.4	103.7
Reference value	60	60	60

Source: *European Commission (spring 2000 preliminary data for that year) and ECB calculations*

(1) European Commission forecast

(2) A negative sign indicates that the government deficit is higher than investment expenditure

As for the fulfillment of the criteria of convergence from Greece that are reported in the four cases of Paragraph 1 of the Article 121 of the Treaty two of them can be seem in Tables 9 and 10. To be more specific, due to the decision 2000/33/EC of Council, December 17th 1999, for the abolition of the decision about the existence of excessive deficit in Greece, Greece has not been the object of decision of the Council about the existence of excessive budgetary deficit (Table 9). Moreover, the average percentage of inflation in Greece during the year that expired in March 2000 was 2.0% which was less than the price of report.

Table 10: Greece: HICP inflation *(annual percentage changes)*

	1996	1997	1998	1999	2000 Jan.	2000 Feb.	2000 Mar.	Apr. 1999 to Mar. 2000
HICP inflation (1)	7.9	5.4	4.5	2.1	2.4	2.6	2.8	2.0
Reference value (2)	2.5	2.7	2.2	2.1	-	-	-	2.4
Euro area average (3)	2.2	1.6	1.1	1.1	1.9	2.0	-2.1	1.4

Source: European Commission

(1) Please note that as of January 2000 the coverage of the HICP has been extended and further harmonized.

(2) Calculations from 1999 to March 2000 are based on the unweighted arithmetic average of annual percentage changes of Sweden, Austria and France plus 1,5 percentage points.

(3) The euro zone average is included for information only.

3. The Greek Statistics over the Last Years (2009-12) and the Reaction of the Eurozone

3.1 Greece's Debt Crisis: The Background

Rossi and Aguilera (2010) pointed out that

"Until October 2009, it appeared that Greece had weathered the global crisis relatively well. Estimates pointed towards a contraction of less than 1% of GDP and public finances. In October 2009, on the eve of the election, the reported deficit for the year officially stood at 5.1%, similar to the EU average predicted at the time. This dispelled the European Commission's frustration with the persistently high historic deficits run by the Greek government. Since 1997, Greece has only met the minimum deficit target of 3% in one year, and the debt-to-GDP ratio has hovered at around 100% throughout the decade despite Greece's relatively fast

growth during the period. Also, there has been a problem of misreporting of statistics" (2010, p. 3).

Although most countries have seen estimates for their budget deficit swell over the course of 2009, the magnitude of the Greek revisions (over both 2008 and 2009) and the implications for already excessive external debt financing have been shocking. The estimated 2009 deficit rose from 5.1% for 2009, as reported to the EC during the spring, to 12.7% by the late autumn while the 2008 deficit was corrected from 5.2% to 7.7%. At that time, the Greek government was therefore pressed to come up with a convincing program for fiscal restructuring, one that would satisfy the EU and the financial markets.

Greece should cut the budget deficit below 3% by 2012 through reduced spending on public sector workers, defense and healthcare, as well as increased tax collection. Furthermore, despite forecasting a -0.3% drop in GDP for 2010, growth was expected to pick up afterward, reaching 2.5% in 2013. Financial markets reacted negatively based on the implausibility of achieving both the tough fiscal target and the forecast rate of GDP growth target as well as the lack of clarity over where spending would be reduced after 2010 (Rosi and Guilera, 2010).

3.2 The Crisis in the Eurozone (2009-2012)

Greece and Ireland faced very significant adverse movements in their yield spreads relative to euro-area benchmark bonds. The market began to ponder whether the crisis could spread further and if the euro system in its current form is sustainable, after the case of Spain. Also, the prospect of very weak growth and high unemployment resulting from fiscal consolidation and years of painful structural adjustment concerned the markets because it makes the temptation to restructure sovereign debt too great to be ignored. Such concerns added to the crisis countries' problems, making it difficult for them to borrow, while the prevailing high interest rates increased their debt service costs (Blundell and Slovik, 2010).

As a basic help for Greece, the Eurozone and IMF allocated 110 billion euro via a three-year loan program. The Eurozone members provided 80 billion euro, allocated in parallel with their relative ECB capital shares, and the IMF provided 30 billion euro (Haydar, 2009). More specifically, according to European Commission (2012) on 2 May 2010, the Eurogroup agreed "to provide bilateral loans pooled by the European Commission for a total amount of EUR 80 billion to be disbursed over the period May 2010 through June 2013. The financial assistance agreed by euro-area Member States is part of a joint package, with the IMF financing additional EUR 30 billion under a stand-by arrangement (SBA)… Also, on 14 March 2012, euro area finance ministers approved financing of the second Greek economic adjustment programme for an amount of up to EUR 130 billion until 2014, including an IMF contribution of EUR 28 billion. Euro area Member States also authorised the EFSF to release the first installment of a total amount of EUR 39.4 billion, which will be disbursed in several tranches. The release of the tranches will be based on observance of quantitative performance criteria and a positive evaluation of progress made with respect to policy criteria in Council Decision 2011/734/EU of 12 July 2011 (as amended in November 2011 and on 13 March 2012) and the Memorandum of Understanding setting the economic policy conditionality, which was signed on 14 March 2012. The finance ministers noted the assessment of the Troika that Greece has implemented all agreed prior actions in a satisfactory manner, and reiterated the importance of further strengthening Greece's institutional capacity. The ministers also based their decisions on the results of the debt sustainability analysis provided jointly by the Commission, the IMF and the ECB. The high private sector involvement (PSI) in Greece's debt exchange offer will make a significant contribution to improving Greece's debt sustainability. Out of a total of EUR 205.6 billion in bonds eligible for the exchange offer, approximately EUR 197 billion, or 95.7% have been exchanged" (see http://ec.europa.eu/economy_finance/eu_borrower/greek_loan_facility /index_en.htm).

Both financial packages aim to reduce Greek fiscal deficit to 3% of GDP by the end of 2014 (however, Greece is asking for an extension of at least two years up to 2016), among other reform measures. Greece also agreed to proceed to adopt an extensive Economic Adjustment Programme, such as an increase in its VAT rate to 23% from 21%, to impose fuel and alcohol taxes by 10 percentage points and to reduce various government-sector wage, pension and employment benefits. In addition to this fiscal tightening, Greece increased the minimum retirement age to 65 years as part of its pension system change and is in the process of privatising a number of state-owned enterprises (Haydar, 2009).

With GDP growth rates lower than the ones observed for PIGS (Portugal, Ireland, Greece and Spain), most of the non-PIGS expose a better performance concerning the budget. For Portugal, the Euro had a strong negative impact which is unique among PIGS: the GDP growth rate decreased dramatically in comparison to the years before the Euro. On the other hand, there were improvements in the positions of Ireland and Spain. These latest results showed that: a) PIGS was not a homogeneous group of countries because Spain and Ireland clearly stand out from the rest; b) the present day problems of Ireland have quite different roots (the failure of the bank system) than those of Portugal and Greece (government mismanagement of public incomes and of the economy in general) (see Fernandes and Mota, 2009).

In addition, having high debt-to-real GDP ratio and slow GDP growth, Greece was unlikely to be able to achieve healthy levels of debt without defaulting. A recent report by the International Monetary Fund (IMF) projected that Greece's public debt would peak from its current level of 143 percent of GDP to 172 percent of GDP in 2012 and remain above 130 percent through 2020. The IMF assumed that Greece would be successful in fully implementing its fiscal adjustment plan. The IMF estimated that if Greece is unsuccessful in implementing its fiscal program or if it fails to fully realize its planned privatizations, debt could remain at unsustainable levels at around 150 percent of GDP through 2020. Additionally, the IMF lowered its projections for Greek real GDP growth going forward, forecasting a decline of 3.8 percent in 2011, an improvement to 0.6 percent in 2012, and a leveling off to 3.0 percent in 2017. The high levels of existing debt and slow real GDP growth suggest that some form of default is likely the only option for Greece, and additional future defaults was very possible (Craig and Koepke, 2011).

On the other hand, the most worrying about the debt crisis in Greece, and the issue of misleading economic statistics by governments, was the failure of the rating agencies to "blow the whistle" in order to warn markets of the serious problems with the credibility of Greek data. The reactions of the rating agencies often followed market reactions. This was a serious failing, since knowledge of the unsatisfactory nature of Greek statistics was not hidden. Membership of the EU meant that the Greek statistical authorities form part of the European Statistical Service, which was coordinated by Eurostat. The Greek case exposed serious limitations in the European Statistical Service, when measured against to monitor fiscal policies across the eurozone. The travails of Greece have focused attention on other eurozone countries exhibiting lax fiscal discipline - in particular, Italy, Spain, Portugal and Ireland. This group of five countries had a weighted average public sector deficit of -8.6% and a total debt to GDP ratio of 90%.

The highly politicised system in Greece meant that the production and dissemination of economic data were not independent. But in the latest European financial crisis, few are blameless. All Greek governments did not tackle necessary structural reforms of the economy nor made any real efforts to control public finances, from the perspective of controlling expenditure and revenue generation. The EU acted too hastily in allowing Greece to enter the eurozone, which was assembled without any consideration of what would happen in the case of default by a member state. No serious attempt was made to this question: why had Greece been able to meet the entry requirement of having a public-sector deficit less than 3% of GDP by 2000 in a few years of high public deficits? Nor were there any effective political repercussions, including the possible threat of expulsion from the eurozone, when revisions to economic statistics showed, from as early as 2002 to 2010, that Greek data were seriously inaccurate. The Greek crisis also casts doubt on the fitness for purpose of Eurostat, in coordinating the statistical output of the national statistical authorities of the member states and in ensuring the quality of economic data published. As in the global financial crisis, investors have been misled by the inadequacies and incompetence of the rating agencies, despite the public information available, to assess the true default risk of Greek public debt (Sturgess, 2010).

In Table 11 we can see the nominal GDP with its percentage change from the previous year (for a time period in 1986-96, and every year from 1997 up to 2012). Specifically, the nominal GDP of Greece has increased 16% in a ten years time period 1986-96, however, there was a worth mentioning increase every year from 1997-2007 with an annual increase of above 5% (in a few years the annual increase was above 8%). The crisis is profound when there is a decrease from 2009 and onwards.

Since 2009, the economic crisis hit especially Estonia (-13.9%) and Ireland (11.2%). But it is remarkable that the Nominal GDP of Poland has increased 5.3% at the same year (2009). Later on, it came as a surprise that the nominal GDP of Turkey increased 16.0% (2010), 13.2% (2011) and 11.7% (2012).

Table 12 presents the real GDP with percentage change from the previous year (for a time period in 1986-96, and every year from 1997 up to 2012). From this Table we can realise that the Greek real GDP growth is different from nominal. The real GDP growth rates are lower than the nominal ones (see Table 11) since it is obvious that there were significant inflation rates in Greece at the same time. So the increases in Greek nominal GDP were much higher due to inflationary conditions. The crisis is profound when there is a decrease from 2009 and onwards.

Also, we can see that in 2009 the real GDP of Estonia (-13.9%) was exactly the same with the increase in nominal GDP (-13.9%), but the real GDP of Ireland (7.6%) was lower than the increase in nominal GDP (-11.2%). On the other hand, the increase in real GDP of Poland (1.7%) was lower than the increase in nominal GDP (5.3%). Finally, the increase in real GDP of Turkey has increased from 2009 and on, but not in such big numbers, thus 8.9% in 2010 (instead of 16.0% as the increase in nominal GDP), 6.5% in 2011 (instead of 13.2% increase in its nominal GDP) and 5.3% in 2012 (instead of 11.7% in its nominal GDP).

Table 11: Nominal GDP in selected countries in the world

OECD Economic Outlook, Volume 2011 Issue 1 - No. 89 - © OECD 2011
Annex Table 2. Nominal GDP
Version 1 - Last updated: 06-Jun-2011

Annex Table 2. **Nominal GDP**
Percentage change from previous year

	Average 1986-96	1997	1998	1999	2000	2001	2002	2003	2004	2005	2006	2007	2008	2009	2010	2011	2012	Fourth quarter 2010	2011	2012
Australia	7,2	5,3	5,3	5,4	7,8	6,5	7,1	5,9	7,6	7,9	7,9	9,1	9,0	0,5	7,8	7,7	7,4	9,0	7,9	7,4
Austria	5,2	2,0	3,9	3,8	4,7	2,5	3,2	1,9	4,0	4,6	5,7	5,7	3,7	-2,9	3,8	4,7	3,7	5,0	3,8	4,0
Belgium	4,9	4,8	3,8	3,8	5,8	2,8	3,4	2,8	5,3	4,4	5,0	5,2	2,8	-1,6	4,0	4,6	4,1	4,5	4,1	4,4
Canada	5,0	5,5	3,7	7,4	9,6	2,9	4,0	5,2	6,4	6,4	5,6	5,5	4,6	-4,5	6,2	5,4	4,5	5,9	5,2	4,6
Chile	..	11,2	5,3	1,7	9,3	7,3	6,5	10,0	14,0	13,5	17,6	10,3	3,9	1,1	15,1	12,0	9,9	14,8	10,5	9,1
Czech Republic	..	7,6	10,2	4,1	5,5	7,4	4,7	4,6	9,1	6,1	8,2	9,7	4,2	-1,6	1,1	2,5	5,1	1,3	2,8	6,8
Denmark	4,3	5,3	3,4	4,3	6,6	3,2	2,8	2,0	4,7	5,4	5,6	3,9	2,7	-4,9	5,4	4,0	3,9	5,5	4,0	3,9
Estonia	..	23,3	12,3	6,5	15,0	13,2	11,6	12,1	11,1	15,5	19,8	18,2	1,8	-13,9	4,6	8,8	7,0	9,7	6,3	8,3
Finland	4,9	8,0	8,8	4,9	7,9	5,4	3,0	1,4	4,7	3,4	5,5	8,3	2,8	-7,2	5,2	5,5	4,8	7,9	3,9	5,3
France	4,3	3,2	4,5	3,2	5,6	3,8	3,5	3,0	3,9	4,0	4,9	4,9	2,7	-2,0	2,2	3,7	3,4	2,8	4,1	3,5
Germany	5,2	2,1	2,4	2,2	2,8	2,6	1,4	0,9	1,7	1,6	4,0	4,7	1,7	-3,3	4,1	4,2	3,8	4,3	4,1	4,1
Greece	16,0	10,7	8,7	6,6	8,0	7,4	7,0	10,1	7,4	5,2	8,5	7,5	4,3	-0,8	-2,1	-2,6	1,3	-5,6	1,1	1,5
Hungary	..	24,5	18,5	11,2	14,5	15,3	12,6	9,2	9,7	6,1	8,3	6,8	4,9	-2,1	3,9	6,7	6,4	4,8	6,8	6,3
Iceland	11,7	8,0	11,8	7,5	8,1	12,9	5,8	3,0	10,4	10,5	13,8	12,0	13,3	0,8	3,0	4,2	5,8	0,4	7,4	5,1
Ireland	8,4	15,7	15,5	15,2	16,2	11,6	11,4	7,3	6,7	8,6	9,3	6,8	-4,9	-11,2	-3,6	-1,3	3,5	-4,6	5,3	3,3
Israel	..	11,5	11,5	9,8	10,9	1,7	3,5	1,0	5,2	6,0	8,1	5,9	5,2	5,9	5,8	6,9	7,3	7,7	6,7	7,0
Italy	7,7	4,6	3,9	3,2	5,9	4,8	3,7	3,2	4,0	2,9	4,0	4,0	1,4	-3,1	1,9	2,4	3,3	2,2	3,4	2,9
Japan	4,0	2,1	-2,1	-1,4	1,1	-1,0	-1,3	-0,2	1,6	0,7	1,1	1,6	-2,2	-6,6	1,8	-2,2	1,7	0,7	-0,7	1,2
Korea	16,5	9,8	-1,0	9,6	9,9	8,0	10,6	6,5	7,8	4,6	5,0	7,3	5,3	3,8	10,1	5,6	7,3	9,5	4,9	8,1
Luxembourg	8,0	4,0	6,1	14,2	10,6	2,6	6,3	7,7	6,3	10,3	12,0	10,5	5,7	-4,0	9,3	5,9	5,6	12,9	1,7	8,1
Mexico	40,1	26,0	20,2	21,5	17,4	4,4	2,7	10,9	13,5	7,9	12,2	9,1	7,8	-2,2	10,1	8,7	8,1	9,4	8,1	8,0
Netherlands	4,5	7,0	5,9	6,5	8,2	7,1	3,9	2,5	3,0	4,5	5,2	5,8	4,3	-4,1	3,4	2,2	3,5	4,4	1,9	3,9
New Zealand	6,2	3,6	1,6	5,1	6,4	6,8	5,9	6,1	8,1	5,4	4,7	7,6	3,3	0,7	4,8	5,2	7,4	6,9	4,7	9,2
Norway	6,1	8,3	1,9	8,8	19,4	3,8	-0,3	4,0	9,4	11,6	11,0	5,2	10,8	-5,4	5,2	11,3	5,9	7,9	10,8	4,9
Poland	..	21,9	16,5	10,7	12,1	5,1	3,7	4,3	9,3	6,6	7,8	11,1	8,3	5,3	5,4	6,9	6,8	6,1	6,9	6,7
Portugal	12,6	8,5	9,0	7,5	7,3	5,6	4,5	2,0	4,1	3,3	4,3	5,6	1,6	-2,0	2,3	-1,1	-0,5	1,7	-2,2	0,2
Slovak Republic	..	10,9	9,7	7,4	10,9	8,7	8,6	10,3	11,2	9,2	11,7	11,8	8,9	-5,9	4,5	5,6	7,2	4,4	5,7	8,6
Slovenia	..	13,8	10,8	12,3	10,0	11,8	12,0	8,6	7,8	6,2	8,0	11,3	7,9	-5,1	1,9	2,8	4,8	2,3	3,4	5,6
Spain	8,7	6,3	7,1	7,5	8,7	8,0	7,1	7,4	7,4	8,1	8,3	7,0	3,3	-3,1	0,8	2,1	2,4	2,0	2,0	2,8
Sweden	6,3	4,3	4,8	5,6	5,9	3,7	4,1	4,1	4,6	4,1	6,3	6,2	2,5	-3,6	6,8	5,8	4,7	9,2	4,1	5,0
Switzerland	3,9	1,9	2,9	1,9	4,8	2,0	0,9	0,8	3,1	2,8	5,8	6,2	4,4	-1,6	2,0	3,1	3,3	2,6	3,1	3,2
Turkey	76,2	95,2	81,1	49,0	59,3	44,1	45,9	29,8	22,9	16,1	16,9	11,2	12,7	0,2	16,0	13,2	11,7	..	..	..
United Kingdom	7,2	6,2	5,9	5,6	5,1	4,6	5,3	6,0	5,5	4,2	5,9	5,8	2,9	-3,5	4,2	4,8	4,0	4,2	5,0	4,3
United States	5,8	6,3	5,5	6,4	6,4	3,4	3,5	4,7	6,5	6,5	6,0	4,9	2,2	-1,7	3,8	4,0	4,5	4,2	4,2	4,7
Euro area	6,1	4,1	4,4	3,9	5,5	4,4	3,6	3,0	3,9	3,8	5,2	5,3	2,3	-3,2	2,6	3,1	3,4	3,1	3,4	3,6
Total OECD	9,2	8,0	6,4	6,3	7,4	4,4	4,2	4,6	5,9	5,2	5,9	5,4	2,8	-2,5	4,3	3,9	4,5	4,5	4,1	4,8

Note: The adoption of national accounts systems SNA93 or ESA95 has been proceeding at an uneven pace among OECD member countries, both with respect to variables and the time period covered. As a consequence, there are breaks in many national series. For further information, see table "National Accounts Reporting Systems, base years and latest data updates" at the beginning of the Statistical Annex and *OECD Economic Outlook* Sources and Methods *(http://www.oecd.org/eco/sources-and-methods)*. Working-day adjusted – see note to Annex Table 1.

Source: OECD Economic Outlook 89 database.

Source: OECD (2011), Volume 2011, Issue 1, No.89

Table 12: Real GDP in selected countries in the world

OECD Economic Outlook, Volume 2011 Issue 1 - No. 89 - © OECD 2011
Annex Table 1. Real GDP
Version 1 - Last updated: 06-Jun-2011

Annex Table 1. **Real GDP**

Percentage change from previous year

	Average 1986-96	1997	1998	1999	2000	2001	2002	2003	2004	2005	2006	2007	2008	2009	2010	2011	2012	Fourth quarter 2010	Fourth quarter 2011	Fourth quarter 2012
Australia	3,4	4,1	5,2	4,3	3,4	2,7	3,9	3,6	3,3	3,4	2,5	4,7	2,4	1,4	2,6	2,9	4,5	2,5	3,7	4,5
Austria	2,4	2,2	3,8	3,7	3,3	0,5	1,6	0,7	2,6	2,8	3,5	3,7	2,2	-3,9	2,1	2,9	2,1	3,1	2,2	2,3
Belgium	2,3	3,9	1,9	3,5	3,8	0,7	1,4	0,8	3,1	2,0	2,7	2,8	0,8	-2,7	2,1	2,4	2,0	2,1	2,2	2,3
Canada	2,2	4,2	4,1	5,5	5,2	1,8	2,9	1,9	3,1	3,0	2,8	2,2	0,5	-2,5	3,1	3,0	2,8	3,2	3,0	3,0
Chile	..	6,7	3,3	-0,8	4,6	3,4	2,1	3,7	5,9	5,6	4,9	4,9	3,2	-1,5	5,1	6,5	5,1	5,8	5,7	4,5
Czech Republic	..	-0,7	-0,7	1,2	3,9	2,4	1,8	3,6	4,3	6,4	7,0	6,1	2,3	-4,0	2,2	2,4	3,5	2,6	2,1	5,0
Denmark	1,7	3,2	2,2	2,6	3,5	0,7	0,5	0,4	2,3	2,4	3,4	1,6	-1,1	-5,2	2,1	1,9	2,1	2,9	2,0	2,2
Estonia	..	11,7	6,7	-0,3	10,0	7,5	7,9	7,6	7,2	9,4	10,6	6,9	-5,1	-13,9	3,1	5,9	4,7	6,8	4,3	5,8
Finland	1,4	6,1	5,1	4,0	5,3	2,2	1,7	2,1	4,1	3,0	4,4	5,3	1,0	-8,3	3,1	3,8	2,8	5,0	2,0	4,0
France	2,1	2,2	3,5	3,2	4,1	1,8	1,1	1,1	2,3	2,0	2,4	2,3	0,1	-2,7	1,4	2,2	2,1	1,6	2,4	2,3
Germany	2,6	1,8	1,8	1,9	3,5	1,4	0,0	-0,2	0,7	0,9	3,6	2,8	0,7	-4,7	3,5	3,4	2,5	4,0	3,1	2,7
Greece	1,4	3,6	3,4	3,4	4,5	4,2	3,4	5,9	4,4	2,3	5,2	4,3	1,0	-2,0	-4,5	-2,9	0,6	-7,5	0,3	1,4
Hungary	..	4,1	4,7	4,1	4,9	4,0	4,1	3,9	4,3	3,4	3,7	0,8	0,6	-6,5	1,0	2,7	3,1	2,5	3,0	3,2
Iceland	1,6	4,9	6,3	4,1	4,3	3,9	0,1	2,4	7,7	7,5	4,6	6,0	1,4	-6,9	-3,5	2,2	2,9	0,1	3,8	2,4
Ireland	5,5	11,5	8,5	10,9	9,7	5,7	6,6	4,4	4,6	6,0	5,3	5,6	-3,6	-7,6	-1,0	0,0	2,3	-0,5	2,1	2,5
Israel	..	3,5	4,1	3,3	9,2	0,0	-0,4	1,5	5,0	4,9	5,7	5,4	4,2	0,8	4,7	5,4	4,7	5,4	4,9	4,6
Italy	2,0	1,9	1,3	1,4	3,9	1,7	0,5	0,1	1,4	0,8	2,1	1,4	-1,3	-5,2	1,2	1,1	1,6	1,5	1,3	1,6
Japan	3,2	1,6	-2,0	-0,1	2,9	0,2	0,3	1,4	2,7	1,9	2,0	2,4	-1,2	-6,3	4,0	-0,9	2,2	2,4	0,3	1,5
Korea	8,6	5,8	-5,7	10,7	8,8	4,0	7,2	2,8	4,6	4,0	5,2	5,1	2,3	0,3	6,2	4,6	4,5	4,7	5,5	4,1
Luxembourg	4,9	5,9	6,5	8,4	8,4	2,5	4,1	1,5	4,4	5,4	5,0	6,6	1,4	-3,6	3,5	3,2	3,9	4,6	1,1	6,9
Mexico	2,5	7,2	5,0	3,6	6,0	-0,9	0,1	1,4	4,0	3,2	5,2	3,2	1,5	-6,1	5,5	4,4	3,8	4,4	3,9	3,8
Netherlands	2,8	4,3	3,9	4,7	3,9	1,9	0,1	0,3	2,2	2,0	3,4	3,9	1,9	-3,9	1,8	2,3	1,9	2,2	2,1	2,1
New Zealand	2,2	2,9	0,6	4,7	3,7	2,5	4,6	4,4	4,1	3,2	2,0	3,4	-0,7	0,0	2,5	0,8	4,1	1,6	1,8	4,4
Norway	2,8	5,4	2,7	2,0	3,3	2,0	1,5	1,0	3,9	2,7	2,3	2,7	0,8	-1,4	0,4	2,5	3,0	1,6	2,3	3,3
Poland	..	7,0	4,9	4,4	4,5	1,3	1,5	3,9	5,2	3,6	6,2	6,8	5,0	1,7	3,8	3,9	3,8	3,9	3,9	3,6
Portugal	3,6	4,4	5,0	4,1	3,9	2,0	0,7	-0,9	1,6	0,8	1,4	2,4	0,0	-2,5	1,3	-2,1	-1,5	1,0	-2,9	-0,7
Slovak Republic	..	5,7	4,4	0,0	1,4	3,5	4,6	4,8	5,1	6,7	8,5	10,5	5,8	-4,8	4,0	3,6	4,4	3,4	3,6	5,1
Slovenia	..	4,9	3,6	5,4	4,4	2,8	4,0	2,8	4,3	4,5	5,9	6,9	3,7	-8,1	1,2	1,8	2,6	2,0	1,7	3,2
Spain	2,9	3,9	4,5	4,7	5,0	3,6	2,7	3,1	3,3	3,6	4,0	3,6	0,9	-3,7	-0,1	0,9	1,6	0,6	1,0	1,9
Sweden	1,5	2,9	4,1	4,4	4,6	1,4	2,5	2,5	3,7	3,1	4,6	3,4	-0,8	-5,3	5,3	4,5	3,1	7,2	3,1	3,2
Switzerland	1,4	2,1	2,6	1,3	3,6	1,2	0,4	-0,2	2,5	2,6	3,6	3,6	1,9	-1,9	2,6	2,7	2,5	3,2	2,5	2,4
Turkey	4,4	7,5	3,1	-3,4	6,8	-5,7	6,2	5,3	9,4	8,4	6,9	4,7	0,7	-4,8	8,9	6,5	5,3	..	..	..
United Kingdom	2,4	3,3	3,6	3,5	3,9	2,5	2,1	2,8	3,0	2,2	2,8	2,7	-0,1	-4,9	1,3	1,4	1,8	1,5	1,7	2,2
United States	2,9	4,5	4,4	4,8	4,1	1,1	1,8	2,5	3,6	3,1	2,7	1,9	0,0	-2,6	2,9	2,6	3,1	2,8	2,7	3,3
Euro area	2,4	2,6	2,8	2,9	4,0	1,9	1,0	0,8	1,9	1,8	3,2	2,8	0,3	-4,1	1,7	2,0	2,0	2,0	2,1	2,2
Total OECD	2,9	3,7	2,7	3,4	4,2	1,3	1,7	2,0	3,2	2,7	3,2	2,7	0,3	-3,5	2,9	2,3	2,8	2,8	2,4	3,0

Note: The adoption of national accounts systems SNA93 or ESA95 has been proceeding at an uneven pace among OECD member countries, both with respect to variables and the time period covered. As a consequence, there are breaks in many national series. Moreover, most countries have shifted to chain-weighted price indices to calculate real GDP and expenditure components. For further information, see table "National Accounts Reporting Systems, base years and latest data updates" at the beginning of the Statistical Annex and *OECD Economic Outlook* Sources and Methods *(http://www.oecd.org/eco/sources-and-methods)*. These numbers are working-day adjusted and hence may differ from the basis used for official projections.

Source: OECD Economic Outlook 89 database.

3.3 How the Revisions of Deficits Led Greece to Economic Crisis: The Case of Absorption of 9.6% of Shadow Economy in the Greek GDP

Greece wanted to revise upward its GDP for the period 2003-2010 by as much as 25 percent a quarter by including parts of its underground economy. This revision would help Greece to meet deficit standards by shrinking its budget deficit as a percentage of GDP. Greece had repeatedly revised budget and national accounts since 2003 and the EU urged the country to improve its statistics in cooperation with the bloc's statistical agency, Eurostat.

The Greek economy minister, George Alogoskoufis, then said that the new GDP figures would not be included in the 2007 draft budget that would be presented. "Most of the revision came after surveys replaced estimations to measure economic activity in several parts of the economy, including construction and trade. A smaller factor was the inclusion of estimations of illegal activities, like drug trafficking and prostitution," said the head of Statistic Service of Greece then M. Kontopyrakis.

Greece's debt was the EU's highest at 107.5 percent of GDP (2005). The country had the lowest credit rating among the 12 countries sharing the euro. Moody's Investors Service ranked Greece's debt A1, its fifth-highest investment grade rating. Standard & Poor's and Fitch Ratings grade the debt one level lower at A (International Herald Tribune, 27/9/2006).

On the other hand, the NSSG conducted a revision of Greek GDP data in accordance with EU Regulation 2223/96, while the last major revision of the Greek GDP data took place in 1994. That revision involved the application of ESA79 to the base year 1988 and led to an increase in GDP of more than 20%. In between the two major revisions there was only one revision, which did not use any new surveys. This means that up to that point national accounts had been using the data of the 1981 Census of Population.

A change took place that added in the nation's robust black-market industries such as prostitution and money laundering. But becoming "richer" turned out not to be as good as it sounded: The revised GDP figures did cost the Greek government as much as $600 million (http://ec.europa.eu/economy_finance/economic_governance/sgp/pdf/20_scps/2006-07/01_programme/2006-12-18_el_sp_en.pdf).

Greece decided to salute the contribution of high class prostitutes to the economy, according to the models of the ancient times. Athens said that its economy was 25% stronger than in reality, in part thanks to the duties of the prostitutes (The Guardian, 2006). The Greek authorities were revising the country's GDP after deciding that the black market should be included in the figures. Greece's economic output was €180bn (£128bn) in 2005 and it would be expected to rise to €194bn the next year (2006). The black economy was estimated at up to €60bn, according to Reuters.

The new figures were the result of Greece's determination to avoid a ticking off from the EU, which had the right to impose hefty fines on a eurozone country if its budget deficit rises above 3% of GDP. By boosting the size of its economy the Greek deficit would fall from 2.1% of GDP to 1.9%. "Without this change, the deficit would have fallen from 2.6% of GDP to 2.4%," according to the Financial Times.

The 2009 budget was outdated before the beginning of the New Year. Especially, by 30 January, the 2009 budget had been completely revised, since the deficit was estimated at 3.7% of GDP. The execution of the 2009 budget went seriously off track, since every single month it was much higher than the previous year, and monthly data were not published, except April and July. Also, the revenue shortfall was 5.4% of GDP, the expenditure overruns 2.6% of GDP and the deficit 12.5% of GDP.

On 27 April 2009, Greece was subjected again to the Excessive Deficit Procedure (EDP) on the basis of 2007 and 2008 deficits, but the Commission stated that these deficits were structural and were not due to the international crisis. Then, Greece was asked to correct the excessive deficit situation by the end of 2010. But insufficient tax measures were taken reluctantly at the latest in June 2009 and the package of measures for EDP was never prepared.

Greece had the last opportunity to send a strong message to the markets as the aftermath of the October election. On 22 October 2009 the new strong deficit was estimated at 12.5% of GDP and published by Eurostat, and consequently Fitch downgraded Greece.

Fitch, S&P and Moody's downgraded Greece again on 8, 16 and 22 of December 2009, since the 3.6% of GDP deficit provided by the 2010 budget did not satisfy the international markets.

In the updated SGP the decline in deficit was envisaged to 4% of GDP and then spreads were at 369 pb on 26th January 2010. On the other hand, the significant fiscal measures didn't appease the international markets and a new round of degradation had begun in April 2010. The next year (April 2010) the Eurogroup decided to help Greece and then began the worst financial-economic crisis in the economic history of Greece.

Some of the most serious reasons of the Greek crisis were the continuous deficits for the last 36 years, the high and rising public debt, no systematic and real efforts to control expenditure or contain tax evasion, the unsuitable fiscal consolidations (1986-1987, 1994-1999, 2005-2006), the continuous worsening of competitiveness after EMU entry, the Greek entry in EMU without adequate preparation, and the magnitude and the frequency of the fiscal data revisions (Manessiotis, 2011).

The revision of GDP by 26% in 2008 was never accepted during the examination of the data by Eurostat, which led to an upward revision of 9.6% (OECD, 2009).

In the decade before the crisis, a significant portion of rising government expenditures was allocated to rising public sector wages and benefits. In 2009, Greek government expenditures accounted for 50% of GDP, with 75% of (non-interest) public spending going to public sector wages and social benefits. Analysts often point out that Greek politicians have traditionally viewed the provision of public sector jobs and benefits as an important way to grant favours and thereby secure electoral support. Among other things, this tendency appears to have helped politically influential public sector unions consistently negotiate generous wage and pension agreements (Nelson, Bekin and Mix, 2011).

Providing financial assistance to Greece has been controversial. Many Eurozone countries, including Germany, had to overcome considerable political resistance to provide support to Greece. Opponents of EU assistance to Greece expressed exasperation with the idea of rescuing a country that, in their perspective, had not exercised budget discipline, failed to modernize its economy, and allegedly falsified financial statistics. Opponents also raised the issue of moral hazard and wished to avoid setting a "bail out" precedent (moral hazard is a situation where a party possibly will take risks because the costs that could incur will not be felt by the party taking the risk). Likewise, providing IMF funds to Greece sparked intense debate because the IMF had not lent to developed countries in recent decades and the IMF program for Greece is quite large relative to the size of its economy (Bekin and Mix, 2011).

On 2 and 21 October 2009, the Greek authorities transmitted two different sets of complete Excessive Deficit Procedure (EDP) notification tables to Eurostat, covering the government deficit and debt data for 2005-2008, and a forecast for 2009. In the 21 October notification, the Greek government deficit for 2008 was revised from 5.0% of GDP (the ratio reported by Greece, and published and validated by Eurostat in April 2009) to 7.7% of GDP. At the same time, the Greek authorities also revised the planned deficit ratio for 2009 from 3.7% of GDP (the figure reported in spring) to 12.5% of GDP, reflecting a number of factors (the impact of the economic crisis, budgetary slippages in an electoral year and accounting decisions). According to the appropriate regulations and practices, this report deals with estimates of past data only. Revisions of this magnitude in the estimated past government deficit ratios have been extremely rare in other EU Member States, but have taken place in Greece on several occasions. These most recent revisions are an illustration of the lack of quality of the Greek fiscal statistics (and of macroeconomic statistics in general) and show that the progress in the compilation of fiscal statistics in Greece, and the intense scrutiny of the Greek fiscal data by Eurostat since 2004 (including 10 EDP visits and 5 reservations on the notified data), have not sufficed to bring the quality of Greek fiscal data to the level reached by other EU Member States. As far as the EDP notification of 21 October 2009 is concerned, the data had not been validated by Eurostat and a substantial number of unanswered questions and pending issues still remained in some key areas, such as social security funds, hospital arrears, and transactions between government and public enterprises.

These questions needed to be resolved, and it could not be excluded that this would lead to further revisions of Greek government deficit and debt data particularly for 2008, but possibly also for previous years. The most recent revisions were an illustration of the lack of quality of the Greek fiscal statistics (and of Greek macroeconomic statistics in general) and showed that the progress in the compilation of fiscal statistics in the country, and the intense scrutiny by Eurostat since 2004, had not sufficed to bring the quality of Greek fiscal data to the level reached by other EU Member States. Even if the existing governance framework for fiscal statistics at EU level functioned satisfactorily and enabled improvements of a statistical and methodological nature, it could not prevent deliberate misreporting of data (http://epp.eurostat.ec.europa.eu/cache/ITY_PUBLIC/COM_2010_REPORT_GREEK/EN/COM_2010_REPORT_GREEK-EN.PDF).

Table 13 presents the Macroeconomic Prospects (2006) of Greek Ministry of Economy and Finance up to 2009. The baseline scenario was based on the assumption that the overall picture of the external environment should remain favourable, despite some uncertainties. Real output was projected to continued to grow at around 4% from 2006-2009. Also, strong domestic demand, the increase in personal income and especially the high rates of growth of investment, which involves spending on imported equipment, will result in an estimated increase in the volume of "imports of goods and services" of 7.2%.

Table 13: Macroeconomic Prospects (in 2006, for the time period 2006-9)

	ESA Code	Year 2005	Year 2005	Year 2006	Year 2007	Year 2008	Year 2009
		Level bn euro	rate of change	rate of change	rate of change	rate of change	rate of change
1. Real GDP	B1*g	117.4	3.7	4.0	3.9	4.0	4.1
2. Nominal GDP	B1*g	181.1	7.5	7.8	7.2	7.1	7.0
Components of real GDP							
3. Private consumption expenditure	P.3	80.9	3.7	3.8	3.7	3.7	3.7
4.Government consumption expenditure	P.3	16.9	3.1	2.1	1.1	0.7	0.7
5. Gross fixed capital formation	P.51	30.5	-1.4	9.1	7.7	7.7	7.8
6. Changes in inventories and net acquisition of valuables (% of GDP)	P.52 + P.53	0.4	0.3	0.0	0.0	0.0	0.0
7. Exports of goods and services	P.6	26.2	3.0	5.1	6.5	7.3	7.6
8. Imports of goods and services	P.7	37.5	-1.2	6.5	7.0	7.3	7.4
Contribution to real GDP growth							
9. Final domestic demand			2.62	5.23	4.81	4.78	4.86
10. Changes in inventories and net acquisition of valuables	P.52 + P.53		-0.03	-0.30	-0.07	-0.01	-0.01
11. External balance of goods and services	B.11		1.07	-0.94	-0.83	-0.77	-0.76

Source: European Union (2006) (http://ec.europa.eu/economy_finance/economic_governance/sgp/pdf/20_scps/2006-07/01_programme/2006-12-18_el_sp_en.pdf)

Table 14 presents that inflation was expected to continue on its downward trend. The average annual rate of increase of the private consumption deflator was projected at 2.8%. Although the output gap remained positive for the whole period, the nominal unit labour cost growth rate was projected to decline gradually from 4.2% in 2006 to 2.6% in 2009.

Table 14: Price Developments

	ESA Code	Year 2005	Year 2006	Year 2007	Year 2008	Year 2009
		rate of change	rate of change	rate of change	rate of change	rate of change
1. GDP deflator		3.7	3.7	3.2	3.0	2.8
2. Private consumption deflator		3.7	3.4	3.0	2.8	2.6
3. HICP		3.5	3.3	3.3	2.8	2.6
4. Public consumption deflator		3.0	3.4	3.5	3.5	3.5
5. Investment deflator		2.6	3.9	3.1	2.2	2.0
6. Export price deflator (goods and services)		4.2	4.2	2.6	2.5	2.3
7. Import price deflator (goods and services)		2.7	5.3	1.9	1.4	1.0

Source: European Union (2006)
http://ec.europa.eu/economy_finance/economic_governance/sgp/pdf/20_scps/2006-07/01_programme/2006-12-18_el_sp_en.pdf

Table 15: Labour market developments

	ESA Code	Year 2005	Year 2005	Year 2006	Year 2007	Year 2008	Year 2009
		Level	rate of change	rate of change	rate of change	rate of change	rate of change
1. Employment, persons (000)		4148,2	1.3	1.7	1.8	1.8	1.8
2. Employment, hours worked (mio)		7918.9	1.3	1.7	1.8	1.8	1.8
3. Unemployment rate (%)			10.4	9.2	8.2	7.4	6.5
4. Labour productivity, persons			2.3	2.2	2.1	2.2	2.3
5. Labour productivity, hours worked			2.3	2.2	2.1	2.2	2.3
6. Compensation of employees (billion euro)	D.1	61.7	7.7	8.7	8.6	7.7	7.5

Source: European Union (2006)
http://ec.europa.eu/economy_finance/economic_governance/sgp/pdf/20_scps/2006-07/01_programme/2006-12-18_el_sp_en.pdf

Table 15 shows that employment for the years 2007-2009 was projected to increase as a consequence of strong economic growth. The forecast for the average annual rate of increase in total employment was

1.8%, while the unemployment rate was expected to decrease gradually reaching 6.5% in 2009 down from 9.2% in 2006.

Table 16: Comparison between the baseline and the alternative scenarios

	Baseline scenario			*Alternative scenario*		
	2007	*2008*	*2009*	*2007*	*2008*	*2009*
GDP growth rate	3.9	4.0	4.1	3.5	3.5	3.5
GDP deflator change	3.2	3.0	2.8	3.1	2.9	2.6
Unemployment rate	8.2	7.4	6.5	8.4	7.8	7.3
General government deficit, % of GDP	2.4	1.8	1.2	2.4	1.9	1.4
General government debt, % of GDP	100.1	95.9	91.3	100.6	97.0	93.3

Source: European Union (2006) http://ec.europa.eu/economy_finance/economic_governance/sgp/pdf/20_scps/2006-07/01_programme/2006-12-18_el_sp_en.pdf

Table 16 presents the alternative scenario, since it was assumed that some of the existing downside risks were realized. These risks were related to the outlook for world trade and GDP, oil price developments, or the impact of worldwide monetary tightening on growth. This alternative scenario projected (2007-2009) a slower annual GDP growth rate of 3.5%. Growth rates for all components of GDP would be lower than in the baseline scenario and thus inflation rate was projected to be lower every year by around 0.1 per percentage on average. Employment growth rates also remained below the reference value of the baseline scenario, while unemployment rates were higher. Public finances were concerned, and a slower growth of government current revenues was projected by about 0.4% to 0.6% each year (2007-2009). Moreover, the alternative scenario assumed cuts on capital and consumption expenditures items. The debt to GDP ratio followed a downward path in the alternative scenario, although the levels were higher than in the baseline scenario.

4. Conclusions

The candidature and the integration of Greece in the EU was a peculiar case, from the beginning to the end. After a lot of fluctuations, in 2000 the equivalence of Greek drachma was revalued at 340.75 GRD against the euro. But the concern remained, because Greece was the only country that failed for two years in a row to enter the EMU. The other countries remained out of the EMU on their own free will, except Sweden (although there was a referendum held in September 2003 (56.1% vote against membership of the eurozone), however, Sweden never met convergence criteria (Sweden is not yet in the euro area, as it has not made the necessary changes to its central bank legislation and it does not meet the convergence criterion related to participation in the ERM II (http://ec.europa.eu/economy_finance/euro/adoption/who_can_join/index_en.htm).

The clues began to become proofs when in March of 2002 Eurostat refused to validate the Greek data, and the same happened in September of that year. The debt was revised for two times in a row and the surplus that was presented from the Greek government appeared as deficit. As a result, in March 2004 Eurostat continued to refuse again to validate the Greek data. Also, the main point was that the accounting method often affected seriously the deficit numbers. The same scene was in 2009 and 2010.

Eurostat in 2010 mentioned that "*Greece's fiscal deficit for 2009 has been upped to 15.4 percent of GDP and the state debt to 126.8 percent of GDP, in revised figures published by EUROSTAT in Brussels. A Greek finance ministry announcement issued later said that "the cycle of dispute and lack of credibility of the Greek statistical data closes today, and one more step in the direction of restoring the confidence of the citizens, the international partners and markets in the fiscal administration of Greece is completed"* (Europe Intelligence Wire, November 15, 2010, p.1)"

In that context, the ministry reassured the public regarding speculation on new additional measures, noting that "the drastic reduction of the deficit by 2014 will be effected in a balanced and fair way and in accordance with the commitments that the country has assumed."

According to the finance ministry, apart from Eurostat's lifting (with its publication of the finalised data for the period 2006-2009) of all its reservations on Greek fiscal data, equally important is the fact that the biggest deficit reduction ever in Greece (6 percentage points of GDP or more than 14 billion euros, much higher than initially planned) was achieved in 2010.

According to figures released by the finance ministry, the fiscal deficit for 2009 had been revised upward from 13.6 percent of GDP to 15.4 percent of GDP, or 66,150 million euros, representing an increase of 1.8 percentage points of GDP. The upward revision was attributed to the inclusion of public organisations to the General Government (representing a deficit increase of 0.7 percent of GDP), adjustment of the social security funds' and OTA (local government) accounts (representing a deficit increase of 0.9 percent of GDP), and a reduction of the 2009 GDP (corresponding to a 0.2 percent increase in the deficit).

The revision also affected the figures of the state debt, into which the accrued debts of the state enterprises that had been entered into the General Government have been incorporated. The 2009 General Government deficit had revised to 298,032 million euros or 126.9 percent of GDP from 115.4 percent of GDP, representing an increase of 11.4 percentage points of GDP, the ministry said.

The revision was attributed chiefly to the incorporation of the DEKO (public utilities and organisations) to the General Government figures (representing a debt increase of 7.75 percentage points of GDP, or 18,204 million euros) and adjustment of the off-market swaps (representing a debt increase of 2.3 percentage points of GDP, or 5,530 million euros).

Following the 2009 debt and deficit revision, the deficit for 2010 was now projected at 9.4 percent of GDP, the ministry said, adding, however, that, in relation to 2009, a fiscal adjustment of more than 14 billion euros had been achieved, from over 36 billion euros in 2009 to approximately 22 billion euros in 2010. As for the state debt, it has now been revised to 144 percent of GDP.

The ministry also said that the figures released by Eurostat was the result of close cooperation and hard and consistent work by Eurostat and the recently-established independent Hellenic Statistical Authority (ELSTAT) and all other agencies involved in the provision of fiscal statistics (Athens New Agency, 2010).

The report by the International Monetary Fund (IMF) projected that Greece's public debt would peak from its current level of 143 percent of GDP to 172 percent of GDP in 2012 and remain above 130 percent through 2020.

All these facts led to members of eurozone to call Portugal, Ireland, Greece and Spain "PIGS" and the worst country of them to be Greece. The fact was that the Greek budgetary statistics have undergone a multiple and great revision and now the eurozone is completely negative against the effort for derotation. If Greece made the best effort to improve its statistics, the control would be complete.

But if we reconsider all these facts, we can realise that in the latest European financial crisis few or no one is innocent. At first, Greek governments had neither tackled necessary structural reforms of the economy, nor made real efforts to control public finances. Also, the EU must have known about real numbers of Greek deficit and debt, but under the pressure of financial market or other reasons, preferred only to refuse to validate the Greek data and not to impose sanctions or to announce the real facts.

References

Adrian, B.-W. and Patrick, S. (2010) A Market Perspective on the European Sovereign Debt and Banking Crisis. *OECD Journal: Financial Market Trends*. 2: 9-36.

Bitzenis, A., (2009), The Balkans: FDI and EU Accession, Ashgate Publishing Ltd, UK, August 2009

Blundell-Wignall, A. and Slovik, P. (2011) A Market Perspective on the European Sovereign Debt and Banking Crisis. *OECD Journal: Financial Market Trends*. 2: 10-36.

Commission of the European Communities (2008), "Report from the Commission to the European Parliament and the Council on the quality of fiscal data reported by member states in 2007", http://eur-lex.europa.eu/LexUriServ/LexUriServ.do?uri=COM:2008:0060:FIN:EN:PDF, [accessed 25/7/2012].

Craig, B. and Koepke, M. (2011) Global Banking System Exposure to the Greek Sovereign Debt Crisis. Federal Reserve Bank of Cleveland. *Economic Trends,* 4 August (0811-http://www.clevelandfed.org/research/trends/2011/0811/01finmar.cfm)

European Central Bank (2000) "ECB Convergence Report 2000", p1-86

European Commission (2012), The Greek Loan Facility, http://ec.europa.eu/economy_finance/eu_borrower/greek_loan_facility/index_en.htm, [accessed 24/7/2012].

European Council (2006), Council Regulation (EC) No 2223/96 of 25 June 1996 on the European system of national and regional accounts in the Community, http://eur-lex.europa.eu/LexUriServ/LexUriServ.do?uri=CELEX:31996R2223:EN:HTML, [accessed 24/7/2012].

—. (2007), "2007/465/EC: Council Decision of 5 June 2007 abrogating Decision 2004/917/EC on the existence of an excessive deficit in Greece", http://eur-lex.europa.eu/LexUriServ/LexUriServ.do?uri=OJ:L:2007:176:0021:01:EN:HTML, [accessed 27/7/2012].

European Union (2006), "The 2006 update of the Hellenic Stability and Growth Program 2006-2009, http://ec.europa.eu/economy_finance/economic_governance/sgp/pdf/20_scps/2006-07/01_programme/2006-12-18_el_sp_en.pdf, [accessed 24/7/2012].

Eurostat (2004), "Report by Eurostat on the Revision of the Greek Government deficit and debt figures", http://epp.eurostat.ec.europa.eu/cache/ITY_PUBLIC/GREECE/EN/GREECE-EN.PDF, [accessed 28/7/2012).

—. (2007) "Europe in Figures – Eurostat yearbook 2006-2007", http://epp.eurostat.ec.europa.eu/cache/ITY_OFFPUB/KS-CD-06-001/EN/KS-CD-06-001-EN.PDF, [accessed 28/7/2012].

Europe Intelligence Wire, (2010) "*Greece projects deficit of 9.4pct of GDP for 2010 after release of revised 2009 figures by Eurostat",* November 15, 2010, http://www.accessmylibrary.com/article-1G1-242176114/greece-projects-deficit-9.html, [accessed 28/7/2012].

Eurostat (2010), "Report on Greek Government deficit and debt statistics", http://epp.eurostat.ec.europa.eu/cache/ITY_PUBLIC/COM_2010_REPORT_GREEK/EN/COM_2010_REPORT_GREEK-EN.PDF, [accessed 28/7/2012].

Fernandes, A.L.C., and Mota, P.R. (2009) The Roots of the Eurozone Sovereign Debt Crisis: PIGS vs Non-PIGS. *PANOECONOMICUS*, 5, pp. 631-649.

Guardian, The. "Greek economy up to 25% - with a little help from prostitutes", 30 September 2006, p.1.

Haidar, J.I. (2009) Sovereign Credit Risk in the Eurozone. *World Economics*. 1, pp. 123-136.

Manessiotis, V. (2011), The root-causes of the Greek sovereign debt crisis, *Paper presented at the 2nd Bank of Greece workshop on the economies of Eastern European and Mediterranean Countries*, Athens 6 May 2011, Greece.

Nelson, R.M., Belkin, P. and Mix. D.E. (2010), Greece's Debt Crisis: Overview, Policy Responses, and Implications, *Congressional Research Service,* pp. 1-18.

OECD (2009), *"OECD Economic Surveys, Greece",* Vol. 2009/15.

Rossi, V. and Aguilera, R. D. (2010) No painless solution to Greece's Debt Crisis. *International Economics*. Chatham House. Programme Paper, pp. 1-23.

Sturgess, B. (2010) Greek Economic Statistics: A Decade of Deceit. *World Economics*. 11: 67-99.

Watt, N. (2006), "Greek Economy up 25% - with a little help from prostitudes", *The Guardian*, 30 September, p. 13.